Improve and Modify Ford Fiesta

Lindsay Porter and Dave Pollard

Haynes ®

A FOULIS Motoring Book

First published 1990

Published by:
Haynes Publishing Group,
Sparkford, Nr Yeovil,
Somerset BA22 7JJ, England
Haynes Publications Inc.,
861 Lawrence Drive,
Newbury park,
California 91320 USA

Produced by:
Porter Publishing,
The Storehouse,
Little Hereford Street,
Bromyard,
Herefordshire HR7 4DE,
England

British Library Cataloguing in Publication Data
Porter, Lindsay, *1949–*
Improve & Modify Ford Fiesta.
1. Cars. Maintenance & Repair.
I. Title II. Pollard, Dave
629.28722
ISBN 0-85429-785-5

Library of Congress Catalog Card No. 90-80219

Editor: Lindsay Porter

Design, typesetting and electronic page make-up
TypeStyle, The Gubbins & Smith Building, Newton Road,
Yeovil, Somerset BA20 1NZ, England

Printed in England by: J. H. Haynes & Co. Ltd.

Contents

Chapter Five Techniques and tools

Chapter Six Fiesta history and development

Chapter Seven Specialists and useful data

Foreword

This book is for those who enjoy ***doing*** things to their cars. Not just fixing them when they go wrong, but making them better than they were, right through from a small, add-on accessory, through to a "hot" engine and uprated suspension.

At the time they leave the showroom the vast majority of new cars are pale, watered down things, when compared with the way their owners – to say nothing of their designers! – would have liked them to have been. The reasons are mainly two-fold: Cost and Choice. Quite clearly, the cost of adding every "extra" would be prohibitive while not everyone would choose exactly the same performance, comfort and "gadgetry" – so do take time to follow the advice given in these pages. In each and every case, instructions have been checked by the manufacturer or supplier, so you can fit the parts you see here in the greatest confidence that the advice you have been given is straight from – or at least, checked by – the horse's mouth.

Done Pollard has written "his" sections of this book – the greater part of it – in clear and relaxed style, while Elaine Hall checked, double-checked and collated material in exemplary fashion. Each and every supplier featured has been most cooperative and we've only featured those products of which we have had "hands-on" experience and which we can fully recommend. To each and every one – many thanks!

Lindsay Porter, Bromyard, Herefordshire

Acknowledgements

Our thanks go, of course, to everyone who has supplied their products, time and experience. For inconvenience above and beyond the call of duty, the following get a special mention.

David Power and Richard Prior (no, not that one!) at Power Engineering who re-scheduled several days work to facilitate us photographing their superb engine conversion, not to mention the fitting of various ancillary items, including the Spax suspension uprate.

Roy Craggs who, once again, clocked up many miles to become "fitter extraordinaire" for the photographic sequences.

Sarah Williams and David Wood, new converts to Fiesta-ism, who gave up their new found friend for many days in the cause of this book.

Gerald Bird and Chris Green of Trimco in Luton, for arranging to fit an RS kit to a 1.6S Fiesta and Tony Lewin, Derek Talbot and Bob Hart of Rye Mill Coachcraft for showing us how colour coding should be done.

Peter Shandley of Zemco for his technical advice in that incredibly complex area of in-car electronics.

As well as putting together an excellent magazine, Dennis Foy managed to take time off from editorship of Performance Ford and provided lots of useful information and hard-to-get photographics.

David Swan of Michelin's technical department for reams of technical information and for his valuable time talking to us.

J. G. Giles & Son of Northampton provided invaluable advice and assistance with regard to the photography and equipment used during the preparation of this book.

Dave Pollard, Buckinghamshire

Introduction

1.1
The XR2 has become the archetypal small "Hot Hatch" and most people's idea of the ideal Fiesta – at least until the Mk III XR2i came along! Most "ordinary" Fiesta owners want to emulate the sporty top of the range model although, by combining many of the modifications shown in this book, you could end up with an even better car!

This book is for Fiesta owners who want to add some of their own individuality to what are already outstanding cars in their own right. Many of the sections cover mods which can be carried out by a reasonably competent owner on a DIY basis. Others set out to show what is available and what magic the specialist can work on your car; the choice, as always, is yours.

Naturally enough, there are plenty of reasons for owners to buy their Fiestas in the first place and as the '80s drew to a close, Ford upped the ante once more with the impressive Mk III version. Fiestas are renowned for being reliable and easy to maintain, although even those models with the smaller capacity engines display a verve and sportiness on the road. When you reach XR2 or XR2i level (or even the mighty Turbo) then you have a vehicle which combines scorching performance with pin sharp handling but is still happy to amble around town carrying large loads of supermarket shopping or collecting the kids from school.

However, regardless of their plus points, the cars are, by definition, very much a mass production vehicle with a distinct lack of identity and individualism. It is this with which the enthusiastic owner will seek to endow his or her steed. This book suggests hundreds of ways this can be done.

The range of improvements is vast and varying enormously in cost and simplicity. Styling stripes for the bodywork and seat covers for the interior are among the simplest whilst relatively easy engine modifications include Dellorto carburettor replacement or fitting an oil cooler.

At the other extreme, you could fit (or have fitted; it's not exactly easy!) a full body kit which will certainly make your car stand out from the crowd. Mechanically, a power uprate from Power Engineering will drastically improve your performance figures.

All of these modifications and many, many more are included in this book although, as previously mentioned, not all are DIY tasks; indeed, we recommend that some are not even attempted by the amateur enthusiast for reasons of safety or specialist skills required.

Improvements and modifications to the Fiesta cover a wide field and we hope that we have done it justice. We have depended heavily on enthusiastic Fiesta owners and certainly could not have done it without the close assistance of the specialists and suppliers in this book.

In every case, we selected the specialist company which we believe has most to offer the Fiesta owner in their particular field; that's why you'll recognise some of the biggest "names" in the business in this book alongside some of those who are less well known but deserve to be more so.

We hope and believe that the combination of top specialists, experienced motoring writing and enthusiastic Fiesta ownership has brought you a book that you, as a Fiesta owner, will want to turn to again and again.

Introduction

The modifications and improvements in this book cover a very wide spectrum, from the smallest item, such as a locking wheel nut, right through to full-blown engine, bodywork and suspension modifications.

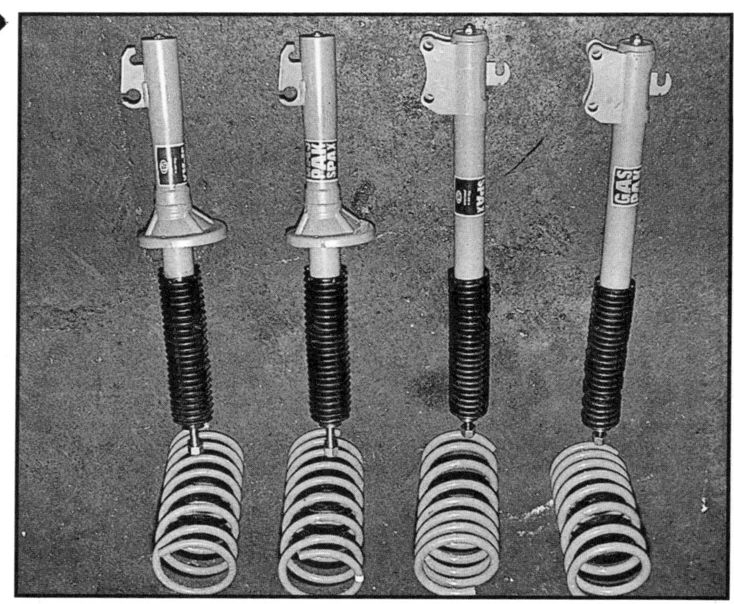

1.2 Changes to tyres and suspension can make exciting improvements, although it's not until the car is on the move that they are apparent. Fitting a Spax sports suspension kit will improve your handling in a big way and is essential if you're going for extra power. *(Courtesy Ford Motor Co. Ltd.)*

1.3 Extra power in abundance is available from Power Engineering's System Two conversion. If you want a real flyer of a Fiesta, this is for you!

1.4 Improving your lighting is certainly a worthwhile modification and few people have as much experience in this field as Hella. Their twin headlamp grille is simple to fit to a Mk I Fiesta.

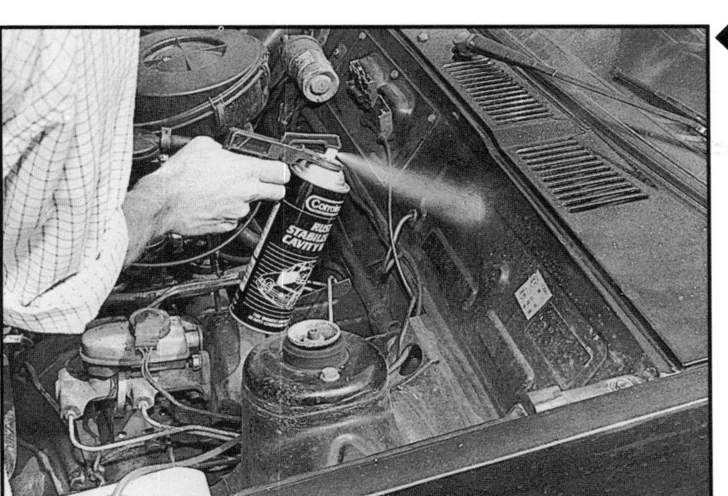

1.5
More practical improvements include rustproofing. Both old and new cars will benefit from the application of Mitchell Marketing's superb rustproofing fluids, shown here.

Although many of the improvements shown in this book relate to cosmetic appearance, it is important that you do not let pride come before practicality: covering your car with stripes when it rides on bald tyres and has leaking shock absorbers is not awfully wise!

1.6
Most modifications can be performed quicker and easier by the use of power tools and those in the cordless, Hitachi range are particularly versatile and well-suited for in-car applications.

1.7
A couple of hours work and just two different Branyl stripes makes a vast improvement to this Fiesta. The variety of stripes available means that you can be subtle or otherwise.

Chapter One
Improving the appearance

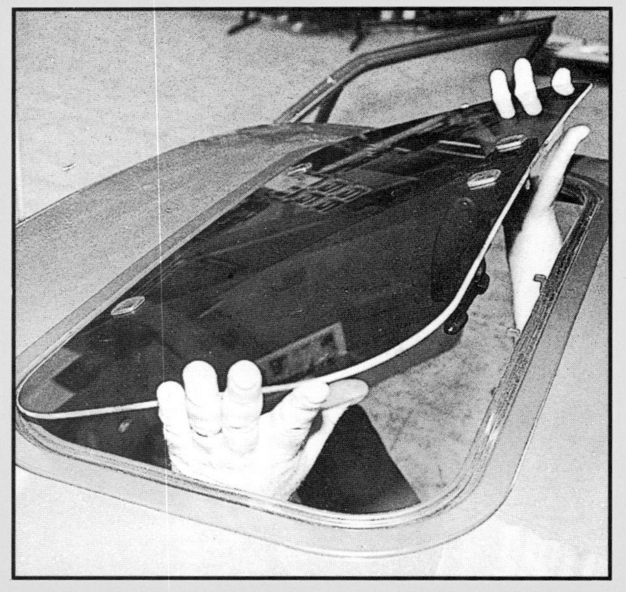

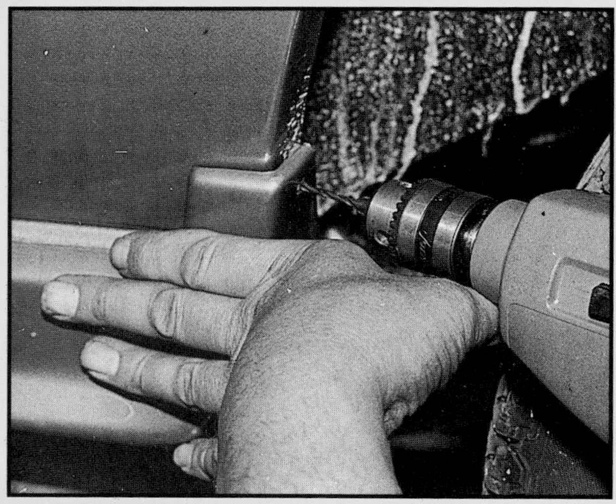

Hints, tips and safety advice

Here are a few dos and don'ts which will help you when working on your car.

IGNITION

Never leave the ignition keys in your car whilst you are working on it, regardless of what you are doing.

MAY THE FORCE ...

Don't force anything ... ever. If a nut won't budge or a part won't come off, there must be a reason. Application of logic, reason and releasing fluid is required in preference to bad temper and brute force!

CHILDREN

Do NOT allow children anywhere near the car when you are working on it. They cannot be expected to know how potentially dangerous it is and could easily find that the most interesting object in the car is the handbrake ... !

OUTDOORS

Most owners will find that much of their work is carried out *al fresco*. Inclement weather is a way of life in the UK but you must remember that water and electrics don't mix at all. Cordless toolsare a good idea when working outside.

INSTRUCTIONS

Most items come with fairly comprehensive instructions often including schematic diagrams and a list of tools required. You can save yourself hours of grief by checking through them beforehand and getting together the tools and ancillaries you will need for the job.

If you enthuse about your motoring, you'll want nothing more on a Saturday morning than to rush back home with your newly purchased goodies and fit them to your Fiesta. Some are relatively simple and require little in the way of preparation. However, if you are doing a more complex task that demands raising the car from the ground, then you should take the precautions mentioned here. Remember also that working under a car will require extra hand and eye protection, particularly with older vehicles which are likely to have falling flakes of rust as well as road dirt.

HT1.1 Whether you're swapping wheels, fitting a spoiler or protecting your existing wheels with locking wheels studs, working on a car without four wheels on the ground is inherently dangerous. So, here's a golden rule: NEVER FIND YOURSELF BENEATH YOUR CAR IF IT IS SUPPORTED ONLY BY A JACK! The one supplied is meant for emergency wheel changing only.

HT1.2 For actually raising the car off the ground, we prefer a brand name trolley jack. One with a safe working load (SWL) of two tons or more will give you ample safety leeway.

HT1.3 Once your car is in the air, you MUST support it other than with the jack. Axle stands can be used but make sure they are securely positioned on parts of the car which are not likely to move or give way.

HT1.4 If the job in hand allows, ramps give much more stability, given that the car is securely positioned. Whichever you choose, you must also chock and block those wheels still left on the ground. If the work allows, leave the car in gear and put the handbrake on. Always ensure that you only raise the car when it is on a level surface; and remember that, as tarmac is relatively soft, the metal edges of the stands or ramps can dig in and cause the car to move, especially in hot weather.

Fitting a grille panel with lamps

Fitting a replacement grille panel with driving or fog lamps is one way of making the standard Fiesta look much more upmarket. The grille featured here is a well-made Hella item which takes little time to fit. Because of the way the Mk II and III cars have been designed, the grille is only suitable for Mk I models.

IA1.1 ➡
As with most Hella items, the grille panel and lamps are superbly made. In this case, ABS (acrylnitrile styrene butadiene) is used during the injection moulding procedure, making the grille panel both incredibly strong *and* very flexible.

IA1.2
The original grille is easy to remove, being held by three crosshead screws. Take some care though, as they may be reluctant to leave home and you don't want to chew up the heads!
⬇

IA1.3 ➡
Being cautious, Hella designed their grille to be fixed with SIX screws, meaning that three brackets have to be fixed into the original three screw holes

⬅ **IA1.4**
At the rear of the grille, the lamps are pre-wired with a bullet connector and an eyelet connector ready fitted to the power and earth leads respectively.

IA1.5
With the wires from the grille passed carefully through into the engine compartment, the grille is fixed to the new brackets.

IA1.6
The Ford badge from the standard grille has to be removed and used on the Hella item. As it is stuck in position, application of heat from a hairdryer will do the trick. A new double-sided "stickie" is provided by Hella.

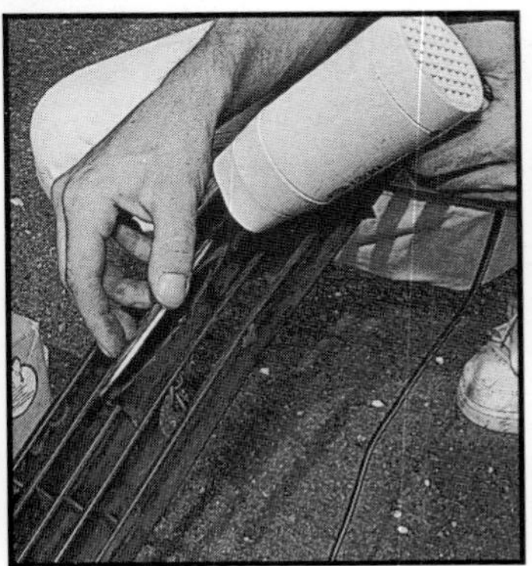

IA1.7
Mounting the relay is the next task. It should be kept out of the way of excess moisture and heat but close enough to the new grille for the various wires to reach.

As always, when dealing with car electrical systems, disconnect the earth lead from the battery before starting work. Once the lamps have been fitted and connected, it is very important that they should be correctly adjusted so as not to blind on-coming traffic. Not only does this ensure legality it makes the fitting of extra lamps more worthwhile; if they are pointing skywards, they're not going to do much good!

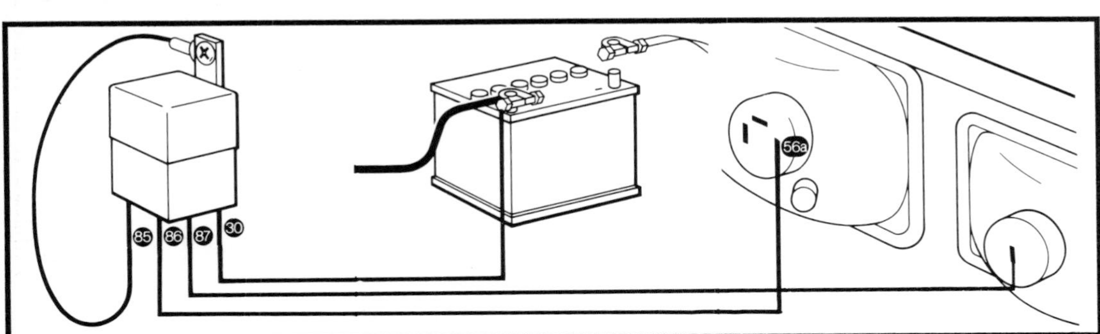

IA1.8
Like the lamps themselves, the relay is ready wired and requires very little in the way of electrical skill. Wired as suggested in the Hella instructions, the lamps will function when main beam is selected. The few Scotchlok connectors needed for this are included in the kit.

(Diagram courtesy Hella Ltd)

IA1.9
The finished result; your car looks better and you'll be able to see better.

Fitting a rear spoiler

The Sedan spoiler shown here is a 95cm roof model, designed to add a touch of sporting style to your humble shopper. It is possible to use one of the larger Sedan spoilers on the rear hatch of your Fiesta, although you would have to do some cutting around the rear wash/wipe.

IA2.1
The Sedan spoiler is made of flexible expanded polyurethane which is very tough and ideally suited to its purpose.

IA2.2
First task, as ever when you are sticking anything to the bodywork, is to give the area in question a good clean. Firstly, a wash to remove dirt and grime and then with a spirit wipe to remove all traces of grease.

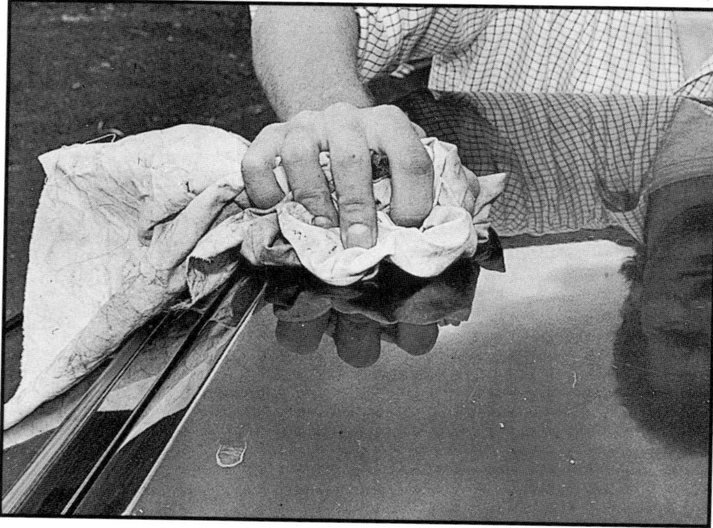

IA2.3
The adhesive strip needs to be fairly warm in order to work properly. Either choose a pleasant day as we did, or employ the hairdryer or domestic radiator technique. Peel away the protective backing and ...

IA2.4
... stick the spoiler into position. In this case, the spoiler looks colour coded on this black Mk I car, although being black it will contrast with any colour and can, if required, be colour matched.

IA2.5
The incredibly strong glue means that even in this topmost position the spoiler will stay firmly in position.

Fitting a set of wheel trims is an inexpensive method of getting the "alloy wheel" look. They will also cover up rusty old wheels that really need a respray! Link Sedan have several styles available to suit the Escort and Orion range, all of which are claimed to be aerodynamically effective.

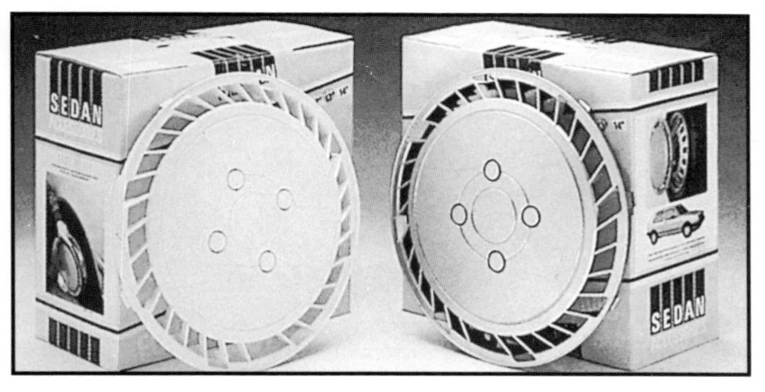

IA3.1 The Sedan wheel trim range is vast and ranges from the simple and subtle to the complex and outrageous. All are manufactured from high quality, impact resistant, ABS resin. Very popular is the Jet trim, with the mock wheel stud covers, whilst ...
(Photo courtesy Link Sedan Ltd)

IA3.2 ... the Sacex is a fairly drastic change in anyone's language. The design is very similar to several wheels in the Ford range.
(Photo courtesy Link Sedan Ltd)

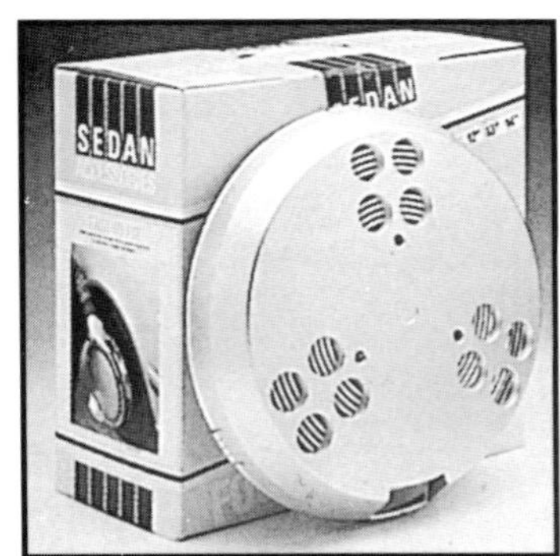

IA3.3 More holes, but completely different. The Monte Carlo features three sets of four holes in a radiating pattern from the centre.
(Photo courtesy Link Sedan Ltd)

IA3.4 The Turbo (at right) and the Daytona are also available for the Fiesta, with the angular patterns blending well with the car's styling.
(Photo courtesy Link Sedan Ltd)

IA3.5 This brand new, Mk III car had no rusty wheels to cover up, but the standard steel wheels certainly needed some improvement. The Basic trims here are available in white or aluminium finish in 13 inch or aluminium only in 14 inch.

Fitting wheel trims

Great care should be taken when fitting wheel trims, for, although the fitting is simple, you must be absolutely sure that they are fully secured; an errant trim flying off the car at speed could be highly dangerous, to say the least!

IA3.6
The trims are fixed to the wheel by means of these extremely strong, plastic clips.

IA3.7
The trim simply pushes into place with the last clip requiring firm pressure from the flat of your hand. You have to be careful that you don't damage the trim, but equally so that the trim is very firmly secured. Note that there is a gap in the "spoke" pattern around the edge which is to allow access to the tyre valve. You must make sure that you have this positioned correctly.

IA3.8
Smooth and stylish, and certainly a great improvement, giving the car a more distinctive appearance.

Fitting windscreen wiper aerofoils

There are few places in the world where the windscreen wiper gets as much use as in the UK. However, you can't help but notice that as your speed increases, especially if it is a windy day, their efficiency starts to fall. This is simply because the wiper blades are being lifted physically from the screen and thus leaving an uncleaned and potentially dangerous area. Fitting the Branyl aerofoils shown here is the work of minutes but the effects will be seen every time it rains.

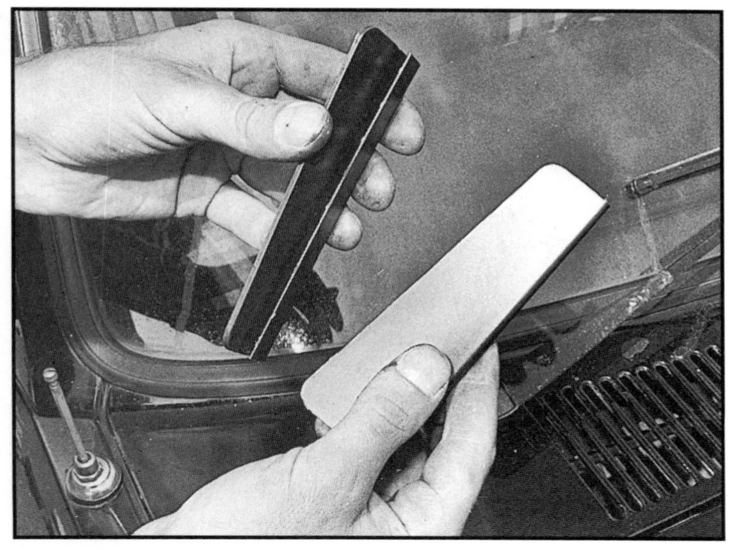

IA4.1 Branyl aerodynamic aerofoils come in bubble packs of two. Once fitted they can stay in place almost indefinitely or until you change your wiper arms and blades.

IA4.2 Fitting them takes hardly any time at all. Pull the wiper arm away from the windscreen and then simply clip the aerofoil into place.

IA4.3 Finished! Nothing to it, but the effects are soon apparent when the rain starts to fall. A clear screen and a much safer car are the result

Adding styling stripes and decals

Branyl recommend a temperature range of 15 to 30 degrees celsius (60 to 86 degrees Fahrenheit) to ensure the stripes stick correctly. If it is any cooler though, you can "cheat" a little by using a hairdryer on the stripes. Any warmer and you'd be advised to apply the stripes in the shade of a garage.

Most of us feel the need to add some individuality to our cars and fitting styling stripes is one of the simplest ways of going about it. We would recommend some degree of subtlety when choosing a stripe, to avoid the "over the top" look of many cars. A simple stripe well positioned will look far better to most eyes.

IA5.1
Branyl produce a wide range of cosmetic body work products suitable for the Fiesta, including their "Sideliner" body trims, shown elsewhere in this book.

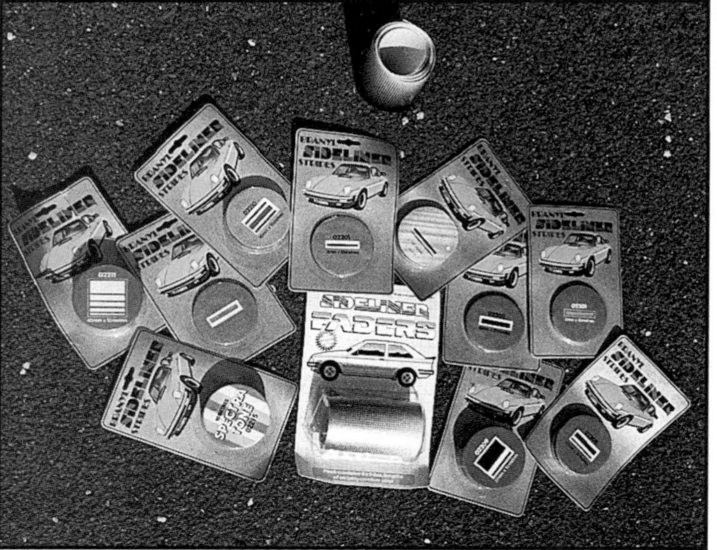

IA5.2
We start with stripes. Just a few from the Branyl range shows that there is a tremendous choice of colour and variety available.

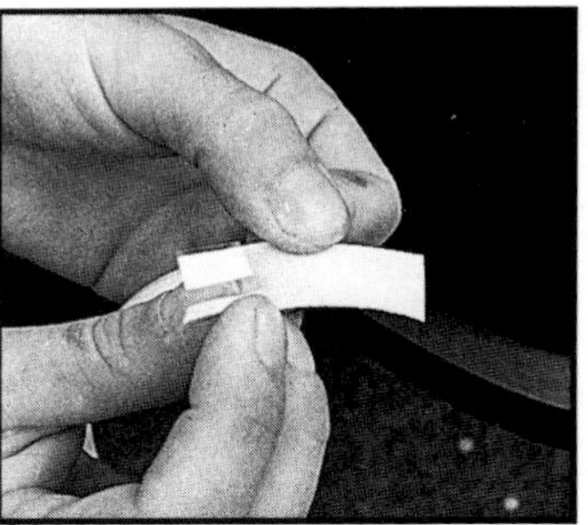

IA5.3
This special edition model 1.1L already had a fairly broad, red stripe along its flanks. However, it was above the waistline and left the lower part of the car looking somewhat slab-sided. So a narrow twin stripe was chosen from the Branyl range. Pulling off the self-adhesive backing ...

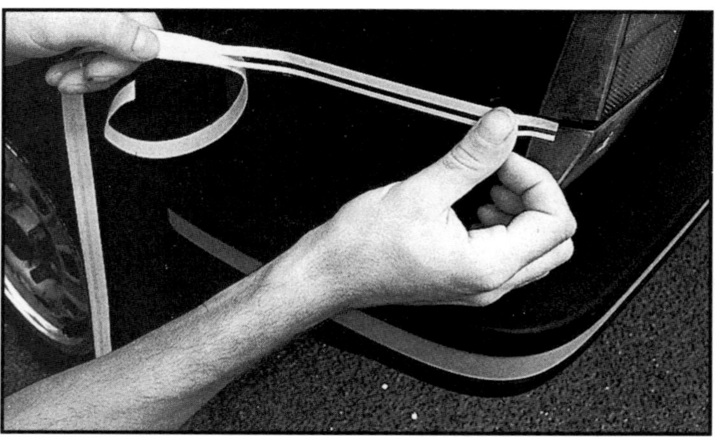

IA5.4
... allows the stripes to be stuck in position. Take care at this point that you get the line of the stripe absolutely straight. An assistant is almost essential here.

Where a stripe has been shaped to a fine point or is in such a position that possible lifting may occur, a small spot of clear nail varnish will ensure that that the end of the tape stays in place.

IA5.5
When you get to the door panel join, carry on over it. If you try to do the line in three sections you'll have a near impossible task getting it straight.

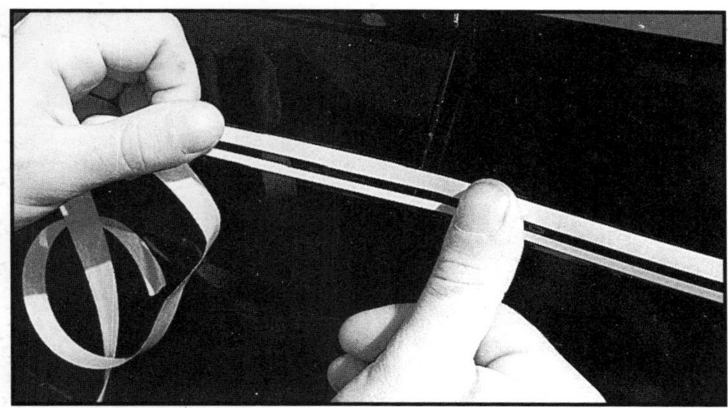

A badly fitted body stripe will look ridiculously wavy as it passes down the length of the car. One way of avoiding this is to align the stripe with a bodywork moulding on your car, if it has one. Alternatively, you could draw a line in felt tip in order to achieve the same result. A helper is always handy, not only to assist with the fitting, but also to stand back from the car and look along its length, checking for accuracy. It is possible for waviness to be detected from an end-on view which is not immediately apparent from the side.

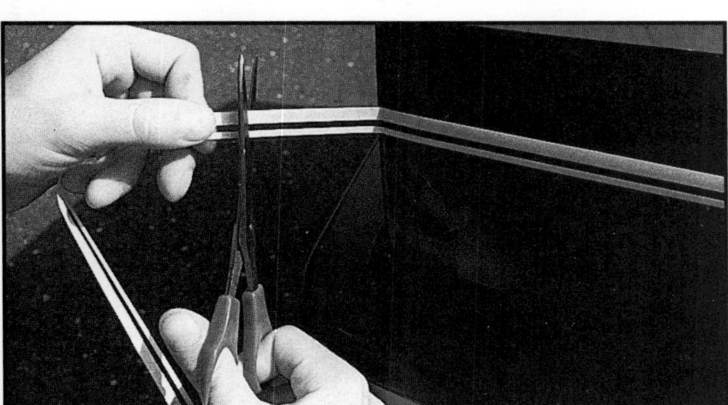

IA5.6
When you get to the front, allow plenty of overlap so that the stripe can be continued around the front of the wing and behind the headlamp unit.

IA5.7
Going back along the stripe, use a sharp craft knife to make a clean cut in the centre of the door and "B" pillar. If you get it right ...

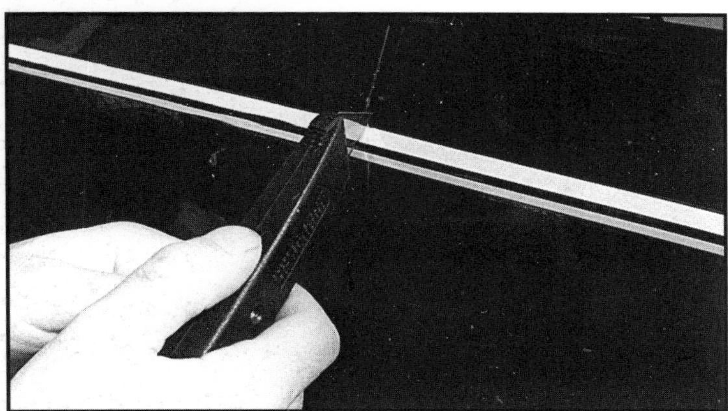

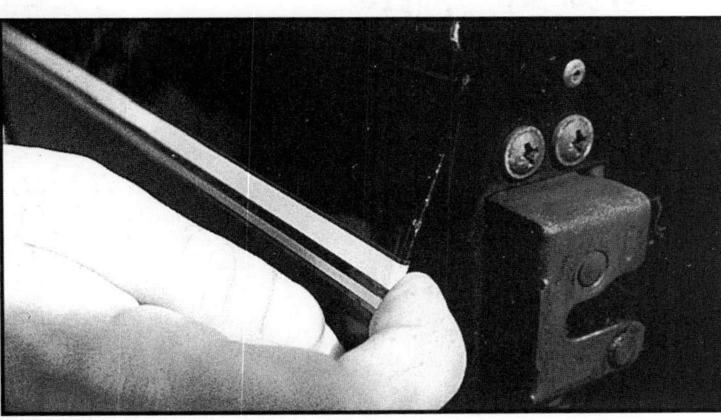

IA5.8
... there should be enough of the stripe left to fold over and stick around the door and actually on the "B" pillar. This operation has to be repeated at the front of the door. Naturally, you will have to use spirit wipe again to ensure that these areas are clean.

Adding styling stripes and decals

In years gone by, the application of a coach stripe was a job for a skilled craftsman and was not something to be undertaken lightly. Nowadays, the addition of a DIY stick-on styling stripe, perhaps in conjunction with a change of wheel trims, can dramatically improve your Fiesta's appearance at a very low cost.

IA5.9
As at the front, cut the stripe long enough to pass behind the rear lamp cluster as shown. It's a little fiddly, so use a narrow bladed screwdriver, but be careful you don't scratch your paintwork.

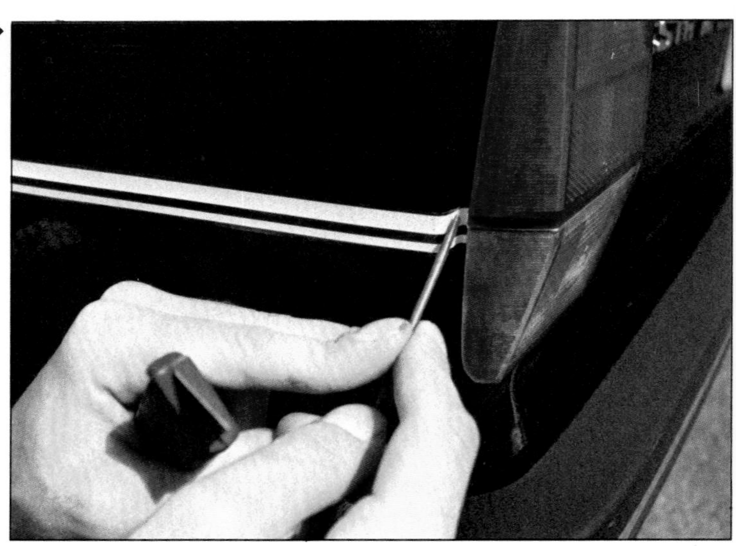

IA5.10
Sure everything is just right? Then the moment of truth arrives: gently pull back the second backing paper to leave just the twin stripes. It pays to pull back short sections at a time, pressing down firmly before peeling back to avoid the stripe lifting.

IA5.11
A well chosen and positioned stripe and without the requirement of a ten year apprenticeship in sign writing!

IA5.12
The Branyl graduated stripes are always popular and justifiably so. As you can see in this close-up, the wide stripe has printed on it a series of coloured dots which are large at the bottom but which fade to nothing at the top.

Those Fiesta owners who have cars with a body moulding have an instant advantage when it comes to fitting stripes. The stripe can be aligned easily against the moulding, thus allowing simple and accurate fitting. However, it pays to make sure that the moulding is actually straight; if your car has been resprayed at any time, you may well find that the moulding was incorrectly replaced and adding another stripe will simply emphasize it!

IA5.13
The first task, after you have decided where you want the stripe, is to measure it accurately. Our black Mk I was again going to be the recipient and we thought this silver stripe would look good along the bottom of the door.

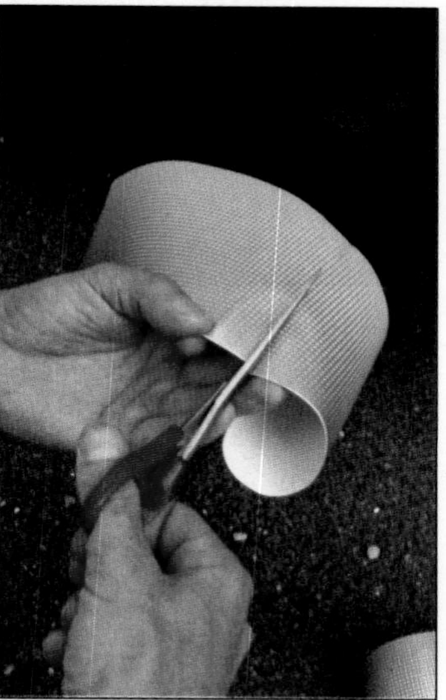

IA5.14
A small overlap is allowed for, the stripe is cut and then ...

IA5.15
... the stripe peels away from the backing paper. Note that there is only backing paper on one side, unlike the stripe fitted earlier.

Adding styling stripes and decals

Any particularly wide Branyl stripes, or those placed a little on the high side, could run across the fuel filler cap. It is essential that the styling stripe passes across the cap, having been cut to the exact shape required. This will give the impression of a clean, uninterrupted line and to some extent disguise the fact that the fuel filler is there at all.

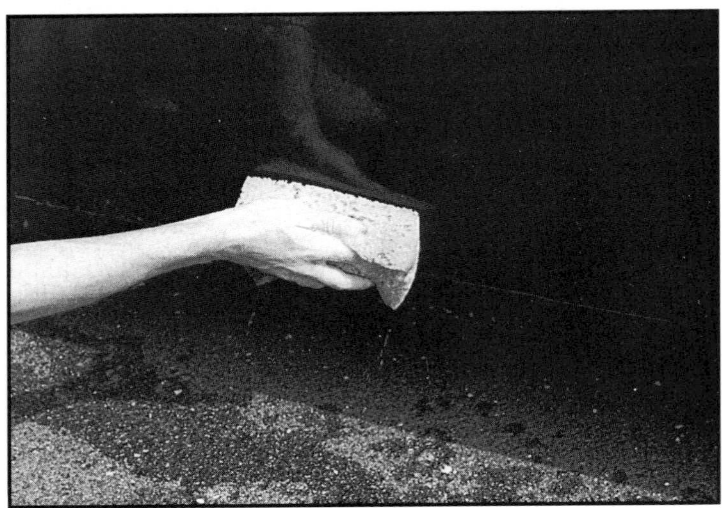

IA5.16
Next, a curious happening, we cover both the lower door and the stripe with soapy water. Not as crazy as it seems, for this allows us to move the stripe around into exactly the right position, an impossibility if no lubricant is used.

IA5.17
The stripe is pressed into place, gradually easing the water out. Once you're happy with the positioning, you can either leave the stripe to dry of its own accord or ...

IA5.18
... use your car squeegee to remove the air and water bubbles.

IA5.19
You can see here the effect of the graduation in the wide, lower stripe. Should it be carried on along the front and rear of the car? That's up to you of course. In terms of accuracy, lining up this stripe was easy as we followed the line of the door. However, it is not always so, depending on where you want your stripe to be. One tip is to place the stripe and backing paper in position and hold it with masking tape. Place further strips of masking tape horizontally along the line of the stripe. By leaving the last pieces of tape in situ, when you come to fit the stripe, all you have to do is realign them and you know that it's positioned correctly.

Several sorts of decals and badges are available from Branyl; some subtle, some amusing and some downright vulgar! The choice is yours!

IA5.20
Ideal for anyone who has a fuel injected, turbo diesel XR3i! Not really, but this does show just some of the wide range of Branyl badges, many of which are just right for the Fiesta.

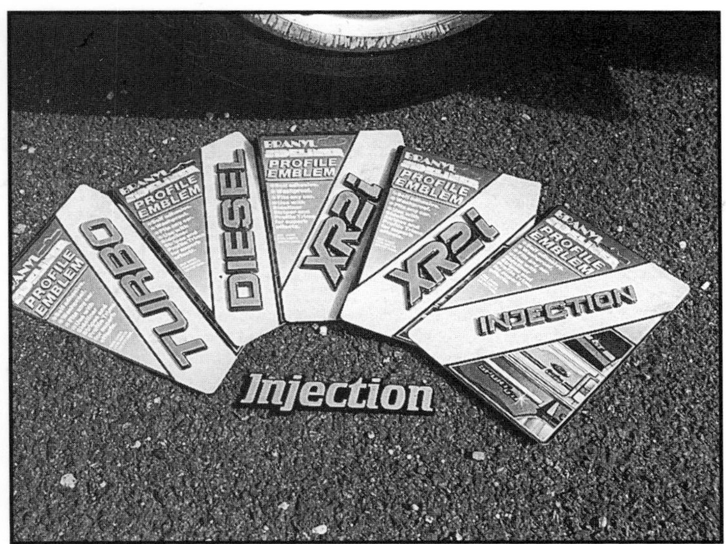

IA5.21
The badges are all one-piece, unlike some which leave you with a bag of litter and the hopeless task of trying to line them up.

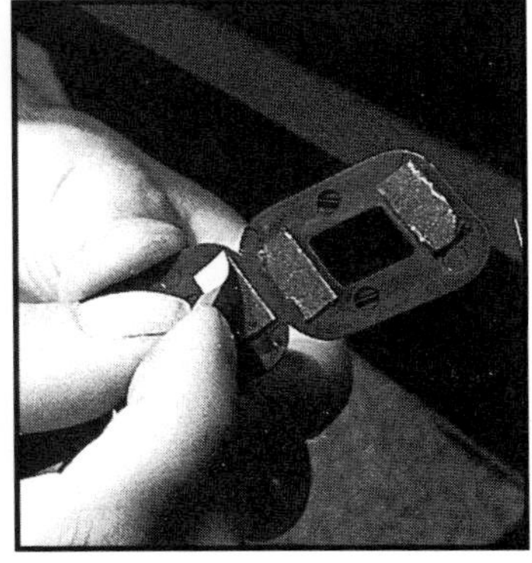

IA5.22
The badges are stuck in place using these double-sided stickies. They peel off easily, but be warned: once in position, they are designed to stay there. Be sure the badge is positioned correctly before you press it into place.

IA5.23
A Turbo Fiesta 1.1L? Stranger things have happened and it's worth it to watch people in the cars following scratching their heads in puzzlement ...!

Colour coding

For this section, we took a Mk II Fiesta to Rye Mill Coachcraft of High Wycombe, to see how the task of colour coding should be approached. The major point that Rye Mill make (and we uphold) is that of safety. So many of the processes and materials involved in the colour coding operation are patently dangerous unless strict safety regulations are adhered to and top class safety equipment is used. Unless you have superlative facilities (most rare for the DIY owner) and some expensive equipment, we would not hesitate to advise that you *do not* attempt two-pack spraying. Rye Mill are most stringent in all aspects of safety and quality, as you will see over the next few pages.

IA6.1
Here, we are covering the partial colour coding of a Mk II 1100cc Fiesta. However, you may have your own ideas of what looks good or possibly want something totally different. At Rye Mill Coachcraft, either Derek Talbot or Bob Hart (both are Glasurit trained) can design the colour scheme of your choice, producing anything from the sublime to the totally unbelievable! However, our choice for this car was to paint the plastic end caps on the front and rear bumpers, the radiator grille and the two door mirrors in the body colour of the car. Check the exact paint reference of your car by looking on the identification plate under the bonnet.

IA6.2
At the Rye Mill/Glasurit paint centre, the heart of the company's 12,000 sq ft premises, the first task is to make sure that the colour being applied to the various parts is exactly the same as the original car colour.

IA6.3
This means first checking with the Glasurit colour guide and then ...

IA6.4
... cross referencing with the Glasurit microfiche system. On this, the constituent colours are listed, telling us exactly how much of each colour is required to make up the specific shade required.

IA6.5
From the Glasurit mixing scheme the various cans are selected and ...

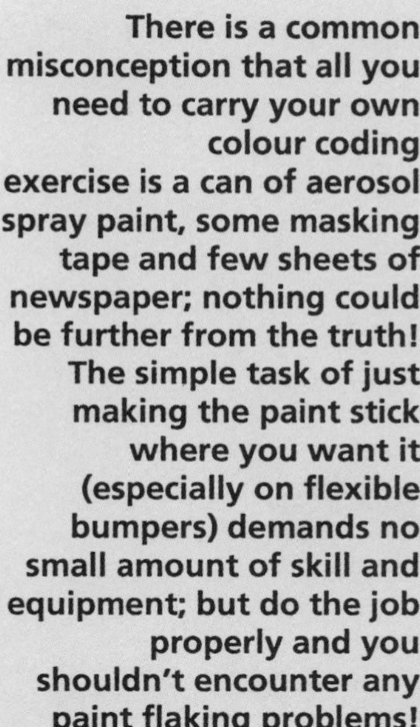

There is a common misconception that all you need to carry your own colour coding exercise is a can of aerosol spray paint, some masking tape and few sheets of newspaper; nothing could be further from the truth! The simple task of just making the paint stick where you want it (especially on flexible bumpers) demands no small amount of skill and equipment; but do the job properly and you shouldn't encounter any paint flaking problems!

IA6.6
... the often tiny required amounts are mixed. The paint is actually "weighed" in grams on this very accurate digital scale to ensure a perfect match every time.

IA6.7
We may be putting the cart before the horse, but we have to show the finished product here, in order to demonstrate, in colour, just how good the end result is, both from the rear ...

IA6.8
... and the front. The owners felt that keeping the centre section of the bumper in its original black, broke up the paintwork nicely and made an interesting colour scheme. They also felt that to have painted the entire bumper sections in body colour would have been "too much" for good taste. However, your tastes may be different and the choice is yours!

Colour coding

Glasurit paint, of course, is widely recognised as being the best available, despite costing a little more than the competition. Those who have had experience of Glasurit always insist on its use, regardless. You can always tell a Glasurit user by the multi-coloured logo which will be much in evidence.

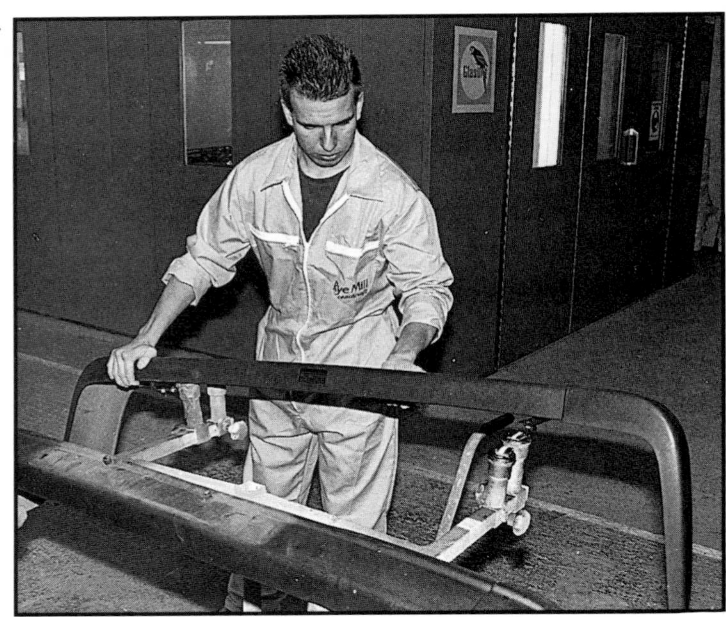

IA6.9 The surfaces to be painted have to be carefully prepared. On some cars, the "stipple" effect on the bumpers is so harsh as to require a coat of primer which has to be flatted down before the operation begins. However, the Fiesta bumpers and radiator grille were quite smooth and so we started by mounting them securely on the purpose made stands ...

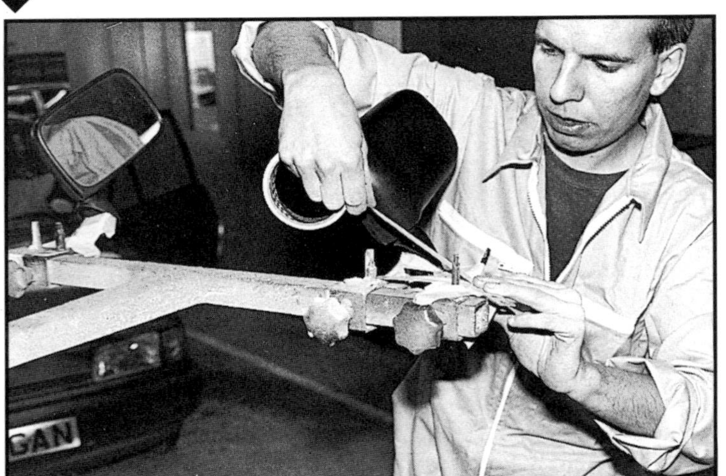

IA6.10 ... though the awkward shape meant that some ingenuity was required in order to hold the mirrors in such a way that held them stable but did not inadvertently mask them.

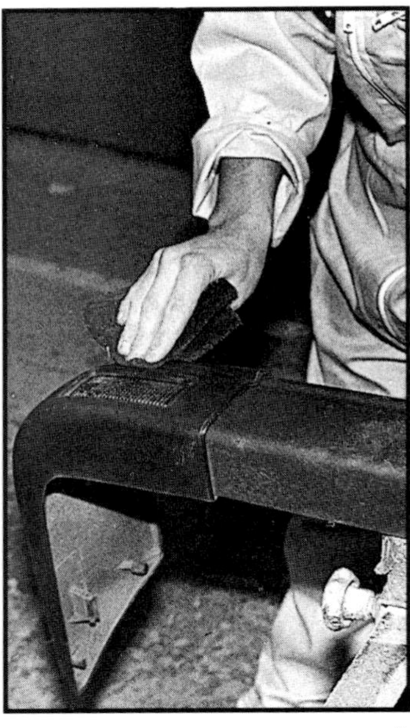

IA6.11 After a light rubbing down with a Scotchbrite cloth (this has to be fairly gentle to avoid making deep marks in the soft plastic) ...

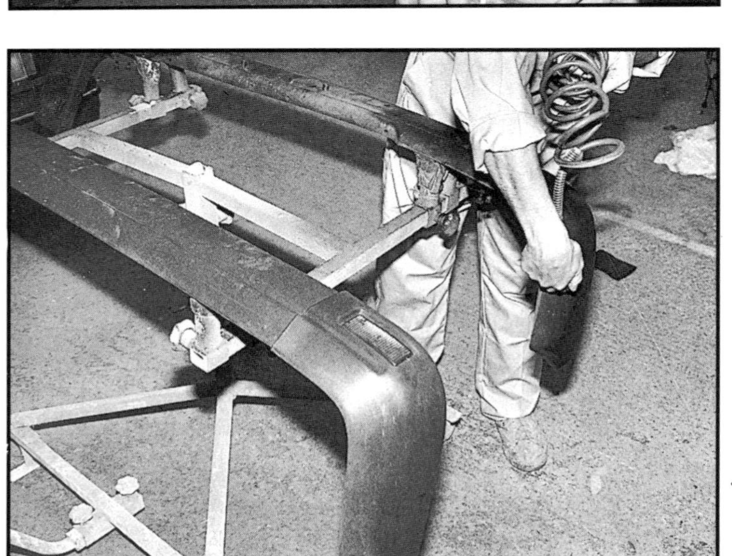

IA6.12 ... the air line is used to blow away the excess dust created by the various sanding processes.

IA6.13

A special Glasurit degreasant (reference 541-5) is used to remove all traces of grease. This is one of the many items carrying a specific warning that it is harmful by inhalation and should not be used in confined spaces without air fed breathing gear.

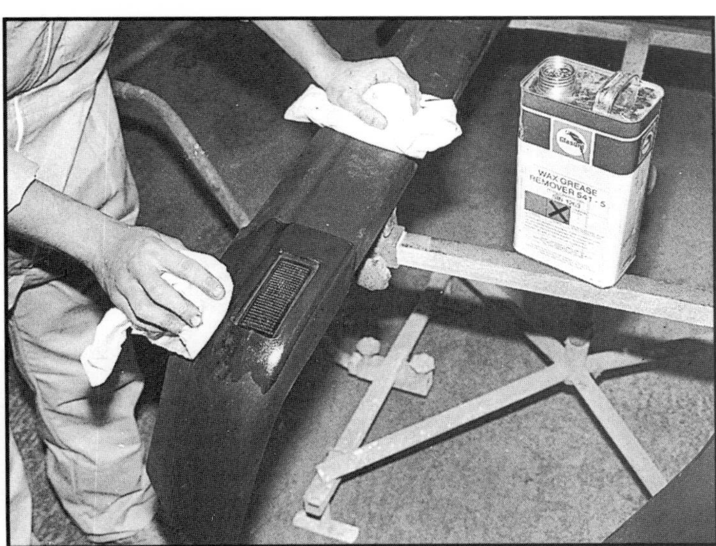

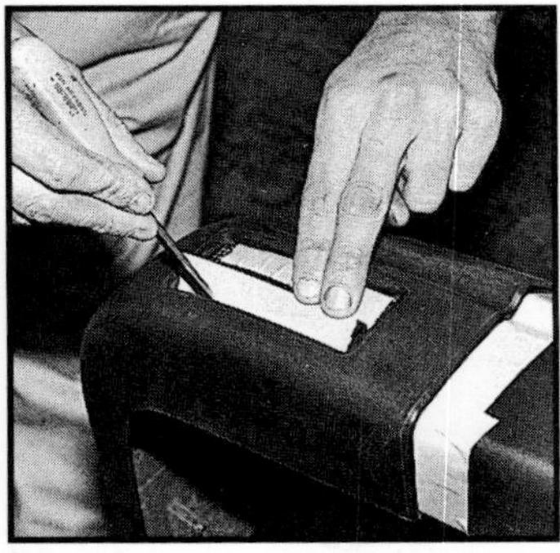

IA6.14

After using the air line again to give the bumpers a quick "blow dry", we started masking off. This is a job which requires some patience and skill. Note how particular care is taken whilst masking the built-in reflectors.

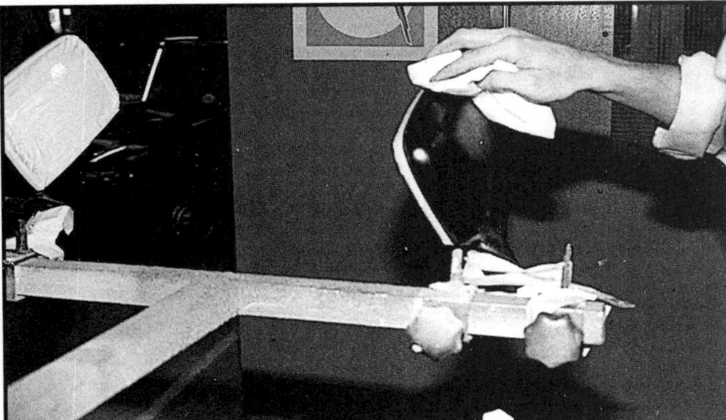

IA6.15

The mirrors were treated in the same way as the bumpers and were masked to leave the edges in the original black, so as to make a contrast which was carried through in the side rubbing stripes. After masking off all relevant items, Glasurit degreasant was once more applied to remove the possibility of fingerprints spoiling the eventual finish.

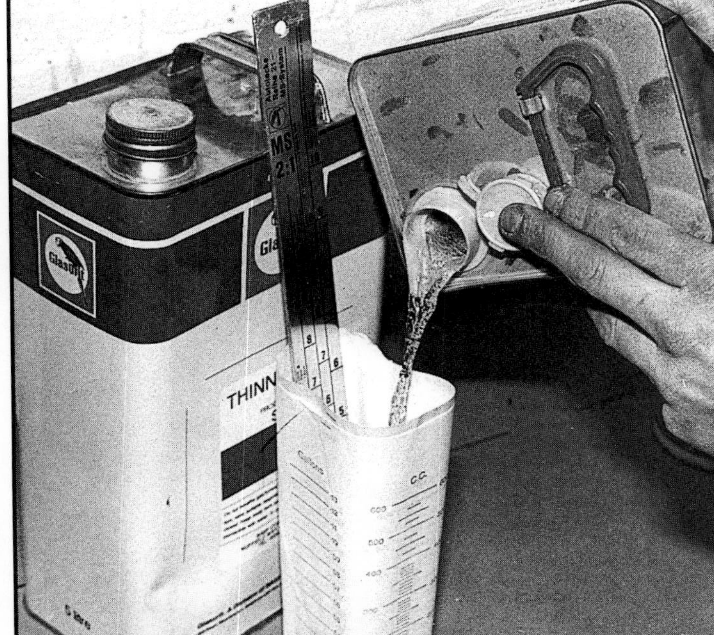

IA6.16

Whilst the various items were left to dry, back in the Glasurit paint bay the two-pack primer was mixed in a ratio of two to one. With the primer is mixed an additive which effectively makes it "go off" and set ...

Bear in mind that the colour coding operation shown here is only part of the whole; dismantling the parts to be sprayed can often take as long as the painting! The door mirrors, for example, require the entire door trim to be removed for access, and bumper removal, especially if they've been in situ for a few years, is likely to be a time consuming job. If you can remove the parts yourself, as we did here, you can save yourself a lot of money. Bear in mind that it took approximately 1.5 hours to complete the removal of the various bits and pieces shown here. Multiply that by two (for refitting) and then again by the average labour cost for your area. An amount worth saving? No doubt about it!

Colour coding

Rye Mill will not only customise your car to your own specification, but they will also repair your bodywork should it be attacked by some other road user! Rye Mill are members of the VBRA (Vehicle Builders and Repairers Association) which is the represenative organisation for the vehicle body repair industry, established in 1914. To retain membership, they have to satisfy a wide range of criteria relating to standards, equipment and expertise and are regularly inspected to ensure that they are providing only the best service available. You owe it to your Fiesta to take similar care when selecting who is to work on your car.

IA6.17
After being mixed, it is filtered before use. Although there should be no foreign elements in either primer or additive, there is always the possibility that dust or dirt could have entered the cans whilst the top was open, and there is never any room for error.

IA6.18
The sign on the Rye Mill bodyshop says it all. Spraying paint or primer is a potentially dangerous task, which is why ...

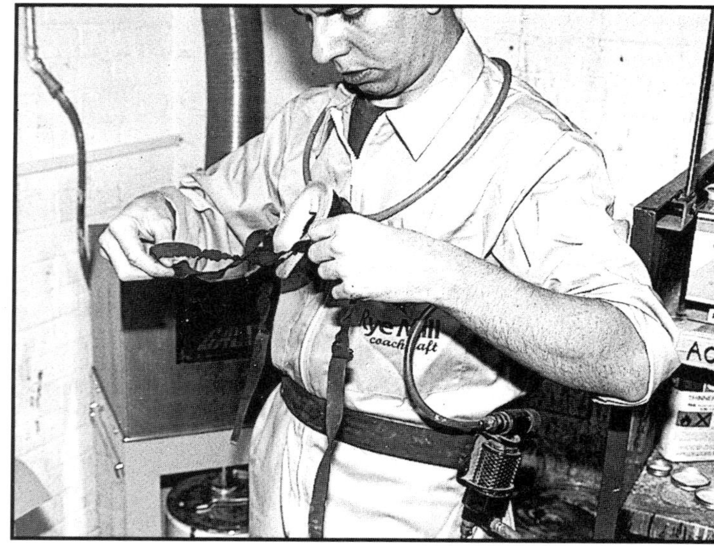

IA6.19
... full, air-fed, breathing equipment with a special charcoal filter was worn. First of all ...

IA6.20
... compressed air was used, together with a wet tack rag to make absolutely sure that there were no dust particles on the items to be sprayed.

IA6.21
Then it was on to the spraying proper. This first coat of primer was left to "flash off" for two minutes before a second coat was applied. This in turn was left for around fifteen minutes. The temperature in the thermostatically controlled spray booth was 20 degrees C whilst spraying was carried out but this was turned up to 55 degrees C for the drying process.

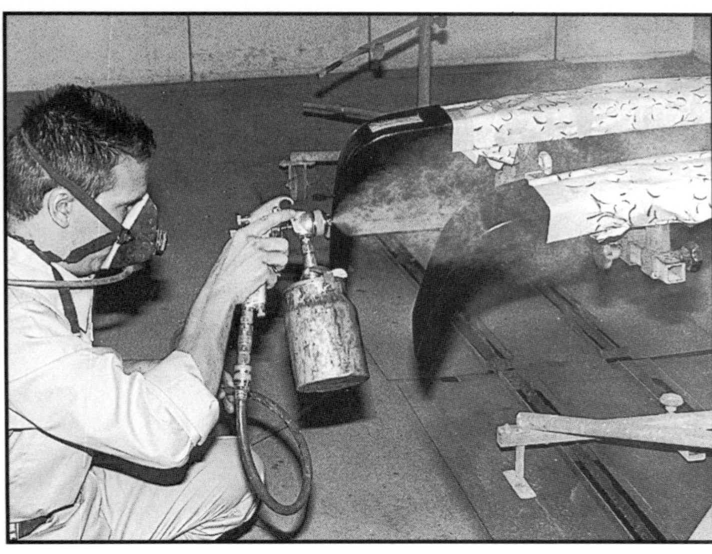

IA6.22
Whilst waiting for the primer to dry, a special hardener was added to the paint mixed earlier. In addition, a soft face additive was mixed in. It is this which allows the paint to remain flexible when dry. Around 5 per cent of the volume should be used, but if too much is added, you could end up with paint that won't dry!

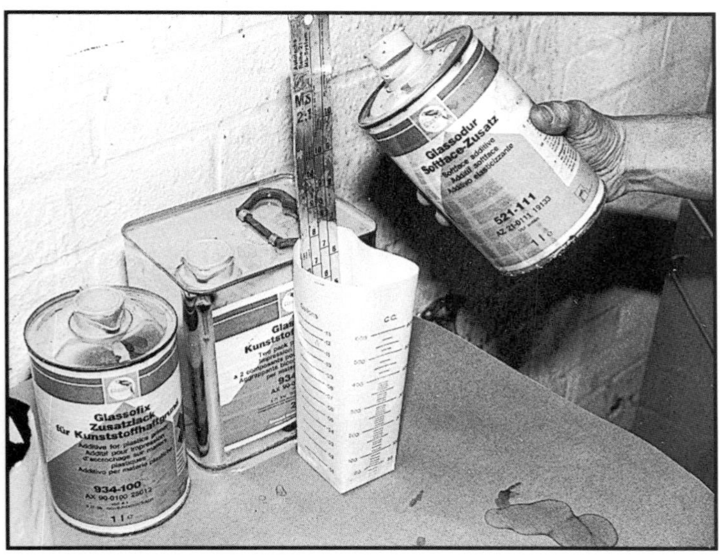

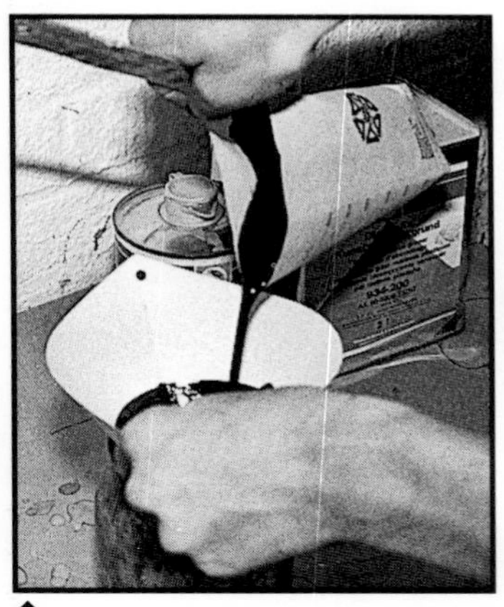

IA6.23
After adding the thinners, the paint is ready to be filtered and poured into the spray gun.

IA6.24
And so it was back into the spray booth. When you watch an expert at work, you cannot help but be slightly amazed at the small amount of paint which seems to leave the gun. However, this is the mark of a professional as the immaculate finish, devoid of runs or drips, shows.

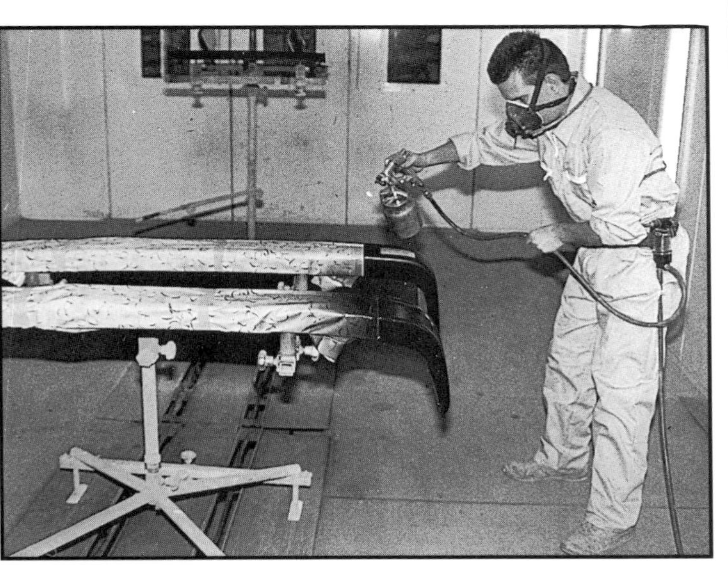

Colour coding

Rye Mill use only Glasurit paint systems, giving the benefit of the highest level of technological development. They are able to accurately reproduce more than 13,000 paint colours from stock. Because of this, Rye Mill proudly assert that they are able to guarantee colour matching. Unless you want the strangest looking Fiesta in the UK, this kind of assurance is something to search out *before* you have your car painted!

Fitting rear screen transfers

Mitchell Marketing claim that these transfers act as a theft deterrent because the car is instantly recognisable as it is being driven away from the scene of the crime. Food for thought indeed! Certainly, no one need be in any doubt as to the make of your car with one of these fitted.

IA7.1
It is essential that the glass area be clean and totally free of stickers. We used a spirit wipe and a razor scraper to attain this. The transfers come on a protective paper backing which is peeled off and ...

IA7.2
... the transfer stuck on the glass.. Take care to ensure that the logo is both central and level. It's possible to do this on your own but an assistant makes it easier. Remember that the transfer has to be put in position with the letters in reversed order (like reading in a mirror!). Look carefully, for it is very easy to end up with a Backflash reading "ATSEIF"!

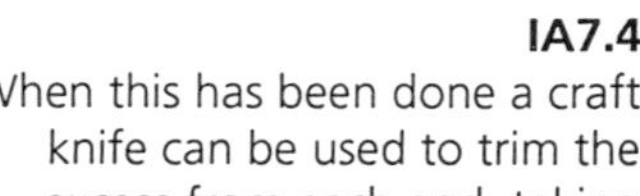

IA7.4
When this has been done a craft knife can be used to trim the excess from each end, taking care not to damage fingers.

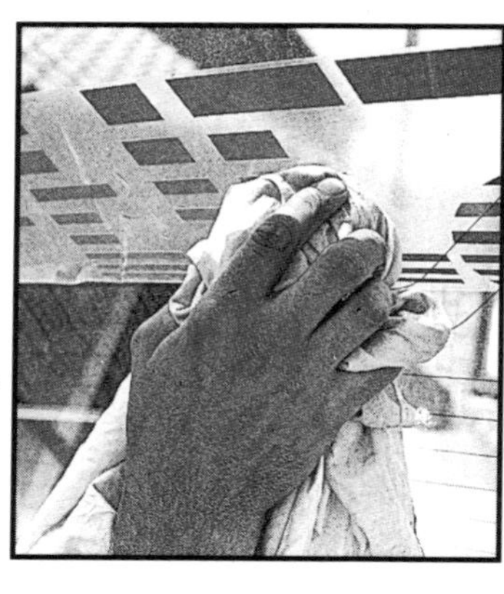

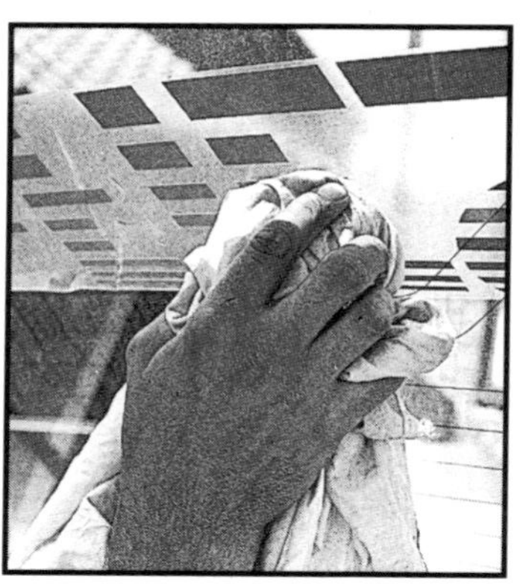

IA7.3
Once in position, the red logo and stripes can be pressed firmly into place, making sure that there are no bubbles or creases.

IA7.5
The clear plastic backing should be pulled back slowly. If the previous instructions have been followed the logo and stripes will be left perfectly positioned. We chose "FIESTA" for this particular car. Mitchell Marketing can also supply other suitable logos in the same style but if none of these is to your liking you can specify your own logo, up to twelve characters in length.

Fitting headlamp transfers

These headlamp transfers, known as "Protectalines" are also designed to give your car a distinctive look. Also, should a headlamp get broken, they will prevent the broken glass from dropping out and you can keep the car on the road until a replacement light unit is fitted.

IA8.1
Protectalines are available in red, black or white which will either contrast or complement the bodywork of your car regardless of its hue.

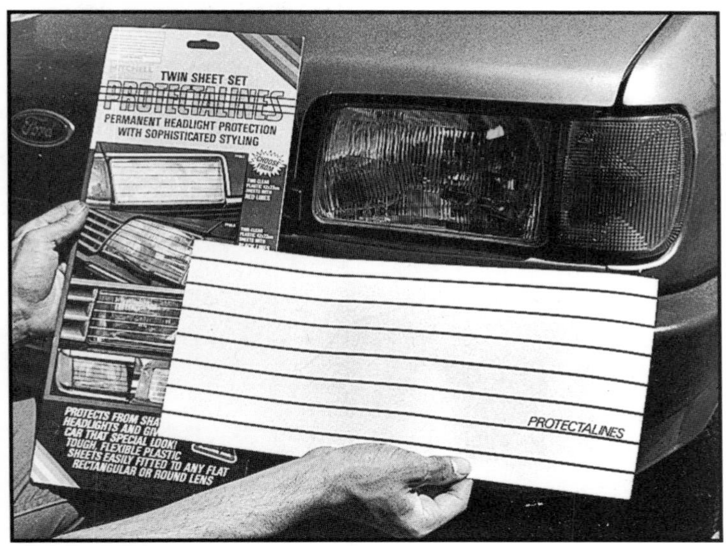

IA8.2
The Protectalines consist of a series of lines on a clear plastic adhesive backing. The first task is to cut the sheet roughly to the size of your particular headlamps. If you have extra lamps, either bracket mounted or possibly in a grille, then you will probably need an extra set.

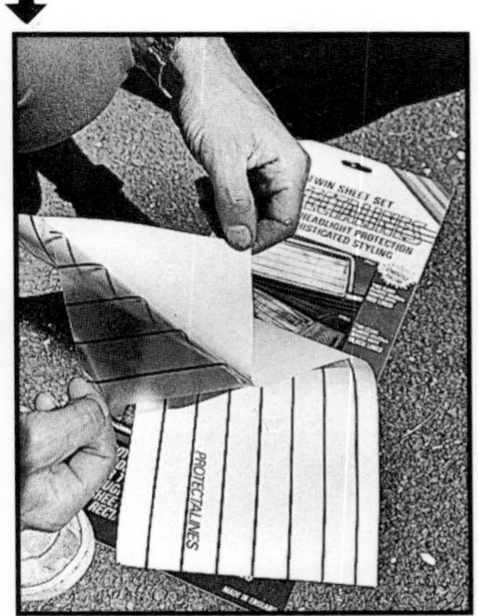

IA8.3
The headlamp has to be very clean, which means getting every splattered insect and every piece of sticky tar off. Having done so, give the lens a good dousing with warm water mixed with a little washing up liquid. This allows a little time ...

IA8.4
... for the Protectalines to be positioned correctly before the strong glue sets. After it has dried, the edges of the sticker can be pressed into place around the headlamp and trimmed with a craft knife if required. And that's it : an end result which is both attractive and functional.

Bodykit options

There are many bodykits available, some of which are shown in this section. However, you should take care to buy a good quality, well fitting kit, for anything that is less than this will be aerodynamically inefficient as well as (eventually) spoiling the look of your car and may even be dangerous. Whichever kit or spoiler you decide to fit, make sure that it is correctly and securely fitted. It's not an easy DIY task, especially if you do not have a good sized garage and facilities to leave your car on ramps for a day or two. If you don't feel confident, take it to a professional.

IA9.1 The chunky, rakish lines of the Mk I Fiesta make it a natural for body kit suppliers. This is the Fibresport XR2/Super Sport kit which, in its basic form, comprises four wheel arches and a front spoiler. All items are produced in black textured finish, moulded in tough GRP. Because of this, even when fitted without colour coding, they will still look good. Whilst the arches are by no means huge, they will allow the fitting of a wider wheel and tyre combination if required. The obvious choice is the standard XR2 wheel or, perhaps, a similar 6 inch wheel. The car shown here has the optional side skirts. Similarly finished, they are designed to link neatly into the front and rear wheel arch mouldings. Naturally, most skirts are purchased mainly for their appearance, but they do serve a definite practical purpose in protecting the lower doors and sills from the damaging effects of stone chips.

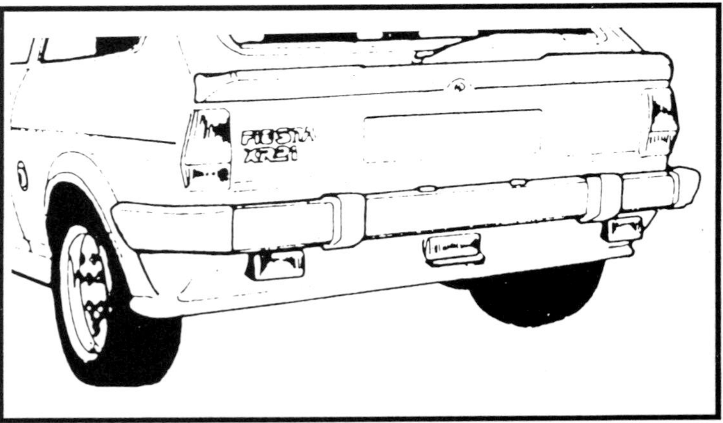

IA9.2
At the rear of the car, a skirt is also available, which gives the Mk I car a Mk II look! Naturally, it is designed to blend in with the wheel arches, skirts and spoiler of the kit shown in photo IA9.1 and features a built-in recess to show the standard reversing light in its original position. Finish is as before, and single or twin fog lamps can also be fitted into this unit.

IA9.3
Not for the shy and introverted! The Fibresports Fiesta Mk I Z-Pack is a radical crowd puller par excellence. It is a 12-piece kit, comprising front spoiler, four wheel arches, two running boards, four inner arches and rear spoiler. Originally produced in conjunction with a major motoring magazine, not surprisingly it has become immensely popular. The various panels lock together to achieve the smooth look and there are internal fixing flanges on the wheel arches for easy, hidden attachment. In order to make the car look right, a wider wheel and tyre combination is required. A 6 inch rim, such as the standard XR2 wheel, would be fine, or a larger 7 inch offset wheel could be fitted. As with all Fibresports kits, spare sections of the kit are available in case you are unfortunate enough to be involved in an accident.

Of course, the manufacturers themselves are hardly backward at coming forward when it comes to customising your Fiesta and there are at present two RS style kits, suitable for the Mk I, II and the latest Mk III models. All of the Ford RS series body kits shown here are made of extremely strong material (ABS), with the skirts and spoilers being flexible and highly resistant to minor bumps and scrapes.

IA9.4 From this angle, Ford's Mk I RS kit is very similar to the Fibresports kit shown previously. Note the addition of the tailgate spoiler. The kit will suit all Mk I cars except the XR2. For those who own an XR2 or a Super S, there is a side skirt kit which complements the standard fitment wheel arch extensions.
(Photo courtesy Ford Motor Company)

IA9.5 From the front, the RS kit gives the standard Fiesta a similar look to that of the XR2, albeit with a touch more aggression. Note that there are no wheel arch sections as such, but rather the front and rear spoilers and side skirts follow the lines of the arches to approximately halfway up the arch. It is noticeable that Ford are not encouraging the use of a wheel wider than 6 inches or taller than 15 inches.
(Photo courtesy Ford Motor Company)

IA9.6 At the rear, the under bumper valance is less pronounced than that of the XR2. The combined roof and tailgate spoiler kit adds a lot of style and can be used independently of the body kit. Naturally, the function of the rear wiper is unaffected.
(Photo courtesy Ford Motor Company)

Bodykit options

Another important point is ground clearance. Almost invariably, fitting an accessory spoiler, whether as part of a kit or on its own, will reduce the ground clearance. Obviously, if you fit the RS spring lowering kit as well as a spoiler, you will definitely have to watch out. Take extra care when parking near high kerbs or when approaching ramps or the dreaded "sleeping policemen". The clearance problem can be exacerbated if lower profile tyres are fitted, as they too will reduce the ride height. At the back of the car, remember that a large rear spoiler could well reduce your rearward vision and that you will need to take extra care when parking.

IA9.7
For those lucky people who have one of the very latest Fiestas (a Mk III, of course), Ford have already got an RS body kit available. The kit shown here comprises: front and rear spoilers, side skirts and rear valance. It should be noted that the front spoiler and rear valance kits are not suitable for the fuel injected XR2. The front foglamps are not standard with the kit but are available as optional extras.
(Photo courtesy Ford Motor Company)

IA9.8
Equally as attractive from the rear, that lower tailgate spoiler gives just a hint of the Sierra Cosworth. Note the change of wheels on this car, which are the 6J x 14 inch "Snowflake" models. For the Mk III series cars, there is also an RS spring lowering kit suitable for all models except the XR2i and vehicles with the SCS braking system.

Fitting a bodykit to your Fiesta is, in theory at least, DIY-able. However, it is not a task to be taken lightly and the ability to work logically and accurately is absolutely essential. As you can see, Trimoco used one of their many two post hoists for the fitting which made the task much easier than grovelling about on the floor, which is usually the lot of the DIY fitter. Also, although the task was completed in less than a working day, this reflects not only the professional equipment used but also the skill and experience. Fitting by the average owner would doubtless take considerably longer. All in all, we would recommend that, having paid good money to buy your kit and have it painted, you spend a little more and have it professionally fitted.

IA10.1
Seen in plan, this is the Fiesta RS bodykit, comprising front and rear spoilers, rear valance and two side skirts. There is also one extra spoiler here, which fits at the top of the tailgate and is standard on the 1.6S model we show in this section. If you have a Mk III car without one, you can buy it as an aftermarket accessory.

IA10.2
First stop was the Trimoco spray booth, where Pete applied the relevant primers, paint and years of experience. Note the use of air fed breathing gear, a definite safety requirement.

IA10.3
After being baked in the oven, we have a superbly finished body kit in Metisse Blue, accurately matching the colour of the car.

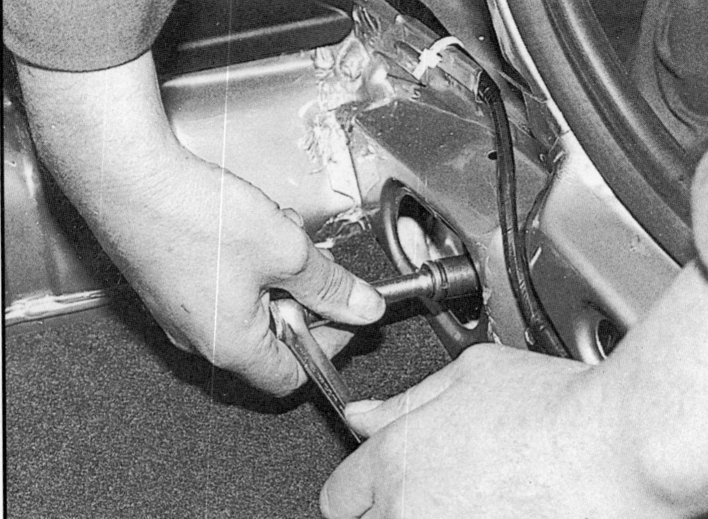

IA10.4
Then the work of fitting began. Starting at the rear, the bumper has to be removed. It is held by two bolts, accessed from inside the hatch and ...

Fitting a full bodykit

All body kits look better if colour coded to match the body colour. However, such painting is a highly skilled operation and, of course, special paint has to be used to ensure that it does not crack as the kit flexes. Using high quality Glasurit primers and paints will ensure a standard of finish equal to that of the car. But remember, these two-pack paints *demand* the use of a professional spray booth, for safety's sake.

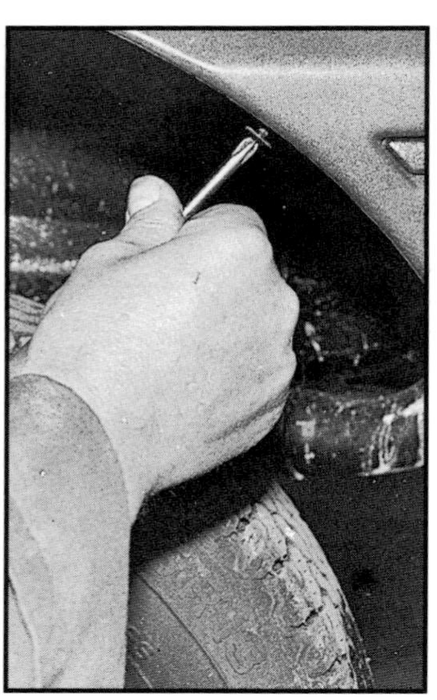

IA10.5
... two self-tapping screws in each wheel arch.

IA10.6
The number plate lamp unclips from the bumper and the two electrical wires unplug, leaving ...

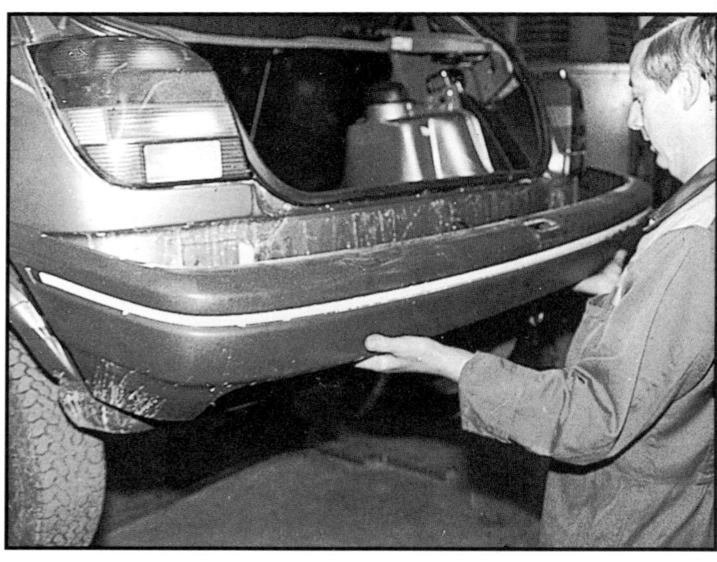

IA10.7
... the whole unit free to slide easily away.

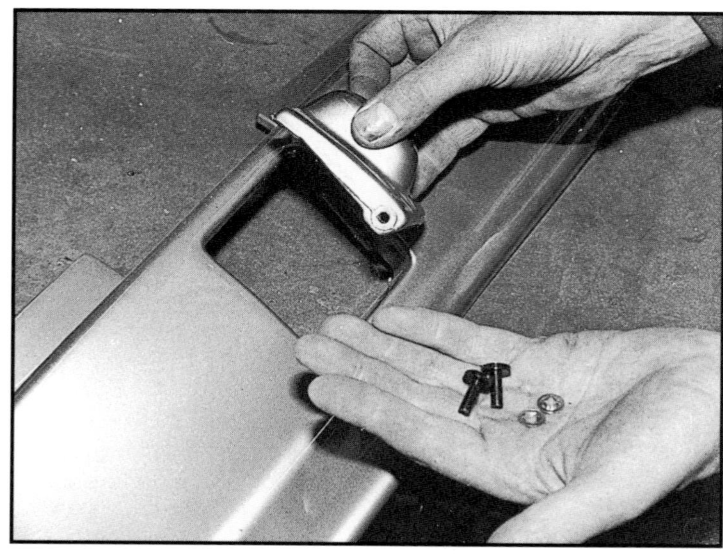

IA10.8
Before starting to fit the rear valance, the towing eye cover has to be fitted. This small cap is kept in place by two plastic bolts which also allow it to pivot, should the eye be required.

IA10.9
When offered up, the RS rear valance fits snugly into the contours of the car, making the measuring and then the drilling of the holes an easier task than on many other kits, which have to be supported in some way. A cordless drill is ideal, especially when there are so many holes to make. For the same reason ...

As you can see, Trimoco sprayed the various bodykit panels before fitting them to the car. This is because the Ford produced RS kit is sufficiently accurate not to need any alterations, however minor. But, not all accessory kits are as accurate and must be "mock fitted" before entering the spray booth so that any imperfections in fit or finish can be rectified beforehand.

IA10.10
... a cordless driver/drill is used to secure the valance with the self-tapping screws provided. Seven screws are used to locate the valance across the width of the car (in a 2/3/2 formation), as well as a further one per side in the rear wheel arches.

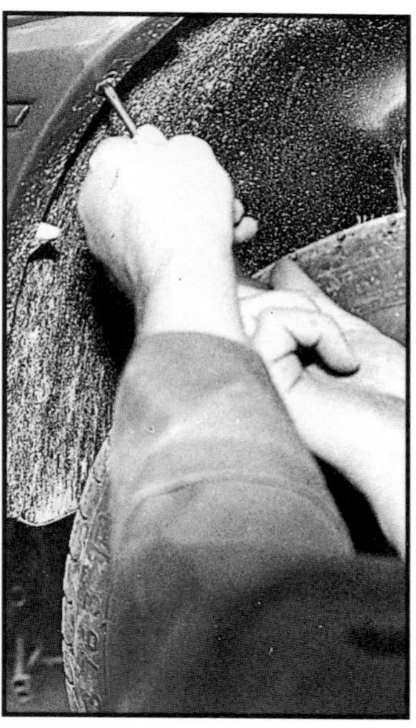

IA10.11
A similar process is followed for the removal of the front bumper, although the two retaining bolts are accessed from under the car, a task made easier by having the car raised on Trimoco's hoist. Then, one screw per side is removed from the wheel arch and ...

IA10.12
... the bumper pulls away. Bear in mind that, with older cars, care has to be taken to ensure that no dirt falls into the eyes.

The thoroughness of the cleaning procedure cannot be emphasized too much. Although the new panels and spoilers will be screwed into place, the glue used for the side skirts won't "take" properly unless all surfaces are totally free from contamination.

IA10.13➡
As at the rear, the towing eye comes in for treatment, though this time with a long prise bar! It has to be bent down some sixty degrees so that it does not foul the front spoiler.

⬅IA10.14
The front spoiler clips into position whilst the hole positions are marked and double checked. When Fred was sure that it was just right, it was time for more drilling, followed by ...

IA10.15➡
... more self-tapping screws. This time, four screws are used across the front of the car, with one either side ...

⬅IA10.16
... being fitted under the wheelarch. As a mark of thoroughness, Trimoco always put a spot of body colour paint, in this case Metisse Blue, over any visible screw heads such as these.

IA10.17
Lots already done, but not yet half way there, the Fiesta sits looking somewhat dejected with extra spoiler but no bumper.

Trimoco always ensure that all steps are taken to prevent the onset of rust from holes drilled in order to fit the bodykit. Both zinc paint and Corroless rust preventative were applied wherever there was the slightest possibility that the dreaded rust bug could get hold.

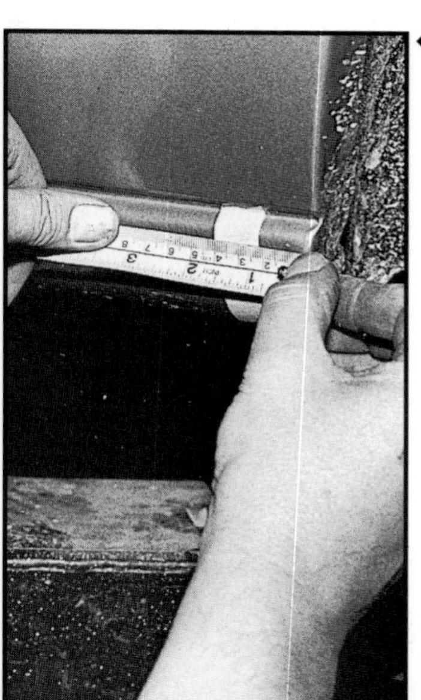

IA10.18
Some very accurate measuring has to be carried out before the side skirts are fitted, for obvious reasons! Masking tape is used to aid location and also ...

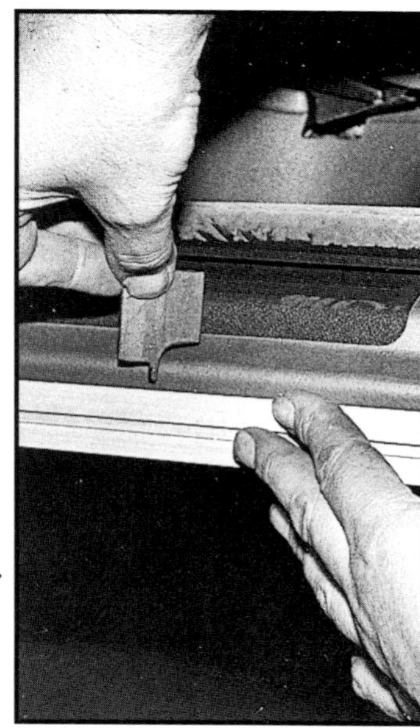

IA10.19
... a special tool is provided to ensure that the skirt is kept absolutely level throughout its length.

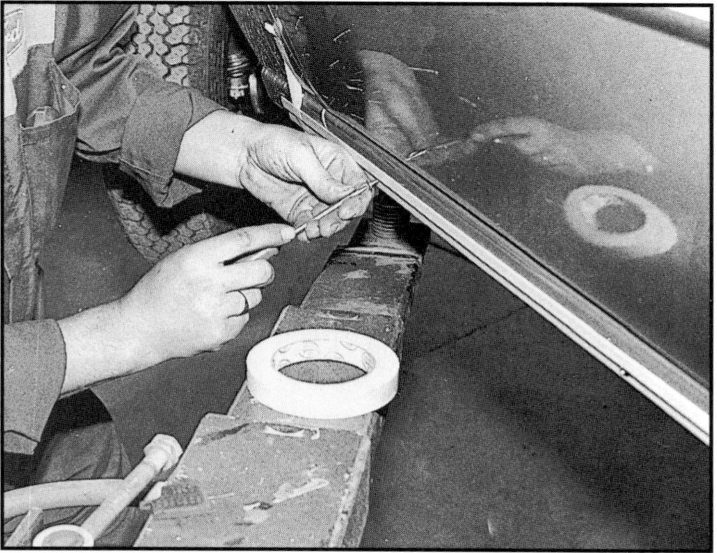

IA10.20
The next item to be fitted is a side skirt retaining rail which looks not unlike a piece of domestic curtain track! Again, this is held in position by seven self-tapping screws.

Fitting a full bodykit

Wherever holes were drilled in the bodywork, the positions were carefully marked with a scriber and then pilot drilled. This is important as it reduces the risk of the drill bit skidding and damaging the paintwork.

IA10.21➔
Careful here – getting this two pack glue on your fingers is not recommended. It's meant to hold the skirts in position through the rigours of many years of motoring and consequently, removing it from human digits can be a very time consuming task! It would be wise to don a pair of surgical gloves for this operation. When mixed, an applicator is used ...

🡐IA10.22
... to squeeze it neatly into the top channel of the retaining rail. Into this channel ...

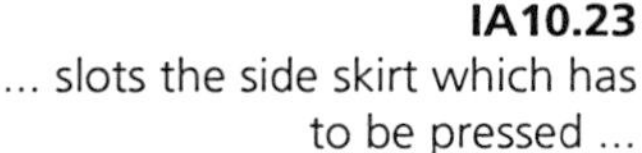

IA10.23➔
... slots the side skirt which has to be pressed ...

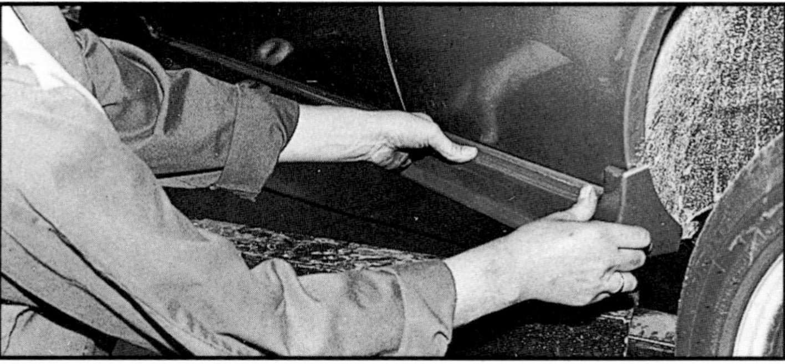

🡐IA10.24
... very firmly into place. If the previous measuring has been carried out correctly, the skirt should be an exact fit to the length of the car and, of course, perfectly level. The fit was perfect.

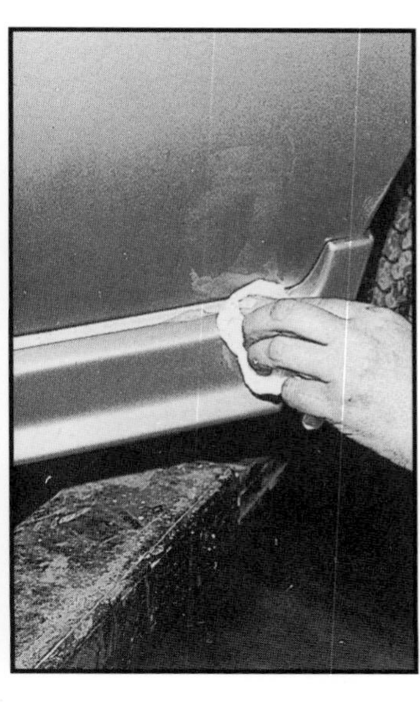

IA10.25
It is vital that any excess glue is wiped away immediately from any visible surfaces, for once it sets, removal is far from easy.

IA10.26
The final touch for the side skirts is the drilling of the ends (which "wrap around" the front and rear wheel arches) and requires yet more self-tappers.

The Fiesta 1.6S shown here comes with a spoiler fitted at the upper edge of the tailgate as standard. However, should you have a model without it, do not despair, for it is available as an accessory and is not difficult to fit, as can be seen in the photos here.

IA10.27
With the other side skirt being fitted in exactly the same manner, we moved to the rear of the car. As mentioned, the Mk III 1.6S has a sporty little spoiler which fits at the top of the hatch window. It had been taken off for colour coding and so replacement was simply a question of linking up the spoiler with the existing holes ...

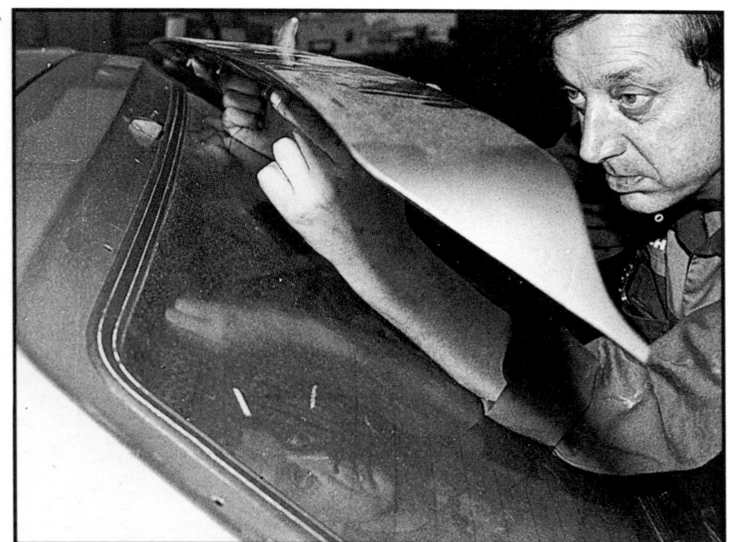

IA10.28
... and then tightening the nuts from inside the tailgate. As well as the top nuts which hold the spoiler across its width, it is also held ...

Fitting an RS bodykit

As you can see, the kit relies heavily on the use of self-tapping screws to hold it in position. When fitting the front spoiler and rear valance, Fred took the wise move of treating them with a coat of grease. This has two benefits, the first being that it adds to the protection against rust, already given to the newly drilled hole and secondly, it means that should either of the spoilers need to be removed at some time in the future, there is less likelihood of the screws being rusted.

IA10.29
... at either end by a large plastic coated rivet, in order to prevent the ingress of water.

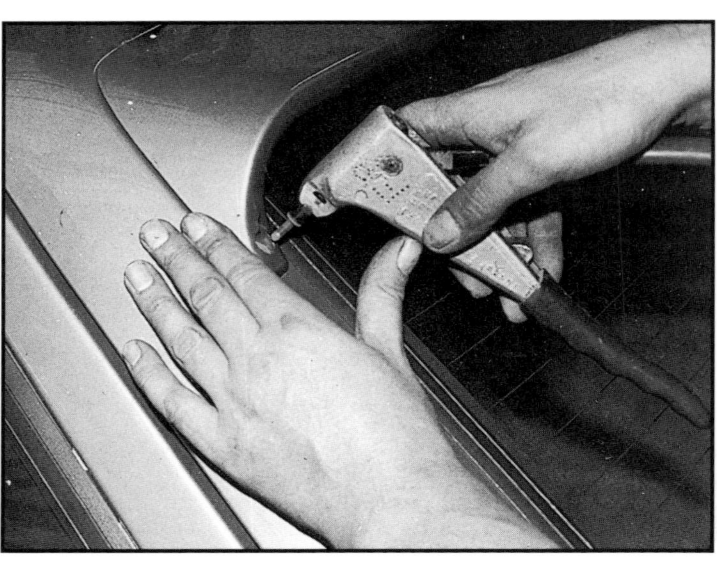

IA10.30
The new RS spoiler requires two holes to be drilled in the lower part of the tailgate and has an ingenious method of fixing which removes the danger of possibly drilling holes in the wrong places. A plastic guide is slotted into the two holes in the spoiler.

IA10.31
Then, the spoiler is held in position and moved around until it is exactly right. Following this, the backing tape is removed from the double-sided stickies attached to the guides, and when the spoiler is lifted away ...

IA10.32
... the guides are left in place. As they are hollow, it is a simple matter to use them to drill directly into the tailgate. Into these holes, strong plastic plugs are placed which will take the studs of the spoiler.

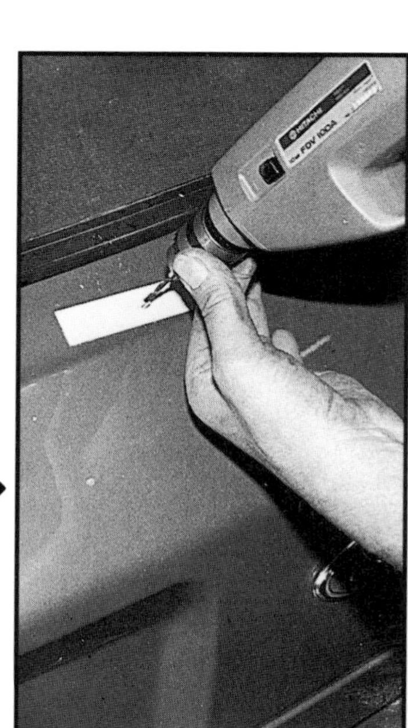

IA10.33
Two studs are inserted in the two centre supports and more glue is used around these and the ends of the spoiler, just to make sure! Note that the spoiler fits over the rear wiper and does not affect its operation at all.

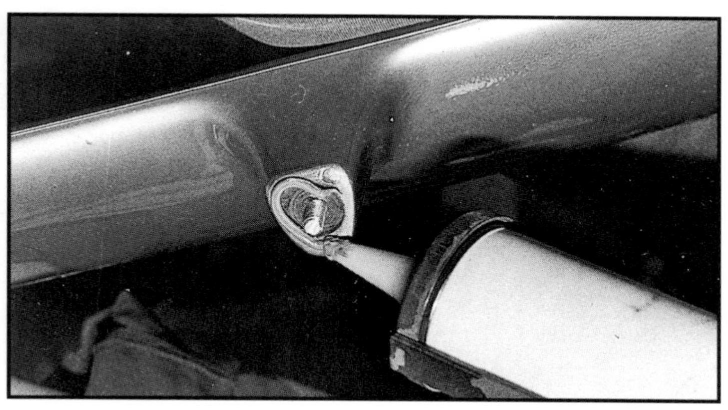

IA10.34
A last clean of all the bodywork sections with the special polish supplied with the kit and the job is complete.

IA10.35
It certainly adds a touch of aggression to the smooth, aerodynamic shape of the new Fiesta, but without the "over-the-top" look of some kits. Next, a set of nice allloys would look good!

Having fitted your colour coded kit, you should be aware that the new paintwork is likely to be "soft" for a few days. Take great care with it and we would recommend not washing the car for a fortnight after fitting. Although such a kit should be able to stand up to the rigours of a good car wash, we would also recommend that you do not take the risk and hand wash in future. Similarly, when you get the inevitable tar splashes on the spoilers or side skirts, refer to your dealer for what is best to use.

Using Holts Autofilm

One thing that won't improve the appearance of your Fiesta is paintwork covered in scratches and other marks. Really bad damage will need to be resprayed, of course, but until recently, the only way to get rid of unsightly paint chips was to use a touch-up brush. However, Holts have developed "Autofilm", which is a unique self-adhesive film which you simply apply to the marked area. With some 300 colours in the range, you're unlikely to find that your car colour isn't covered and its very nature means that you can carry it around in the glovebox and repair minor paintwork damage as and when it occurs.

IA11.1
First and foremost you must know the exact colour of your car. Just saying "red" is not enough, for in the catalogue shown here, there are already ten Ford "reds" listed! If your local accessory shop does not have your particular colour, then you can buy an Autofilm voucher. There is a simple form inside which you complete and return to Holts HQ in the prepaid envelope supplied. They will then send you your Autofilm direct.

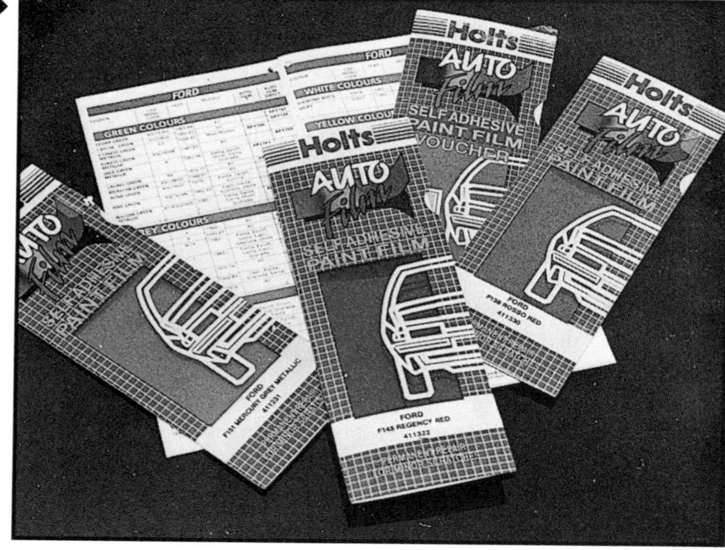

IA11.2
Before you start, your paintwork must be clean with no traces of dirt, flies, road dirt or grease; otherwise the adhesive film will not stick properly.

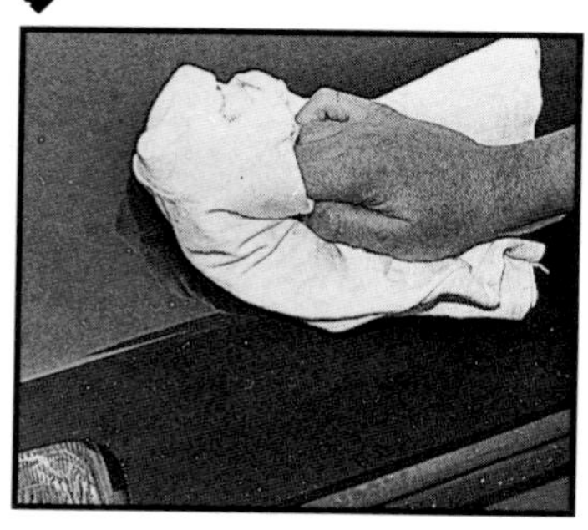

IA11.3
What looks like a single large sheet of coloured film is actually scored into many different sized pieces. So, whether you need to repair a small chip or a large one, there will be a size ready cut. They peel off like this and ...

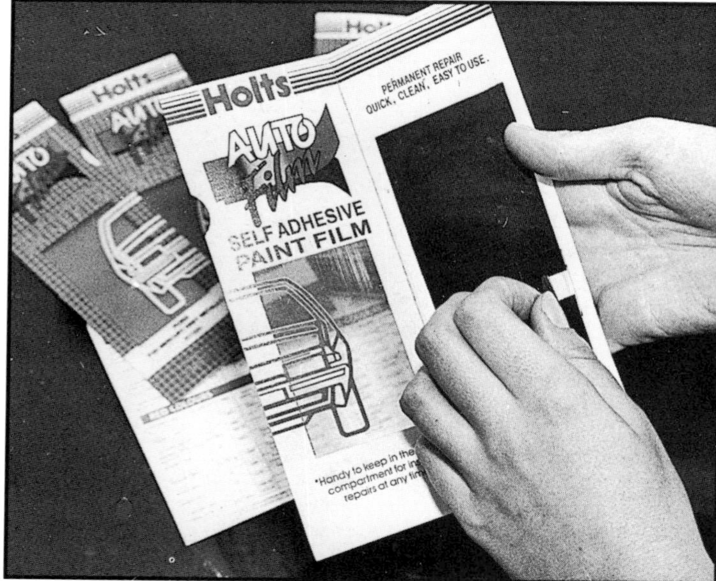

IA11.4
... you then simply have to place the piece of film in position. The maximum adhesion is reached after approximately five hours. The repair is permanent and just as resistant to weathering, heat, petrol, washing and waxing as the normal paint surface of your Fiesta.

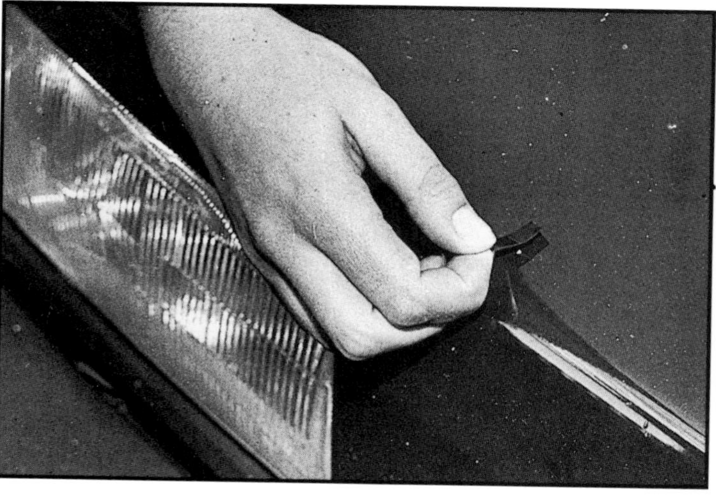

Fitting sideliners

IA12.1
The Sideliner trim comes in large reels and is ready to apply. The colour you choose will depend on the colour and trim of your own particular car. The Fiesta shown here was black and so red was chosen to contrast. The trim sticks into place and so it was necessary to clean the area beforehand with a spirit wipe.

IA12.2
Once the Sideliner has been measured, it can be cut with a sharp craft knife ...

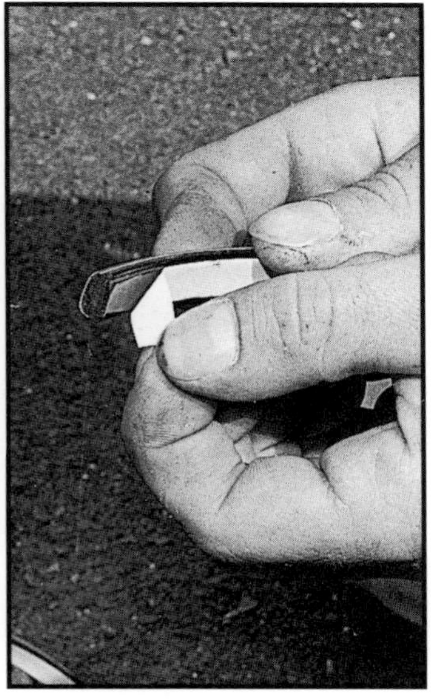

IA12.3
... the protective backing film pulled off and ...

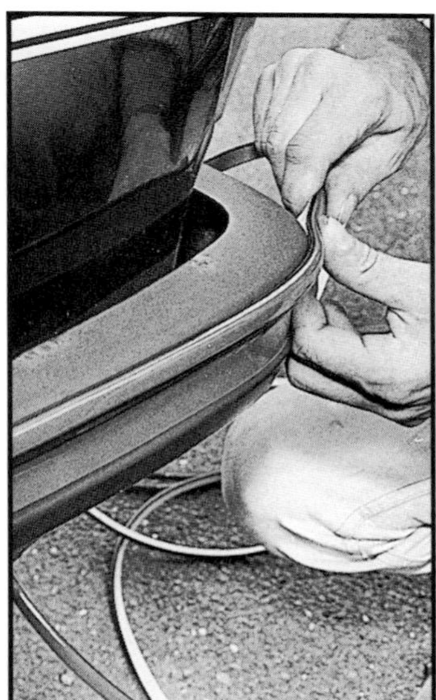

IA12.4
... then placed in its final position. This can be a little nerve-racking as it's got to be spot-on, first time. Take your time as a badly fitted Sideliner will make your car look absolutely awful. As you can see, it requires either four hands or a helper!

IA12.5
A quick and easy way of protecting and smartening your Fiesta in one fell swoop.

Branyl describe their self-adhesive trims as impossible to reposition once they are in place. From the DIY point of view, this means that much care has to be taken to ensure that they are correctly positioned before being pressed into place. Branyl recommend that the car is not washed for a week after the Sideliner trim has been fitted and that a temperature of 20 degrees or more is required for successful fitment. Sideliner car trim can be used both to protect your Fiesta (by using them on the edges of the doors, for example), and to improve the looks when used around rusty wheelarches. It is available in chrome, red or black finish.

Fitting a sports door mirror

This section shows just two of the Sedan range of sports mirrors, any of which will improve the looks of your Fiesta. If you are replacing a standard mirror (rather than adding a new one altogether), then you should ensure that the new mirror mounting bracket will cover the original hole in the door.

IA13.1
The "Sebring Racing" door mirror is a stylish, tinted unit which, like all Sedan mirrors, comes complete with a fitting kit. Available in black only, it is universal (and thus will fit either left- or right-hand doors) and can be adjusted to any comfortable angle. It is extremely stable and will not vibrate, even at high speed.

IA13.2
This diagram shows that fitting is not at all difficult. Just two holes need to be drilled, after which the mirror mounting bracket screws into place. Don't forget to rust proof any holes you drill.
(Diagram courtesy Link Sedan Ltd)

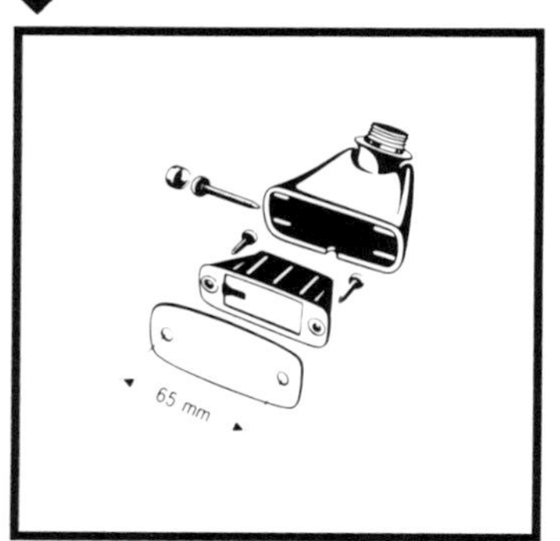

IA13.3
A definite improvement on the rather staid, standard issue. It can be left in the self-colour black or, if required, painted to match the body colour (see Section 6).

IA13.4
The "Sports" is another smart mirror, although, unlike the "Sebring" it is available in either black, red or white. It, too, is universal.

Fitting a sunroof

The sunroof fitted here is the Automaxi Mistral "Prestige", which measures 770 x 400mm (approx 30 x 16 inches) and has a toughened and tinted glass panel. The panel is instantly removable if required and is made of Solar reflective glass. We see it here being installed by a highly trained and very skilled fitter at the Leighton Buzzard HQ of Automaxi, who talked us through this quick and professional fitting of the sunroof to a Mk I Fiesta.

Fitting a sunroof to your Fiesta is, in theory at least, DIY-able, provided that the fitter is very accomplished and able to work to the fine tolerances involved. In practice, however, you would be well advised to leave the work to an expert, such as Automaxi's top fitter, Kelvin Oliver, shown here. The risks involved if things go wrong, from a mistake in cutting the roof to a trim-spoiling leak, are not worth encountering.

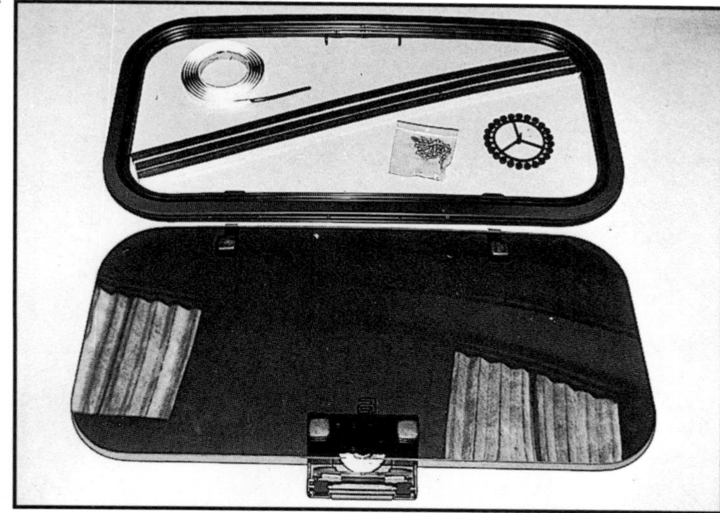

IA14.1→ The sunroof kit comes with everything necessary to complete the installation, including all fastenings and the sealant. Note that the latter is not the usual, gooey type, but is in the form of a solid roll; far less messy!

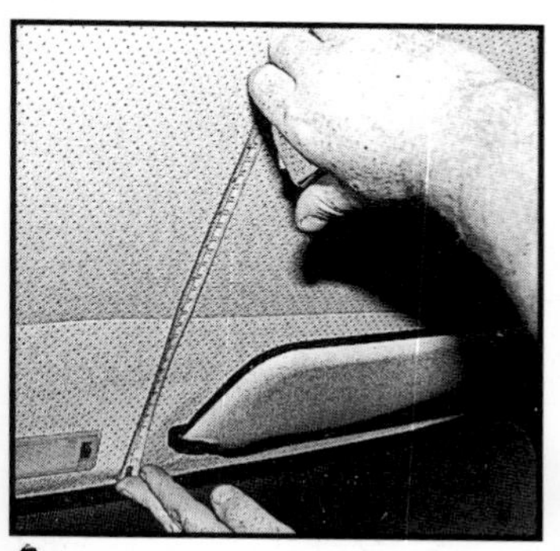

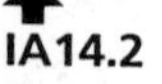

IA14.2 First and most important job is measuring. This is followed by checking, more measuring and then checking again! Here, Kelvin is measuring approximately one inch beyond the back of the sun visors, in order to have the sunroof in the correct position – over the front two occupants rather than the rear!

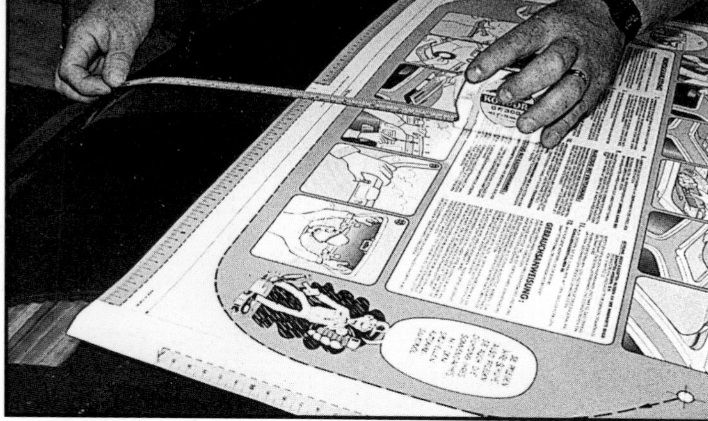

IA14.3→ This measurement is then transferred to the top of the car to give a basic start for the template which comes with the kit.

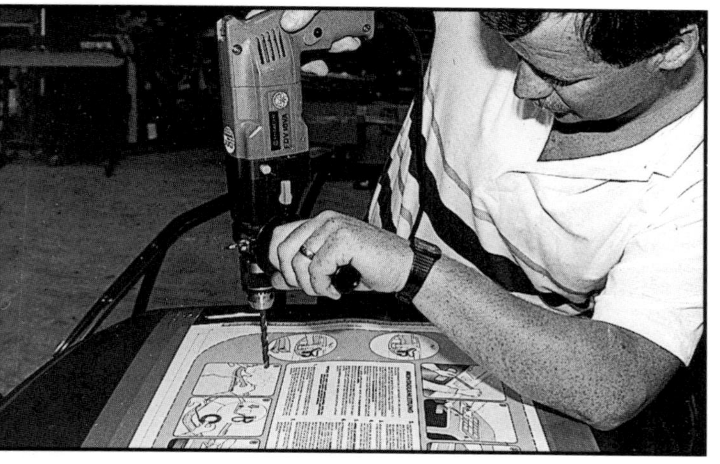

IA14.4→ Having checked that the template is sitting square, it is securely taped down and a pilot hole drilled for the hole cutter to start in. Note that the hole was drilled only through the metal, not the headlining, which has a natural tendency to wind itself around the drill bit.

Fitting a sunroof

Although like many glass sunroofs, the Automaxi Prestige is totally removable, the company do not offer a carry bag or a wind deflector as options. However, the reason for this becomes obvious when you check out the very wide opening aperture. As they say, most people only remove the roof altogether in order to get more fresh air; with this roof, you don't need to!

IA14.5
As you can see, a high quality metal shear is used, as jig-saws tend to create a lot of messy and dangerous swarf. Note that Kelvin is taking no chances and pulling out the sliver of roof with a gloved hand.

IA14.6
A neat and tidy cut means that the roof panel can be lifted out easily. Underneath, there is some sound-deadening material laying on top of the headlining, which has to be removed.

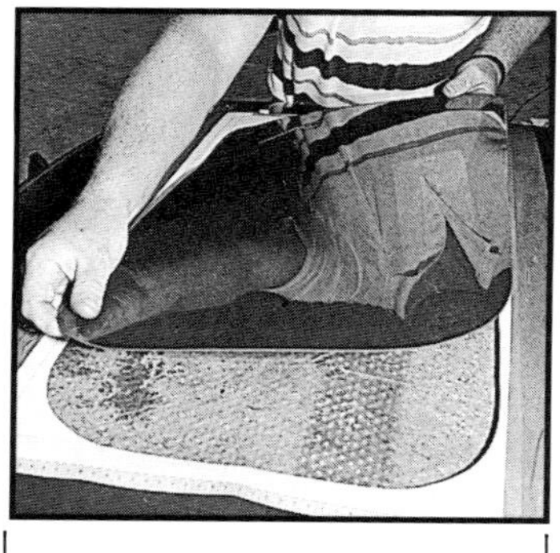

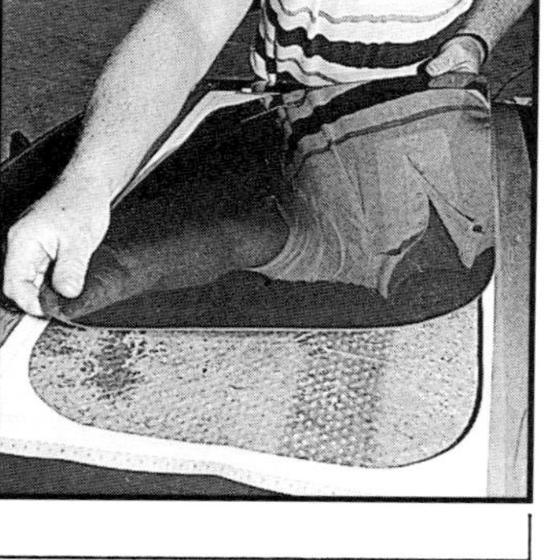

IA14.7
In this model, there is a bracing rod across the top of the car, holding the headlining taut. When removing this, it is important that the sewn join should not be cut, or the whole headlining would fall down.

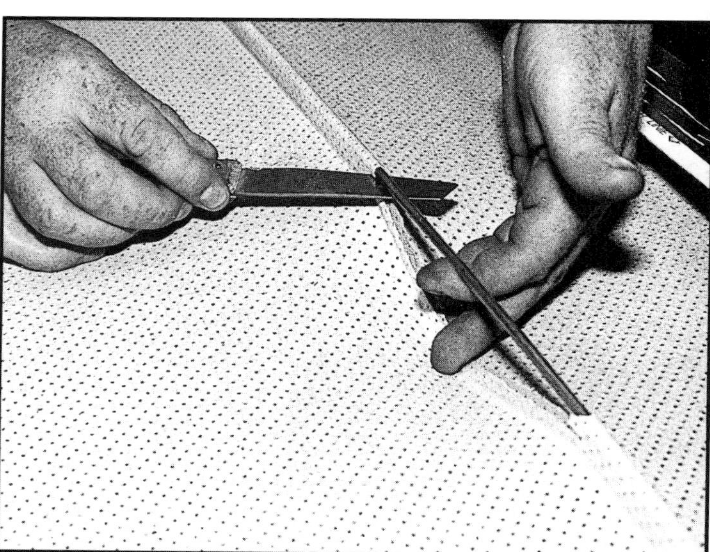

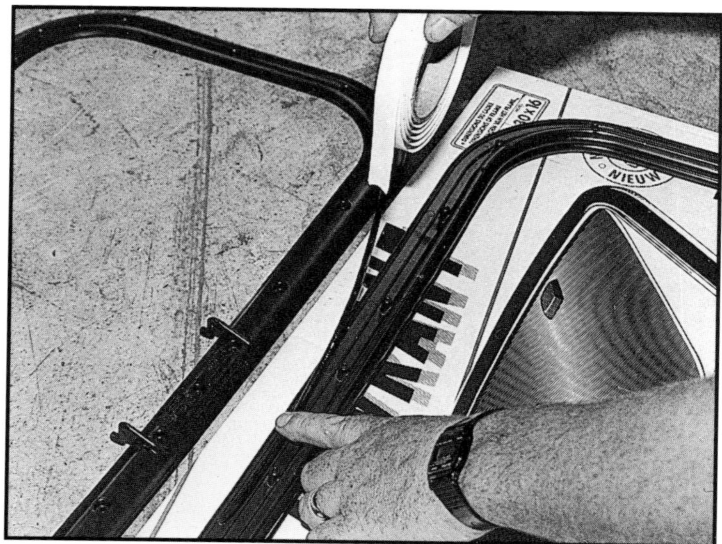

IA14.8
A double check on the accuracy of marking out and cutting is to let the top frame rest in place. It should fit easily, and not be forced. With this confirmed, it is now time to apply the butyl sealant. As you can see, it is far easier and much less messy than conventional, gooey liquid sealants. The join is always made at the back of the roof frame.

IA14.9
Double-sided, self-adhesive strips of foam are used to provide a means of controlling compression between the top and bottom frames and also to hold the soft headlining in place. No less than 28 "torque" screws hold the two frames together and a power screwdriver literally saves on elbow grease here! (see Chapter Five: Power Tools). Part of the fitting kit is a "carousel" of plastic screw caps which leave a nice neat finish to the inside of the roof.

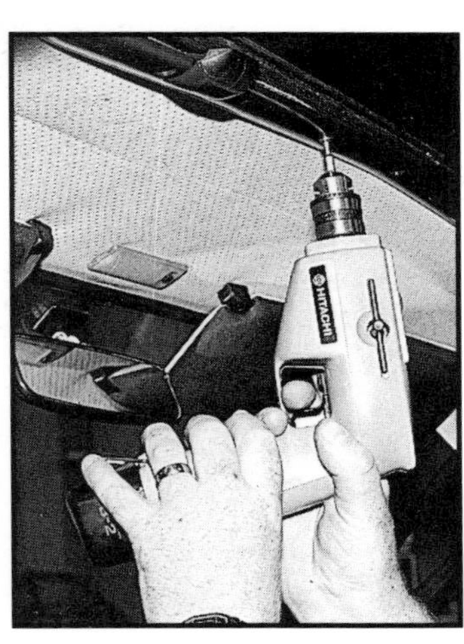

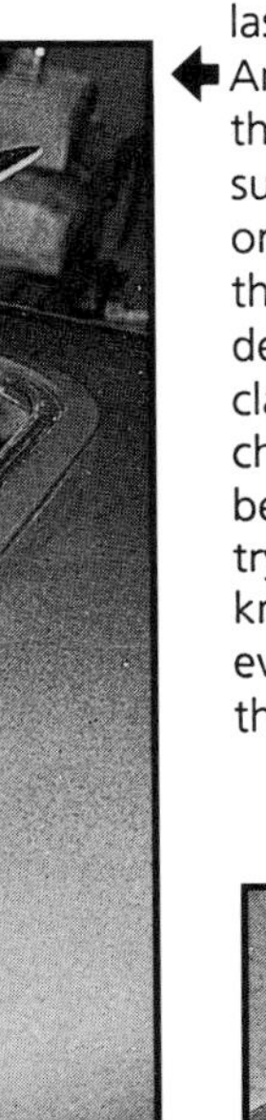

IA14.10
A key feature of the Prestige model is the impressive lockable handle, a rarity indeed and perfect for the security minded Fiesta owner. Not only that, but the design allows the roof to open to a massive 11cm at the last of its four opening positions. An additional safety feature is that should the handle be subjected to a loading of 100 lbs or more whilst the roof is open, the handle will break at a pre-determined overload position. A classic example of this is where children are left in a car (not to be recommended anyway) and try to shut the roof without knowing how to do it, eventually pulling so hard that they damage the roof!

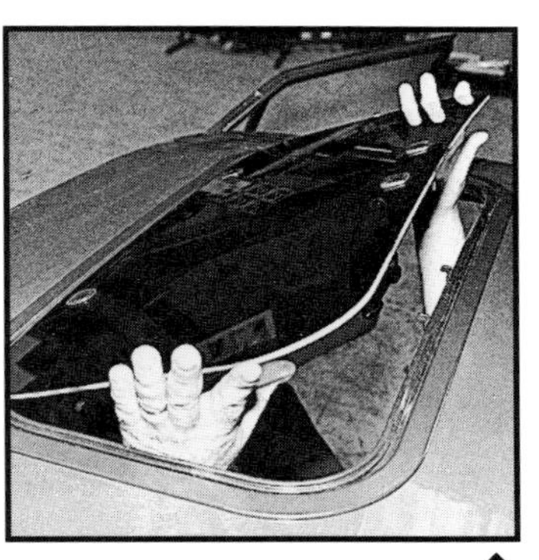

IA14.11
The roof simply slots into position at the front and two pins engage on the handles at the rear. And so we have ...

IA14.12
... a practical and attractive way of improving any Fiesta.

Whether you fit your own roof or choose to have it professionally fitted, it is important to carry out the water test. Hose the top of the car down from all angles, to ensure that there are absolutely no leaks whatsoever. It's best to find out now than in a sudden thunderstorm halfway round the M25!

Fitting front fog lamps

When it comes to producing automotive lighting equipment, Hella have a reputation second to none. Their excellent quality products are the end result of many years research and development and this has been spurred by their massive involvement in motor sport. Hammering down a Keilder Forest single lane cart track, at 90mph in driving rain, is no time to find out that your lamps are no good! If anyone needs good, no-nonsense lighting it's a rally driver! The number of manufacturers (including Ford) who fit Hella lamps as standard equipment, is the best testimony of their ultimate worth.

IA15.1
The Hella Comet range of auxiliary lamps is the latest in a long line of products designed to increase your night-time vision. The Comet 500 models, seen here, are round in shape and available as fog and driving lamps, as are ...

IA15.2
... the Comet 550 versions which are rectangular. All of the Comet range comes equipped with H3, 55 watt halogen bulbs and utilise the latest advances in CAD/CAM with a new backing shell and advanced reflector design for improved safety. Preference for 500 or 550 models is likely to be based purely on personal taste or other modifications you have made to your car. To some, fitting rectangular lamps to the angular Fiesta makes a great deal of sense, as they match well. To others, fitting the round, Comet 500 lamps, makes a nice contrast.

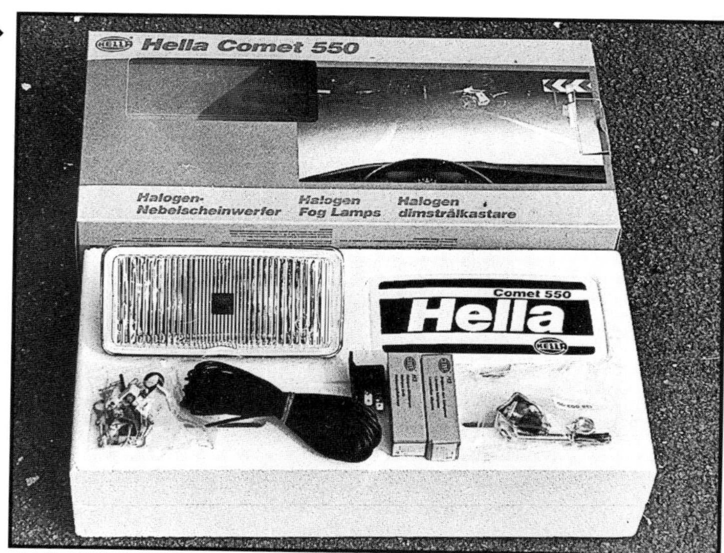

IA15.3
You must **never** touch Halogen bulbs with your fingers. Like this is safe enough, but only remove the bulbs from their protective boxes just before you are ready to put them in the lamp.

IA15.4
The lamps can be fitted to any model Fiesta and if preferred, the bumper can be drilled to take them or brackets used to mount them under the bumper. However, we took the easy route and chose these standard Ford brackets, which were very reasonably priced.

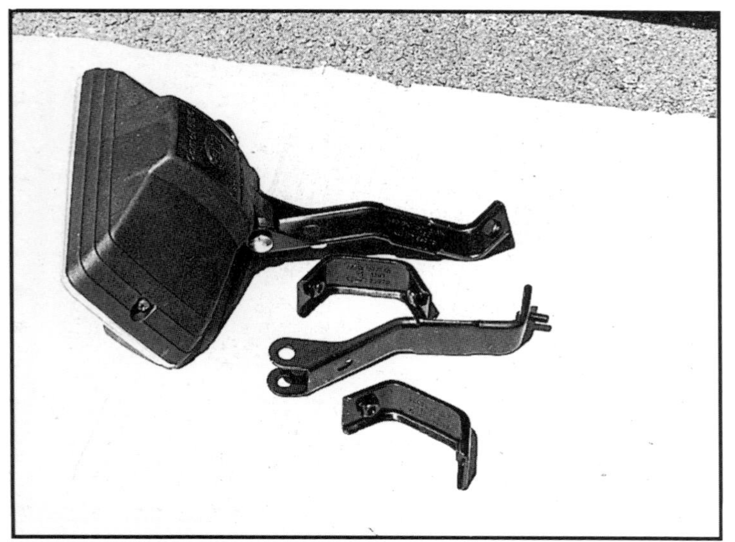

The lighting effect of fog lamps is greater the lower they are mounted and the further they are to the outer edges of the car. Whether you attach the lamps upright or pendant fashion, you must comply with the legal requirements, as shown in this table and diagram.

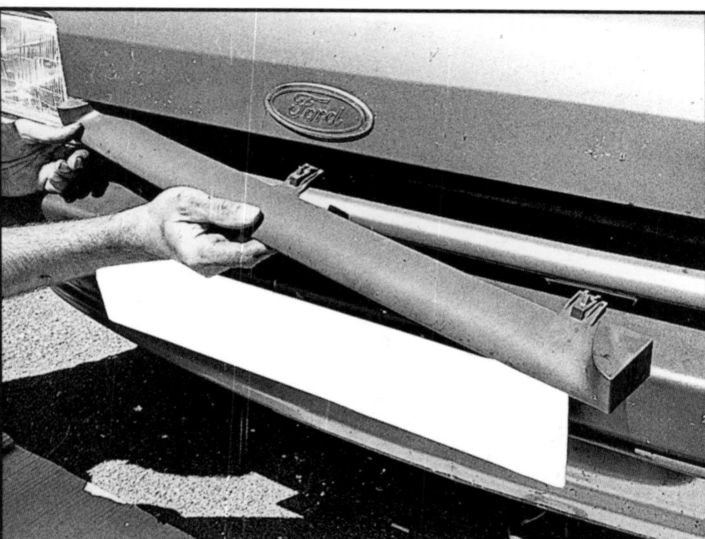

IA15.5
Although it looks as if you have to remove the bumper, you don't! First task is to remove the plastic grille as shown. This is held by a series of three clips, released by *gentle* pressure from a small screwdriver.

1 **Overall height must not be higher than the dipped headlamps.**
2 **The two lamps must be at least 350mm apart.**
3 **The two lamps must be at least 250mm above ground level.**
4 **Each lamp must be no more than 400mm from the very edge of the vehicle.**

If you are unsure about any aspect of fog lamp fitting or legality, you should consult your Hella dealer before you fit them.

(Diagram courtesy Hella Ltd)

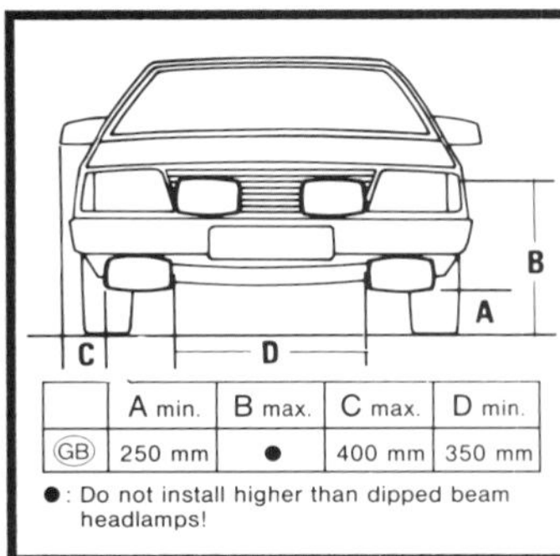

	A min.	B max.	C max.	D min.
GB	250 mm	●	400 mm	350 mm

● : Do not install higher than dipped beam headlamps!

IA15.6
You need to have access to the area just behind the bumper. The simplest method is to undo the two radiator mounting bolts and ease it back slightly which ...

Fitting front fog lamps

The final wiring permutation of the Hella lamps is very much down to the individual, although in order to be fully legal, you must ensure that the lamps can only be switched on with the side lamps and not used on their own. The diagram below shows how the wiring is achieved. Having fitted your lamps, you should pay a great deal of attention to keeping them clean; according to Hella, up to 80 per cent of light from the lamps can be absorbed by dirt on the lenses.

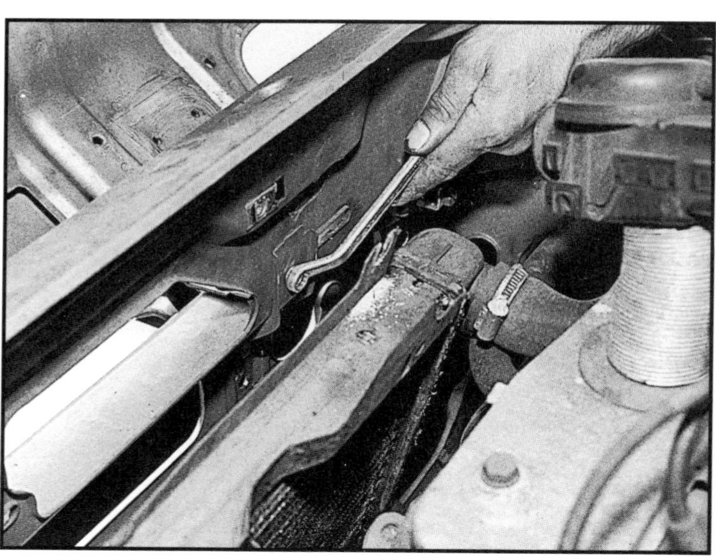

IA15.7
... gives sufficient room for a spanner to be placed on the securing nut for the lower bracket. It should not be attempted with anything but a cold engine!

IA15.8
Like the lower bracket, the other half fits snugly into pre-drilled holes in the Fiesta's front valance and then the two halves of the bracket are joined as shown here.

(Diagram courtesy Hella Ltd)

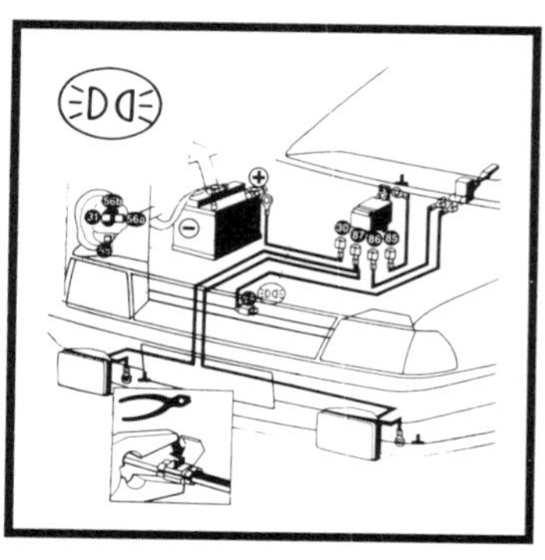

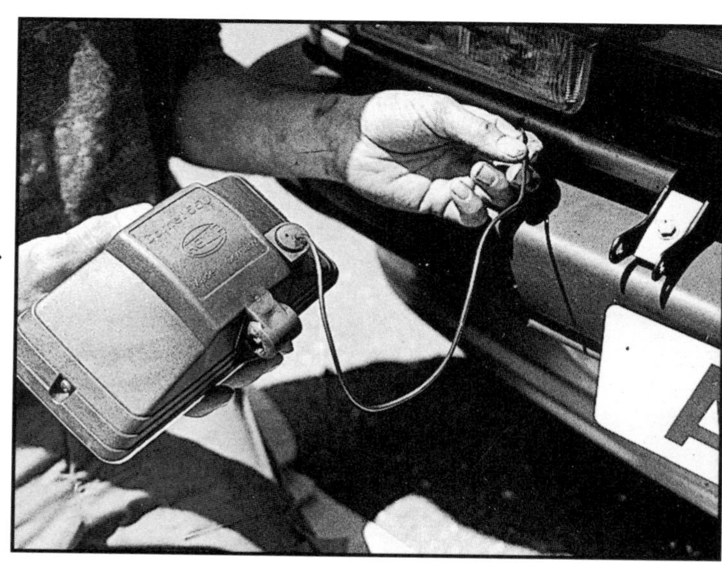

IA15.9
The wiring exits the rear of the lamp via a strong rubber grommet and should be carefully routed whilst the grille is still out. Do not route the wiring where it will be affected by extremes of heat and cold. A relay is supplied with the lamps, which should also be mounted with similar care.

Fitting front fog lamps

IA15.10 ➔
The finished result, vastly improving the car's candlepower and a great safety aid in conditions of reduced visibility. The strong, white plastic covers serve to protect the lamps whilst not in use, and add greatly to the appearance of the car.

This is what you will need to fit the foglamps, as per the handy Hella list in the instructions.

1 A ruler or tape measure
2 A pair of combination pliers
3 A pair of electrical crimpers
4 A Philips screwdriver
5 Spanners, size 13mm, 17mm & 19mm
6 Drill and bits, size 3mm, 10mm and 12mm (unless you use a purpose made bracket)

Fitting fog lamp locking nuts

IA16.1
If you are fitting fog or spot lamps, you should be aware that they pose an often irresistible temptation for those Fiesta "enthusiasts" with light fingers! One way to protect them is to use the Cosmic locking nuts which ...

IA16.2
... work in a similar manner to locking wheel nuts. Once in position on the foglamp mounting bolt (shown here out of situ for clarity), the Cosmic nuts are locked into place with a key. Removal of the mounting nut is then impossible, as all that will happen is the whole of the locking mechanism will rotate.

It might sound obvious, but do remember where you have stored the locking key! Otherwise ...

Fitting specialist roof racks

Gone are the days when a roof rack was just a few bits of angle iron bolted to the top of the car. Automaxi have a complete range of racks to suit all Fiesta models for all reasons, whether personal or commercial. These racks can be fitted with an incredible variety of accessories including a lockable ski carrier for four pairs of downhill skis or five pairs of the cross-country type, a cycle carrier, a windsurfer carrier and a towing spoiler made of steel with an adjustable plastic lip.

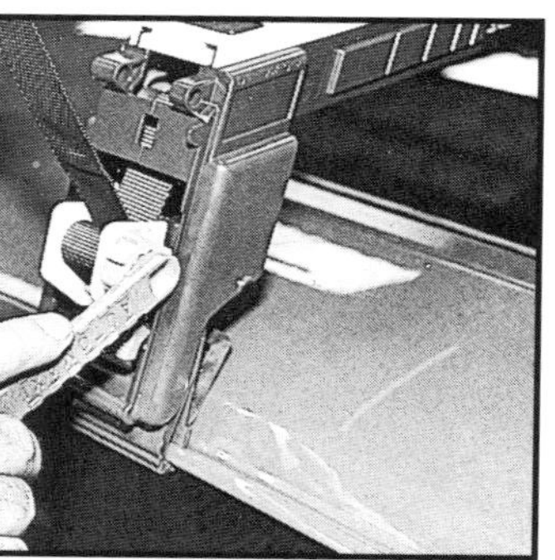

IA17.1
The Automaxi Universal rack clips into the roof gutter and is tightened and secured in seconds. This webbing strap passes from one side to the other where it is pulled tight and then held with the ratchet mechanism as shown here. The webbing has a breaking strain of 1000lbs and the design means that as it is tightened, the bars become taut in two directions, thus making them much stronger.

IA17.2
The ratchet key slots into the plastic cover which then clips over the mechanism and is locked with a small key, which effectively means that the bar cannot be removed.

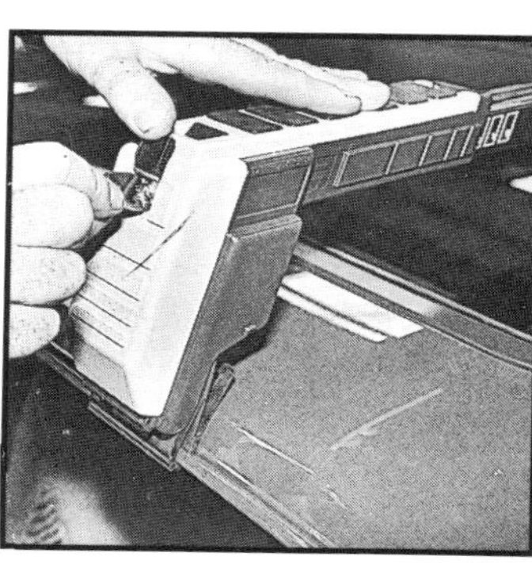

IA17.3
Fitting both bars takes only a few minutes and they are both stylish and practical.

IA17.4
Onto the basic rack can be attached a variety of specialist accessory racks. Swiftly becoming all the rage is windsurfing. The Universal will hold one or two boards complete with sails and can be secured in minutes using the tether straps as shown.

IA17.5

Bicycles are becoming increasingly popular and this single safety cycle carrier fits easily onto the Universal; up to three of these could be carried on the Fiesta roof.

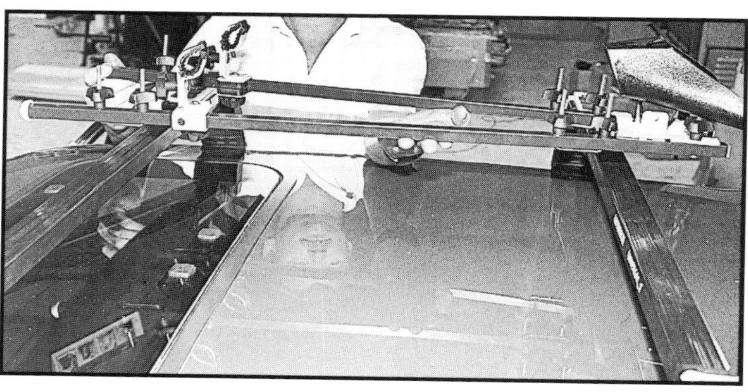

Fitting a rear fog lamp

IA18.1
First point to check is the EEC approval. If you look at a lamp which doesn't have it, don't buy it! The Link Sedan lamp comes with bulb and bracket ready for mounting. However, you'll need some wire and a switch as they are not supplied. Whatever you do, don't use the same colour wire for both live and earth connections.

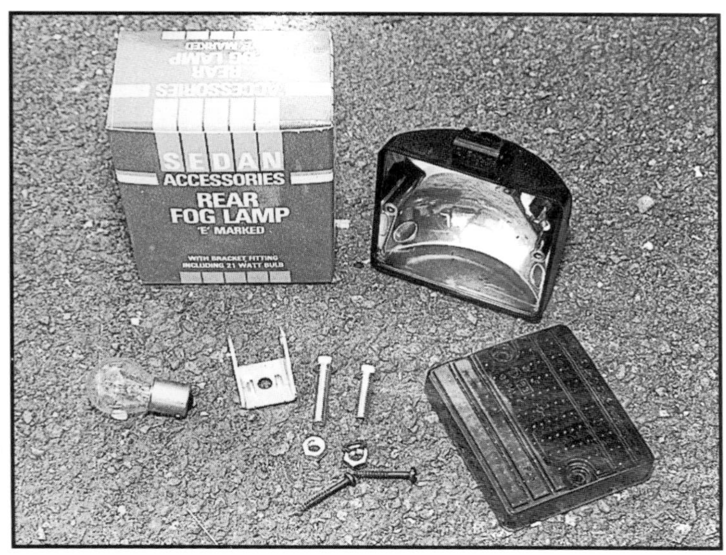

IA18.2
Remember that the law requires you to have some form of warning on the dashboard that the rear fog lamp(s) are on. These Sedan switches come with a built-in bulb which serves the purpose admirably and , as you can see, there are several types to choose. Either a "flick" switch, or one of two sizes of "rockers". Your decision will depend largely on how they fit in with the rest of your car's interior.

IA18.3
The bracket supplied is simple to fit to the lamp. Check carefully the positioning of the bracket hole before drilling the bumper.

IA18.4
To run the wiring into the car you will have to drill a small hole. Don't forget to rustproof the hole (see Chapter Five) and fit a grommet to prevent the wiring from chafing. One of the wires from the lamp goes to earth, either by Scotchloking into an existing earth lead or by using a ring terminal and using a screw passing into the body of the car. Make sure that the ring terminal makes good contact with bare metal, rather than paintwork. The other wire can be taken direct to the switch, or Scotchloked into the wire from the front foglamps to the switch, depending on which diagram you are following.

You don't have to drive many miles to know that the biggest minus point of rear fog lamps are those drivers who put them on when they aren't required, leave them on after the fog has disappeared or switch them on accidentally. We would suggest, therefore, wiring your rear fog lamp(s) in one of the two ways shown below.

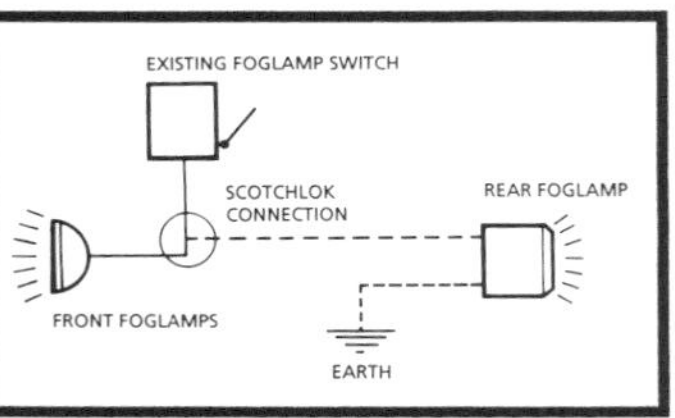

DIAGRAM 1
If you have fitted front fog lamps (page 48), then you should follow the diagram here. By doing so, you ensure that the rear fog lamp(s) cannot be switched on unless the front ones are also illuminated.

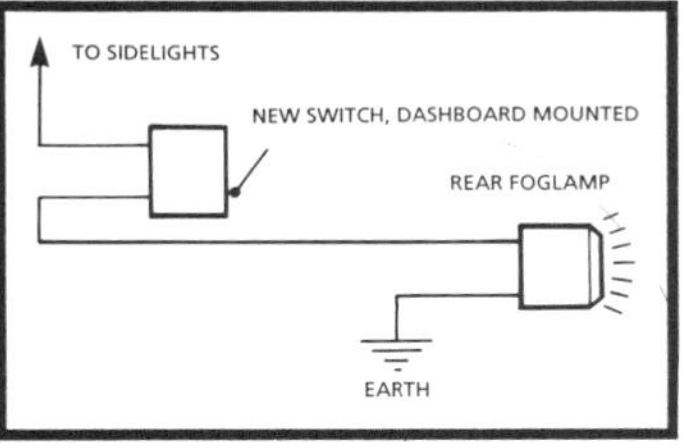

DIAGRAM 2
If you don't have front fog lamps, then follow this diagram. By doing so, it means that the fog lamp(s) will not come on unless your sidelights are switched on.

It should be noted that neither of these diagrams will prevent you leaving your lamp(s) on when not required and that at the end of the day, it is your responsibility to make sure you are not inadvertently blinding the driver behind!

Fitting wiper arm covers

Those of us of a certain age will well remember the days when cars had acres of chrome to polish. One of the worst areas to clean were the windscreen wiper arms and you couldn't leave them otherwise the resulting rust would be sitting right in front of your eyes! The change in trend to matt black wiper arms helped, but even they can rust. Fitting a set of the Mitchell covers shown here will achieve three goals:

a) Cover up any rust already present,

b) keep the elements from the wiper arms to prevent them from rusting in the first place and,

c) improve the appearance, especially if the colour of your car is one of the standard Mitchell colours (red, black or white) – instant colour coding, no less!

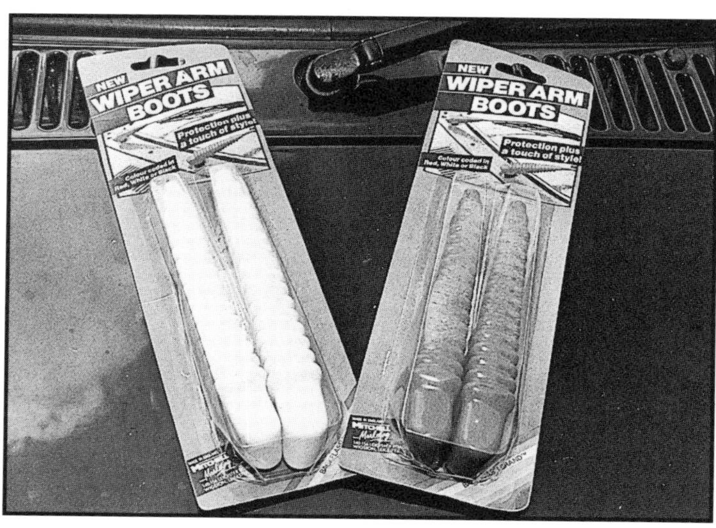

IA19.1 The wiper arm covers will fit any model Fiesta and come in white and red (shown here) or black. Your choice is either to colour co-ordinate them with your Fiesta body colour or do the opposite and choose a contrast.

IA19.2 The wiper blade has to be removed. This unclips from the end of the arm and is slid back and away. Take care not to scrape the matt black paintwork of the arm (or the car's paintwork) as you do them.

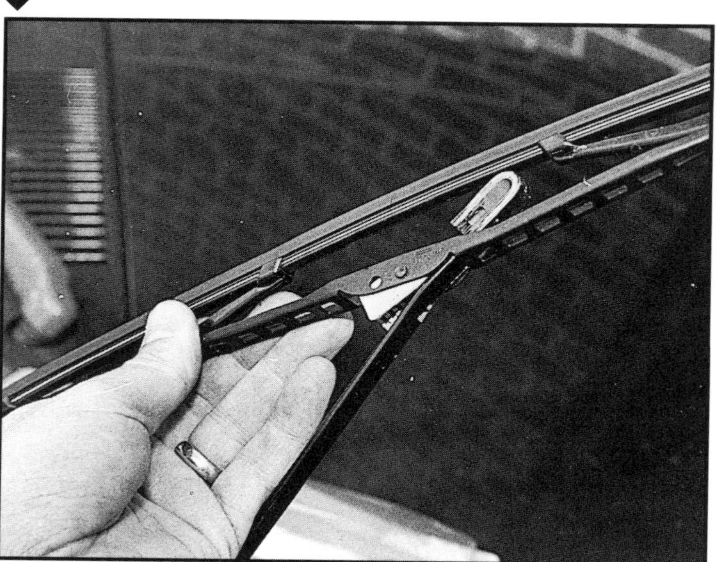

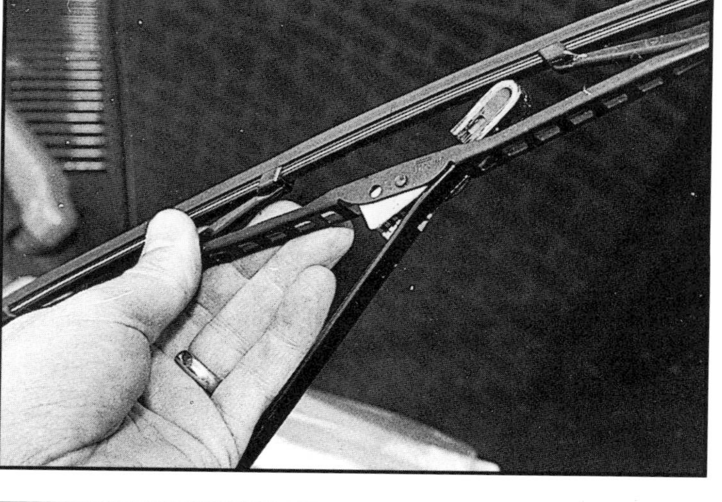

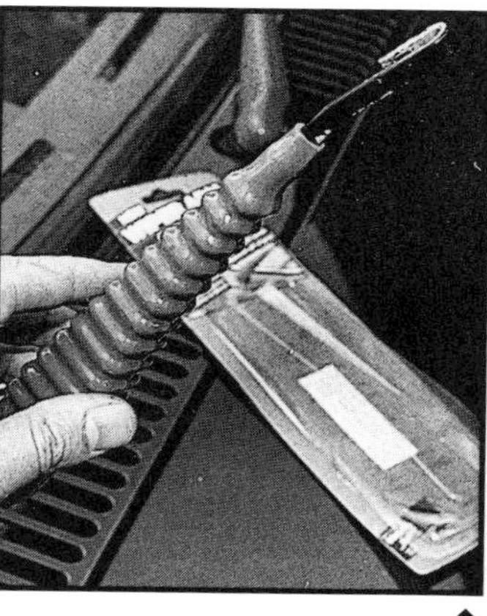

IA19.3 The flexible covers are a tight push fit over the ends of the wiper arms. Warming them slightly helps but **don't** use excessive force, otherwise you'll run the risk of splitting them.

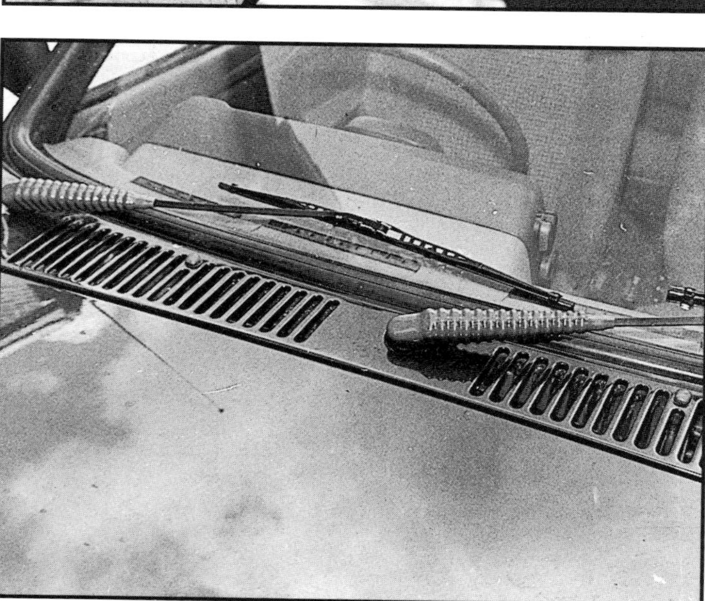

IA19.4 The work of minutes is rewarded by a more interesting look to the wipers and if your original arms were rusty, no-one will know now!

Fitting mudflaps

Fitting mudflaps to your Fiesta, either two or four, is always a good idea. They protect the bodywork against damage from stones and cut down the amount of dirt and mud which encourages rust on the paintwork. They also reduce the amount of tar from the road splashing up and sticking to the paintwork. Thus for a relatively small investment, they could add considerably to your car's resale value.

IA20.1
These Cannon mudflaps are well made and look good. They come complete with all necessary clips and fastenings.

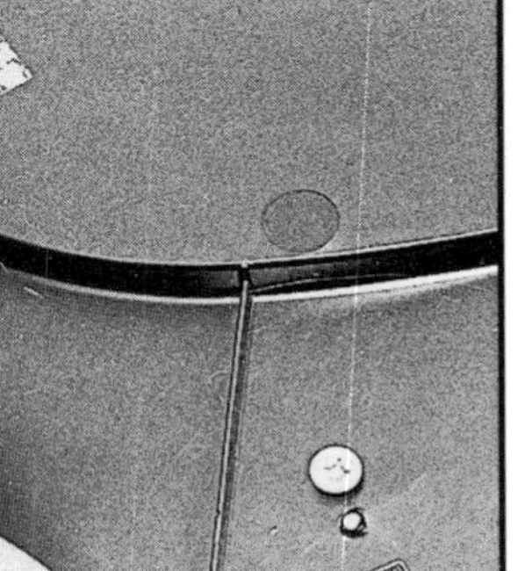

IA20.2
The optional reflective strips are an excellent safety idea. There are two pegs in the rear of each one which push through pre-marked holes and are secured by the clips shown here.

IA20.3
The flexible outer edge of the mudflap extends around the edge of the wing. It has to be held in position and the topmost point marked in some way. The simplest method we found was to use masking tape.

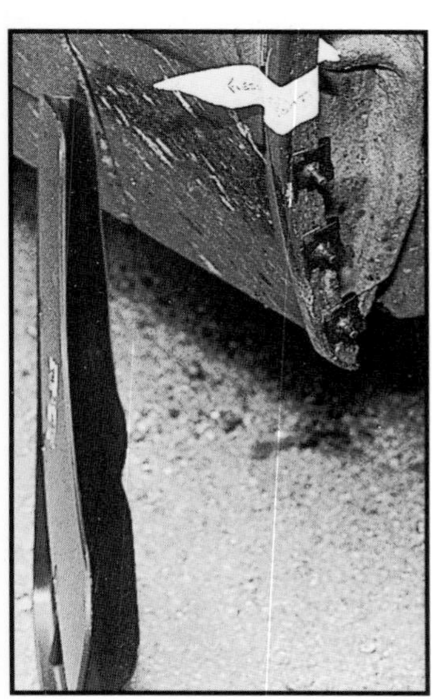

IA20.4
The three fixing clips are then positioned on the metalwork. When the position is correct, corresponding holes are drilled in the flap.

IA20.5
With the final clips in place, the job is finished and with three clips per flap they are very secure.

Fitting an exhaust pipe extension

Fitting an exhaust pipe extension is an easy task which should only be attempted when the exhaust system is cold. Although fitting is simple, it is important that it should not protude beyond the bumper line, as shown in this diagram.

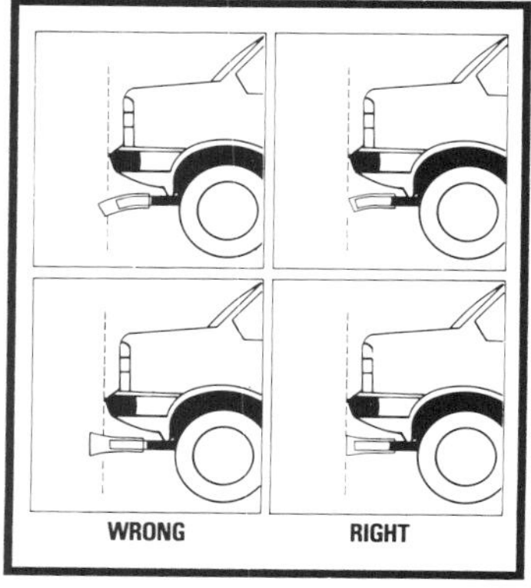

(Diagram courtesy Link Sedan)

One thing guaranteed to spoil the look of your otherwise immaculate Fiesta is a rusty tailpipe. Fitting a Sedan accessory extension is a simple way to solve the problem. If the end of the original pipe is rotten or if the original pipe protrudes too far from the rear of the car, it may be necessary to cut the original pipe (see Power Tools section). Extensions are available for all models of Fiesta.

IA21.1
Link Sedan produce a range of extensions, some of which are seen here. There are single and twin tailpipe versions available in either chrome or chrome and black. All models are made of pure brass in order to prevent rusting and corrosion.

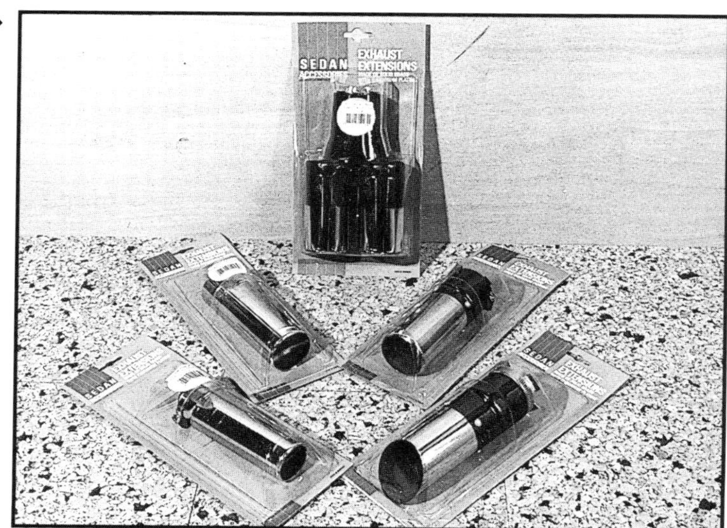

IA21.2
There are two basic methods of fixing the extensions. The first is with a simple jubilee clip, as supplied with the single pipe extension or ...

IA21.3
... with an integral locking device for the twin tail pipes, which, like the jubilee clip, requires only a screwdriver to fix into position.

IA21.4
Decisions, decisions ... which looks best is up to you! This is the plain chrome finish, single pipe ...

IA21.5
... whereas this is the more sporty black and chrome version, with the end cut away slightly and painted red on the inside of the pipe.

Fitting a towing bracket

The major point to consider when fitting a towbar is stress. Clearly, by harnessing your Fiesta to another vehicle, be it a small camping trailer or caravan, a whole new set of complex stresses and strains are placed on your car. Two things are necessary. Firstly, the towing bracket should be strong enough for the job in hand and, secondly, it should not place any undue strain on the car.

Unless you have in-depth engineering knowledge, you are best advised to buy a bracket from a well-known manufacturer. C. P. Witter Ltd is a well-respected company having produced over two million towing brackets (and nothing else) since its formation in 1950.

All Fiesta towing brackets meet the relevant International Standards, one of which is a test cycle of two million alternating push/pull loads on each new towbar design! Among the 600 different brackets they produce is one for every model in the Fiesta range.

Whatever you tow with your Fiesta, the one thing you must never do is carry more than the manufacturer's recommended weight. The maximum trailer weight for all 1.1 litre models is 245kg (540ib) and for all others it is 408kg (900lb). Whilst carrying more than these figures is not strictly illegal, it is far from being wise and could possibly be classed as a dangerous load, which *is* illegal

IA22.1 There's more to a towing bracket than meets the eye! The Witter bracket shown here meets the very exacting International Standard ISO 3853 (BS AU 114). This standard unit was fitted to a Mk II diesel by Martin Clews of trailer specialists, Indespension of Northampton.

IA22.2 With the rear of the car on ramps (remember the safety procedures if you're fitting your own), the first job is to place the inner rear flat bracing strap in position, mark and dot punch the holes accurately and then drill the holes. Fastening up the bolts on the XR2 model does not involve removal of the rear spoiler; simply remove the rear foglamps.

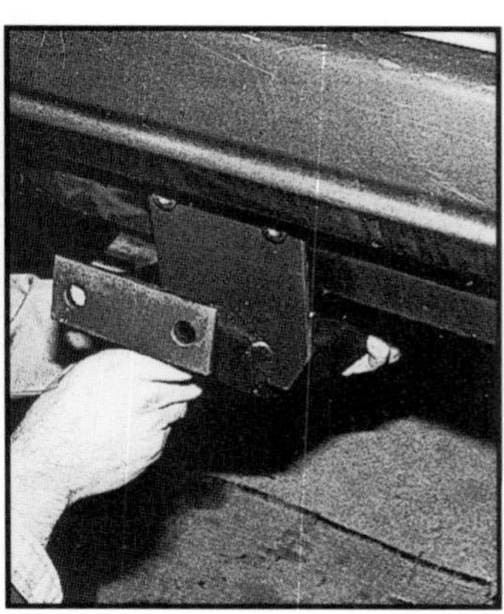

IA22.3 Next, the extremely strong, tubular section centre strut is fastened at the rear and then ...

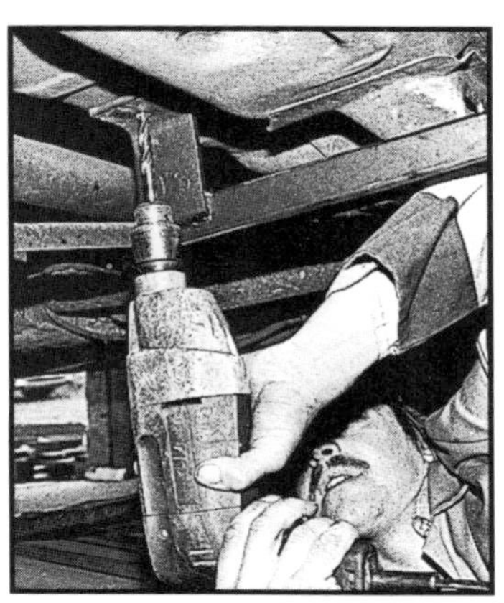

IA22.4 ... used as a template for drilling the holes in the hatch floor. Again, dot punch and pilot drill first and take care that you do not get any debris in your eyes.

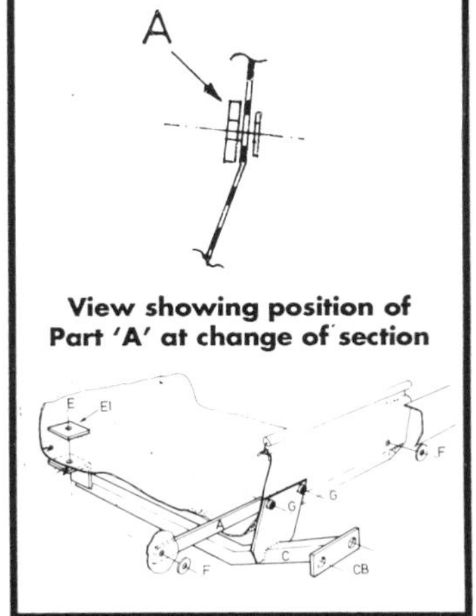

Witter towing brackets all come with a clear and concise schematic diagram to make DIY fitting easier. ***(Diagram courtesy C. P. Witter Ltd)***

Fitting a towing bracket

One point that Indespension stressed was that when fitting a towing bracket, each fixing point *must* have metal-to-metal contact. This means that thick underseal, etc, must be removed before the bracket is tightened into position.

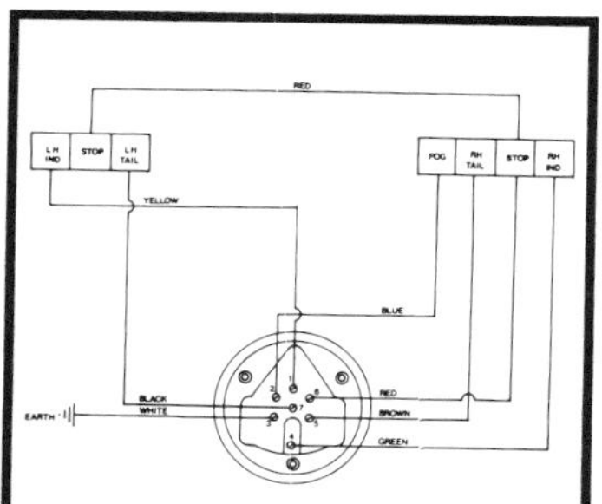

12N ROAD LIGHTING

INDICATOR LEFT HAND	L	YELLOW
REAR FOG LIGHT	54G	BLUE
EARTH	31	WHITE
INDICATOR RIGHT HAND	R	GREEN
TAIL LIGHT RIGHT HAND	58R	BROWN
STOP LIGHTS	54	RED
TAIL LIGHT LEFT HAND NUMBER PLATE LIGHT	58L	BLACK

Wiring the standard, seven-pin socket is not particularly difficult nowadays, with the advent of Scotchlok connectors. A clear diagram, a stock of connectors and a 12 volt tester is all that is required. This diagram shows the wiring for a standard socket. If you intend to run your caravan's internal lighting/heating or ancillaries from your car, then you'll need to wire a second socket.

(Diagram courtesy Indespension Ltd)

IA22.5
The strengthening plate for the central strut **must** make direct contact with metal and for this reason, the underseal and paint have to be scraped away. There are no exceptions to this rule as it is a load bearing fastening.

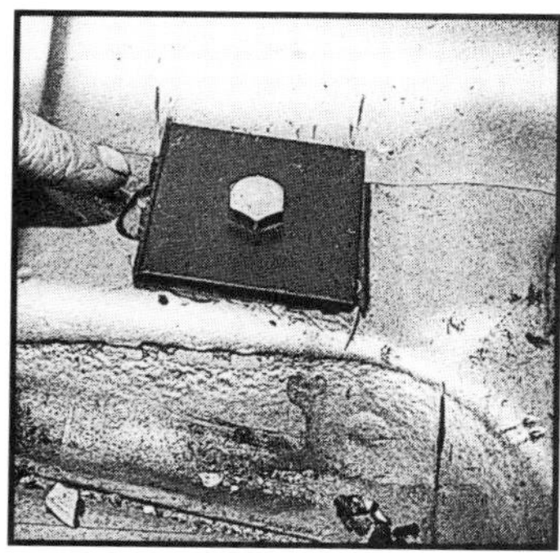

IA22.6
Although it may seem a shame to pull off your car's paintwork in this way, safety demands it. Don't forget to rustproof this area together with all the holes drilled along the way.

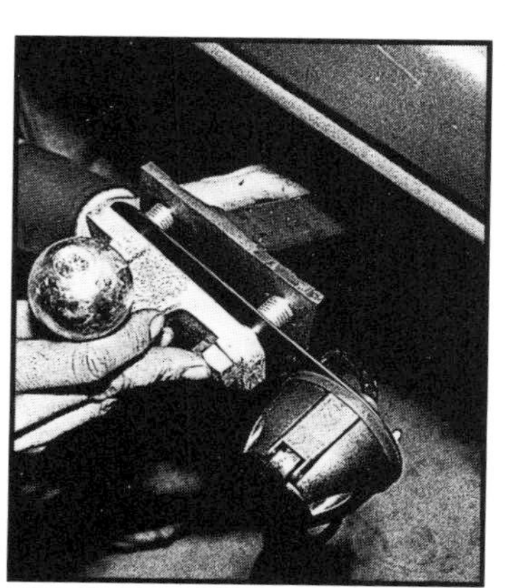

IA22.7
This socket is ready wired, it makes life simpler and reduces the possibility of errors for the DIY fitter. Don't forget that the hole drilled for the cable should be rustproofed and fitted with a rubber grommet. The socket is bolted in position on a simple bracket via the towball itself. The towball used is a standard 50mm unit which has become the standard European size for trailers up to 3500kg capacity. Always remember to grease the towball well before use and ensure that it is never left to run dry. Martin also used an ingenious device, called a "Master Flash" which warns the driver of an indicator failure (a legal requirement) without the need to trail wires the length of the car and install a warning lamp.

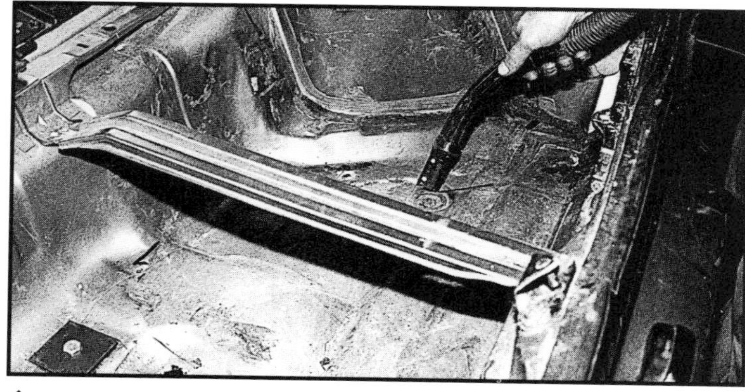

IA22.8
A good move: hoovering up not only makes the car tidier, it also prevents pieces of swarf collecting, rusting and ultimately rotting your Fiesta from the inside out.

IA22.9
The finished bracket, unobtrusive and totally safe. Note the towball cover, most necessary if you are to protect your clothing from grease every time you open the hatch!

Fitting a wide-view overtaking mirror

IA23.1 Branyl offer two different overtaking mirrors – circular or oblong – to suit your taste and the shape of your existing door mirrors.

IA23.2 We decided to fit the circular mirrors to this Fiesta 1.1L largely because the owner liked them! It has a simple, peel off backing which reveals a sticky pad.

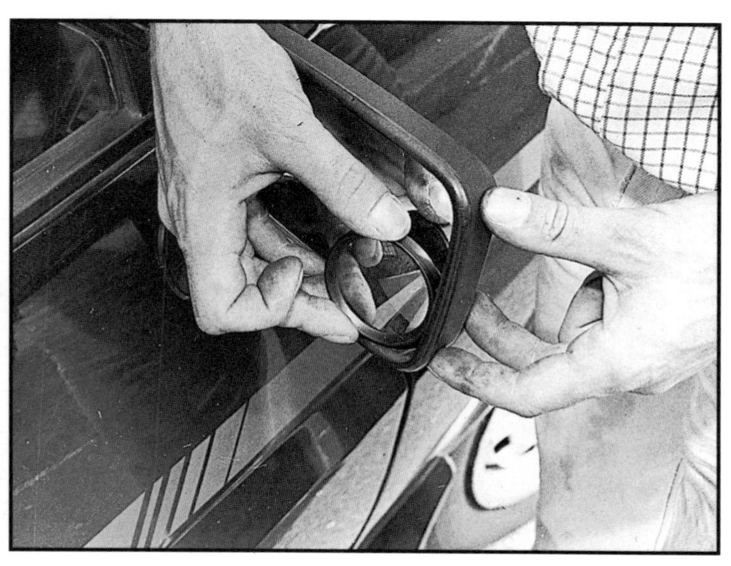

IA23.3 The original mirror should be cleaned with spirit wipe before attempting to stick the mirror into place. But, be warned, this sticky is never meant to come off! Make sure that you position the mirror exactly before pressing the Branyl mirror in place.

The increasing use of wing mirrors on both doors is something which we must applaud. On many occasions it is more important to know what's behind you than what's in front! Ideally your door mirror should serve two main functions; first to give you a good idea of exactly what is going on behind and second, to give an overall view of the general traffic situation up to half a mile away. The problem here is, that in order to do this, you really need two mirrors, a concave and a convex. The answer is to do just that. By using the small Branyl convex mirror shown here, you can have the best of both worlds. It is particularly useful for those who drive Fiesta vans, or who have caravans in tow, and all drivers will benefit when motorway driving where the wide view allows the driver to take note of fast traffic coming up in an outer lane.

Choosing alternative wheels

When Ford made your Fiesta they fitted road wheels (steel or alloy) designed with specific requirements with regard to their dimensions, stresses and operating loads. Similarly, the wheel studs are engineered to very exacting tolerances and are produced to match specific wheels. It is most important that they have the correct length, cone seating dimensions and torque characteristics. Using an incorrect wheel stud is potentially very dangerous indeed. Therefore, when changing wheels, great care should be taken to ensure that only the recommended studs are used. A six inch rim width is just about ideal. You should certainly question quite seriously whether you need to go any wider. If you *do* want to go wider than this, we would strongly recommend that a visit to a wheel specialist is called for before you proceed. The choice of wheel is a personal and subjective matter but don't forget that any wheels will soon become dirty with the combined effects of the elements and brake dust. There is no doubt that any spoke effect wheel will take an awful lot of time and effort to keep in pristine condition, especially when compared to the much simpler and smoother, seven-spoke designs.

(All photos on this page courtesy Ford Motor Company)

When changing wheels it is very important to consider the tyres as well. Obviously, if the new wheel is a larger diameter, as is often the case, then a completely new set of tyres (and spare, don't forget) will be required. Equally obvious, this will add a great deal to the cost; in some cases, more than the wheels themselves! Similarly, even if the diameter of the wheel remains the same, an increase in the width of the rim may mean that the tyre is not wide enough to sit safely on the new wheel rim. In addition, a new wheel and tyre combination can alter the gearing of your car. This will affect top speed, acceleration and most important, speedometer accuracy. This is usually avoided by using a lower profile tyre in conjunction with a larger diameter wheel, although you should check before you fit the tyres. Remember that larger wheel and tyre combinations will also effect the handling of the car. Whilst it is true that a larger tyre area will give more grip in the dry, it is also true that the car will be more prone to aquaplaning in the wet. With this in mind, we would not recommend going wider than six inches if you wish to keep the practicability and civility of your car.

The price of new alloy wheels may prompt you to purchase a secondhand set. Take great care here, for they are easily damaged and a layer of road dirt and brake dust could easily hide a potentially lethal hairline crack.

IA24.1
Available from Ford main dealers are the RS series, seven-spoke wheels, which come in two variants.

IA24.2
This one is similar but with the very useful addition of a locking centre cap covering the wheel studs.

IA24.3
Still in the RS series are the spoke effect wheels which, like the previous examples, also come with the wheel nuts exposed ...

IA24.4
... or covered, as shown here.

IA24.5
Another option is to uprate your car by fitting alloy wheels fitted as standard to a more upmarket model. These "pepperpot" style wheels grace many an XR2, but there's no reason why you shouldn't fit them to a lesser model.

There are few items which will transform the overall look of your Fiesta more simply than a set of alloy wheels. Of course, some Fiestas have alloy wheels as standard, notably the XR2's. Hard though it may be, it is best to be practical when changing your wheels and you should ask yourself just how easy they will be to clean. However attractive a wheel may look when it is new, it will look somewhat different after two weeks of winter driving. Cleaning some wheels can be almost a full time job, although it's often the way that the best looking wheels are the most complex and most likely to ruin your fingernails.

IA24.6
The XR2i (Mk III, of course) benefits greatly from these 6J x 13 inch alloy wheels. They look excellent and are not too difficult to clean.

IA24.7
The smooth alloy look is one favoured by many and you can see why on the Stella wheel and also ...
(Photo courtesy Wheelwright)

IA24.8
... this Khamsin model. Note that both feature locking centre caps which help from a security and an aerodynamic efficiency point of view. Both are available in 14 and 15 inch sizes.
(Photo courtesy Wheelwright)

IA24.9
The Windy is available in 13 inch and 14 inch sizes for the Fiesta and, as you can see, comes in either 9 or 10 spoke versions, both of which have different locking centre caps.
(Photo courtesy Wheelwright)

IA24.10
Another stylish wheel, from the German Borbet company, is the 5 spoke, which combines classic good looks with lots of practicality; it's easy to clean!
(Photo courtesy Borbet GmbH)

Using a tyre dresser

Using a tyre dresser is a simple and fairly cheap method of adding that certain something to your car. Picking out the maker's name on the tyre wall is usual, especially if you have the latest, high performance low profiles fitted. However, bear in mind that by drawing attention to them you could well be attracting the wrong sort of enthusiast! Locking wheel studs (see next page) are to be well advised.

IA25.1
As can be seen here, there are several colours of tyre dresser to choose from, including white, silver and gold. Naturally, white is the most popular, but there's nothing to stop you experimenting with the others – colour coded tyres, perhaps?

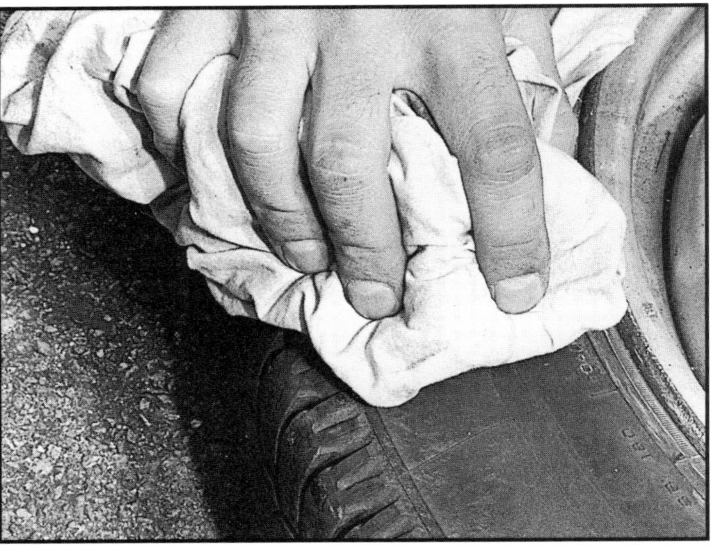

IA25.2
First things first. Because of their place in life, tyres get dirty, greasy and covered in all sorts of thoroughly unpleasant substances! You should thoroughly clean the area in question before starting. If you really want a good looking tyre, you could paint the rest of it with Comma's Tyre Black.

IA25.3
When using the tyre dresser remember that the pen has to be shaken very vigorously before use. A steady hand is needed and ideally the wheel should be taken off the car and placed horizontally on a work-bench for best results.

Fitting locking wheel bolts

IA26.1
Carflow Lock-bolts look like the originals except that they have a pattern of holes in the top. These correspond exactly with the prongs in the special socket provided. Without this socket, none of the four wheels can be removed. Four Lock-bolts are provided and are fitted one per wheel. It is obviously important to remember to keep the socket in the car at all times in case of a puncture. Equally, it is just as important to make a note of the code number of the socket, which will enable you to order a replacement should you lose the original.

Safety note from Carflow: please avoid using an air gun or impact wrench if you are not familiar with these tools.

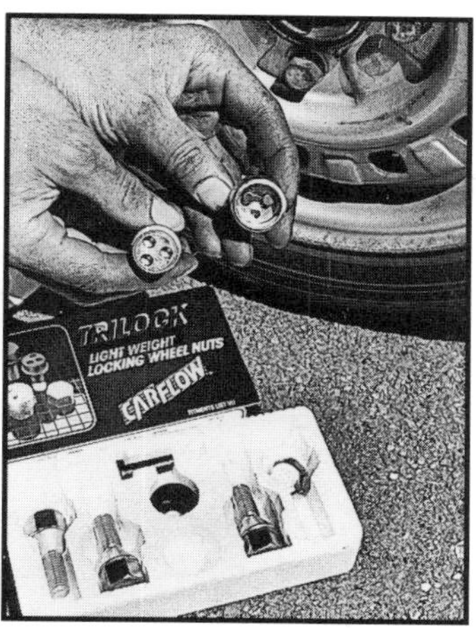

IA26.2
The bolts are fitted in exactly the same manner as the standard ones, except, of course, that the special "key" is used in the wheel wrench. For each new bolt fitted there is a metal cover, shaped to look like a standard head. This is a nice touch for those who have wheel bolts exposed rather than covered by a wheel centre, as in many cases. There are Carflow bolts for all Fiesta models, but you should check carefully the fitting code and refer directly to the manufacturer if you have any doubts as to their compatibility with your particular wheels.

Having fitted alloy wheels and probably a new set of tyres as well, you will doubtless want to keep them. Even those who have steel wheels may well have some expensive tyres which would be tempting to the would-be thief. The Carflow locking wheel bolts make it almost impossible for anyone to take your wheels away without the special socket "key". In the interests of safety it is *vital* that you always ensure that the bolts you use are of the correct length and that the seating is the correct type for the wheels you have fitted. Not all wheels have the same standard seatings.

Fitting Wheel Clean Discs

Most Fiesta owners know the annoyance that the fine layer of brake dust upon the front wheels can cause, especially those with complex patterned alloys! One way to alleviate the problem is to fit a set of Carflow Wheel Clean Discs, which fit inside the wheels and protect them.

IA27.1
The Wheel Clean Discs are sold in pairs and have a metal centre with holes suitable for 3, 4 and 5 stud applications up to 130mm PCD. Note the moulded circles which are used as a guide should any need to be trimmed off.

IA27.2
With the wheel removed from the car, the inside of the wheel should be brushed down to remove road dirt. The disc should then be aligned with the stud holes and centralised. If, when it is pushed well into the contour of the wheel, the rubber is too big, it can be trimmed with normal household scissors. If fouling of the calipers is a problem, Carflow suggest that it may be possible to glue the Wheel Clean Disc to the inside of the wheel. They also advise that the wheel bolts should be re-torqued after 100 miles as a precaution.

We had a natural concern about fitting these items, with regard to the effect they may have on braking safety. However, they are fully approved by the extremely demanding German TUV organisation. The tests insist that the discs must not cause brake fade, overheating of hubs and brakes under extreme conditions or the fouling of braking or suspension parts.

During fitting of the wheel clean discs, all of the usual safety precautions should be taken whilst the car is jacked up.

Cleaning and protecting bodywork

Washing the car is only half the job. Take note of Fiestas which have never been waxed or which have never had the tar spots cleaned off; they look grubby and dull even when they are supposedly clean! Apart from the obvious pride of ownership, when you come to sell it, a clean and obviously well looked after car will sell much easier and for much more!

IA28.1 Washing the car is made easier by using the Cosmic Turbo Wash. This simple yet effective device is designed to fit onto the end of an ordinary hosepipe. To start with, it has to be "loaded" with car shampoo, in this case, a special pack provided with the Turbowash with a nozzle ...

IA28.2 ... which allows the shampoo to be poured easily into the barrel of the Turbo Wash unit. Whatever you do, don't use washing up liquid to clean your Fiesta. The salt it contains will cause corrosive problems.

IA28.3 By fitting the special adaptor to the end of your garden hose, the Turbo Wash can be connected to the water supply and with the tap turned on ...

IA28.4 ... the device turns a mild trickle into a torrent. The settings on the Turbo Wash are for Wash and Rinse, so start by giving the whole car a going over with the former and then, when the shampoo has been thoroughly spread, rinse on the latter setting. Do remember to shut the windows.

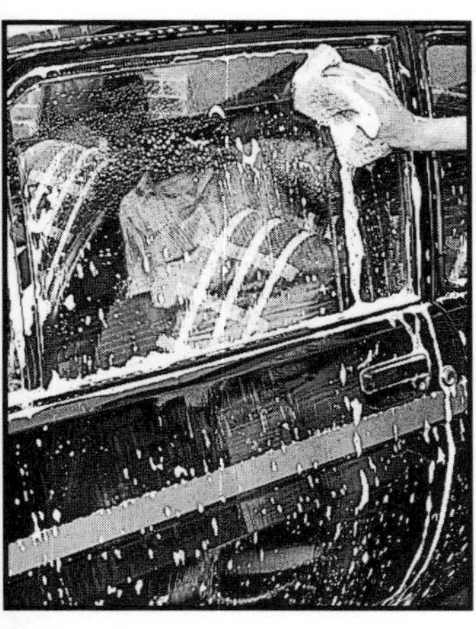

IA28.5
Having given the bodywork a good cleaning with water and shampoo, you will now have to resort to good old fashioned elbow grease; there's no substitute! A mixture of warm water and Comma's Super Wash 'n Wax will bring out the true colour of your car. You should follow this up with the Turbo Wash again, this time on the "Rinse" setting and resort once more to old fashioned techniques ...

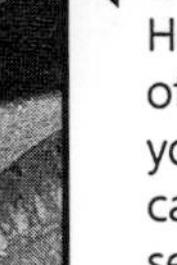

IA28.7
Having washed away the layers of dirt and grime, look closely at your paintwork. Even on a black car like this one, you're bound to see those nasty black spots – tar! The longer they stay on your paintwork the more damage they will do. Remove them simply and quickly with Comma Tar Remover, applied with a soft cloth and then wiped over with a clean one. Having removed the tar, then it's time to wax the paintwork.

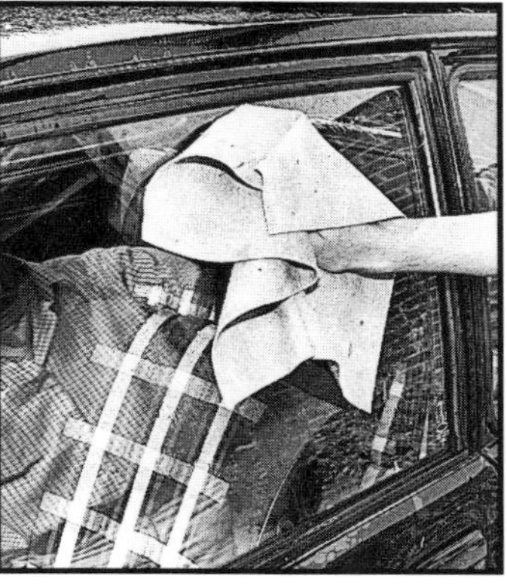

IA28.6
... by using the chamois to wipe away excess water and prevent "streaking".

IA28.8
Comma's Quick Wax comes in handy trigger packs and couldn't be easier to use; spray on, wipe off. It gives a high gloss sheen and at the same time, protects against oxidisation and the ever increasing acid rain. Do not polish your car in direct sunlight or if the heat from the engine has made the bonnet warm.

IA28.9
If you've let your paintwork get a little out of hand, then use a combined cutting polish and wax polish or, if it's really bad, Comma Top Cut, followed by Comma Quick Wax (but not on metallics). For those who can still find some chrome on their Fiesta, there's a good chrome cleaner in the Comma range.

Always take care not to get wax-based products onto the glass, particularly the windscreen, where it could smear and be potentially very dangerous. From this point of view, it is usually best to make glass cleaning the last job when smartening up your Fiesta. A purpose-made cleaner, such as Comma's Clean Glass, will make short work of it.

It may sound obvious, but there is a correct order to follow when washing your car – useful to tell the kids before they smear the underbody mud over the windscreen with the wash sponge! Start with the windows; go to the roof, bonnet and upper hatch/boot. Wash down to the body moulding and finish off with wheel arches, sills, valances and wheels.

Cleaning and protecting bodywork

A handy tip for the preservation of chamois leathers is to squeeze, rather than wring them out. Also, they should not be allowed to dry out thoroughly; best achieved by putting them into a sealed container whilst still damp.

IA28.10
It is surprisingly easy to forget the large area of the car that isn't metal ... the glass! Comma Clean Glass can be used inside and out and is particularly useful for the windscreen, where it removes traffic film and squashed insects. After spraying a thin film over the glass area ...

IA28.11
... it can be wiped clean with a soft cloth.

IA28.12
For those bits of your Fiesta made of black or grey plastic, Comma produce Trim Black and Trim Grey. They should be rubbed onto a whole area in one application with a soft cloth. When dry, buffing with a soft cloth will bring back to life a "new look" wheelarch, bumper or what-have-you. It can also be used on tyres, mudflaps and rubber mouldings.

IA28.13
Here's a car which hasn't been fitted with Wheel Clean Discs! The owner should turn to page 63 but we'll stay here and watch Comma's Clean Wheels get rid of that brake dust and road dirt. It comes in a trigger pack and is suitable not only for steel wheels but also alloys because of its non-corrosive nature. Spray it on as shown and then ...

All of the Comma products shown here are environment friendly, with no aerosol CFCs to damage the atmosphere. Certainly, this is to be commended and hopefully, all manufacturers will soon follow suit.

IA28.14
... when you are sure that you have covered everywhere, leave it to do its job for a minute or two before giving it a good rinsing. The Turbo Wash helps again here, especially getting into those awkward nooks and crannies. If you've been lax and let your wheels get very dirty, you may need a second or even a third application, agitating with a brush for best results.

IA28.15
Whilst you have the Turbo Wash out and in the area of the wheelarches, it's good sense to fit one of the three optional angled nozzles ...

IA28.16
... and spray underneath the wings to remove the build-up of road dirt, which can harbour rust-inducing moisture.

Chapter Two
In-Car Comforts

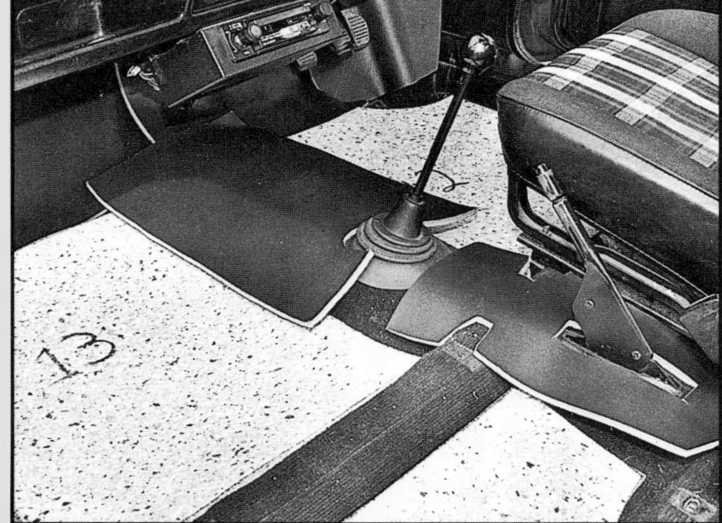

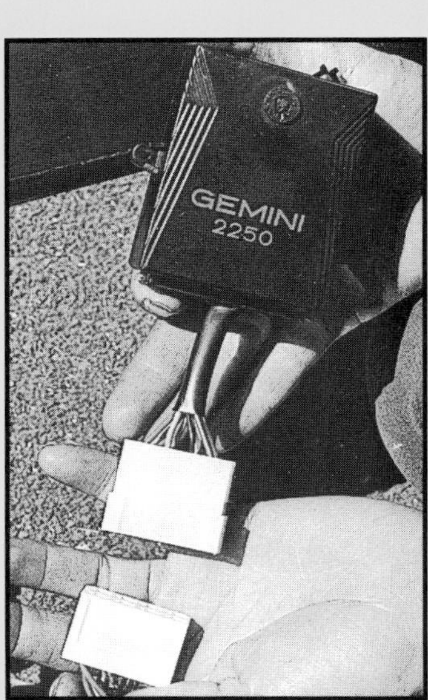

HT1.1
Many of the items shown in this section are electrical. Before you even think about tampering with your Fiesta's electrical system, you should find your fuse box, seen here in the driver's side cubby hole on this Mk II model.

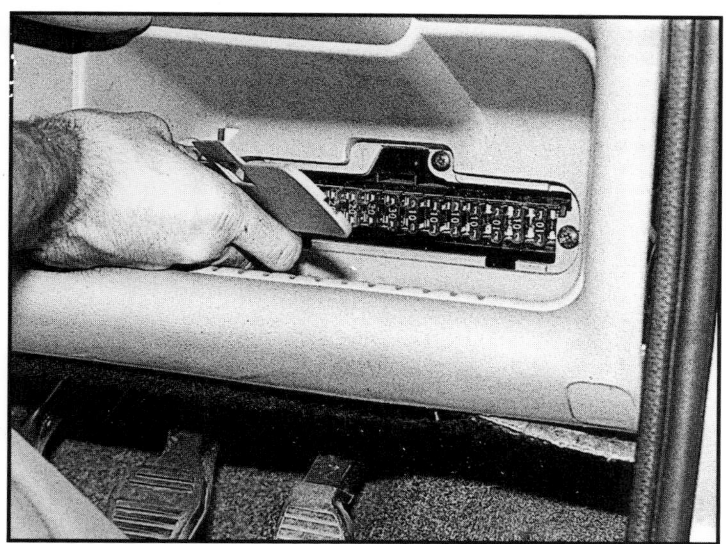

HT1.2
Make sure that you have a supply of spare fuses and that you can identify which fuse is which. Your handbook or Haynes manual should show this. As with most modern cars, the Fiesta uses these flat-bladed type. Don't use anything but the correctly rated fuse: not cigarette paper, or randomly chosen pieces of wire; just the right fuse. The fuses are colour coded according to their rating and you should never change this rating.

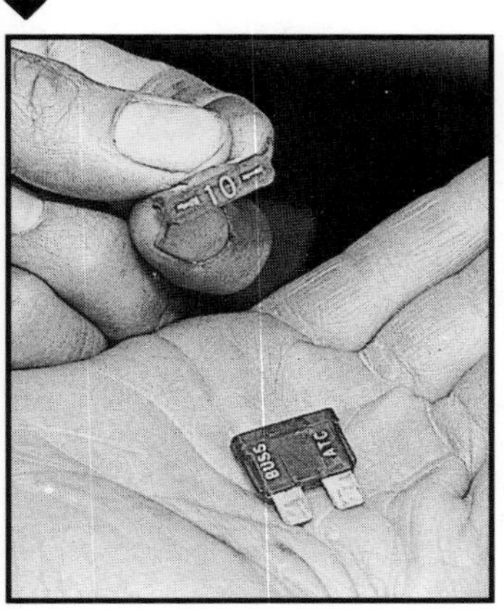

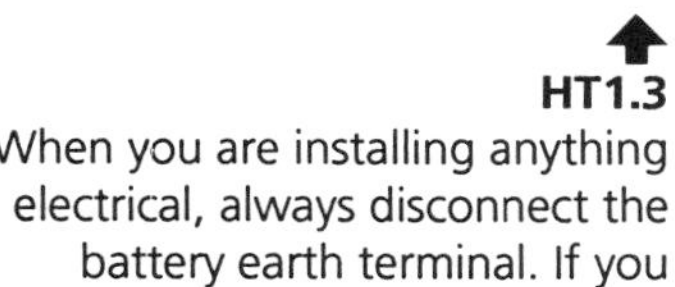

HT1.3
When you are installing anything electrical, always disconnect the battery earth terminal. If you need to locate a live wire ...

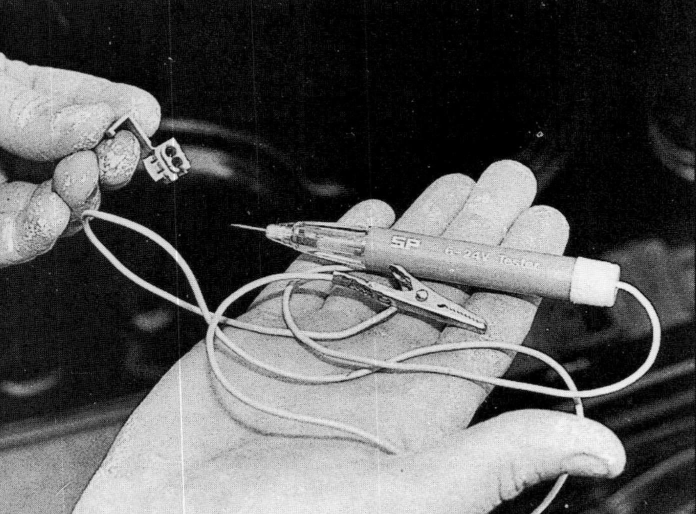

HT1.4
... check with your 12V tester first, mark the wire and then remove the battery earth lead. Also, it is the modern way to make many connections using "Scotchlok" connectors. If you do use them, make a habit of checking every connection AS YOU DO IT. This way, you can save yourself hours of frustration locating "faults"!

Some of the modifications shown in this Chapter make use of the very popular double-sided "stickie" pads. Obviously, this means there is no need to drill holes or make screw holes in your interior trim. However, some items have to be fitted this way and when doing so, you should always check out the practicalities first. If you drill a panel, make sure there is nothing behind it. If you are using a self-tapping screw, are you going to self-tap into part of the wiring loom? You wouldn't be the first! Check also whether ancillary items will still function when you're finished. It's no use fitting Sharp speakers in the rear side panels if you can't then pull the rear seat forward!

Fitting a replacement steering wheel

Replacing the standard steering wheel is one of the most popular ways of improving the look of your Fiesta's interior. Also, the feel of a well designed leather wheel, such as the Mountney models featured here, can make a world of difference to the pleasure derived from driving.

There is certainly no shortage of steering wheels suitable for your Fiesta, but as Mountney produce the largest range in Great Britain, it is probable that there will be something to suit most tastes. Vinyl wheels are available, but most owners find leather replacement wheels preferable. The leather used by Mountney is of excellent quality and to the high standards set by leading luxury car manufacturers. These standards include Fogging, Martindale abrasive, Tensile strength and Anti-perspirant tests.

IC1.1
Every wheel requires a boss which is specifically made for the car to which it is to be fitted. Mountney can apply bosses and adaptors to suit most Fiesta models.

IC1.2
All Mountney bosses are designed to allow the normal use of the existing indicator stalks with the usual self-cancelling facilities.

IC1.3
The centre of the original wheel prises free with fingernails or a thin-bladed screwdriver. Take care not to damage the plastic edges!

IC1.4
A socket and extension bar are required to remove the steering wheel nut. Take care to ensure that the steering wheel is in the straight ahead position before you actually remove the steering wheel from the splines; this can save an awful lot of headaches later on!

It is important to have the correct size of wheel. We would recommend no bigger than 14 inch diameter and not much smaller than 13 inch diameter. If your needs are specialised (racing, for example), the Mountney range extends to diameters as low as 10 inches.

IC1.5
Once the nut is off, the steering wheel follows suit. It should only require fairly gentle pulling. If it sticks on the splines, it is natural to want to apply pressure to the back of the wheel, that is, towards yourself. **Don't** ... you could damage the wheel, the splines and yourself! All you have to do is tap gently around the rim of the wheel downwards, towards the facia and the wheel will free itself.

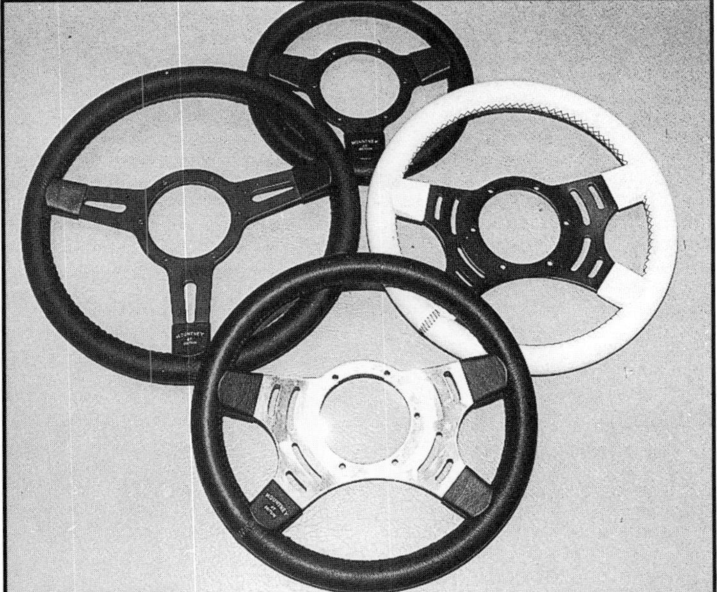

IC1.6
The number of styles and various connotations in the Mountney range would take far more space than we have here. These four represent the sublime to the not-so-sublime as far as Fiesta owners are concerned. The tiny 10 inch rim at the top is not recommended.

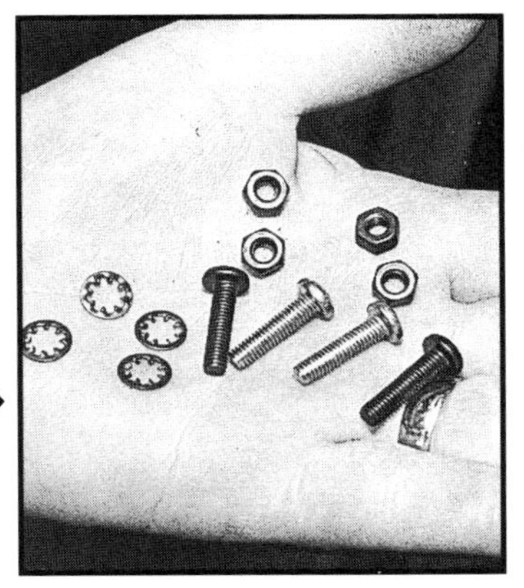

IC1.7
Mountney provide two sets of screws with each boss to enable you to match the colour of the wheel spokes on your particular wheel, in this case, matt black. Note the provision of shakeproof washers which ***must*** be fitted

Fitting a replacement steering wheel

Which wheel you choose is a matter of personal taste. The standard wheel was deemed far too bus-like so a 13 inch diameter, semi-dished model with matt black centre spokes and grey leather rim was chosen, being something different from the usual all-black. The Mountney range includes white, red, brown or wood rims! We checked carefully that the ancillary controls would still operate with the smaller wheel.

IC1.8
The six crosshead screws that hold the wheel to the boss are secured on the underside by a nut and a shakeproof washer. Once the wheel is fully tightened onto the boss ...

IC1.9
... the centre nut can be tightened up. It is very important that this should be to a maximum torque of 20 lbs/ft: no more, no less, either of which could be potentially very dangerous.

IC1.10
Each Mountney wheel comes with a centre cap. Although not required here, it serves the purpose of horn button on some models. The embossed centre logo is "Mountney", but many others are available reflecting the make and model of car.

IC1.11
The finished article. Smaller and more manageable without going to extremes, the new wheel is thicker rimmed and adds greatly to the pleasure of driving.

You don't have to drive 30,000 miles a year to realise that a comfortable seat is more than just a luxury. The Cobra range of high quality seats is extensive and the company has taken great care to ensure that they are both comfortable and supportive in the right places. For "sporting" drivers particularly, a good quality seat, with more support, is essential when cornering enthusiastically!

IC2.1
The top of the range is the Instyle SL (where SL stands for "Super Luxury"). As well as the adjustable backrest, pump-up lumbar support can be specified and the base central cushion can be extended one or two inches for extra thigh support.
(Photo courtesy Cobra Superform Ltd)

IC2.2
The most popular Cobra seats can be ordered in hand-crafted, Connolly leather and there's little that will give your Fiesta a more "up-market" look, not to mention that glorious fragrance. Some of the leather trim options are complemented by American stitching in a contrasting colour. The seat shown here is the Montreaux, fitted with the open type headrest.
(Photo courtesy Cobra Superform Ltd)

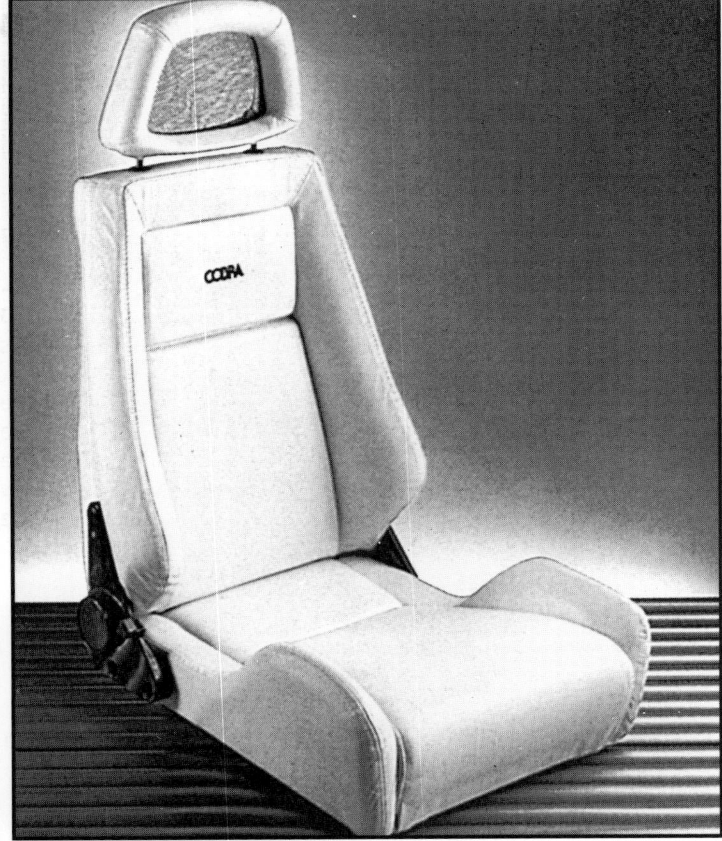

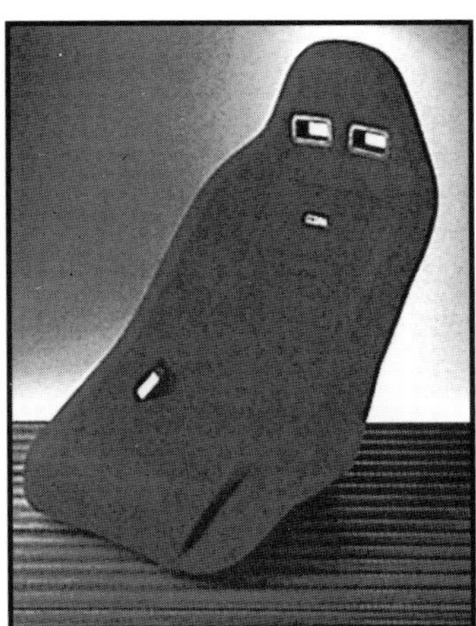

IC2.3
Whilst most seats in the Cobra range are recliners, there is a wide range of sports seats, all of which can be used in standard, road-going vehicles. The Clubman is a tough, sporty seat at a budget price, offering excellent lateral support. If you race, rally or otherwise compete in your Fiesta ...
(Photo courtesy Cobra Superform Ltd)

Fitting replacement seats

The combination of trim and style of seats in the Cobra range is extensive and all are of excellent quality and designed to give the maximum ergonomic support for your body. The main factors are that the support should be in the right places and of the right amount. It is important that the lumbar support should not "give" as you sit on it and there are adjustable backrest controls on most models.

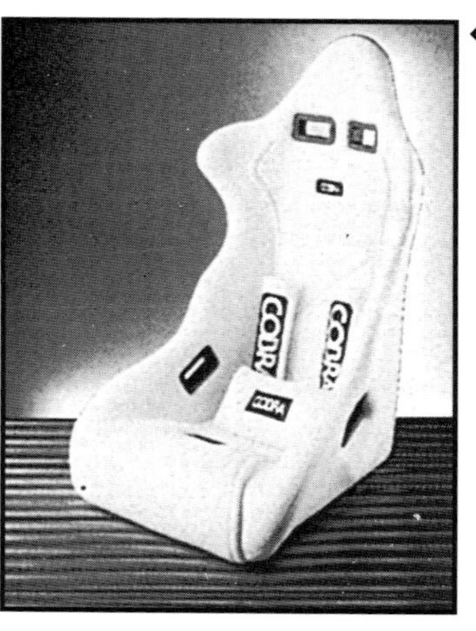

IC2.4
... then you will need the Cobra Kevlar competition seat. It is constructed to the highest standards with driver comfort and safety being paramount. It comes in red, black or blue, with provision for a full racing harness and, available as options, extra harness pads and a lumbar support.
(Photo courtesy Cobra Superform Ltd)

IC2.5
At the Cobra factory, the seats are made to exacting specifications, evolving from a basic frame. It's hard to believe that this rather uncomfortable looking mass of metal and wood will eventually be transformed into a superb sporting seat.

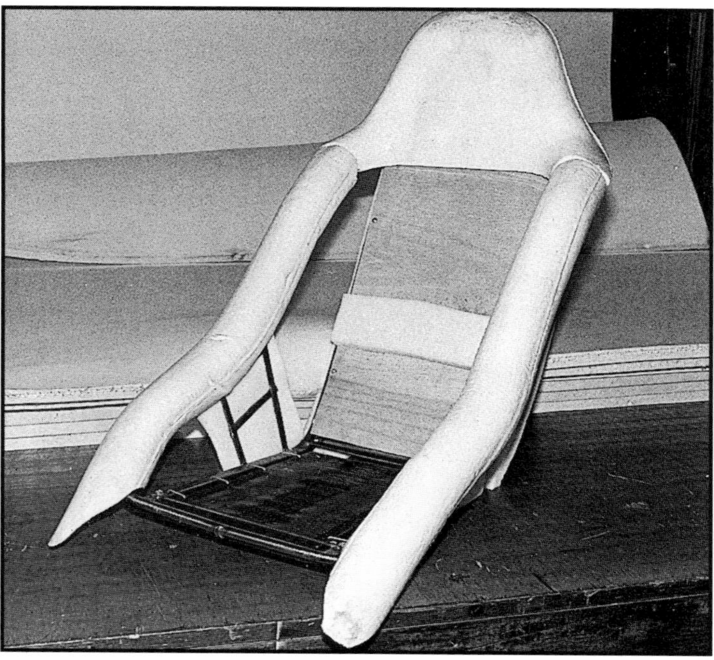

IC2.6
Once some of the padding is added, this latest Cobra begins to take shape and before long ...

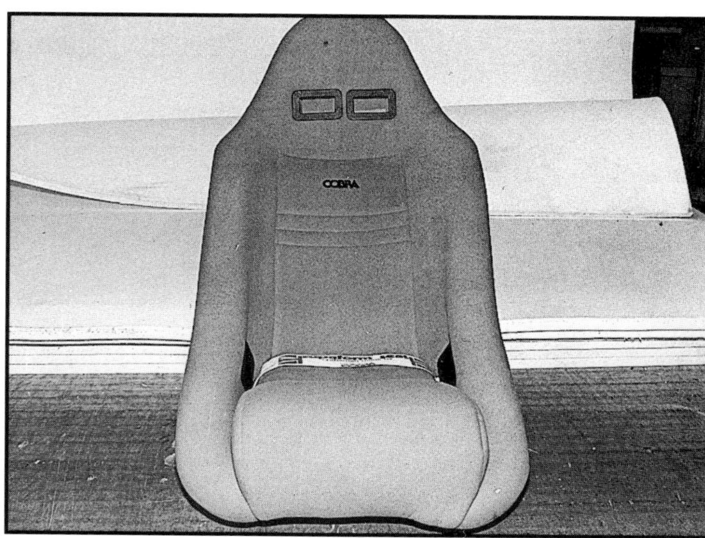

IC2.7
... we have what is obviously a fixed back, bucket seat. At this stage, the trim has to be finished before the seat is passed to Cobra's rigorous, quality control department.

IC2.8
We fitted Montreaux seats to this 1.1 model Fiesta, a task which proved surprisingly easy. First task is to remove the old seats. Not hard at all, requiring only a 10mm socket to take care of the four bolts involved, two at the front and two at the rear.

IC2.9
The Cobra adaptor brackets are quite ingenious, enabling the seat to be fitted to any Fiesta. By re-using the standard sub-frame, the original seat adjustment controls are used and it makes changing the seats from car to car incredibly easy.

As you can see, swapping seats in your Fiesta is far from being difficult. However, you must not become lax in your attitude to safety because of this. You *must* ensure that all retaining bolts are replaced correctly and tightened up fully. The dangers of driving a car with a seat not properly secured are obvious and not very pleasant!

IC2.10
The standard seat subframe unbolts (10mm again) and lifts off, allowing the Cobra brackets to be fitted in their place.

IC2.11
The new seat is then fitted onto the subframe and into the car in the same manner as the standard seats. Seen against the original driver's seat, the Montreaux greatly improves the interior of the basic Fiesta, as well as providing comfortable and supportive seating. It is manufactured using dual density moulded foam and finished in the highest quality Polyester/Wool, making it easy to care for. It looks a little out of place, however, without ...

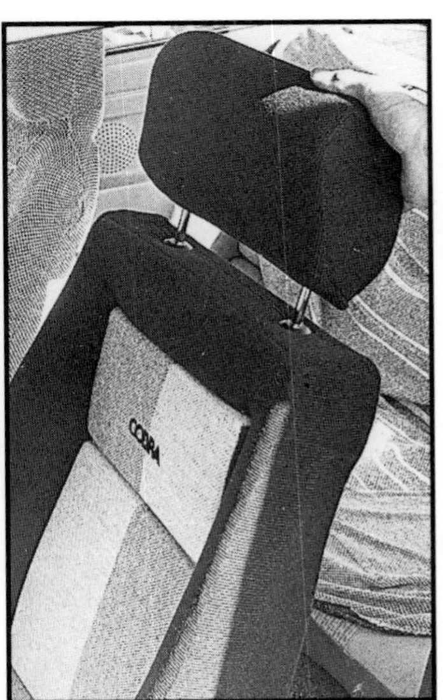

IC2.12
... the optional head-rest. Always to be recommended as it is likely to be a great safety aid in reducing the effects of whiplash injuries for front seat passengers. The Cobra head-rests are available in either solid (as here), or netted styles and simply slot into place.

Fitting seat covers

Fitting your Fiesta with seat covers is almost invariably a good idea. If your seats are fairly new and in good condition, then a set of seat covers will protect them, thus improving the car's resale value. If the previous owner has not looked after the seats, you may need seat covers to improve the general appearance of the car. The Sedan covers shown here are available for all models of Fiesta. They can be purchased for front seats only, rear seats only, with or without head-rests, or as a whole package, as fitted to the Mk II in this section. They are made of 80 per cent polyester and are machine washedable.

IC3.1
The Sedan range of car seat covers is wide indeed, ranging from subtle checks to not-so-subtle stripes. The covers are named after different parts of the world, from Miami to Milano, of which the former is shown here. Which to fit? It's your car – you choose! *(Photo courtesy Link Sedan)*

IC3.2
In this section, we fitted a complete set of "London" Sedan covers to this Mk II Fiesta. This comprised two covers for the front seats and the two optional head-rest covers, together with one for the rear back-rest and one for the rear squab. This particular design is rather attractive, featuring the effect found in the XR2.

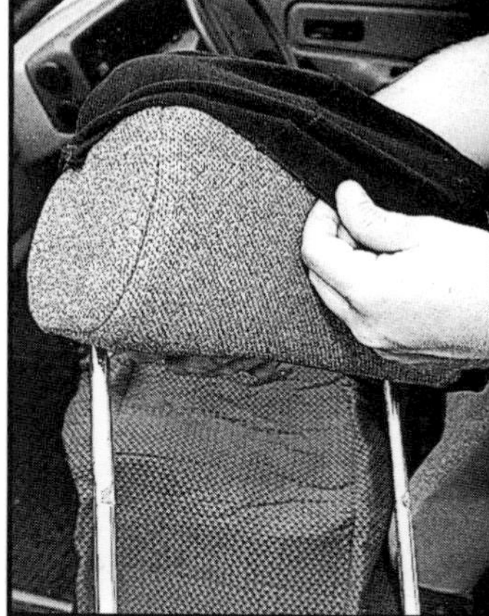

IC3.3
We started with the easiest bit – the head-rests, which simply required the covers to be pulled tightly into place.

IC3.4
The cover for the front seat is in one piece and is designed to fit both the back-rest and the squab. The back-rest section has to be pulled down until it is really tight and the pattern straight.

IC3.5
Before performing the same stretching routine on the squab. Around the bottom of the cover are a series of elasticated loops which have to be stretched under the seat and ...

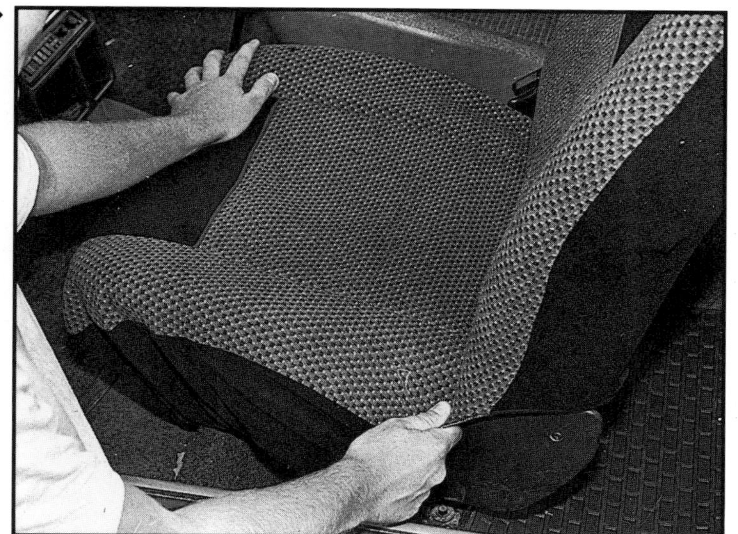

When using the metal clips to secure the covers under the seat, great care should be taken, as there is a lot of tension in the loops. Should your fingers slip, the flying metal clips could be very dangerous, especially with regard to the eyes.

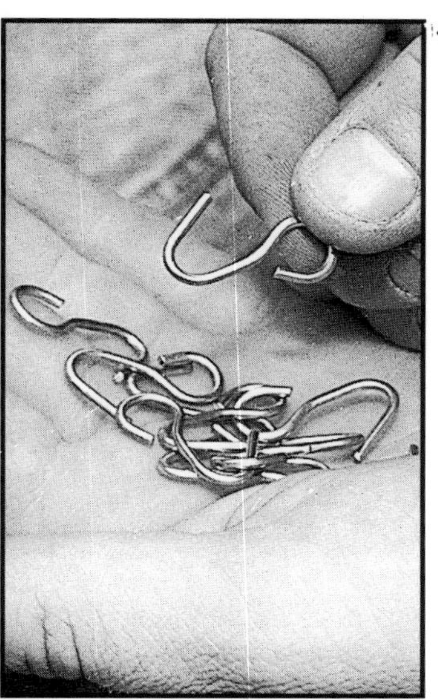

IC3.6
... joined diagonally by these metal hooks.

IC3.7
The front seat cover, being one piece, has no holes for the head-rest. You have to make them using these two-part plastic circles.

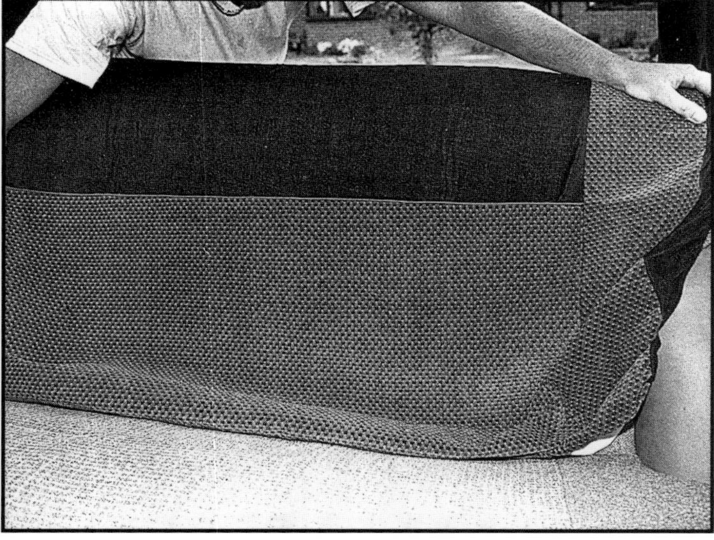

IC3.8
At the rear, fitting is similarly performed, although the squab is held in position by two crosshead screws. As with the front, you should take care to line up the pattern precisely.

Fitting a sound deadening kit

Although the modern Ford is a much quieter beast than its predecessors, engine noise, exhaust boom, transmission whine, body drumming and tyre noise are all present in any Fiesta and can mean that an ambient noise level of over 80db is possible. And you wonder why passengers can't hear you at motorway cruising speeds! There are Autosound "tailored-to-fit" sound proofing kits to suit Mk I and II Fiestas and in addition, all their soundproofing materials are available separately, sold by the foot, roll or litre.

For this section we fitted the Autosound kit to an 1100 Fiesta which was more than a little noisy even at fairly low speeds. The time taken was about two hours, which included removal of much of the interior trim (carpets and so on). We would recommend that you use some form of barrier cream before commencing this job. This will help to get your hands clean after fitting the sound deadening, for the glue, of necessity, is very strong. Comma's "Manista" hand cleaner is especially effective in removing tenacious glue from your skin.

IC4.1 There's lots of material in the box, as you can see! No less than twenty pieces, cut to fit the Mk II Fiesta, complete with a tin of powerful glue, a roll of airseal tape and six strips of sealing mastic. There are three basic materials: Neoprene coated felt for the underbonnet area, Sound Barrier Mat (which has a shiny black surface bonded to a layer of grey foam) and the Autosound Acousticell, sound absorbing foam. Following the comprehensive instructions is made simpler by the fact that all the panels are numbered.

IC4.2 Starting at the front, the underbonnet area was first for the Autosound treatment. There are four neoprene coated felt panels to be fitted here. The layout (on a cold engine, of course!) shows how they fit exactly. You ***must*** make sure that the area you are working in is well-ventilated before using the glue.

IC4.3 In the engine bay, there are three sound barrier mats to be glued to the bulkhead. Ensure the bulkhead is totally free of oil and grease. The glue has to be applied to both metal and pad and allowed to go tacky before positioning.

IC4.4 Working inside the car, the seats have to be taken out (a simple task, just four 10mm bolts to remove), and the carpets removed, following which the whole floor and bulkhead should be thoroughly cleaned. Any holes or badly sealed joints should then be filled using the mastic strips supplied. As can be seen here, there are four pieces which have to be glued against the inner bulkhead, one which is stuck to the centre tunnel and two for the driver's and passenger's floor sections.

IC4.5
At the rear, a similar layout is followed, with the central tunnel being covered with three more pieces of sound barrier mat, neatly cut to fit the car exactly. Like those in the front, the mats for the rear passenger floor sections are only laid in position (rather than glued) so that they can be taken out and dried should the floor become wet.

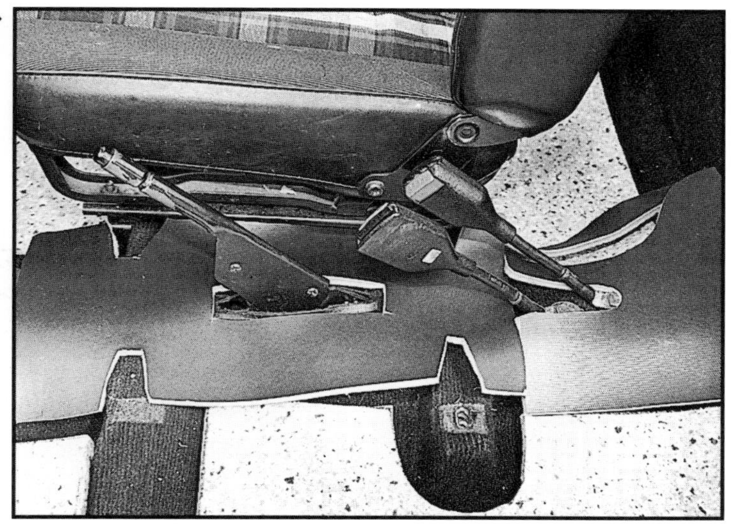

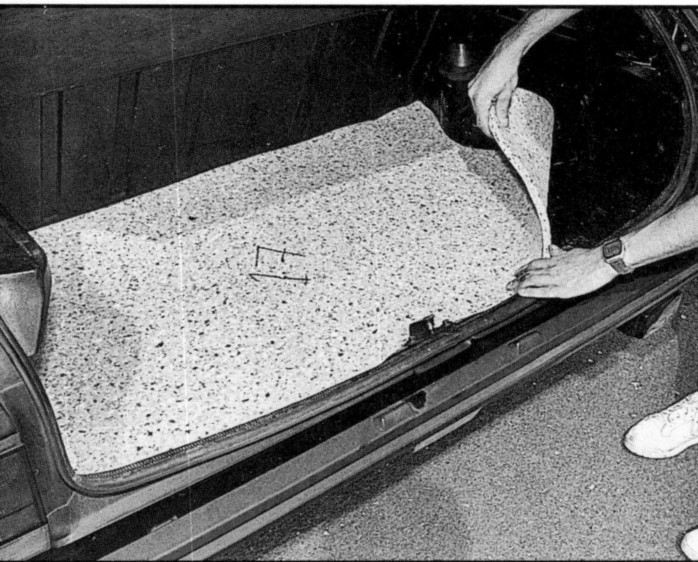

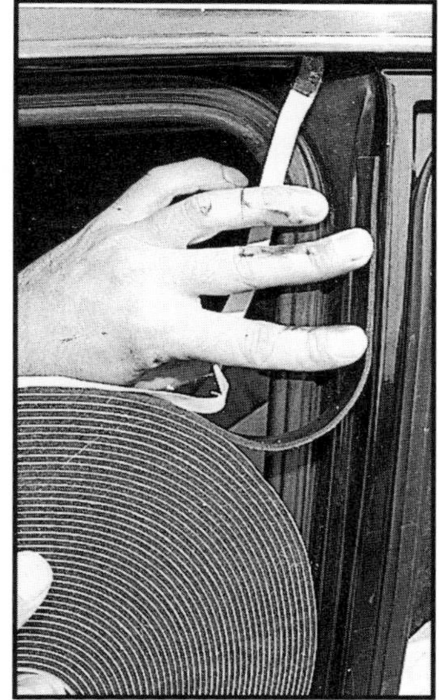

IC4.6
In the hatch there are two panels to keep things quiet. This one lies inside the spare wheel well.

IC4.7
Whilst there is a separate piece which is stuck onto the underside of the rear parcel shelf.

IC4.8
Not often considered is the amount of noise which can enter a car via the door and hatch seals. Sound Services have and provide a roll of Airseal tape to keep out wind noise. This should be applied along door and hatch seals. We suggest leaving the car outside with the doors and hatch open for an hour or so to allow the glue to dissipate before replacing the carpets and interior trim. The before and after noise levels have to be heard to be believed, with the "boominess' and resonant droning sounds very much reduced.

Sound Services point out that before carrying out the fitting of the Autosound sound deadening, a check should be made to ensure that there is no noise coming from such sources as faulty steering or suspension or unbalanced wheels. Split rubber gaiters and missing grommets could also produce extra decibels. As can be seen from the graph below, most of the ambient noise in your Fiesta is well down the frequency range, producing a low, booming effect. It shows a typical "before and after" situation, with the Autosound treatment drastically reducing the noise levels. Now you'll actually be able to hear your sound system!

(Courtesy Sound Services Ltd)

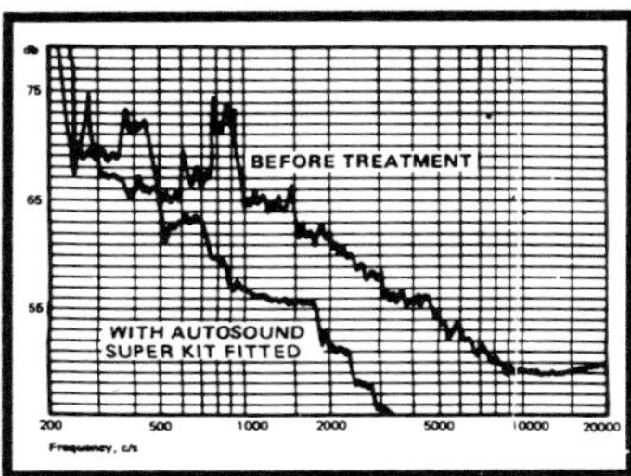

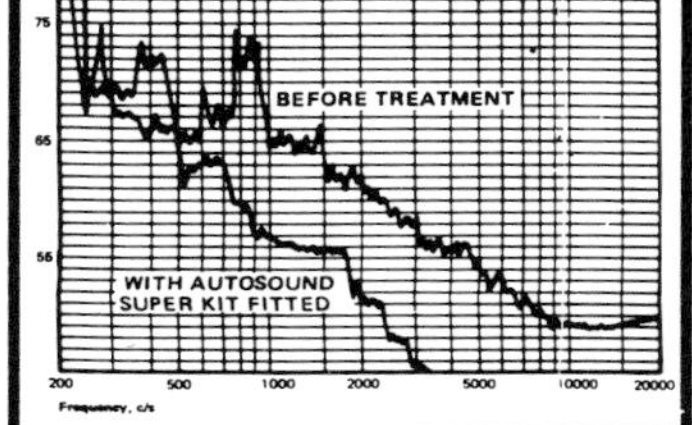

Fitting a carpet set

Using a made-to-measure carpet overmat set in your Fiesta has many advantages. The Autostyle Unique mats shown here are tailored to fit exactly and, as such, do not move around, even though they are easily removed for cleaning. Not only will they make your car interior look better whilst they are in position, they will also offer greater protection to the carpeting already in your car. Clearly, this will pay dividends when you come to sell it. These particular mats have the "XR2" logo on them, although there are many others available, to suit your own model. The sets are available in either tough loop pile or luxurious cut pile and both carry a comprehensive, one-year or 20,000 mile warranty.

IC5.1➡
Several colours are available, but we decided to fit a black carpet set to contrast with the grey interior of this XR2. All mats have a bound, contrasting edging to both mat and heel pad and the backing is non-slip. An optional embroidered heel pad is also available for the passenger side.

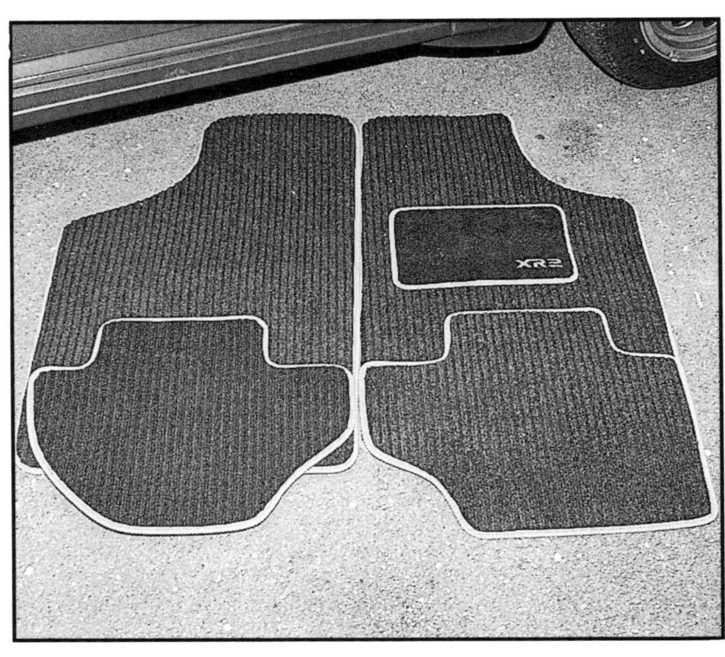

⬅IC5.2
As can be seen here, the driver's side mat is a perfect fit and has the legend "XR2" embroidered in red on the strengthened pedal mat.

IC5.3➡
The mats fit just as snugly in the rear, offering much needed protection for the car's original carpets. You should also note that it is Autostyle Unique who are responsible for the Fiesta clothing and regalia seen throughout this book, and indeed, they have produced a special "Improve and Modify" range, just for us! After all, there is not much point in vastly improving your car's appearance if you don't match it!

Fitting a dog guard

He may be your best friend (after your Fiesta, of course) and your ever faithful companion but you can only stretch friendship so far. When your dog has seen fit to dive all over your newly fitted seat covers with his newly muddied paws, you may find your friendship becoming somewhat strained. The hatchback configuration of the Fiesta makes it ideal for the transportation of a quadruped, with or without the rear seats folded, but only if you have some method of keeping him where the mud doesn't matter! The Cosmic dog guard is just such a device; well made (he won't chew his way through this one!), attractive and, above all, totally safe.

IC6.1
In these days of increased safety awareness, it makes a lot of sense to restrain your dog, and indeed any large or bulky loads you may be carrying, in case you are unlucky enough to be involved in an accident. After all, the thought of even a medium sized pooch being thrown around the inside of your Fiesta is pretty scary. The Cosmic guard shown here comes as seen, together with ...

IC6.2
... the only fitting required, the protective rubber feet. The upright rails are adjustable to suit the height of your car so that it can be installed in the hatch itself (leaving the rear seat in place) or actually on the back of the rear seat when it is folded.

IC6.3
We fitted the guard with the seat folded, to give any animal in the back much more room to move around. Rearward visibility is not impaired to any great extent. The Cosmic guard comes in the black epoxy coated finish seen here, or in an optional chrome finish. The dimensional details are as follows:

Max width	56 inch (1420mm)
Min width	34 inch (860mm)
Max height	43 inch (1090mm)
Min height	25 inch (630mm)

Fitting rear sun blinds

By installing Sedan sun blinds, the car will stay cooler, particularly when it is left with the windows shut. In addition, it can stop the interior trim from fading and will help to keep driver and passengers much more comfortable. Although they look totally black from the outside, they actually do not reduce visibility by much and it is quite safe to drive with them in position, at least in daylight. However, we would recommend that for night driving or travelling in bad weather conditions, the blinds should both be open.

IC7.1
Most car owners fit sun blinds on the rear parcel shelf and Sedan blinds are sold in pairs for this purpose. However, they can, if required, be fitted to the rear side windows in a similar manner to that described.

IC7.2
They are similar in design and operation to the normal domestic roller blind (and just as powerful; watch those fingers!). "Our" car was fitted with a non-standard, wooden rear shelf (ideal for large speakers) and so a small pilot hole was drilled to make life easier for the self-tapping screws which hold the blinds in place. Note that the blinds were slightly longer than the width of the car. As such, a slight overlap in the centre was necessary.

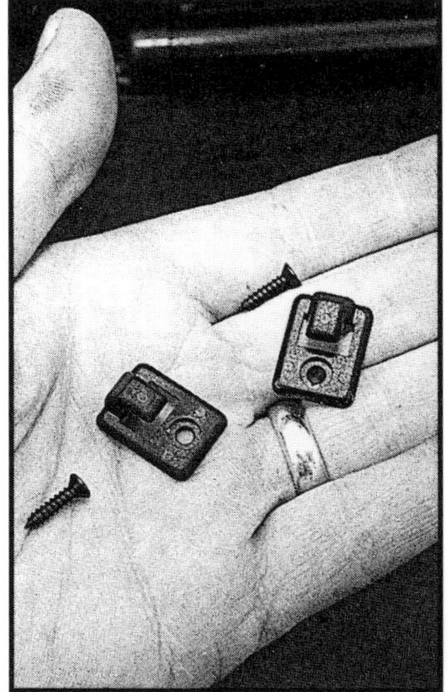

IC7.3
The blinds are held in position by means of these plastic hooks which are self-tapped into the edge of the roof near the tailgate.

IC7.4
The mechanism is tested to ensure that all is well. Note that you must allow for the tailgate to be opened and closed. Also, you should ensure that the self-tappers don't protude through the rear shelf or worse, through the roof! make sure that there's no wiring there either.

Fitting a centre console

A good quality centre console can really improve the look of your Fiesta's interior, as you can see from the photos here. Quickfit 70 make various models including the "Tailor Made Designer" range, trimmed in black vinyl with mock wood centres and the "New Generation" range finished in either charcoal or brown. It is the latter style which is used in this section. There are consoles available for all Mk I and II Fiestas although you must state the precise year of your car.

IC8.1
The first task is to remove any tray or console already fitted. The standard Ford console comes out easily, with the coin tray section unclipping from the main unit. With this removed, the new console is affixed to brackets on the centre tunnel by two crosshead screws on each side.

IC8.2
Two styles of console in the "New Generation" range. Both well made with padded cloth sides. The consoles here are charcoal (blending in with the grey trim of the car), but are also available in brown.

IC8.3
Installation is relatively simple, using the brackets and self-tapping screws supplied. If you do not have a radio/cassette deck, leave the simple, push-out DIN-sized panel in place. This diagram shows component parts and the bracket mounting positions.
(Diagram courtesy Quickfit 70 Ltd)

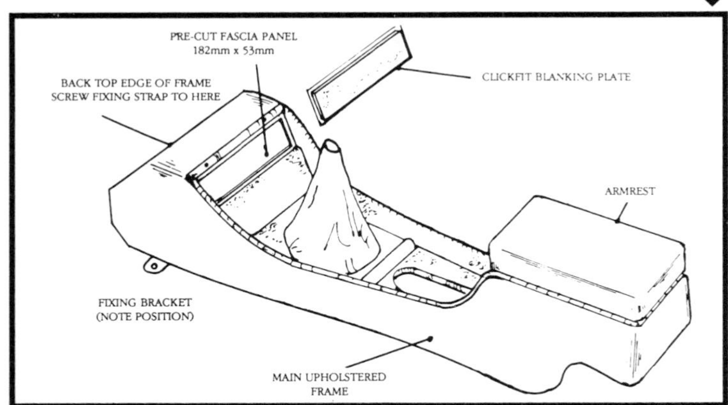

IC8.4
The armrest lifts up and down and reveals a handy little cubby hole.

IC8.5
If you have a good quality radio/cassette unit, like this Sharp 558E, it will slot directly into the aperture. Don't forget to use the bracing strap to support the unit at the rear. The effect of the console is to give this Mk II Fiesta a definite luxury feel. Note that the carpets are being protected by a strong set of Cannon Multifit "S" car mats which have a non-slip backing for safety and deep patterns to retain the dirt and grit which would otherwise get into your carpets and ruin your car's interior and resale value.

Fitting a cassette storage module

Apart from making your car considerably tidier, the use of a Fischer C-Box cassette storage unit will help to preserve your tapes. It will protect them from sunlight and dust and prevent damage to both case and mechanism.

The in-car cassette player (more usually a radio/cassette player) is a boon to those of us who regularly have to make long tedious journeys. It does mean, however, that cassettes have to be carried in the car and as most of us like to have a reasonable selection, this poses a storage problem. Fischer C-Box have acquired an eniviable reputation when it comes to in-car cassette storage and so we took a look at what this German company could provide.

IC9.1 ➡
Fischer make a wide range of C-Boxes and seen here, left to right, are the six-cassette horizontal, the six-cassette vertical and the twelve-cassette portable.

⬆
IC9.2
The first two are meant for in-car fitment only and this can be achieved by either screwing the box in place or using the double-sided sticky pad provided. The bracket is cleverly designed to allow the box to be mounted either way up and ...

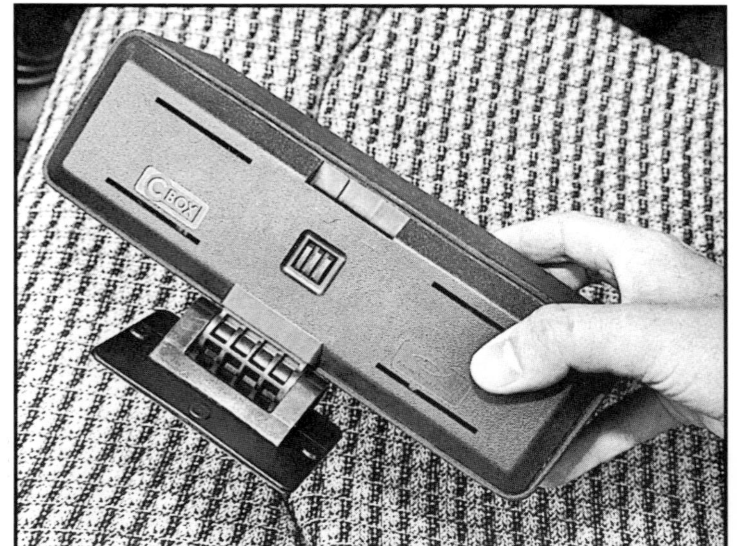

⬆
IC9.3
... simply slots into position on the back of the box. Wherever it is practical we would always prefer to stick the C-Box in place as in the case ...

⬅ **IC9.4**
... of this Mk III model. Mounted here, it is easily accessible for both driver and passenger, but does not obstruct the driver's view.

IC9.5
Alternatively, it could be suspended under the centre of the dash. If you intend to do this, you would probably be better advised to use the self-tapping screws provided. Don't forget though, that when you sell the car, you'll leave holes in the dash.

IC9.6
The vertical model can be positioned and mounted in the same manner. Both of these universal boxes hold six cassettes, so choice comes down to personal preferences and what looks and fits best in your particular Fiesta.

In common with many safety conscious German manufacturers, all Fischer C-Box storage units, whether specific or universal, are made of extremely strong, shatter resistant plastic.

IC9.7
For those who have a lot of tapes and use them alternately in the car and in the home, the C-Box carry case could be the answer. It holds twelve tapes and ...

IC9.8
... features ingenious small red "cassettes in place" markers, showing which drawers are in use. It can be mounted in-car by using the two brackets provided which hold the unit firmly in place but allow its quick removal when required. The latter is recommended as a loose box in the car could easily turn into an unguided missile in the event of a crash.

Safety equipment

Fitting a fire extinguisher and safety kit

Take temperatures of several hundred degrees, a ready supply of highly flammable fluid and a number of high voltage electrical systems and you have the makings of a fairly powerful bomb. Whether you realise it or not, you are actually driving around in this high incendiary device every day of the week! With ever more complex electrical systems being installed in modern Fiestas, it makes sense to carry a fire extinguisher.

IC10.1
Little and large: at left is the Gloria, PG2A, 2kg extinguisher and at right is the PG1A, a 1kg version. Both come complete with a mounting bracket as standard and both are powder discharge models, ideally suited to in-car use. Naturally, their usefulness extends over into associated areas, such as boats and caravans. Like most extinguishers of this type, once used, they should be refilled and ***not*** kept in a partially filled state. Refills are also available from Hella.

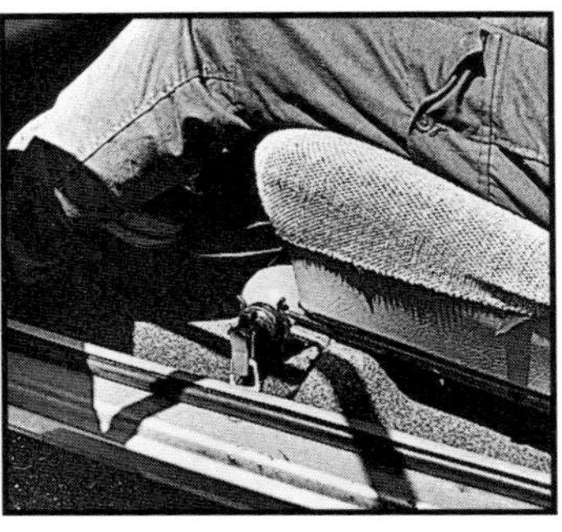

IC10.2
Mounting the extinguisher calls for some thought. It needs to be readily accessible and so a hatch or boot mounting comes a poor second to installing it in the cabin. Don't fix the extinguisher onto the dash or on the parcel shelf. However well secured for normal driving conditions, it could easily cause injury in an accident. Also, even if it doesn't hit anyone, at the very time you're likely to need it, it will doubtless have wedged itself under the seat! We found that screwing the bracket to the floor, just in front of the passenger seat, is perfect; easily reached in an emergency, but does not interfere with the passenger's comfort.

IC10.3
Another safety item, also marketed by Hella, is this Safety Kit. It comes in a very strong, plastic carry case and contains just about everything you would need to deal with a roadside emergency. Each side of the case is secured by one of these plastic covers which ...

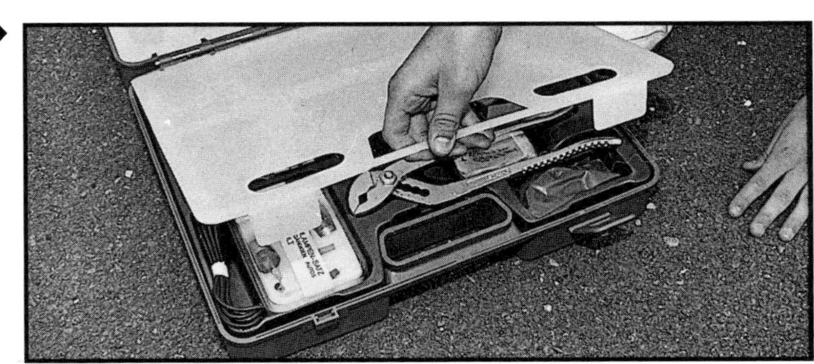

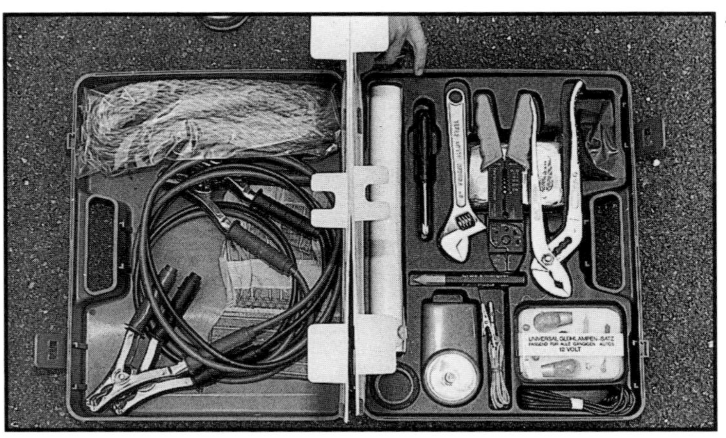

IC10.4
... when released gives access to following items: an SOS window sticker, a roll of electrical tape, a crosshead/slotted head screwdriver, a 9 inch adjustable wrench, a yellow crayon, a large adjustable spanner, a small torch, a 6–24 volt electrical tester, a universal light bulb kit with fuses and wire, a crimper with a selection of connections, a plastic raincoat, heavy duty jump leads, protective gloves and a strong nylon tow rope.

Fitting child car seats

IC11.1

The seat you choose will depend largely upon the age and weight of your child. The Britax Babysure is intended for use by children aged up to approximately nine months (and weighing up to 10kg), and is one of the new generation of child seats. Designed to be used facing rearwards, the manufacturers state very clearly that it should ***never*** be used facing forwards. It uses the Fiesta's standard lap and diagonal belts which thread through the various points, as shown in the diagram.

(Diagram courtesy of Britax Ltd)

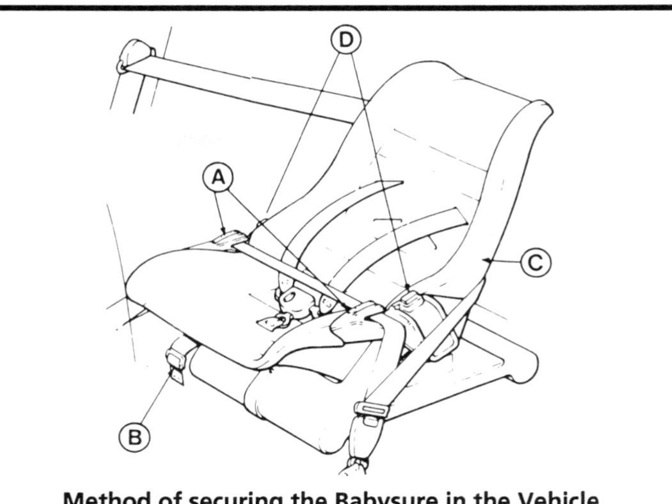

Method of securing the Babysure in the Vehicle

A – Webbing guide hooks
B – Crotch strap adjuster
C – Removable cover
D – Recliner buttons

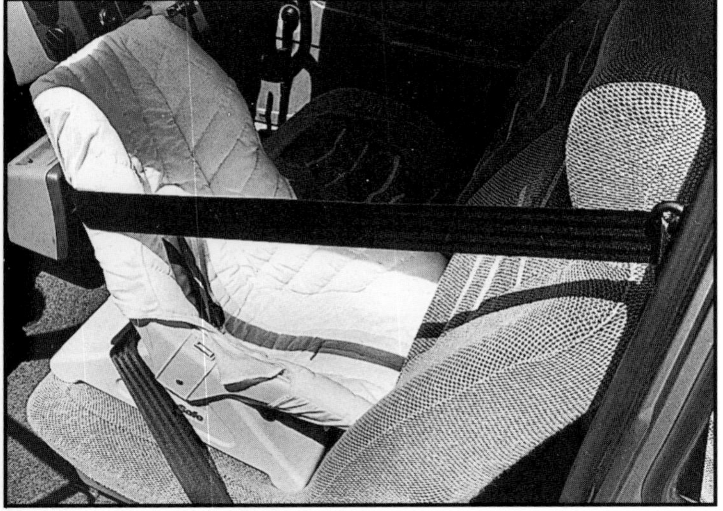

IC11.2

The seat can be used on either the front or the back seat but ***not*** with a lap only belt. The Babysure is a strong and comfortable item and (by utilising the carrying handles), can quite easily be removed for use in the home. However, it should not be used in any other manner than that prescribed in the fitting instructions.

IC11.3

Another easy to fit seat is the Bobby which, again, can be used in either front or rear of the car. It should only be used with a lap and diagonal belt. With the child in the seat, the belt should be fitted as normal and then the adjustable guide strap, shown here hand held, can be used to ensure that the seat belt is comfortable and does not touch the neck area or the stomach. It is designed for use by children aged approximately eight months to seven years and weighing 9 to 25kg.

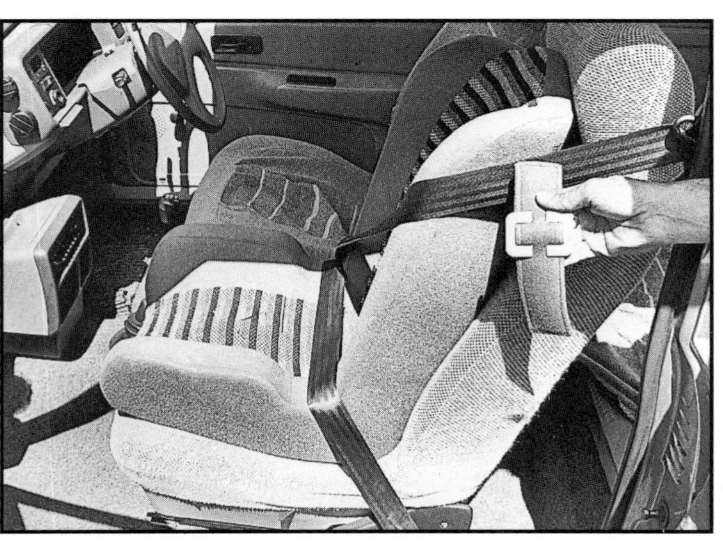

It seems to us amazing that there should be such controversy over the restraint of children (and adults for that matter!) when travelling in cars. Official accident figures show clearly the beneficial effect of compulsory front seat belts and, after 1989, doubtless the figures will show similar improvements with regard to rear seat passengers because of new legislation which became effective during September. Of all passengers, surely children must be the most at risk and yet time and time again one can see cars being driven, often at speed, with children on the back seat, totally unrestrained. Even quite a minor accident can have tragic results, where children can be catapulted into the back of the front seat or even worse, between the front seats and through the windscreen. If you need convincing, even a brief look at some of the sickening photographs taken of hospitalised cases will soon change your mind. We would always recommend that *anyone* travelling in any motor vehicle should be restrained in some manner.

Fitting child car seats

When looking to buy a child seat you should always look for the British Standard "kite mark" or European "E" mark, meaning that the product you are buying is fit for its intended purpose. All Britax seats are approved to either of these levels and, as you would expect from one of the top manufacturers, are produced to a very high standard.

IC11.4
The StarRiser car booster seat is intended for children from approximately four years upwards, who may otherwise be sitting too low down for the proper use of conventional seat belts.

IC11.5
Full instructions are included with the StarRiser and must be followed carefully. This drawing shows how to position the cushion on the seat. The StarRiser is used in conjunction with a lap and diagonal seat belt, or with a child harness.
(Courtesy of Britax Ltd)

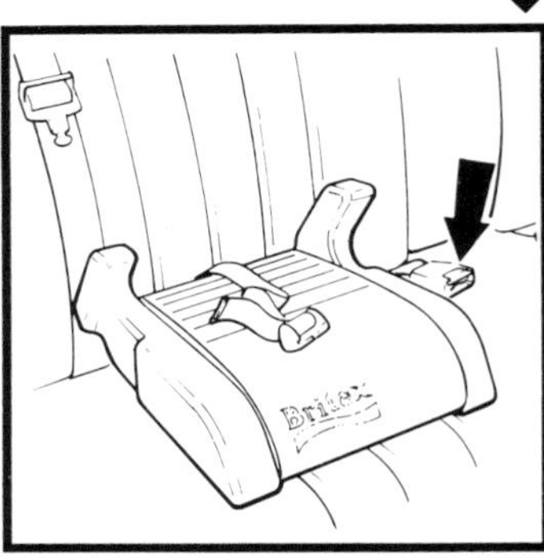

IC11.6
The Recliner looks like everyone's idea of a child seat, being much akin to a scaled down rally car seat. It is fitted with a full harness to hold the child securely in position. It has a parachute type central release mechanism which allows the child to be withdrawn quickly in case of emergency. It is suitable for children aged approximately six months to four years and weighing between 9 and 18kg.

To be effective, a child seat must, of course, be correctly fitted following the manufacturer's detailed instructions. Fitting any of the seats shown here is within the reach of most DIYers, but if you have any qualms, then either take your Fiesta to a specialist for fitting or checking before use. You simply *cannot* afford to take risks.

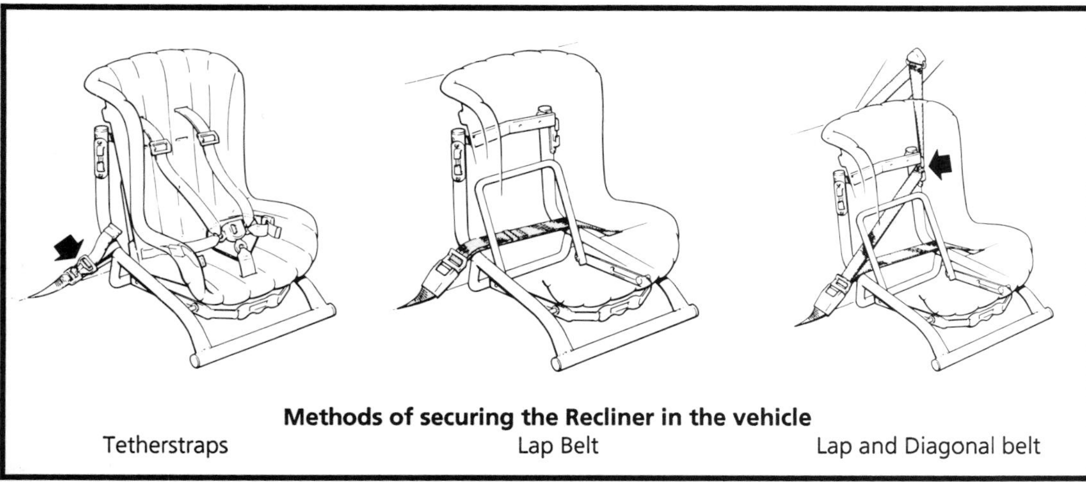

Methods of securing the Recliner in the vehicle

IC11.7
As can be seen from these diagrams, fitting can be either by means of tether straps, a lap belt or a lap and diagonal belt. As an added bonus, the seat can be fully reclined (as the name suggests) thus encouraging your child to sleep the journey away; not just properly restrained, but peaceful too!
(Diagrams courtesy Britax Ltd)

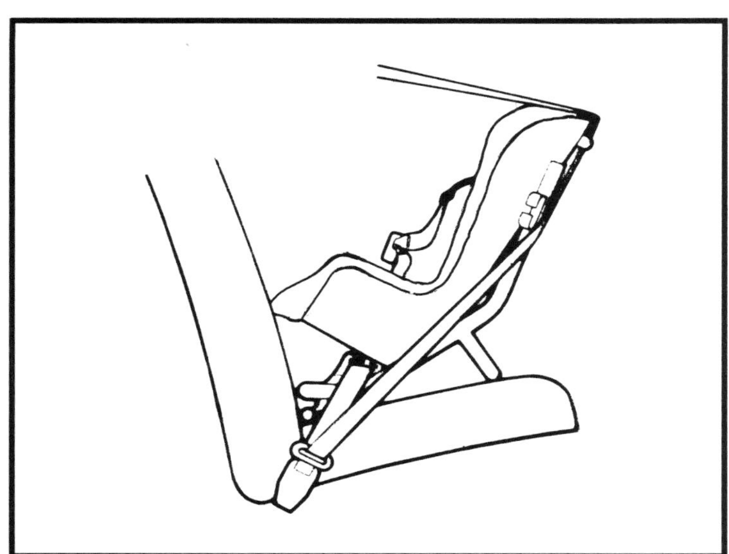

IC11.8
The Britax 2-Way can be used in a rearward facing position (with a lap and diagonal belt) and is suitable when used this way for babies up to 10kg.
(Photo courtesy Britax Ltd)

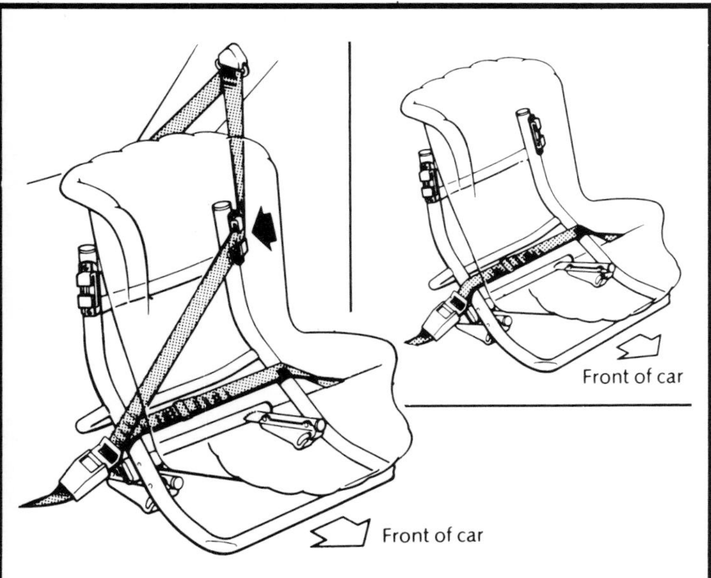

IC11.9
As the name suggests, it can also be used facing forwards. When fitted in this manner it is suitable for children weighing between 9 and 18kg. When facing forwards it is used with a lap and diagonal, or lap seat belt (or even with a separate fitting kit).
(Photo courtesy Britax Ltd)

Fitting a roll cage

Given the tremendous interest in racing the Fiesta XR2 since the early 80s, it is little wonder that demand for suitable roll cages continues apace. Safety Devices can cater for any model of Fiesta and if they haven't got what you want; they'll make it! It is a terrifying fact, but statistics show that in 15 per cent of serious accidents, the car actually overturns. Such figures make one think very carefully about the possibility of installing a roll cage for pure road use.

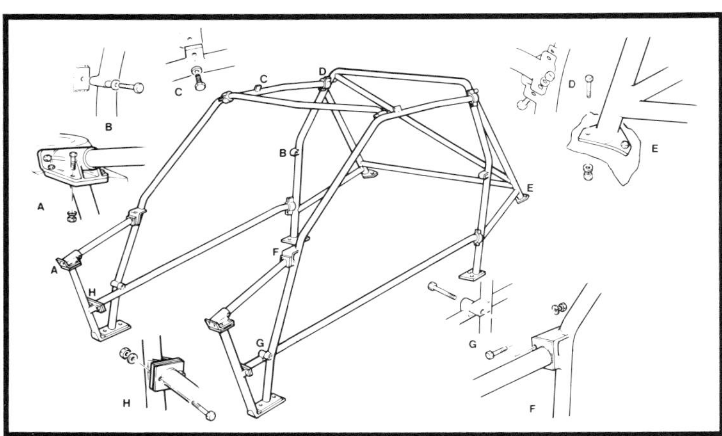

IC12.1
This is it! The ultimate in roll-over protection is the Safety Devices Multipoint model. The complete structure integrates with the Fiesta for which it has been designed and adds to the inherent strengths and compensates for its weaknesses. *(Diagram courtesy Safety Devices)*

IC12.2
This stunning creation was prepared by Autocross of Bracknell for their rally crossing boss, John Cross. With rear wheel drive and some 250bhp from the BDA engine, a good roll cage is something of a necessity.

IC12.3
The demands of rally cross are extreme, not least the very real possibility that you could end up on your roof! Seen here, the tubing extends all around the inside of the car to protect its precious contents ...

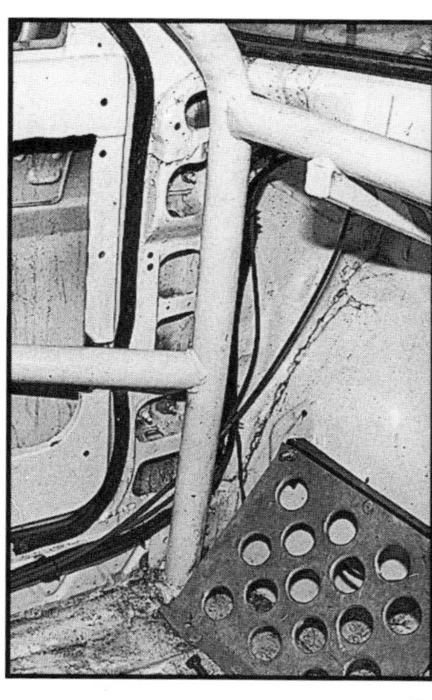

IC12.4
... and is actually welded to the car at many points, as here in the passenger side.

IC12.5
The shell of the car is also specially strengthened: a strong roll cage is not a lot of use unless the car itself can stand the pace.

IC12.6
Where necessary, the roll cage is thickly padded in order to protect the occupants' heads

Technically, Safety Devices roll cages are most impressive. All feature computer aided design and aerospace standard welding, and come with a comprehensive fitting kit incorporating reinforcing plates and high tensile steel bolts, washers and nuts.

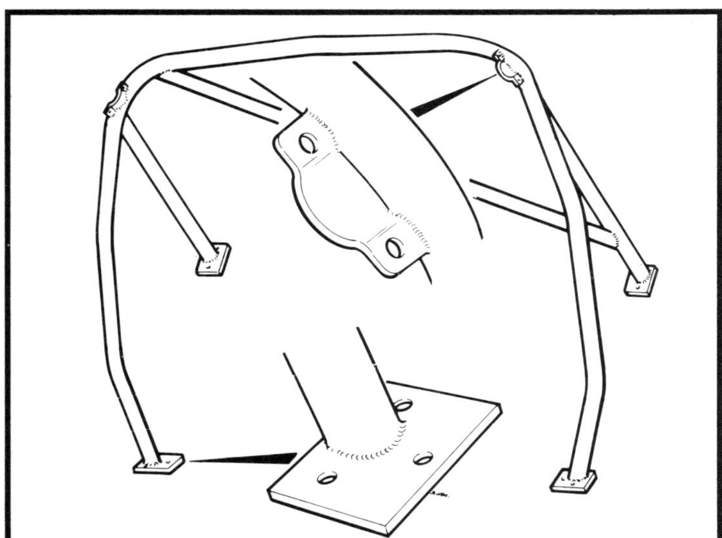

IC12.7
If your competition requirements are not so demanding, then there are a variety of other cages to suit the specific sport in question, whether it's hill climbing, rallying or out and out racing. The Type 5, for example, is a rear bar and is compulsory for all vehicles competing in speed events (racing, sprints and hill climbs), run to FIA appendix J regulations.

(Diagram courtesy Safety Devices)

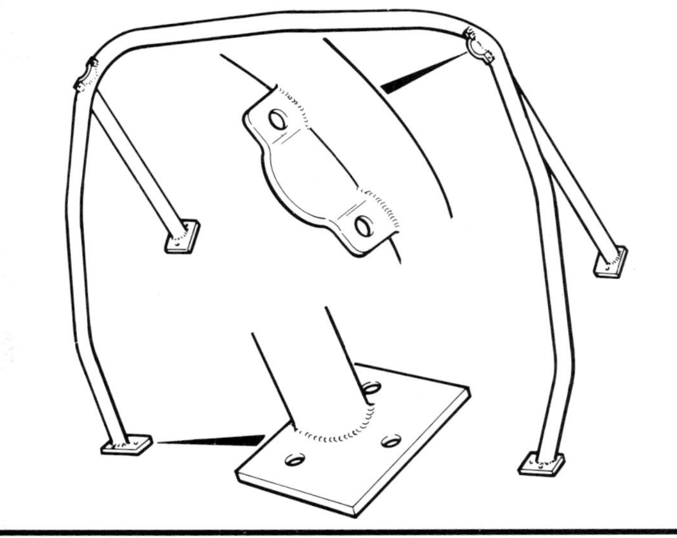

IC12.8
Whilst the Type 2 is a simpler cage (albeit designed and made to the same high standards), it is suitable for saloons under 1000kg (competition weight) competing in club and restricted events. It comes with fittings ready-made to accept the matching front cage (Type 3).

(Diagram courtesy Safety Devices)

Electrical accessories

Fitting a fuel computer

As microprocessor technology makes more inroads into modern motoring, it is common nowadays to find trip computers fitted to many cars as standard. For those who agree with us that such a device is worthwhile, Zemco manufacture an impressive range of driving computers suitable for all models except those with mechanical fuel injection. These range from extremely complex units which combine the normal features with a cruise control, to the (relatively) simple Zemco DCS 350E "Fuel Manager".

The Zemco DCS 360E fitted here has an impressive list of features including:
Fuel management –
Instant mph/mpg on a trip/fuel used/fuel left in tank.
Distance –
Mileage since last fill-up/ on trip/to empty.
Time –
Real-time or spent on trip.
Speed –
Actual instantaneous or average for trip.
As with all models in the range, it provides instant change-over from litres to gallons, for those who do not yet consider themselves to be "European"! So, you can buy your fuel in litres but measure your consumption in mpg.

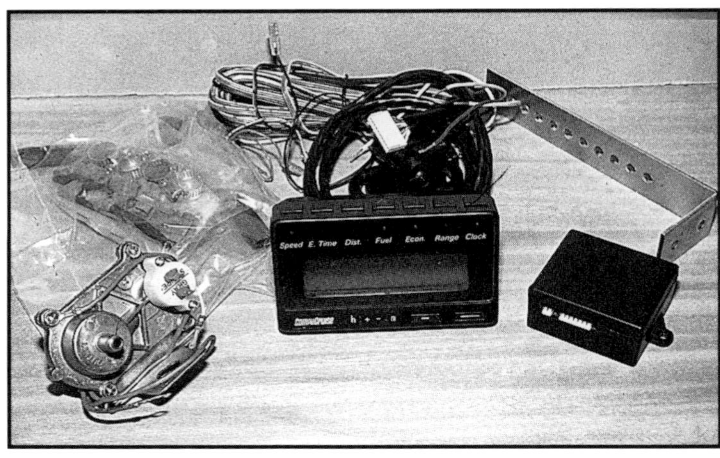

IC13.1 The kit comes complete with all items required to fit the computer as well as two very thorough instruction and installation manuals. Complex though it looks, the wiring is all neatly assembled in two looms and fitted with multi-plugs where possible.

IC13.2 First job is to mount the command module. It is possible to obtain a bracket which would enable it to be mounted on the dash, or any flat surface. However, standard fitting is by means of this flexible stalk. The wiring runs up the centre of the stalk and is then simply plugged into the module. The module is then affixed to the stalk by two self-tapping screws.

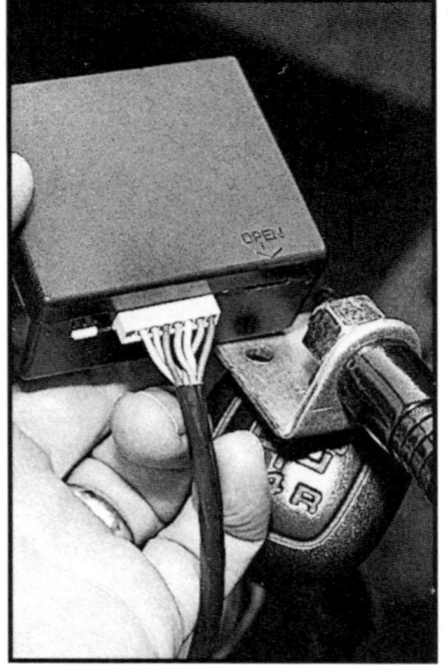

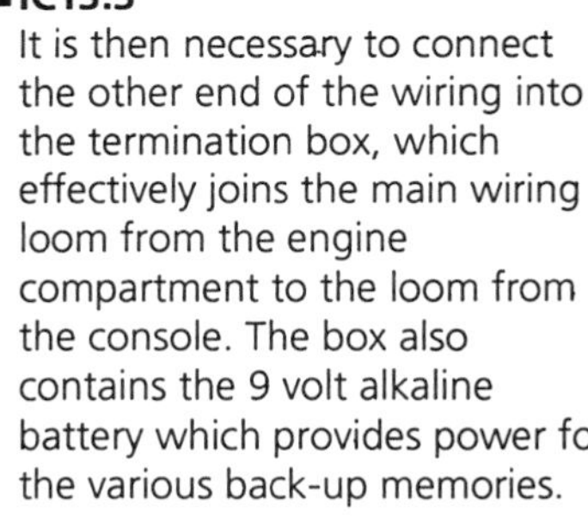

IC13.3 It is then necessary to connect the other end of the wiring into the termination box, which effectively joins the main wiring loom from the engine compartment to the loom from the console. The box also contains the 9 volt alkaline battery which provides power for the various back-up memories.

IC13.4 The stalk has a mounting bracket which accepts two self-tapping screws. These can be used for mounting it on the side of the transmission tunnel or the centre console. The passenger side is probably preferable, as shown here, so as to be easily seen by the driver but without physically getting in the way. However, where and how you put it, is purely down to personal choice.

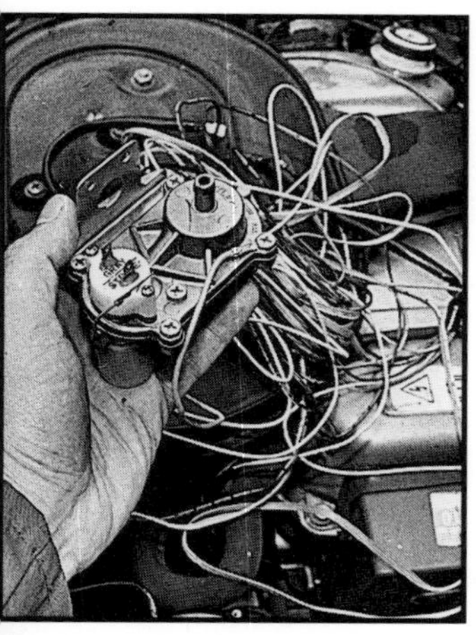

IC13.5
The fuel sensor measures the rate and amount of fuel passing from the tank into the carburettor, thus giving the consumption. It is important that it should be mounted the correct way up, although this is clearly marked.

IC13.6
Selection of metric or imperial measurements is by means of a switch on the back of the module.

IC13.7
The information about road speed is fed to the computer via this speed sensor. Mounted on the bracket shown here, it picks up impulses from the magnets which have to be attached to the driveshaft. Care should be taken to ensure that the magnets are stuck to a spotlessly clean surface and that they are then bound securely to the driveshaft with the stainless steel wires provided. Having finished the installation, the procedure of calibration is thoroughly covered in the operation manual.

For those unimpressed with some car manufacturers digital displays, the Zemco DCS 360E presents two readouts for instant mpg figures; one is the normal display and the other is in the form of an easy-to-check digital bar graph. All Zemco kits are available with a choice of fuel sensors for carburettored engines, or electronic fuel-injected engines. Those owners with mechanical fuel injection cannot fit the DCS 360E.

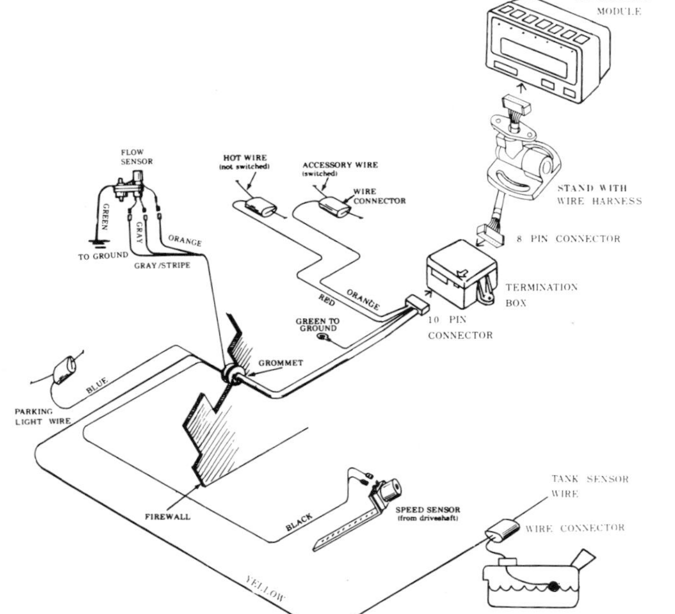

IC13.8
The wiring connections are very simple, as this diagram shows. This is just one of dozens of such diagrams taken from the installation guide.

(Diagram courtesy Zemco Ltd)

Fitting electric windows

Even though they are increasingly being fitted as original equipment, electric windows will still give your car that certain air of luxury as they slide gracefully up and down at the flick of a switch. The windows we fitted here, to a Mk II Fiesta, are Gemini Spal units. One very important feature is the inclusion of a clutch mechanism, which comes into play when the window is fully closed or open and thus ensures a long life for the motor as well as making the windows safer in use. There are Gemini Spal kits available for both two- and four-door Fiestas, which require fitting in the same way, the only difference being a little, simple additional wiring.

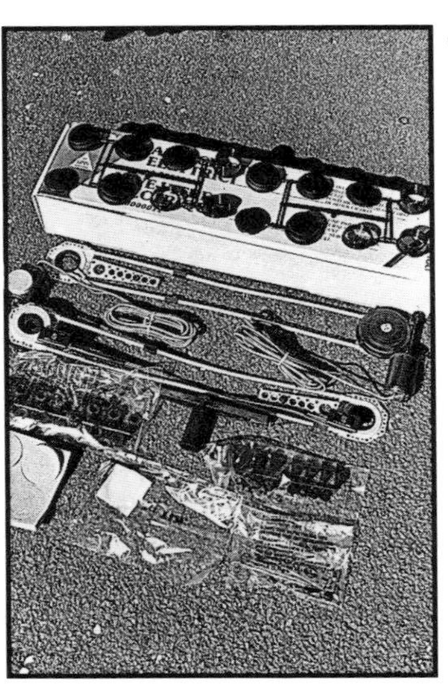

IC14.1
The kit is truly universal and comes with a variety of blanking plugs as well as the various necessary plugs, wiring, nuts and bolts. This is a two-door kit with twin mechanisms and motors and, perhaps most important, a separate handle for winding the windows manually in case of a car electrical problem.

IC14.2
With the door trim panel removed, the first task is to select the correct sized toothed wheel from the selection provided and place it into the driven end of the drive unit. Then ...

IC14.3
... a second, smaller wheel is selected to match both the first one and the splines of the Fiesta's window winder.

IC14.4
This is secured to the original spindle by a small self-tapping screw and the whole assembly can be offered up to see how and where the motor is to be supported.

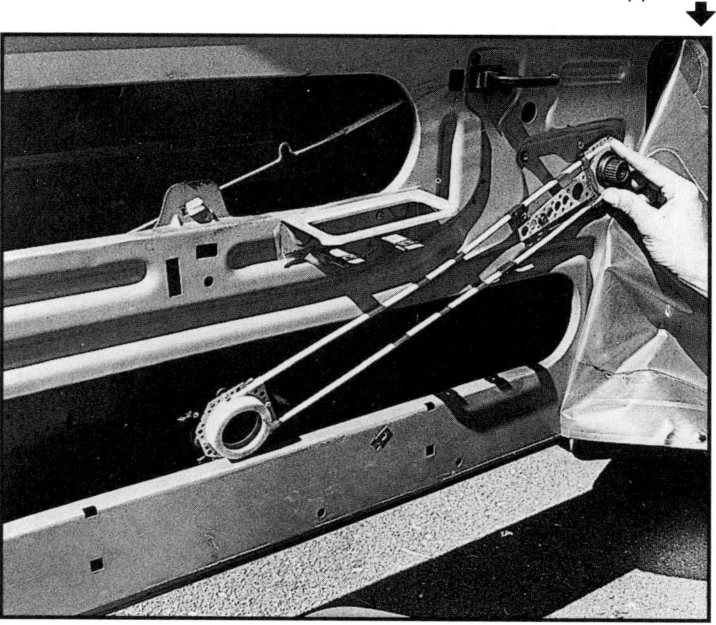

IC14.5
Gemini Spal provide a good selection of brackets which simply self-tap onto the relevant holes around the motor.

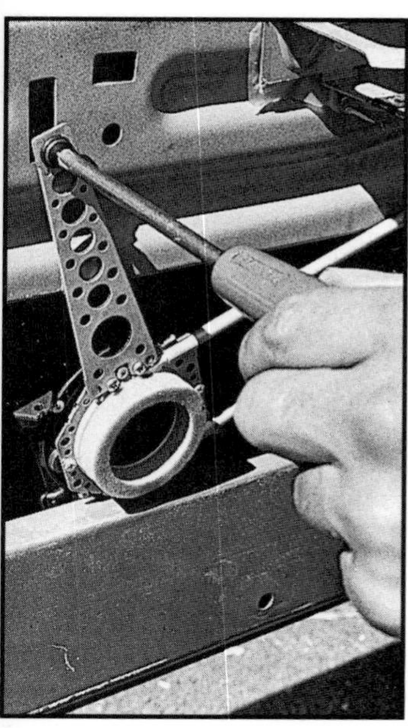

IC14.6
For the first bracket, an existing hole in the door was used. The multi-hole design makes the brackets very versatile.

IC14.7
At least one more bracket should be added and this means drilling a hole. Mark the position carefully and dot punch before drilling with a small pilot drill. Apply some form of rustproofing before you screw everything into place. With most of the trim removed, it is an ideal opportunity to rustproof the whole of the inner door. (See Chapter 5.)

IC14.8
The switches are designed and produced to look like original equipment units, rather than aftermarket fitments, adding to the "upmarket" image. No soldering is involved, as the switches come complete, with six inch lengths of wire connected at the switch terminals. In a small car like the Fiesta, it makes good sense to locate the switches in the armrests, although mounting both in the centre console is also a popular choice.

IC14.9
And what happens if you have a power failure? Not to worry, a manual winding handle is supplied and fits onto the splines after the blanking plug has been removed.

Should you wire the switches through a permanently "live" power supply, or one that is only "live" when the ignition is turned on? On the one hand, windows which operate with the ignition off, could be a danger if children are left in the car alone. Conversely, windows which are ignition fed, could be potentially quite dangerous in the event of an emergency, such as a serious accident. It's a decision which will depend on the individual. If it helps, we chose to wire these windows to a permanently live source. Be sure to protect your power supply with a fuse of appropriate size – see instructions supplied – and always use an in-line fuse, sited near the unit, when wiring to a permanently "live" source. As can be seen, the wiring is not difficult.

(Diagram courtesy Gemini Eletronnica Ltd)

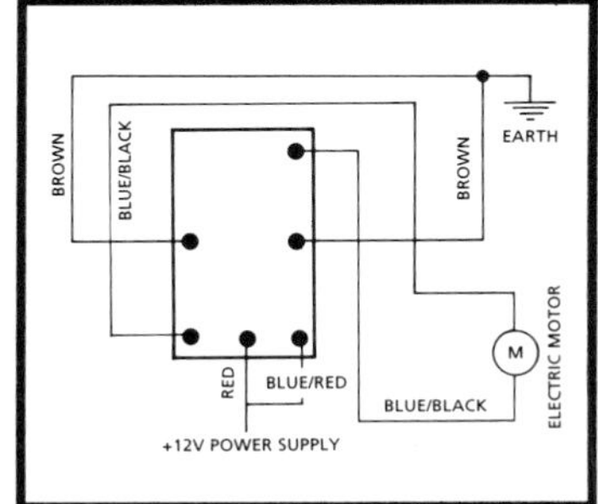

Fitting an interior light delay

Some of the simplest ideas are the best. The micro switch controlling the courtesy light is one of them, but the trouble is that it cuts the light the instant you shut the door. No problem in daylight, but at night, it can be most inconvenient when the light goes out, leaving the driver and passengers fumbling around with seat belts and ignition keys. You can, of course, leave the door open, but what if it is raining, snowing or blowing a gale? The Cosmic interior light delay is easy to fit and prevents "instant darkness". Unlike some similar devices, it cuts the power to the light slowly, so that the change from light to dark is somewhat gentler than usual.

IC15.1
A small black box and two wires ... your task is to connect the box between the door switch and the courtesy light. In this Mk I car the wire to the courtesy light was easy to pull out from its position beneath the dash.

IC15.2
If you have problems unscrew the switch from the door pillar, pull it out and the wire is there. Pull off the spade connector and pull the wire back into the car.

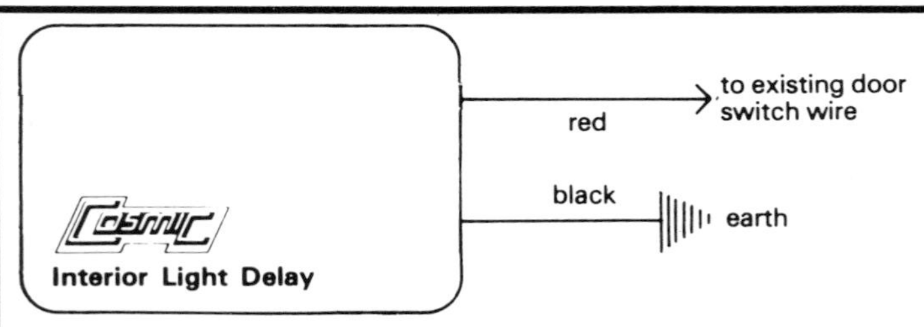

IC15.3
This diagram shows that all you need now is an earth to connect the black wire to (either Scotchlok into a convenient wire or fix the lead under an earthed screw) and then ...

(Diagram courtesy Cosmic Car Accessories Ltd)

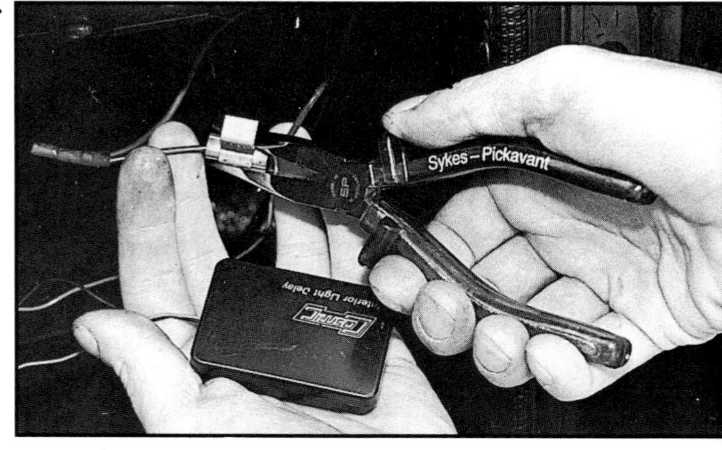

IC15.4
... Scotchlok the red wire into the lead coming from the back of the door switch. The easiest way to do this is to take off the switch altogether by removing the single, crosshead screw as mentioned earlier.

IC15.5
Because it is so light, a double-sided stickie is ample to hold the unit in place against the side of the inner dash.

Fitting an intermittent wiper control

This is a very useful device which is relatively easy to fit. The control can be fitted, as the makers intended, to the front wipers or, with a slight modification, to the rear wash/wipe system. The Hella unit shown here allows intermittent operation between two and twenty sweeps per minute. It can be fitted to any model of Fiesta.

As can be seen in the accompanying diagram, the wiring for this item is quite straightforward and all necessary Scotchloks, are provided in the kit. However, a test lamp is almost essential for establishing which lead is which.

IC16.1
This is a comprehensive package including full instructions, which should be studied carefully before starting to fit. The system is manufactured by Hella for the front wiper system and so a small relay, shown here, is also required to allow its fitment to the rear wiper.

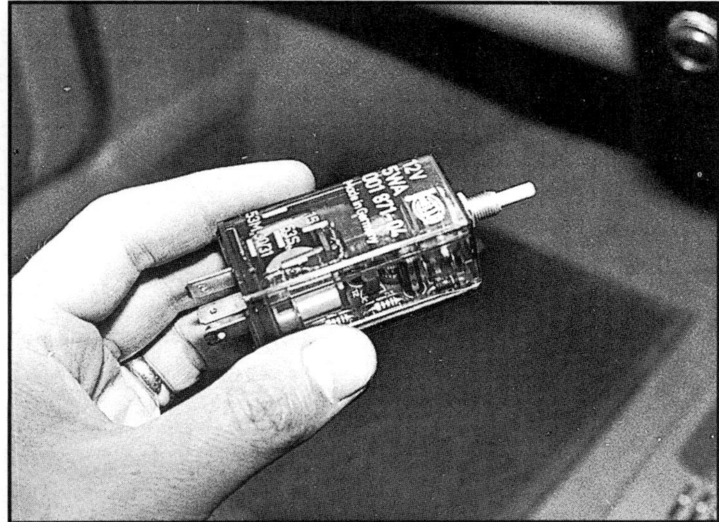

IC16.2
The heart of the system is this "see-through" control box, on the end of which is mounted the infinitely variable control knob.

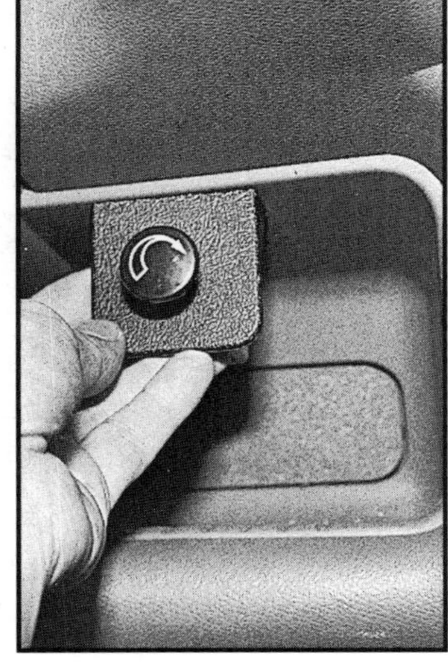

IC16.3
A mounting panel is provided with the kit and so all you have to do is find somewhere convenient to mount it. Naturally, it has to be within easy reach of the driver and in the right-hand cubby hole is ideal. The panel can be screwed into position here (it's a bit too heavy to be stuck in place), where it still allows space to be used for odds and ends.

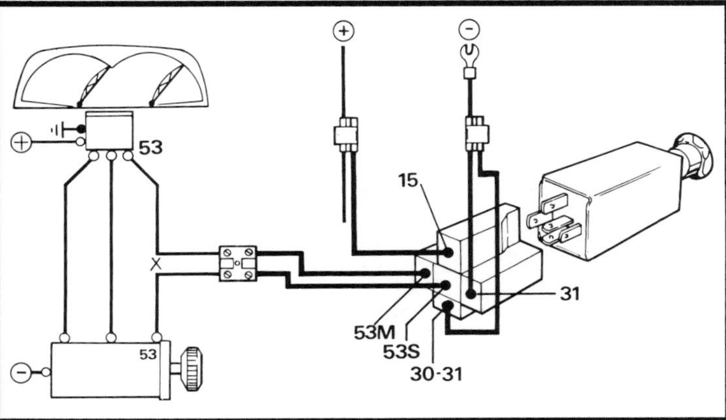

IC16.4
As usual with Hella equipment, the diagrams are clear, concise and, above all, schematic, for those non-electricians among us!

Fitting an alarm system

We would always recommend the use of an alarm system which has a battery back-up, as with the Zemco unit featured here. This means that should the main power leads be cut, the alarm will still function. The back-up in this case being by means of twin alkaline PP3s.

If you have fitted even a few of the items featured in this book, then you will have a very desirable Ford indeed. The problem is that there are those with less than honest intentions who may also admire your handiwork and taste! Statistics for car theft (and theft from cars) show steady increases in the numbers of such incidents, so it makes sense to try and protect your pride and joy.

In this section, we show the fitting of a Zemco "Smart" alarm system to a Fiesta XR2. However, it would fit just as easily to any other Fiesta. The "Smart" refers to the fact that the alarm is passive, arming itself without any action from the driver.

Their consultation with the police and insurance companies led Zemco to the conclusion that this was the only real way to guarantee protection; after all, even the best alarm in the world is useless if it isn't set!

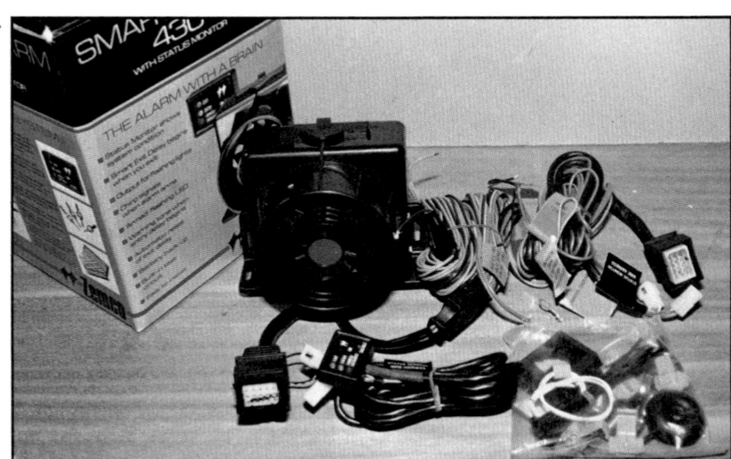

IC17.1 The kit comes complete with all the necessary fixings and clear instructions. The standard 430 model here does not have remote switching ...

IC17.2
... so we fitted the 432 remote control system at the same time. Although not a necessity, because of the way the "Smart" alarms work, it adds a further flexibility. The keys are radio, rather than infra red, which makes them less directional, and gives a longer range.

IC17.3
Wherever you mount your alarm, it is easiest to insert the PP3 batteries in the lower compartment before you tighten everything up.

IC17.4
Similarly, the adjustments to the shock sensor and entry delay can be made with the main unit out of the car. Again, if you mount it where it is accessible, you could do this after installation. The shock sensor needs to be sensitive enough to detect sudden, large impacts but not so much that it triggers when next door's cat walks by! The entry delay can be set between 0–25 seconds. With no remote control switching, you should leave between 5–10 seconds to allow you to get the key into the ignition. When using the remote switching, it could be set at zero, meaning that it would trigger the instant a door, bonnet or hatch were opened.

IC17.5

Space is at a premium under any Fiesta bonnet, but the XR2 has less than most. The siren has to be mounted securely where it will not be subjected to extremes of heat or damp. Here on the nearside bulkhead is ideal, not least because there are a couple of holes ready-made in the right position!

There is a wide range of Zemco products to choose from including: radio remote control "keys", an ultrasonic sensor, central door locking interface, motion detector, shock sensor and various bonnet and boot switches. This "pick-n-mix" makes the systems particularly versatile both from the point of view of personal taste and cashflow!

IC17.6

The wiring is detailed in the instructions and each wire on the wiring loom supplied is clearly marked as to its destination.

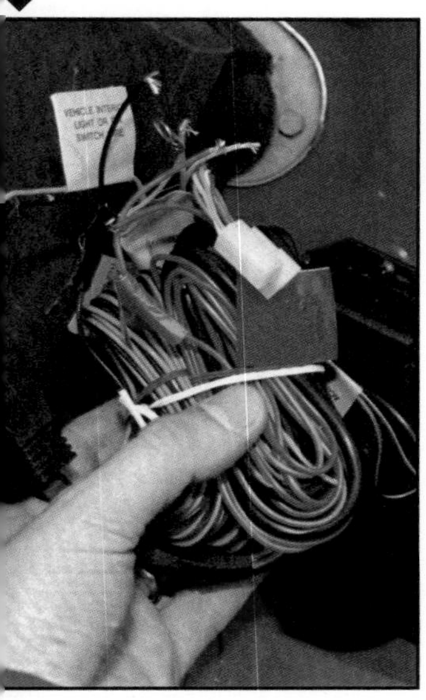

IC17.7

The remote control plug-in module has to be mounted inside the car, in this case under the passenger side dash which is warm and easy to wire through the bulkhead. It is also awkward for a thief to reach in a hurry.

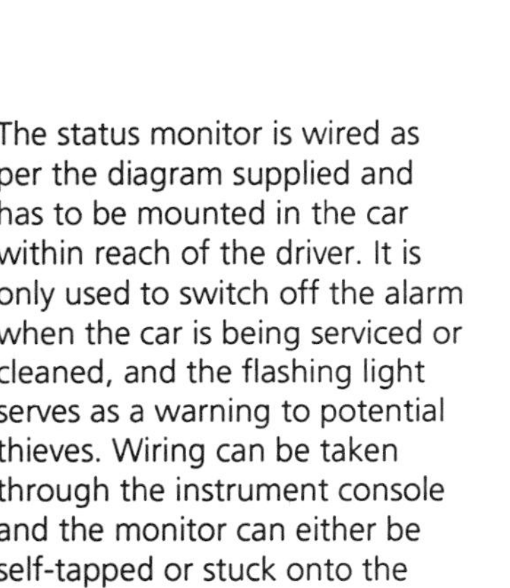

The status monitor is wired as per the diagram supplied and has to be mounted in the car within reach of the driver. It is only used to switch off the alarm when the car is being serviced or cleaned, and the flashing light serves as a warning to potential thieves. Wiring can be taken through the instrument console and the monitor can either be self-tapped or stuck onto the switch blanking plate.

IC17.8

IC17.9

Once connected, the alarm will set itself within 20 seconds every time you remove the ignition key and close all the doors. Should you open any door within the 20 seconds, it will wait until it is shut again, then reset itself within another 20 second interval. Note the sticker in the rear window warning potential thieves not to waste their time on this Zemco protected XR2.

Fitting door floodlights

There are two problems with car interior lights; one is that they go off as soon as you shut the door, and this can be solved by fitting a light delay unit as described earlier in this Chapter. The other problem is that they only illuminate the interior of the car; you pull up in a car park, switch off the engine, open the door and ... Splash! You step into the largest puddle this side of Lake Windermere! Fitting a small Cosmic door floodlight will save your shoes, clothing and credibility!

IC18.1 The Cosmic lights are packaged in pairs, one to be fitted on each side of the car.

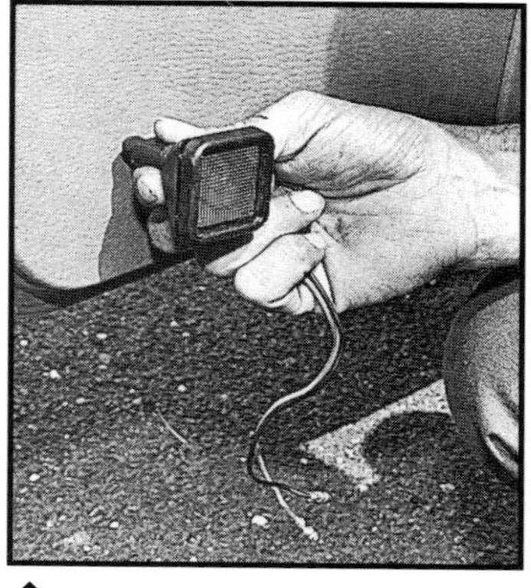

IC18.2 The lights are intended for use here, in the lower rear of the doors, where their light will be of most use. There is no reason why you shouldn't fit one in every door, whether you have two, four or ...

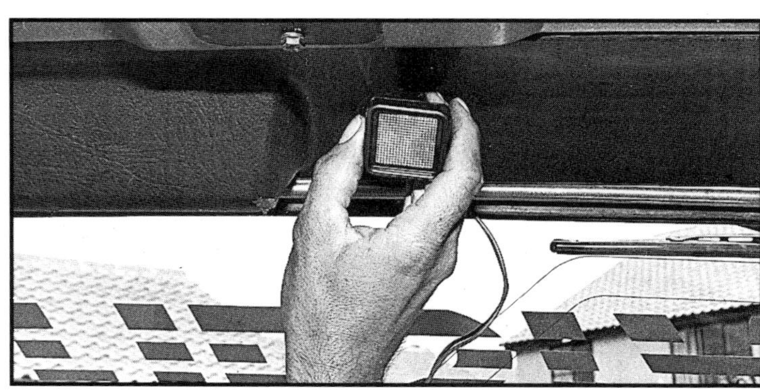

IC18.3 ... five, for that matter. In the tailgate would be a good place to fit one, providing excellent lighting for unloading in the dark.

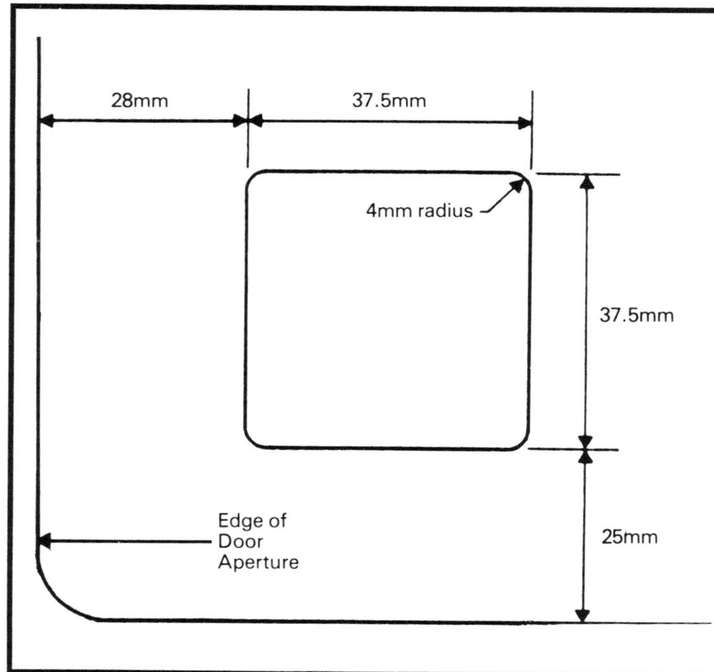

IC18.4 The diagram supplied shows clearly the dimensions of the floodlights and the amount of clearance needed all round. Obviously, you should take great care when cutting and drilling your interior panels to avoid damaging other trim underneath, or worse, electrical wiring. The wiring couldn't be simpler. Take one wire to a fused power supply (not governed by the ignition switch) and the other to the lead from the interior lamp to the door switch. Thus connected, the floodlights will come on with the interior light. Instructions are also included to facilitate wiring if you have a light delay unit fitted.

(Diagram courtesy Cosmic Car Accessories Ltd)

The Zemco Cruise Control Kit featured here has two main advantages: it allows a constant cruising speed to be maintained easily and in so doing, allows a higher mpg figure to be returned. Zemco claim that figures of 10 to 15 per cent improvement are quite easy to obtain! Fitting is not overly difficult, although some time and patience is required to carry out this task and for safety's sake it must be fitted correctly. Seek professional assistance if you are not fully competent to carry out the work. However, the Zemco kit is unique in our experience in that a video is enclosed with the AP120 model, showing in detail exactly how it should be fitted. An excellent feature which more manufacturers would do well to copy. We were fortunate to have the services of two of Zemco's own engineers for this section of the book.

IC19.1
The Zemco kit contains all you need to fit, except tools and enough time. Our experts took around an hour but you should allow at least a leisurely Saturday morning to ensure it is fitted correctly.

IC19.2
The wiring to the throttle actuator is made easier by the use of a labelled wiring loom and a multi-plug which plugs into the back as shown. If you are mounting in a confined space, it is best to plug this in beforehand.

IC19.3 
Similarly, there are several adjustments to make with a small screwdriver on the back of the unit (number of cylinders, for example), which may be easier to carry out before mounting.

IC19.4
The throttle actuator has to be mounted in the engine bay. The XR2 doesn't have much space under the bonnet but here on the nearside bulkhead was just right, particularly as it gives the cables a neat and smooth run to the carburettor.

IC19.5 
The actuator has to be linked into the car's servo system by using this T-piece, meaning that ...

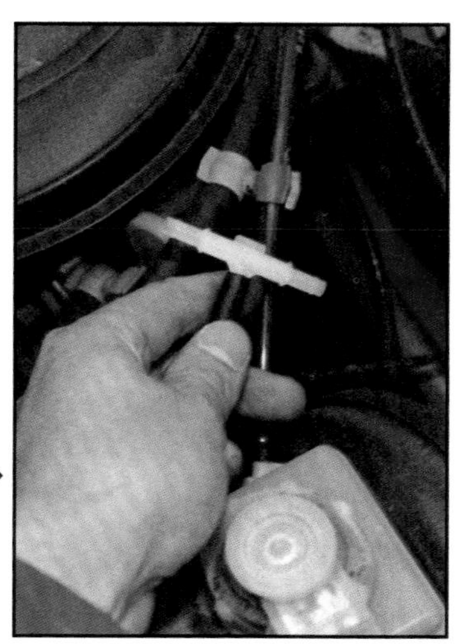

The heart of the Zemco Cruise Control is, not surprisingly, a microprocessor. It memorises the chosen speed and then actuates the throttle regulator to maintain it. Programming the speed is simply a question of pressing the "set" button; the magic "chip" does the rest. For safety reasons, the cruise control will not operate below 25mph. It can be switched off at will by the driver and is automatically disconnected by touching the brake pedal or by changing gear on a manual car. Having been disconnected, the "resume" button can be pressed and the car will smoothly accelerate to the speed set previously and maintain as before. Although the standard unit works with a vacuum operated throttle actuator, there are now models available for diesel Fiestas with electric actuators.

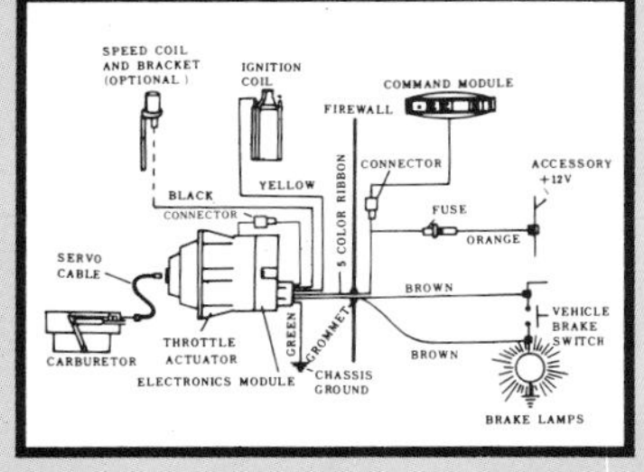

Zemco include a simple, schematic diagram which makes the situation much clearer.

(Diagram courtesy Zemco Ltd)

When fitting this cruise control unit, it is essential to check that the brake lamp switch is in good condition and is adjusted so that the lights come on at the start of the pedal movement. Also, the connectors need to be totally secure, as a touch on the brake pedal is the primary method of turning off the system when in use.

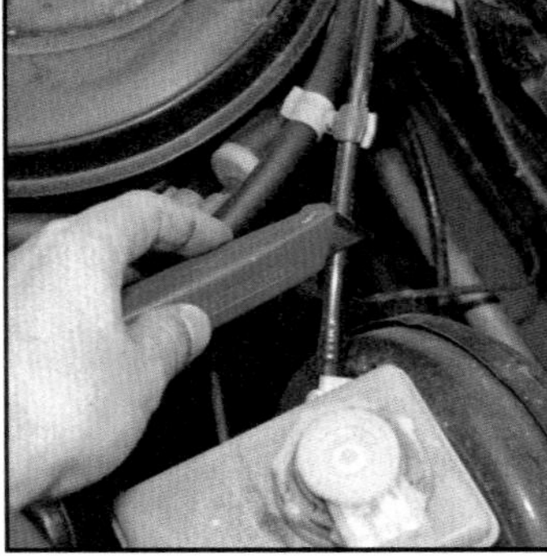

IC19.6
... the vacuum hose has to be cut. Make sure that the cut is straight and that the new connections you make are absolutely airtight.

IC19.7
Here the connection is being made to the coil which is fo ignition speed and electroni clutch switch sensing. Both functions are vital to the safety of the cruise control and so you must be careful to connect to the correct side of the coil, as per the instructions.

DRIVING

The Zemco AP120 is an excellent accessory for those who have to make long, tedious journeys. The electronic "brain" of the system checks the speed several times per second and adjusts the throttle accordingly. This not only makes the car more economical, but also it could save your driving licence; but only if you set it at a legal limit!
As most of us know, when driving on a motorway, there is a tendency to increase speed without realising, no matter how much we try not to. The Zemco AP120 has no such tendencies and keeps the vehicle at the same constant speed. Some owners have fears about the throttle sticking open and the car going out of control. Because of the many safety features incorporated by Zemco, there is no danger at all of a *properly fitted* cruise control being anything but totally safe.

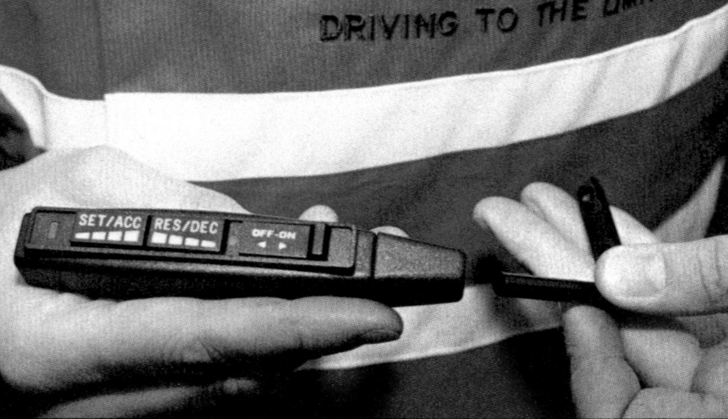

IC19.8
The command module is an attractive looking unit, which wi blend in well with any model of Fiesta. It can be mounted on its own separate stalk, seen here ...

IC19.9
... or on its own, stuck or self-tapped on to the dash. Here, we found that the lower right-hand switch blanking plate was an ideal place, with the wires running directly down into the console. When fitting and wiring is completed, it is important that you run through the full checking procedure advised by Zemco; preferably on a quiet, straight road!

Fitting a screenwash level indicator

It is a legal requirement that your Fiesta should have working windscreen washers. Clearly this means that the windscreen washer bottle has to have some water in it! It is all too easy to run out, especially in particularly foul weather and although we have all done it, it doesn't make it any more legal and it can make the car positively unsafe in certain situations, such as driving at night. A regular underbonnet check is one answer but a simple (and less messy!) answer is to fit the Cosmic Screenwash Alarm, shown here. Because the warning light is an LED, there can never be a bulb failure and the system is designed to reset every time the bottle runs dry and is refilled.

IC20.1➡
As usual, the workings of the system are contained in this little black box from which sprout four wires. Two of them are for power and earth.

IC20.2➡
The other two are attached to small strong pins which have to be inserted into the lower part of the screenwash bottle. To do this, a couple of 3/16th inch diameter holes have to be drilled, one at half an inch from the bottom and the other, two inches from the bottom. The best method is to remove the bottle altogether and drill when dry. The green wire goes to the top hole and the white one to the lower. A dab of strong glue should be placed around both holes in order to maintain a good seal.

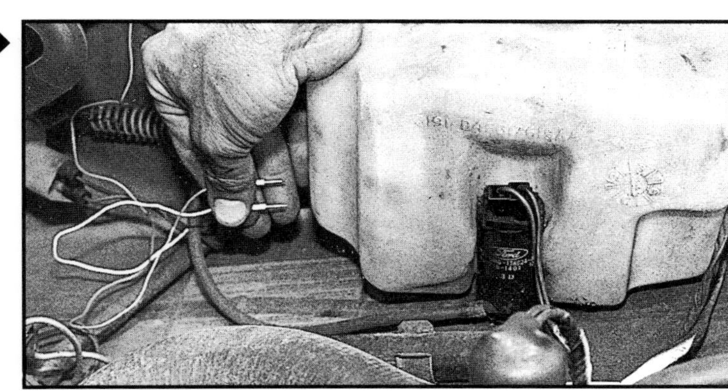

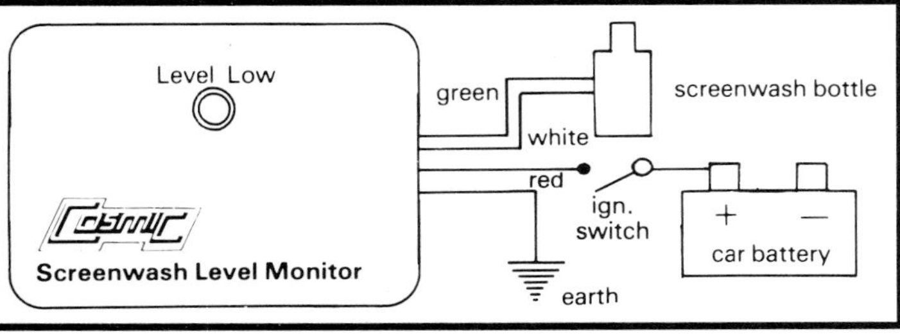

⬅IC20.3
The diagram shows how the wiring should be carried out. Note that the power is taken from an ignition fed source.

IC20.4➡
The wires have to be fed through the bulkhead and the monitor mounted within sight of the driver. On this 1.1 Fiesta, the lower RH switch position blanking plug on the console was prised out, the wires routed through and the monitor mounted using a double-sided stickie. No hole to drill and so no untidy dashboard, and ideally placed for the red warning light to catch the driver's eye when the screenwash fluid level is low.

Fitting a high level brake light

With the ever increasing number of cars on the road and the "nose-to-tail" driving which seems prevalent on Britain's motorways nowadays, the fitting of a high level brake lamp has to be a definite safety aid. When braking, the light can be seen several cars back thus reducing the possibility of a serious accident in yet another multi-car pile up.

IC21.1
The Hella kit comes complete with all nuts, bolts, brackets, bulb and wiring, to do the job. Nice and simple diagrams help, too! It can be suspended on the rear screen or alternatively, mounted on the rear parcel shelf. We chose the latter route for the Fiesta.

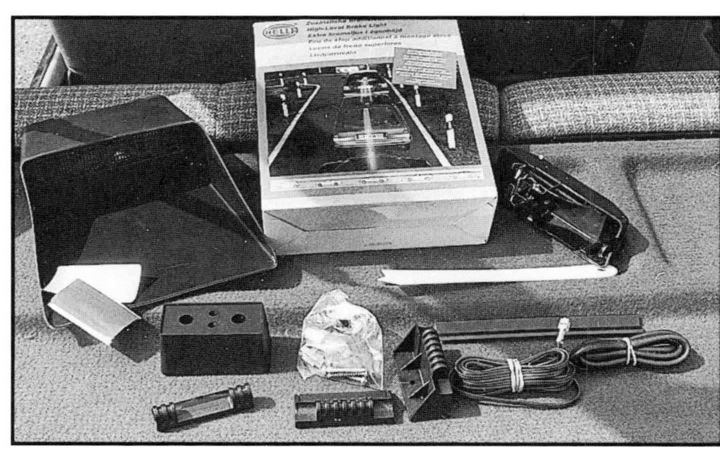

IC21.2
The first task is to cut the lamp housing to match the angle of the rear window. A bevel square is provided in the kit and so this is used to ascertain the angle of the window and transfer it to the housing.

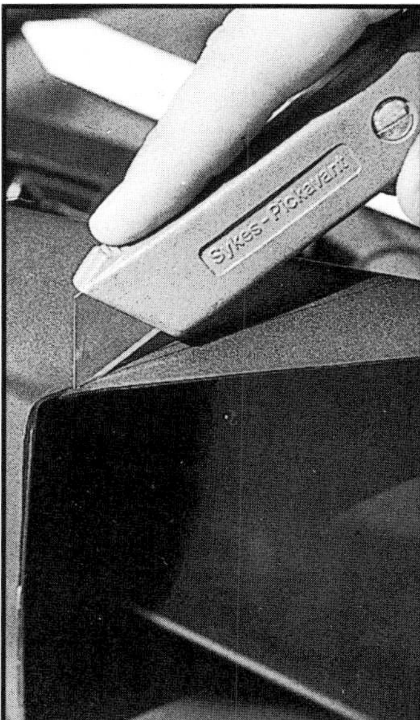

IC21.3
The plastic housing has to be cut to suit. Be careful here, as the craft knife (sharp as it is) requires quite a lot of pressure and could easily slip.

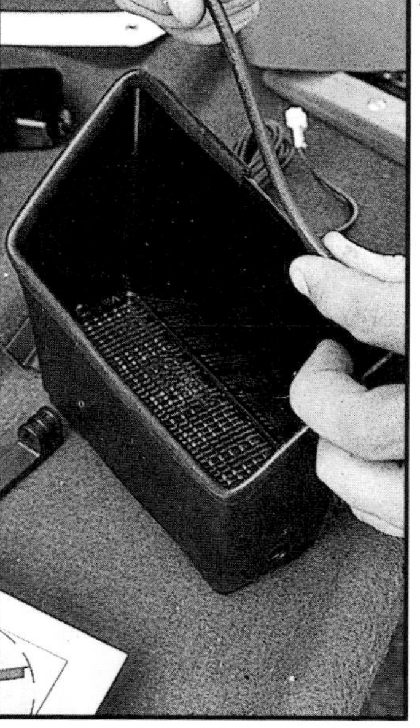

IC21.4
Once the housing has been cut to size all the way round, the edge can be covered with the protective rubber strip provided.

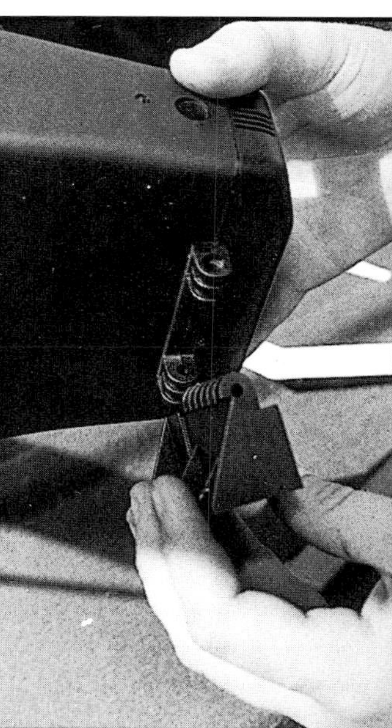

IC21.5
We had decided to mount the lamp actually on the parcel shelf and so the housing had to be fixed to a special mounting.

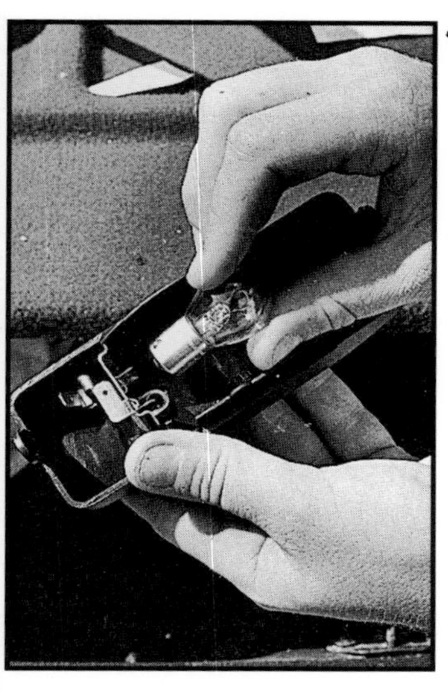

IC21.6
The bulb holder clips into place on the back of the housing so the bulb and wiring has to be connected before the holder.

IC21.7
A couple of small holes have to be drilled in the shelf. The simplest way is to use the bracket as a template. You'll also need a small hole for the wire.

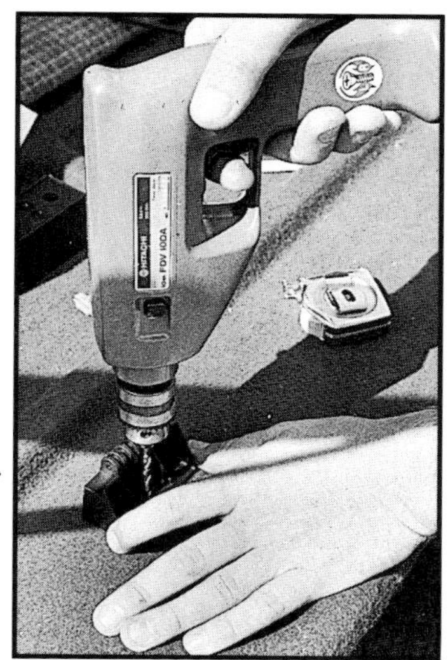

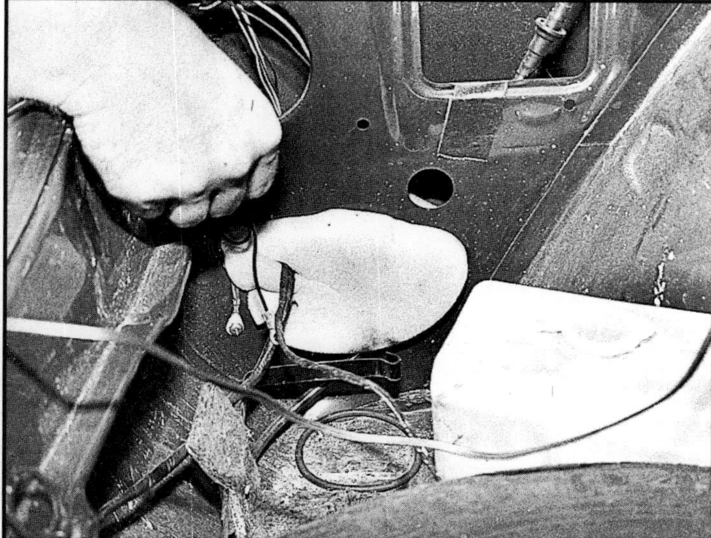

IC21.8
One of the wires goes to earth. On this car, an earth wire was already taken on a self-tapping screw on the lower part of the spare wheel well. By fitting a connector from the Hella kit, we were able to add our wire as well.

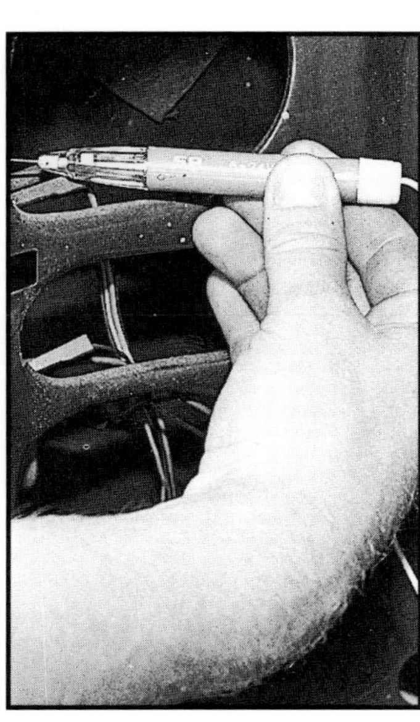

IC21.9
The live feed is, naturally enough, taken to the brake lamp wire on the back of the lamp cluster. Test which is which by using the Speedline 6–24 volt tester with someone pressing the brake pedal. When the right lead is located, just Scotchlok into the wire with the remaining lead from the high level lamp. Make sure that you route the wiring carefully so that raising the shelf does not damage anything. If you wish, you can put a join in the cable itself at shelf height by using bullet connectors. This allows the shelf to be removed altogether if required.

IC21.10
Mounted above the two standard lights, it is unobtrusive from the point of view of rearward vision and very visible, not just to the car behind, but to ***several*** cars following.

It is important to take note of any local regulations regarding the fitment of high level rear brake lamps. In the UK, the *minimum* height of the lamps from the road should be 400mm. The *maximum* height should be 1500mm.

As can be seen from this diagram, the wiring should pose few problems, with only two connections (brake lamp live and earth), to be made.

(Diagram courtesy Hella Ltd)

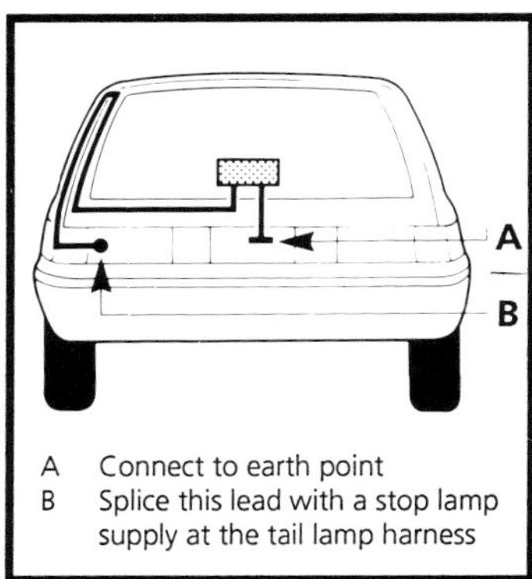

A Connect to earth point
B Splice this lead with a stop lamp supply at the tail lamp harness

Fitting a map reading lamp

If you can't see the need for a map lamp, then you've never been lost in the dark! Even with the interior light on, it can be very difficult for a passenger to read a map or instructions and it is always invariably distracting for the driver. Hella have used their considerable experience in the field of rallying to produce the excellent quality lights shown here which are suitable for all Fiesta models.

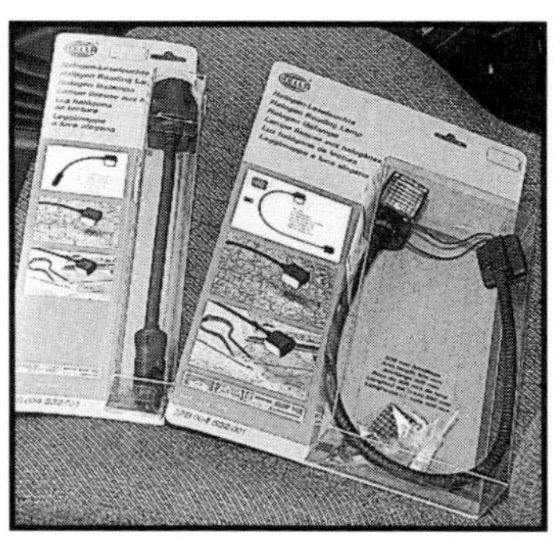

IC22.1
Hella have two different map reading lamps available.

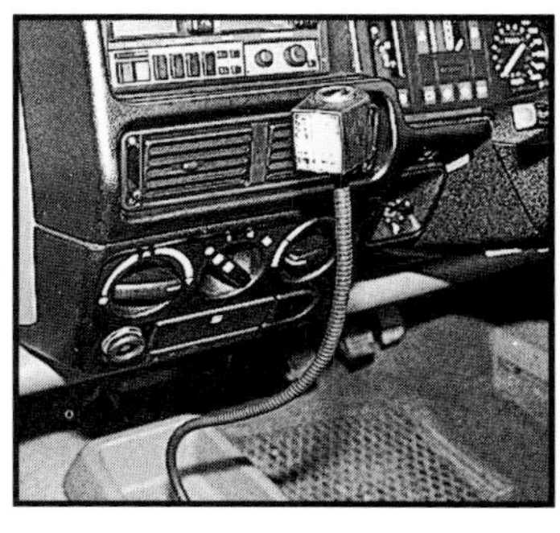

IC22.2
The first is this one, made to be wired permanently into the car's electrical system and mounted conveniently for both passenger and driver. Here, on the transmission tunnel, would seem to be a good position. By giving up a couple of coin holders, you can thread the two wires (earth and live), through them instead of drilling extra holes. The flexible, 500mm neck is metal and will stay in whatever position is required and a spare red lens is supplied.

IC22.3
Alternatively, this smaller version simply plugs into the cigar lighter socket. Although the neck is not as long as with the previous lamp, it has all the benefits including a 12V/5W bulb, highly polished reflector head and a lens which gives a glare-free beam. Both lamps are made from glass fibre reinforced plastic and have the on/off switch mounted conveniently in the top of the lamp unit.

Fitting a "lights-on" warning buzzer

This diagram shows how simple the "lights-on" buzzer is to fit. It requires only two Scotchloks to complete.

(Diagram courtesy Hella Ltd)

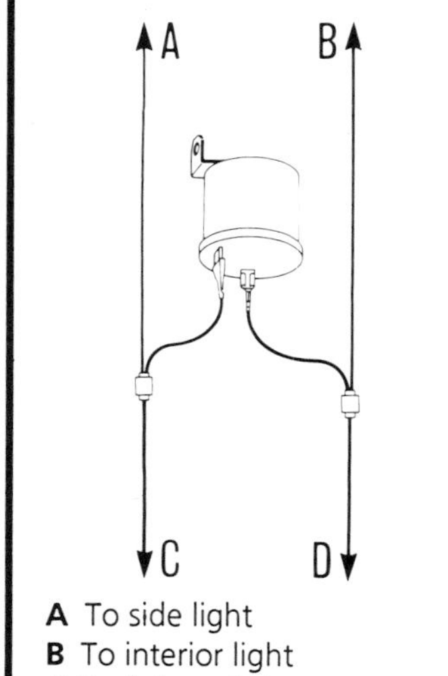

A To side light
B To interior light
C To light switch
D To door contact switch

Driving with lights on in daylight when visibility is poor is now a legal requirement, and that is certainly no bad thing. The problem for many comes at the end of the journey when the driver gets out and forgets about the lights. Usually, the memory is only jogged at the end of the working day, when a turn of the ignition key brings no response from the engine! With the addition of the Hella "lights-on" warning buzzer, it is unlikely that you will ever leave the lights on again; it is loud! The buzzer is suitable for all models of Fiesta.

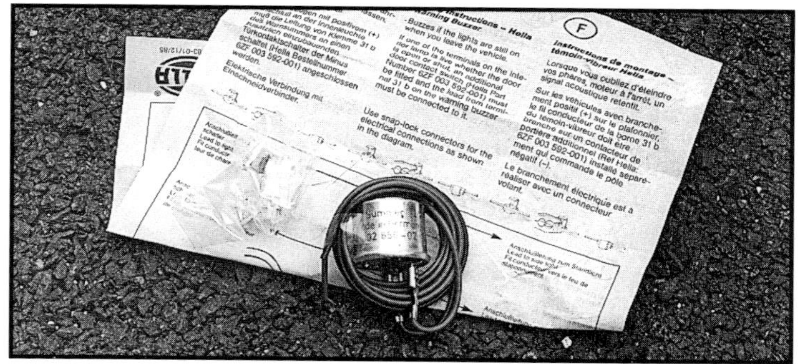

IC23.1
This is what you get. The buzzer is connected into the side light and courtesy light circuits. As the diagram shows, the Hella buzzer simply needs Scotchloking into the electrical system.

IC23.2
Access to the electrics can be gained by pulling down the under-dash felt on this late model XR2. The buzzer has an integral bracket and is designed to fit under a convenient trim screw. Alternatively, you could use double-sided tape or Velcro to hold the unit firmly in position.

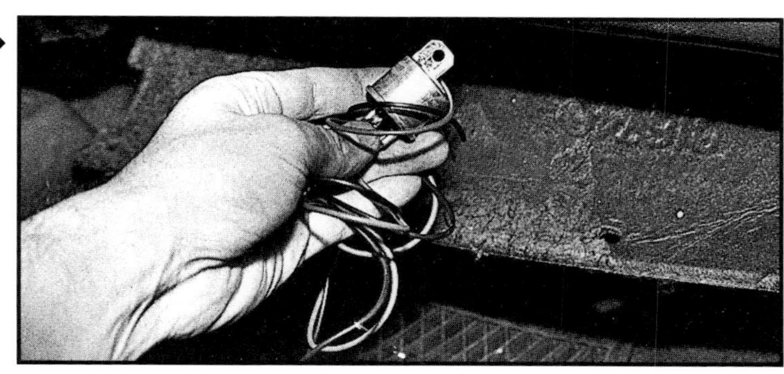

Fitting a central locking system

Central locking is becoming more and more popular on Fiestas, although it wasn't that long ago that it was only the most luxurious of Granadas that were so fitted. We show here how to fit the Gemini central locking kit to a two-door Fiesta but it is also available as a four-door version. The kit includes electric drive solenoids, relay switching unit, cable looms, all connectors, plugs and sockets and linking rods to attach to existing door lock mechanisms. When installed, the system can be operated from *either* the driver or passenger door. This is an important point when considering your choice of systems, as not all have this feature. If you're wondering how you include your boot or hatch, the answer is that a single unit has to be purchased separately.

The fitting of a central locking system may sound a little daunting, but this Gemini kit should pose few problems for the keen DIY Fiesta owner. The wiring isn't as complex as it may seem at first acquaintance!

IC24.1➡
The kit as it comes. This is the two-door version, differing only in quantity to the four-door kit, the latter, of course, only being of use on Mk III cars. The bane of many a DIY Fiesta owner is the wiring, so the ready-made wiring loom will be most welcome.

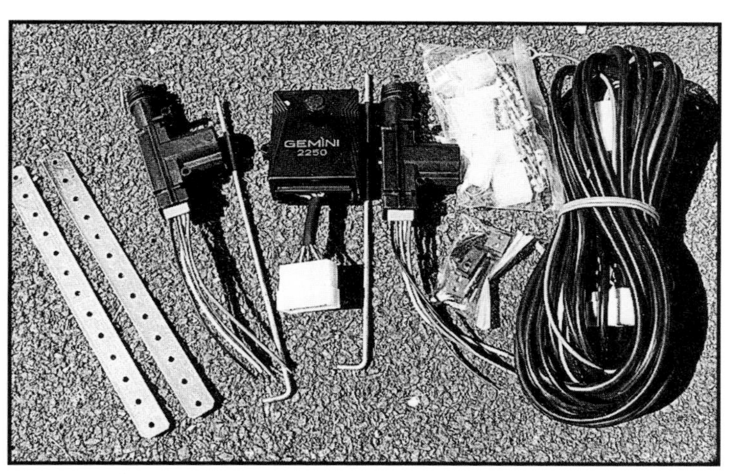

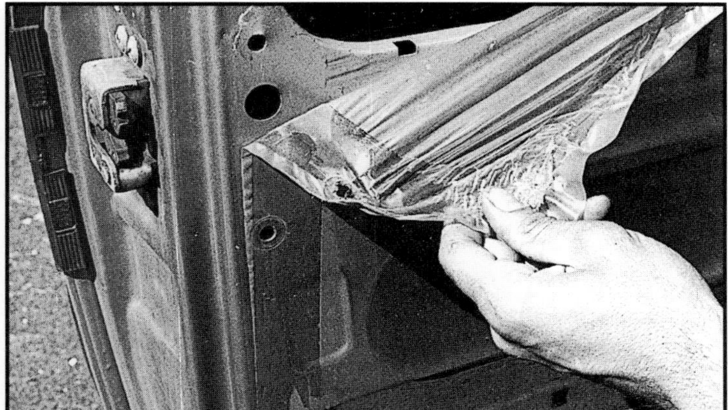

⬅IC24.2
You have to gain access to the inner door frame, which means removing the outer trim. This varies slightly with the model and age of the car but if you have any doubts as to what fits where, consult your Haynes manual before you set about it with a screwdriver! With the trim removed, the plastic lining sheet should be pulled back. If you are careful enough you will be able to stick it back in position without damaging it.

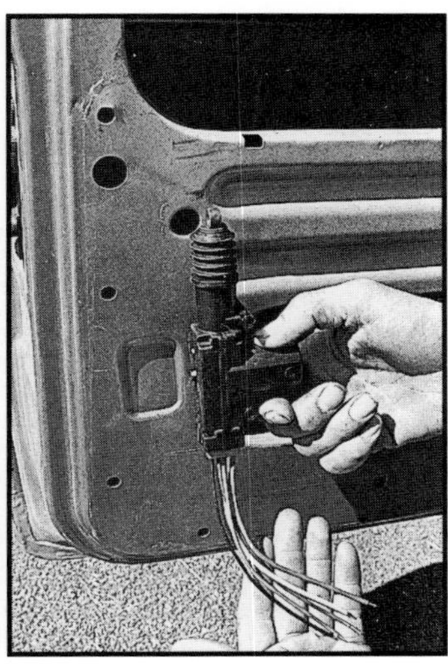

⬅IC24.3
Each door has to be fitted with an electronic solenoid. It has to be mounted inside the door pressing at approximately the position shown here. If you have problems fitting it, Gemini supply some mounting straps with the kit.

IC24.4➡
The solenoid is linked into the car's locking system by means of this rod which can be bent and cut to suit. Check carefully that the operation of the door lock also operates the solenoid.

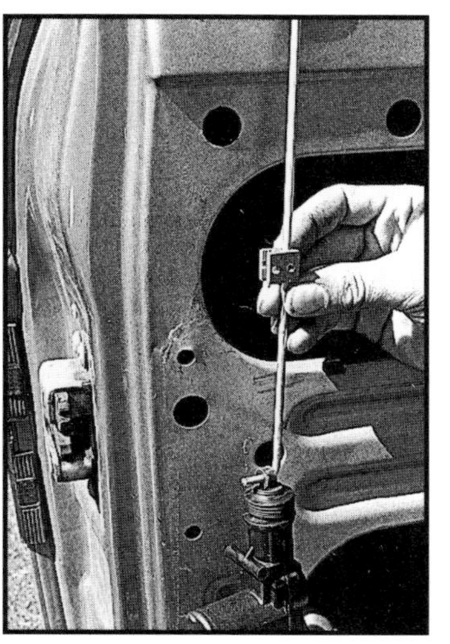

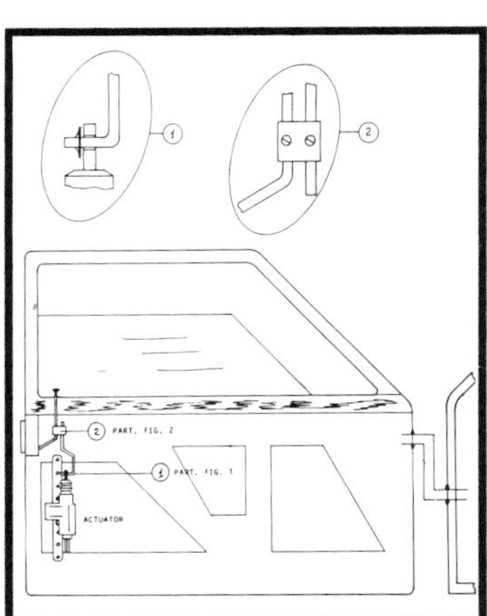

This diagram shows how the door locking solenoid has to be mounted in the door and connected into the locking mechanism.

Fitting a central locking system

Central locking offers many benefits. Apart from ease of operation (having to physically take a tour of the car and lock each door in turn can be somewhat wearing, it gives any car an immediate air of luxury. In addition it offers security benefits, in that once the driver's (or passenger's) door is locked, all the others follow suit. The Gemini kit is electric, rather than pneumatic, as on some systems, and thus locking is as near instantaneous as can be. Once fitted, the Gemini central locking kit can be linked up with an alarm system, via a clever electronic interface, so that, with the single press of a button, your car is locked *and* alarmed.

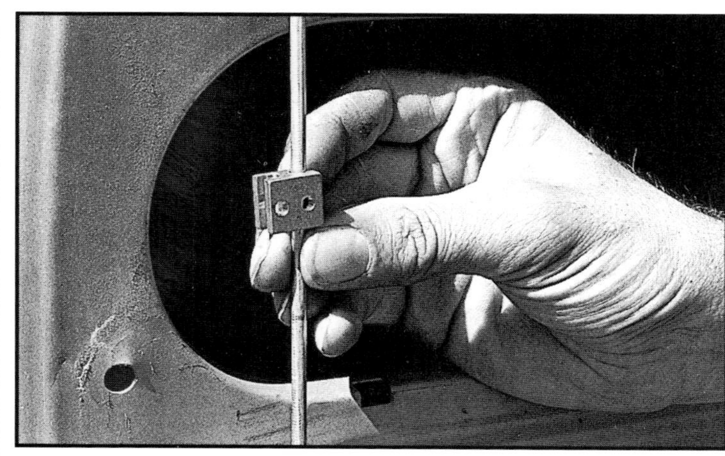

IC24.5
The operating rod is joined to the Fiesta's locking rods by this simple, but very effective brass connector. When you are absolutely sure that you have measured and marked the position correctly ...

IC24.6
... the two mounting holes for the solenoid can be drilled. Don't forget to rustproof the holes before you finish off.

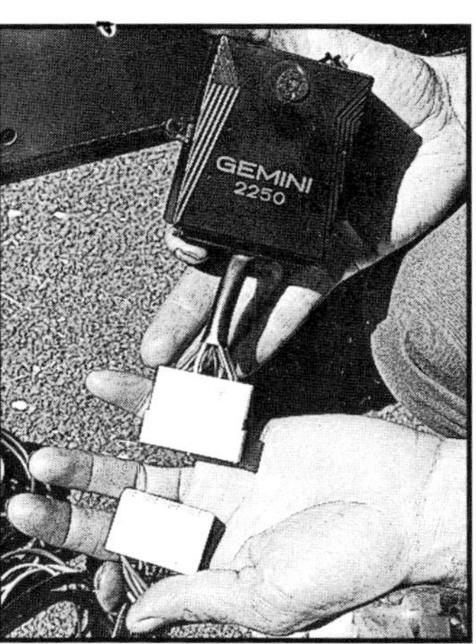

IC24.7
The wires from the solenoid and those from the main loom have no connectors fitted. However, they are all included in the kit and, better still, are designed to become part of two purpose built plugs and sockets. The small black box is the brain of the whole operation. It should be mounted equi-distant between the two doors, preferably under the dash as it is relatively cool and dry. Take care when moving the wiring loom from the car to the door. Don't trap wires or route them so that they are taut.

GEMINI 2249
FRONT DOORS
+15/54 POSITIVE UNDERKEY
SOLENOID +30
15 AMP FUSE
EARTH
GREEN
PINK
YELLOW
BLACK
BROWN
VIOLET
BLEU
RED

IC24.8
The wiring diagram looks much worse than it is, as the wiring comes in a ready-made loom, requiring only correct routing and a few crimped connections to complete. You must be very careful, when making up the plugs and sockets, that the wire colour codes correspond; red to red and so on.

(Diagram courtesy Gemini Elettronicca)

Fitting side indicator repeater lamps

Later model Fiestas are already equipped with indicator side repeater lamps and a very good idea they are too. They Scotchlok easily into the car's indicator system and give visible warning to vehicles approaching from the side. Not surprisingly, perhaps, they are yet another idea inherited from our American cousins. However, you should be very wary of using them as American style "running" lights, the legality of which is in some doubt.

IC25.1
The Cosmic lamps are packaged individually although you'll need at least two to be of any use. Bulb, holder and basic wiring to the lamp is included, but you'll have to provide the necessary wire and Scotchloks to connect them into the indicator circuit.

IC25.2
The standard mounting position is on the front wing, meaning that the rear of the lamps would be exposed to the elements up through the inside of the wing. Not here, for they are protected by this tough rubber shield which fits snugly into place preventing water and dirt from entering the lamp.

IC25.3
Measure and mark the position of the lamp very carefully before you drill your hole. Obviously, it is particularly important that the lamp on the nearside matches the position of the one on the offside. If required, they can also be mounted at the rear.

Fitting an electronic compass

The Zemco DE710A electronic compass absolutely bristles with advanced technology, despite its user simplicity. If you're sitting comfortably ... it computes the vehicle heading by measuring the earth's magnetic field with a two-channel flux gate magnetometer. The field is measured in two directions, one direction parallel to the vehicle and one perpendicular. Using basic trigonometry, the relative angle of the earth's magnetic field can be calculated and displayed. Simple, isn't it!

Finding your way from A to B isn't as easy as it used to be. Ring roads, one-way systems and infrequent road signs all conspire to make sure that your journey is as fraught as possible. The Zemco compass shown here will ensure that you always know in which direction you are heading. Using aircraft technology (see accompanying note), and an aircraft style LCD display, it is immune to the effects of stray magnetic fields.

IC26.1
The attractive display unit comes with the simple wiring (just one lead) and two brackets which facilitate mounting in a variety of different positions.

IC26.2
In this case, we decided to wire the unit in permanently, not least because the position of the cigar lighter (on the left-hand side of the console), would have meant a dangling wire. By unscrewing the plate on the centre console, we fed the wire in and Scotchloked it to the required leads.

IC26.3
At the display end, the wire simply plugs into the back.

IC26.4
Mounted thus, on the top of the console, we found the compass to be reasonably sited for viewing by both driver and passenger. The display is back-lit in attractive and relaxing orange-red, again another aircraft based idea. Unlike many such items, the task of calibration is a matter of a few minutes and pressing a button on the back of the display. Once the compass has calculated where it is, neither it, nor you, have any excuse for being lost.

Fitting extra instruments and switches

IC27.1
For many owners, the thought of cutting the dashboard of their pride and joy is totally alien. Fear not, for Sedan produce a wide range of instrument mounting pods which can be mounted on or under the dash, without the need for extensive surgery. As can be seen here, you can mount either one, two, three or four gauges in whatever way you choose.

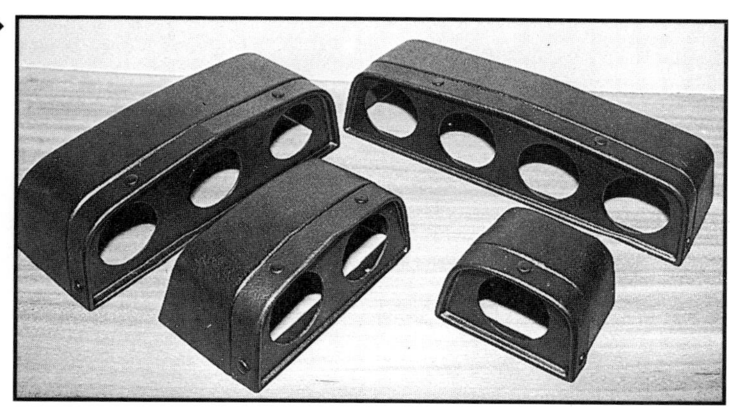

IC27.2
In the case of the three-instrument mounting pod, push-in pegs locate the front of the mounting pod to the rear of the case. The two are easily separated ...

IC27.3
.. allowing the instruments to be pushed home into the front panel. This can then be refitted to the pod which hides the wiring and pipework coming from the instruments quite neatly. This is shown out of situ for clarity.

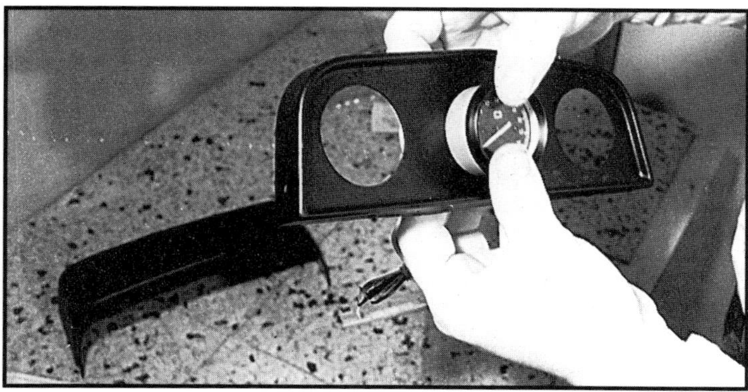

IC27.4
Sedan also produce a wide range of gauges to suit, including voltmeters, water and oil temperature gauges, tachometers, ammeters, an econometer and an outside temperature gauge. Many are also available in different diameters, to suit individual cars or the tastes of their owners.

Some of the functions offered on the Sedan instruments and gauges seen here are covered by the Fiesta's warning light system. However, they usually only come into play when a major disaster has occurred and, for example, your engine has parted company with all of its oil! Clearly, it would be far better to know that something of that nature was happening well before it reached the point of no return. In addition, they constantly monitor and measure the engine's functions and provide the intelligent Fiesta owner with an accurate picture of exactly what is going on in the engine bay and elsewhere.

Fitting extra instruments and switches

In addition to the Sedan instruments and switches shown here, there is also a wide range of warning lights, illuminated switches and other instruments available. Where electrical connections have to be made, we would suggest using the Sykes-Pickavant crimping tool with Sedan's own range of connectors. See Chapter Five for some wiring hints and tips.

IC27.5
As an alternative to selecting individual gauges, Sedan produce a "three-in-one" series, such as this set of "electric" gauges. They are all carefully matched and even before they are connected up, they will improve the look of any Fiesta.

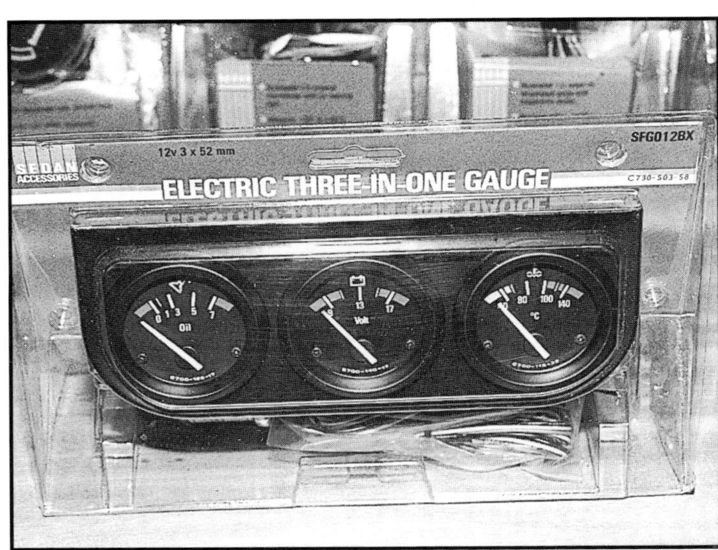

IC27.6
Sedan pride themselves on producing accessories suitable for the DIY enthusiast. The kit of parts which comes with the Sedan econometer, just as with all the other instruments in the range, contains a very clear set of diagrammatical instructions.

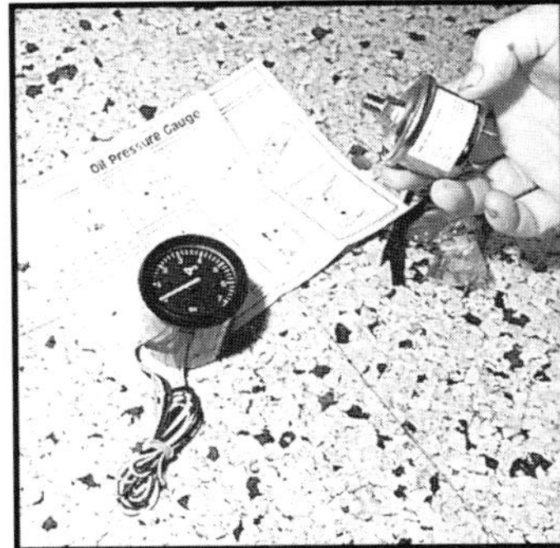

IC27.7
The Sedan oil pressure gauge is a popular addition and with good reason. It is the best indicator of whether an engine is wearing out and can provide advance warning (ahead of a warning light) of an imminent, engine wrecking, oil pressure drop.

IC27.8
As well as instruments and mounting pods and brackets, Sedan also manufacture a wide range of in-car switch-gear, well suited to the DIY Fiesta owner. Once again, the choice is yours; switch brackets which hold between one and four switches, rocker switches (illuminated or not), standard flick switches or extended. Whatever you want, there is something there to suit your purpose and the layout of your dash.

Cleaning interior trim and surfaces

For many owners, cleaning the inside of the car is one of those tasks that always seems to go to the bottom of a priority list. Usually, by the time three weeks mud and dirt have been removed from the outside of the car, there is not the time (or energy) left to do the interior. By doing the job regularly, however, it does not have to take long. Also, it means that you can keep a check on the general condition of the trim and if any new stains have appeared, there may be some chance of removing them before they become too ingrained.

Cleaning the interior of your Fiesta is made much simpler by emptying the car before you start. Just take out any mats or additional carpets, rubbish, loose cassettes, pieces of paper, maps, sweets, scrapers, pens and parking tickets, and you're halfway there!

IC28.1
The dashboard is a place where dirt and dust accumulate slowly and are usually not noticed until disturbed. Here, a paintbrush (dry, of course!) is being used to remove dust in those tricky-to-get-at places, which abound on the Fiesta dash. Another good idea is to use an air brush, as used by photographers for lens cleaning.

IC28.2
Clean dash and interior surfaces with Comma Interior Valet, which removes the various stains and marks that accumulate. Follow this with Comma Cockpit Spray, which gives a deep, anti-static sheen. It is sprayed on as shown here ...

IC28.3
... and spread along the surface by using a cloth. A final polish after five minutes will finish the task. The Comma product also restores that aromatic "new car" smell. Being anti-static, it will be good news to the many who frequently suffer from "shocks" in the car. However, perhaps the best news of all is that Cockpit Spray is CFC-free and that by using this particular aerosol, you will not be making any extra holes in the ozone layer!

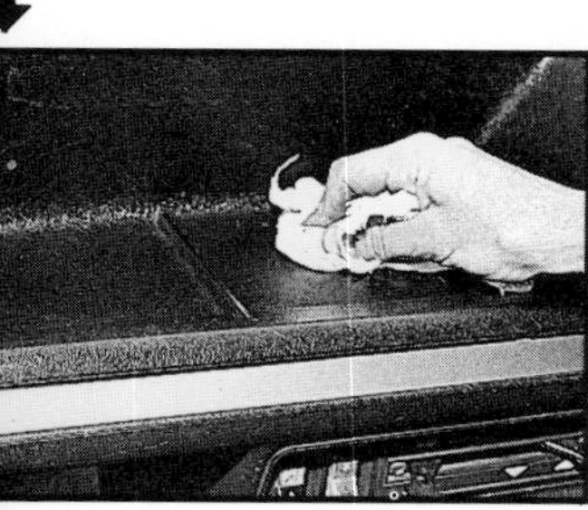

IC28.4
Replacing a full set of carpets in a Fiesta is an expensive business, so it pays to take good care of them. A set of Autostyle Unique tailored mats will help to protect them (see page 80). The easiest way to clean your carpets is to use a vacuum cleaner. The Link-Sedan vacuum seen here is particularly handy.

Cleaning interior trim and surfaces

By using high quality products, such as the Comma range featured here, the appearance of your Escort will remain much as it was when it rolled off the production line. Don't forget also that an "as-new" interior is one of the greatest factors in maintaining the resale value of your car.

IC28.5
It is operated from a 12 volt supply, namely the cigar lighter socket. Simply plug in and clean away!

IC28.6
The long nozzle means that you can get into your car's important little places. You won't believe the amount of dirt and grit that accumulates where the eye can't see. Take this opportunity to clean down the back of the seats and under them too.

IC28.7
When the carpets are really dirty, or if you have bought a car with stained carpets, vacuuming alone will probably not be enough. One of Comma's latest products is Interior Valet, which is also suitable for fabrics, vinyl and leather. You should always test for colour fastness first before spraying the foam onto the surface.

IC28.8
After a minute it can be wipe off with a damp sponge Stubborn marks will need second application and som assistance from a stiff brush. No only does it bring the life back t tired carpets but it also adds lemon scent to your car

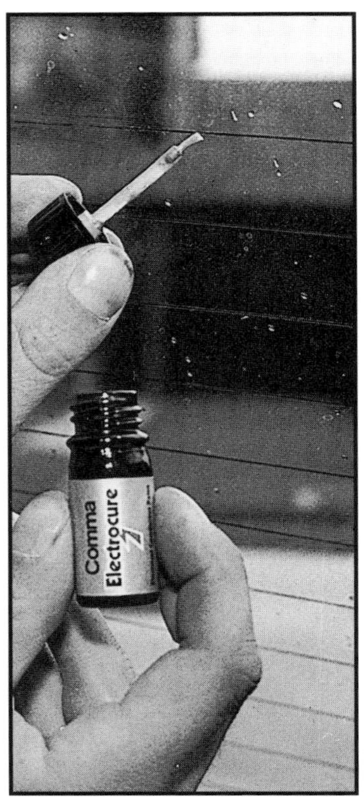

IC28.9
What have dogs, children, luggage and old age got in common? They can all damage the heated rear window element of your car, and replacement of the window isn't cheap! Using Comma Electrocure *is*, however, and what's more it's simple to use. It is a silver-based liquid which is "painted" onto the affected areas, using masking tape to keep a straight line or the stencil supplied in the Electrocure Kit. In some cases, a second coat will be required after twenty minutes.

Chapter Three
In-car Entertainment

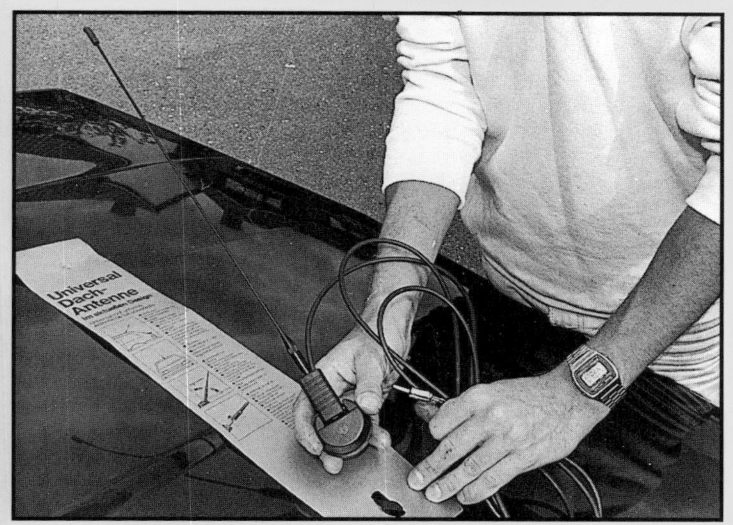

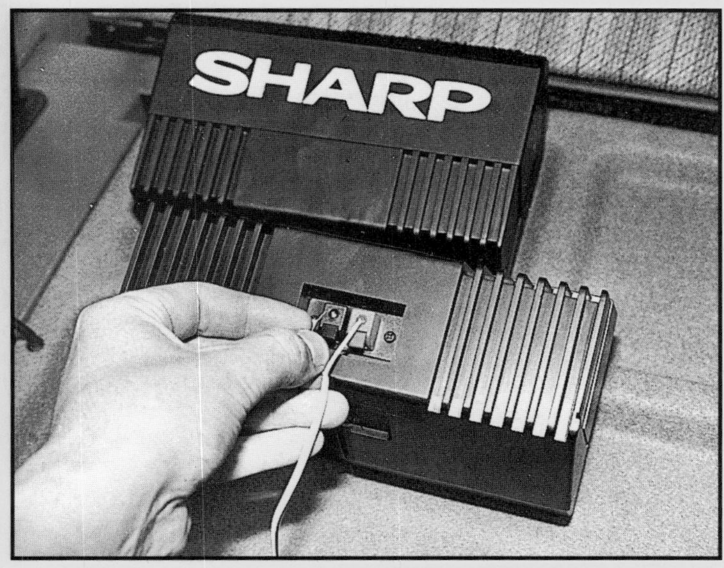

Introduction

In this Chapter many technical terms and abbreviations are used. In order to save repetitious explanations, we have included a glossary in the "Choosing ICE" section. It pays to try and understand some of the jargon attached to the in-car audio market. Although advertisers love to load their copy with impressive-sounding terminology, it doesn't actually help until you know what the jargon means!

Over the past few years, "music on the move" has increased massively in popularity. This is best illustrated by a glance at the 1989 Fiesta brochure, which shows that all models except the Popular come equipped with some form of in-car audio equipment. In this section, we will be looking at some of the options offered by Sharp from their wide range of radio/cassettes.

The standard of fit and finish is always high and it is pleasing to note that this applies uniformly to all of the model range and not just the top priced sets. Their attention to detail and in particular to the ergonomics of the sets matches the high standards set by Ford in the production of the Fiesta.

Because of this, Sharp equipment will not look out of place in any model, whether "cooking" Popular or sporting XR2. Similarly, all sets are DIN sized which means that there will be no wasted hours spent with a hacksaw making a hole big enough to suit!

HISTORY OF SHARP

For a company which has such a high standing in the world market of electronic products in general and in-car entertainment in particular, it is strange to relate that their success began with a mechanical pencil! This relatively simple device, commonplace in most homes and offices today, was the first invention of the Sharp Corporation back in 1915.

It was three years earlier that Tokuji Hayakawa founded the company, known today as the Sharp Corporation, marking the beginning of over 75 years of innovative, technological developments.

The next Sharp milestone occurred in 1924, when the company produced Japan's first radio set; a crystal device, no less. Readers will be pleased to learn that their current in-car range is slightly more sophisticated!

Over the years, Sharp maintained its technological lead over the opposition and in 1953 began mass production of TV sets and microwave ovens.

By 1964, they had introduced the world's first transistor diode desktop calculator, and throughout the '60s the name of Sharp began to be seen more and more across the world, starting with a subsidiary company in the USA, followed by one in Germany in 1968 and in the UK in 1969.

Another turning point came in the change of name. In 1970, it was changed from Hayakawa Electric Industries Co. Ltd. (quite a mouthful in anyone's language!) to simply, the Sharp Corporation, thus linking the brand name with the company name. Since then, their continual research and development has led to ever more complex, yet reliable, electronic items, not just in-car but in the home and in commercial markets too. Their expertise in utilising the mighty micro-chip can be seen (and heard!) in their range of in-car entertainment products.

Advising which equipment to fit to your Fiesta is difficult, almost to the point of being impossible. Everyone has different opinions as to what constitutes a good in-car audio system, from the simple and straightforward to the incredibly sophisticated. There are a number of limiting factors, not least of which is the amount you have available to spend, and good quality sound does not come cheap at any level. There is also usage to consider. If your Fiesta is only driven four miles a day throughout the year, it makes little sense to load it up with the latest high tech stereo system. Another major point is to judge which is best for your personal listening. Most "front end units" produced today are combination radio/cassette players.

So, if you're one of those people who prefer to listen to the radio and seldom use the cassette deck, a set with particularly advanced radio features but less sophisticated cassette facilities will appeal. Conversely, those who prefer cassette listening will be looking for some form of noise reduction (typically Dolby "B" or "C"), metal tape facility, track search and so on. It is worth noting that, by and large, in most combination units the radio is more advanced than the tape deck and thus a high performance cassette player will usually be accompanied by a high quality radio.

As a sign of the times, the 1989 Sharp catalogue includes only combination units. This is a measure of the popularity of in-car entertainment equipment generally, as it is not that many years ago when just a radio fitted in the dash would have been the very height of chic. Whatever your personal choice, it is worth sitting down for a while and deciding exactly what YOU want from a car audio system. Bear in mind that when improving your in-car audio, uprating one item will almost certainly mean that another link in the chain will also have to be uprated. For example, an uprated radio/cassette deck may require uprated speakers to cope with the extra power.

GLOSSARY

With the help of Sharp Electronics (UK) Ltd, we have listed here some of the most frequently used words and phrases which should prove useful in deciphering exactly the capabilities of any given set.

Auto Stop
A cassette deck feature used on sets which do not have auto-reverse and whereby the cassette will stop automatically when it reaches the end of one side.

Auto Reverse
A system whereby the tape direction is automatically changed at the end of the cassette.

ANSS
A tuner feature which listens for extraneous noise and suppresses it automatically before it reaches the speakers. Stands for Automatic Noise Suppression System.

APSS
A clever cassette deck function which will fast forward or reverse the cassette to the start of the next or previous track. The deck will then revert to play mode. Stands for Auto Program Search System.

Balance
The control which "moves" the sound from side to side, the feature being standard on stereo sets.

Bass
The sound which occurs in the low frequency range, up to approximately 600Hz.

Chrome Dioxide Tape
This is cassette tape which has a magnetic coating of chrome dioxide (Cro2) in order in give better reproduction.

Dolby* Noise Reduction
A system developed by Ray Dolby as a means of reducing the tape hiss inherent in the cassette format. There are now two types, Dolby "B" and the higher grade Dolby "C".

Fader
A balance control allowing the sound to be regulated between the front and rear of the car with a four speaker set-up.

Ferric Tape
A tape with a magnetic coating of iron oxide particles. Improves the quality of the tape reproduction, though not by as much as chrome dioxide.

Graphic Equaliser
Basically a sophisticated tone control capable of altering individual frequency ranges. Highly desirable in the un-acoustic box of the motor car.

Hertz (Hz)
A measurement of frequency in cycles per second.

Music Power
The maximum (peak) power available from an amplifier for a short period of time, whether separate or as part of a radio/cassette deck. See also rated power.

Nominal Power Rating
The maximum electric power in Watts that a loudspeaker can handle continuously.

Phasing
An odd sound effect caused by incorrect wiring of the speaker terminals where one speaker cone is moving out as the other is moving in. A loss of bass response is one side effect.

PLL Circuit
PLL stands for Phased Locked Loop, an electronic circuit with a quartz stabilised frequency scanning system into which frequencies are "locked" and held with high stability.

Rated Power (RMS)
The average continuous maximum output of an amplifier.

RDS
A system of electronic codes sent with certain FM signals. These can be decoded by sets equipped with special tuners and provide such services as traffic information and automatic same station following.

Sharp Guard
A Sharp anti-theft system, whereby the radio/cassette deck is automatically locked into its dashboard position when the ignition key is removed.

Sharp Safe
Another Sharp security measure available only on certain sets. On the front of the radio/cassette deck is a small removable panel which houses several vital functions. When leaving the car the panel is removed thus disabling the set.

Spectrum Analyser
A graphic equaliser function showing visual display of how the sound is made up throughout the frequency range. The display is usually in the form of LED lights.

Treble
The sound which occurs in the high frequency range, approximately 4,000 to 20,000Hz.

Tweeter
A loudspeaker, usually very small, for reproducing high frequencies.

Two-Way Loudspeaker
A speaker which has two speakers of different types in a single housing, for example, a mid-range and a tweeter.

Woofer
A speaker which is designed to handle bass frequencies, up to approximately 600Hz.

Wow and Flutter
Uneven sounds caused by speed variations in the cassette deck tape transport mechanism.

** Dolby is the trademark of Dolby Laboratories Ltd.*

When buying a radio/cassette player, you should always remember that, at some time in the future, an upgrade of some kind may be desired. The sets featured on these pages are all capable "front end units" with varying power outputs ranging from the adequate to the mind-blowing!

Choosing your in-car entertainment

Whereas lots of extra features may be totally superfluous on a domestic audio unit, the same features could well be literally life savers on a similar in-car player. Most features included on in-car audio equipment are there to make life easier and, more importantly, to help keep the driver's attention on the road, where it should be.

ICE1.1

The entry level radio/cassette deck is the RGF 272E. With no Long Wave reception, it still features an FM/AM radio with Sharp's automatic noise suppression system (ANSS) and an FM stereo/mono switch for when reception is patchy. The cassette deck features lockable fast forward and an auto stop mechanism. The power output is 8W maximum. If you want to have Long Wave as well, but still only require limited cassette facilities with a small power output, the RGF 274E unit will suit you admirably, being almost identical to the previous set in other respects.

ICE1.2

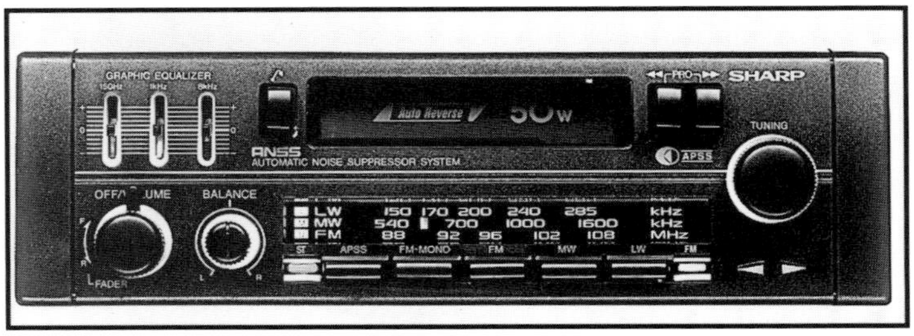

The RGF 284 model is a definite move upmarket, certainly from the power point of view, for it produces no less than 50W maximum which can be put through either two speakers or four, via the built-in front/rear fader. The tuner has three wavebands but no preset facility. Tone control is by means of a built-in three-band graphic equaliser with auto-reverse and APSS on the cassette deck. Although it does not have any form of noise reduction, this is compensated for to some extent by the graphic equaliser which can be used to "dial out" any unwanted tape hiss.

ICE1.3

If you want a high-power set with plenty of advanced tuner features, then you can start with the RGF 558E. The total power output of 36W maximum can be put through a two or four speaker system. The tuner has the very useful SCAN facility with Automatic Station Program Memory, Automatic Noise Suppressor System and an LCD digital frequency display. Most importantly, perhaps, it has a 16 station memory, comprising 8FM, 5MW and 3LW, reflecting the general usage of each waveband in the UK. If this set has the facilities you want, but you fancy a little more power, then the RGF 822E will fit the bill, being similar in basic design, but offering a power output of 50W maximum and auto reverse on the tape deck. Both of these sets have the Sharp Guard anti-theft system, an excellent idea which is discussed later.

ICE1.4

Getting towards the top of the Sharp range, the RGF 810 combines a high power output with both advanced tuner and cassette features. With 50W maximum there's plenty of power coming through the four-band graphic equaliser, whether the signal is coming from the Dolby "B" noise reduced cassettes or the 16 station preset tuner.

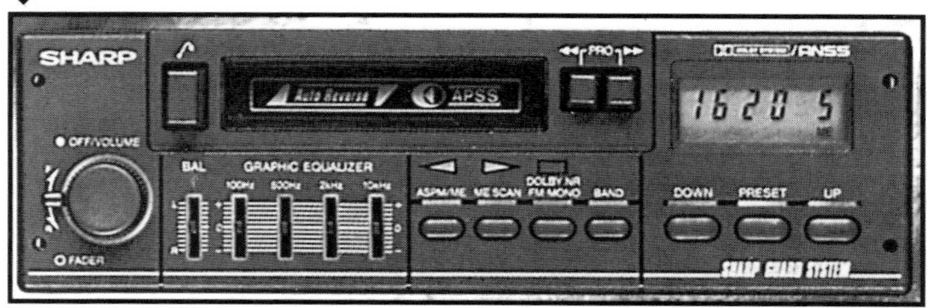

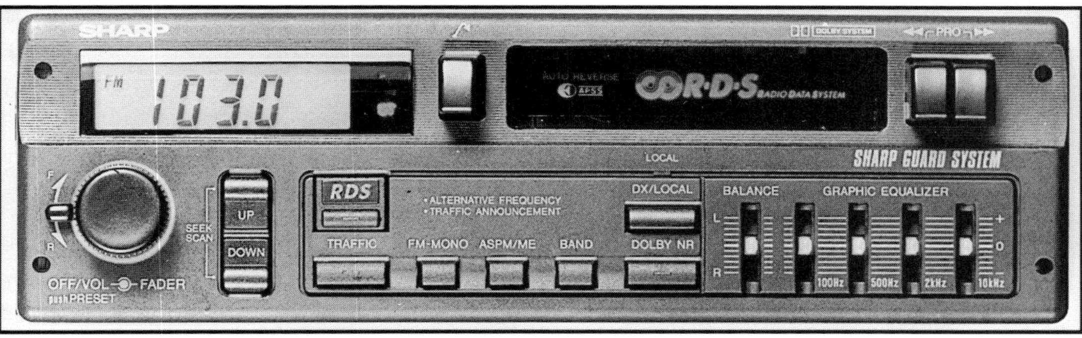

RDS is the latest technology to grace the motorists' ears and, once again, it is a very useful feature, not only by removing the need for constant retuning to a particular wavelength, but also because of the advance traffic information available.

ICE1.5
RDS stands for Radio Data System and it is as revolutionary as FM stereo was. It offers many advantages over conventional radio receivers but poses no extra problems in terms of fitting or operation. The extra information required to operate the system comes from a signal which is broadcast along with the normal FM signal.

The main features of RDS are:

Network Indication
The set displays the name of the radio station being received, rather than just the frequency. Where a programme is split (for example, where a radio station is broadcasting educational programmes on FM but normal programmes on Long Wave), it will show which part of the split you are listening to when tuned into FM.

Automatic Same Network Following System
With this, the set will automatically search and receive the best frequency for a particular station in a given area. Thus, as you travel around the country, you can listen to a consistently good signal without the need to constantly retune.

Traffic Information Reception
At present in its infancy, this is likely to be the biggest boon to drivers for years. The RDS signal will interrupt a programme on the radio or even a cassette in order to receive a traffic information bulletin. The implications are clear, in that the driver can be warned of all possible trouble spots, traffic jams and accidents, before he reaches them, thus allowing time to select a different route. Alternatively, he could just use his in-car phone to call ahead and say he's going to be late! Not surprisingly, Sharp are heavily involved in developing a range of sets capable of decoding the RDS transmissions, the set shown here being the RGF 872E.

Quite apart from the RDS functions, it is a well qualified set, with a built-in four-band graphic equaliser, 16 preset memories, Dolby noise reduction, auto-reverse and a power output of 25W per channel.

ICE1.6
At the top of the RDS tree is this little beauty, the RGF 896E which, in addition to the features found on the previous set, has a record and timer record facility for RDS messages. With this, special Sharp circuitry means that every time you get into the car, the machine will play back the most recent traffic information flash, recorded on a built-in integrated circuit. Naturally enough, both RDS sets have the full Sharp Guard security system.

Fitting a radio/cassette player

To many, the thought of wiring up a radio/cassette unit is unbearable – all those wires, all those complications! Whilst it's true that some care has to be taken, it should not be beyond the reach of the average DIY Fiesta owner. Sharp have taken a lot of trouble to ensure that the instructions are easy to follow, as this diagram for the basic wiring of the RGF 284E shows, and all wires are clearly marked.

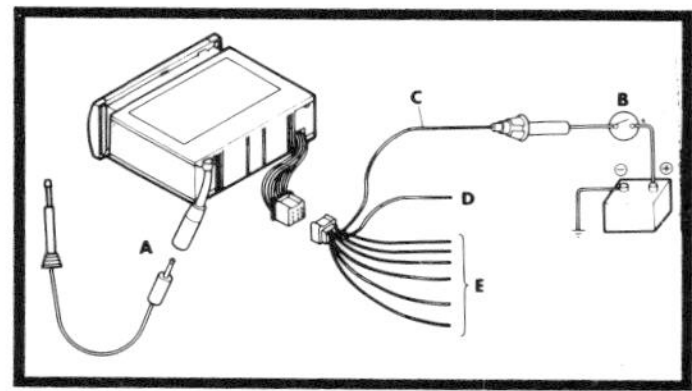

Diagram ICE2.A
[Diagram courtesy Sharp Electronics (UK) Ltd.]

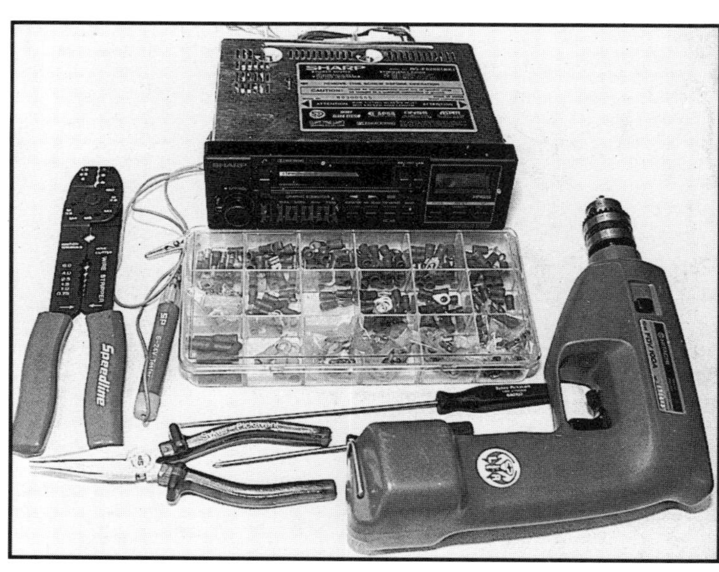

ICE2.1
In this section we will be showing how we fitted a Sharp RGF 284E into a Mk II, 1.1 Fiesta. The principle can be applied to other models, of course. The tools you are likely to need are shown here, including the most useful box of Sedan connectors and the Speedline crimper. The cordless drill will only be used if you need to drill holes for mounting under the dash (where there is no centre console) or for mounting a stabilising bracket. If you do use a drill, don't forget to check that you are not drilling through lots of electrical wiring!

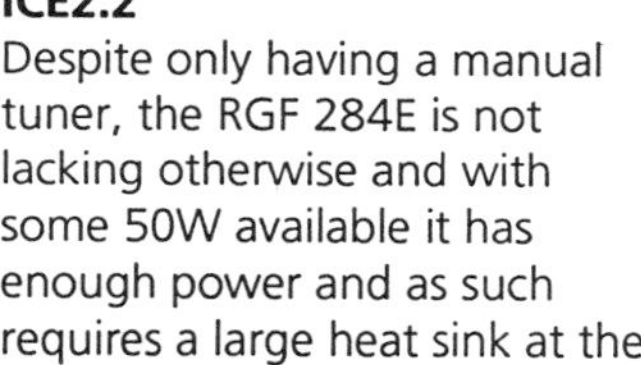

ICE2.2
Despite only having a manual tuner, the RGF 284E is not lacking otherwise and with some 50W available it has enough power and as such requires a large heat sink at the rear of the set to disperse the excess heat produced.

ICE2.3
If you already have a standard Ford radio/cassette or tuner-only unit, removal is quite simple. Insert the two special "hooks" in each side of the set and it will pull out as shown here.

ICE2.4
The standard Ford wiring uses DIN plugs for the speakers, so as to suit the standard Ford sets. As the RGF 284E does not use DIN speaker plugs ...

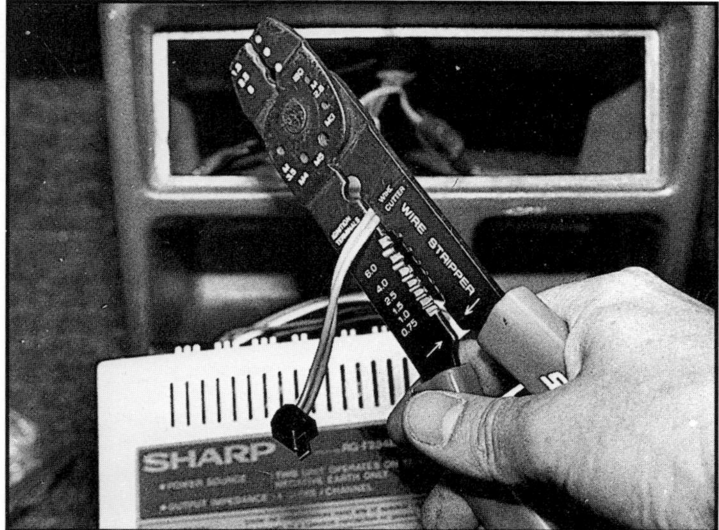

ICE2.5
... they have to be removed. If you leave around 3 inches of wire; you will be able to re-use them, should the need arise.

ICE2.6
Next, the ends of the speaker leads were stripped and bullet connectors crimped on. Note that on the end of each speaker lead (ie, the ones from the speakers and the others from the set), a male and female connector should be used. Also, each connector requires **two** crimps; one which holds the bare wire to the metal and one which traps the insulation. Make sure that the polarity remains the same by lining up the white stripe in both sets of wires.

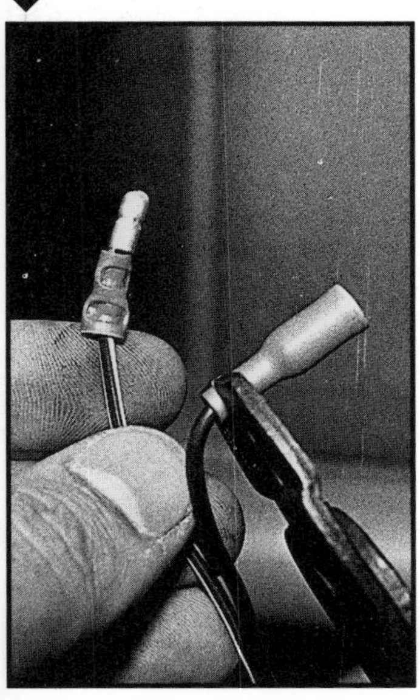

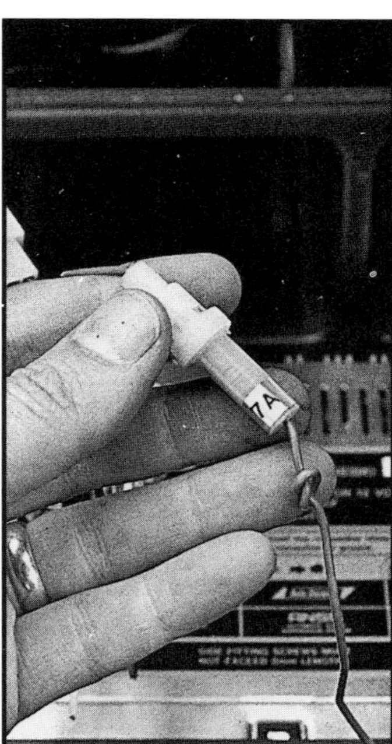

ICE2.7
The power/earth leads are connected into the car's system by fitting connectors in a similar manner. Naturally, the main power lead is protected by an in-line, 7 amp fuse. The various wires all culminate in this multi-plug which simply plugs into the socket in the back of the set. Apart from the obvious ease, it means that the wiring can be completed without the usual situation of the set hanging around at all angles on the end of a speaker whilst you crimp away! Don't forget to plug in the aerial lead; a common mistake.

ICE2.8
This particular Sharp model is held in situ by two small mounting brackets on each side. When the set is placed into the DIN slot ...

We've said it before; make sure that the speaker polarity is right! The Sharp sets shown in this section can be wired for either two or four speakers. Sharp provide two diagrams showing the relevant wiring requirements. Note that in a two-speaker fitment, it is important that the two wires not used (orange and white) are taped securely out of the way, to prevent any danger of damaging speakers or the set.

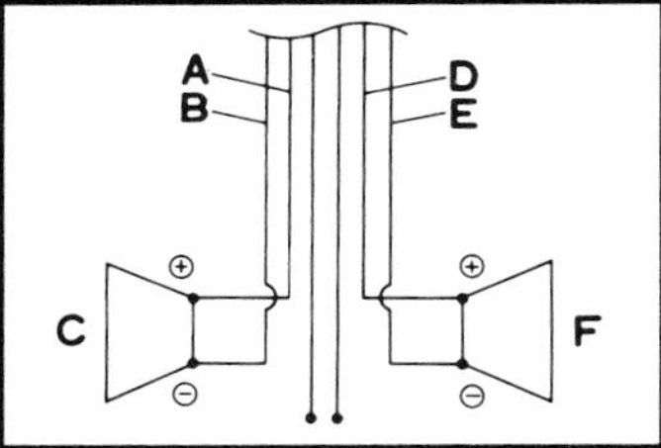

Diagram ICE2.B
Two-speaker system

A	**Green +**
B	**Brown –**
C	**Left Speaker**
D	**Blue +**
E	**Grey –**
F	**Right Speaker**

Diagram ICE2.C
Four-speaker system

A	**Orange +/–**
B	**Green +**
C	**Brown –**
D	**Front Left Speaker**
E	**Rear Left Speaker**
F	**White +/–**
G	**Blue +**
H	**Grey –**
I	**Front Right Speaker**
J	**Rear Right Speaker**

[Diagrams courtesy Sharp Electronic (UK) Ltd.]

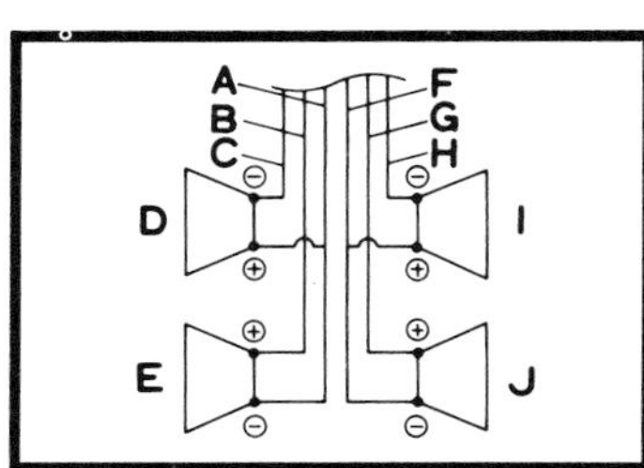

Fitting a radio/cassette player

All but four of Sharp's wide range of radio/cassette decks are fitted with graphic equalisers. A graphic equaliser is best described as a more versatile tone control switch. Effectively, your car is its own tone control and because it modifies the sounds at random due to the effects of engine, wind and tyre noise, etc, the chances of getting the sound you would really like, without using a graphic equaliser, are minimal. However, by using a graphic equaliser, you can tune out the problem frequencies more accurately.

ICE2.9
... the small screw is tightened and the set effectively "clamps" itself into position. This means that thieves will find difficulty in just pulling the set out in a hurry.

ICE2.10
The finishing touch is a couple of plastic end plates to cover up the screws and brackets and ...

ICE2.11
... that's it: fitted, working and extremely powerful. In this particular instance, the car was wired for only two speakers, but we would recommend that four be used in order to make best use of the unit's capabilities.

ICE2.12
The RGF 828E is also 50W max output, but is much nearer to the top of the range, with more advanced features in evidence. Unlike the RGF 284E, this set ***does*** use the DIN speaker plugs used by Ford. There are four sockets on the rear of the unit and a two-speaker loom complete with ready-wired plugs is provided.

ICE2.13 ➡
Because the set is equipped with the Sharp Guard anti-theft system, a supplementary bracket is used in the DIN size aperture. The set fits in here and these pins lock the set into position. The set cannot be removed unless the correct procedure is followed.

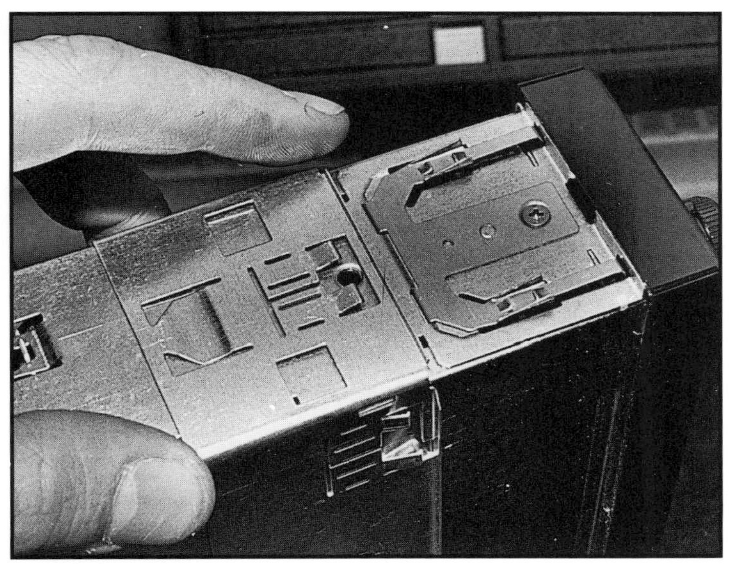

When considering any of the improvements mentioned in this section, you should always remember that in order to have a good overall sound system in your Fiesta, you need to match speakers to the set and vice versa. A really competent set, such as the RGF 828E, will sound absolutely awful if you run it through a set of "bargain" speakers. Although a more complex set, this diagram shows that Sharp have made the wiring just as simple to follow.

⬅ **ICE2.14**
Wiring, as per the easy to understand diagram, is fundamentally the same as the RGF 284E unit. Installed, the unit looks as goods as it sounds – you'll have to take our word for it!

⬅ **ICE2.15**
Like the Ford standard radio/ cassette decks, the RGF 828E can be removed by using these two special tools. They slot into holes on each side of the set and release catches on the supplementary frame.

ICE2.16 ➡
Prevention is better than cure and once your Sharp set is installed, this sticker in the window will warn the light-fingered "enthusiasts" to look elsewhere for their "free" ICE equipment!

Diagram ICE2.D

1. **A/B Front Speakers**
2. **C/D Rear Speakers**
3. **Aerial**
4. **Earth Lead**
5. **DC Power Supply (Memory)**
6. **DC Supply Lead**
7. **Guard Lead**
8. **Ignition Switch**
9. **Aerial Control Lead (for Auto Aerial)**

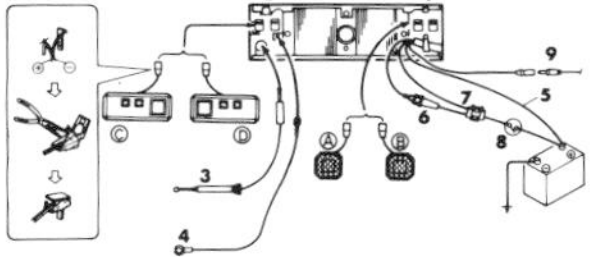

[Diagram courtesy Sharp Electronics (UK) Ltd.]

Speaker selection and fitting

The Golden Rule:
On no account should speaker leads be connected together! To do so could ruin both speakers and amplifier. Speaker cable is usually coded by a stripe of some description down one of the wires. This is so that you can get the phasing of all the speakers in the system the same, that is, ensure that the positive side of the set is connected to the positive terminal on the speaker. Naturally, this has to be continued throughout the system.

The loudspeaker could possibly be regarded as the Cinderella of in-car audio. Time and again we see (and hear!) impressive systems with expensive radio/cassette units, amplifiers and graphic equalisers which are drastically let down by using sub-standard speakers. This is the audio equivalent of turbocharging your XR2 and then running it on 4.5 inch wheels and 155 section tyres!

Essentially, a speaker is a device for converting electrical impulses, emanating from the radio tuner, into sound waves, capable of being picked up by the human ear. The amplifier causes the speaker cone to move in or out and thus create sound waves. In terms of speaker selection, you should always take some time to contemplate your decision. Obviously, if you have a set with, for instance, a power output of 20 watts per channel, then you will need speakers capable of handling at least this amount of power. However, what of the future? If you are thinking of a future upgrade then it may pay you to buy better speakers now. Check also the manufacturer's quotation of power output; there is a difference between maximum and nominal figures. Also, the "watts per channel" figure is usually quoted for stereo, ie, two channels. If you have a four speaker set-up, then you will have half as much power through each speaker.

ICE3.1
There's plenty to choose from in the Sharp range, created specifically to suit the modern motoring environment and ideal for any model Fiesta. From 8W to 80W is quite a span and should meet all but the most impressive of hi-fi set-ups.

ICE3.2
If you have a modest set (possibly the standard Ford fitment) and are unlikely to progress much further up the power scale, then the CP53 loudspeaker could be for you. These pod mounted speakers come in pairs (as do all the Sharp range) and ...

ICE3.3
... are ideal for mounting on the rear parcel shelf. The speakers are 4 inch (100mm) diameter and are useful for uprating a two speaker system into a four-speaker set-up. They have a maximum power handling capacity of 8W and an impedance of 4 ohms. Note that the speaker leads are soldered onto the terminals and the short wires have bullet connectors.

ICE3.4 ➡
The CPS 41 is capable of handling much more power, up to 25W maximum. Don't forget that with a four-speaker system, this means up to 100 watts! It is a flush-fitting speaker of 4 inch (100mm) diameter with dual cones for better sound separation. They come with two rolls of speaker lead, sufficient to run from front to rear of the car. Note that the speaker terminals are pre-fitted and are of different sizes (to prevent getting the polarity wrong), and the other ends are fitted with DIN plugs, although some sets will not be so equipped and the leads will need fitting with new plugs. Fitting means either cutting holes in the trim or parcel shelf or replacing the standard door units.

⬅ **ICE3.5**
The CP41s are intended for use mainly in doors and so we fitted them to this Mk II Fiesta. Ford blessed this model with factory fitted speakers which saved us a lot of work! Removing the door trim gives easy access. Note how well the speaker is mounted, being held securely with four screws passing through re-inforced metal in the door frame. Were this not so, the speaker may be able to move and the resultant sound would be distorted. Four crosshead screws hold the standard unit in place. They will be tight, so take care that the screwdriver does not slip and damage the speaker.

⬅ **ICE3.6**
With the screws removed, the speaker will pull out. Before you remove the speaker leads, make sure that the set is not on (remove the negative battery lead), for accidentally touching the leads together is a recipe for disaster!

ICE3.7 ➡
The CPS 41 comes complete with water shield. In this case, ord provided a built-in shield so the Sharp one wasn't needed. However, some protection gainst water penetration is vital where the speaker is mounted vertically in any panel.

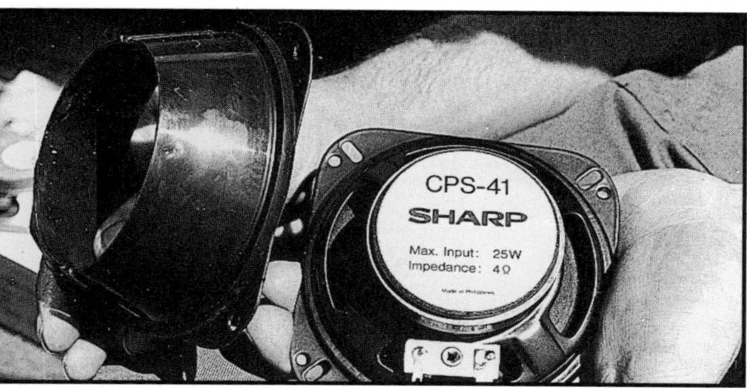

Speaker types

There are three basic speaker types. The broadband speaker is the one most usually fitted as standard, either by manufacturer or owner. As its name suggests, it is something of a compromise and handles frequencies from the base, middle and treble ranges. The next step up is a dual cone speaker and almost any improvement to the audio system will require at least an upgrade to this type. This speaker is, in fact, two speakers in one, with the main cone being either a bass or a mid-range and a tweeter in the middle. A component speaker is one designed to handle just one set of frequencies – bass, midrange or treble. The table below gives a guide as to which speaker handles which frequency.

Speaker	***Frequency Response***
Bass (Woofer)	**35/4,00Hz**
Mid-range	**300/12,000Hz**
Treble (Tweeter)	**2,000/ 25,000Hz**

Speaker selection and fitting

Wiring speakers in a car is something of an art. Not only must all the connections be correct, but also the routing of the wires must be carefully considered, so as to avoid using hundreds of yards of speaker cable! The basic rule is that the power handling capacity of the speakers must at least equal the output. In the two diagrams here, the output is 4 ohms.

Diagram ICE3.A
Two speakers have to be wired in series, as shown.

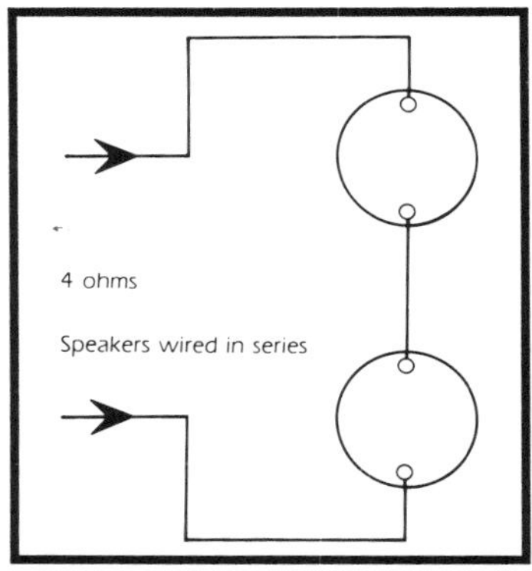

Diagram ICE3.B
However, with four speakers, a parallel arrangement is called for, in order to stay within the output level (4 ohms) of the amplifier. Note that the speaker terminals are of different sizes.

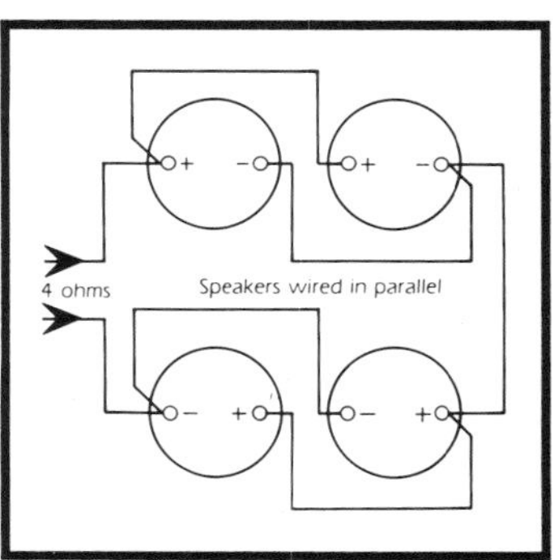

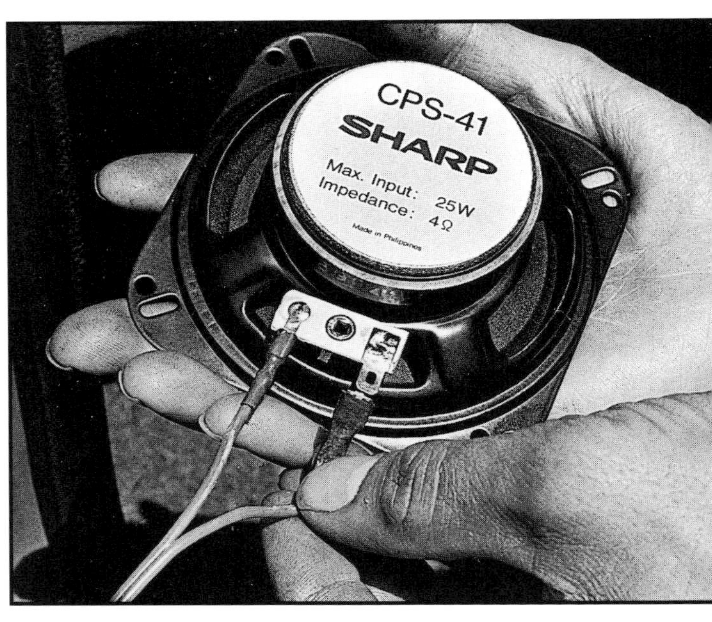

ICE3.8
The terminals on the CP41 are standard female spades of differing sizes. These match the standard speaker leads in the Fiesta and the different sizes of terminals ensure that polarity is correctly maintained.

ICE3.9
Once you are sure that the terminals are secure, you can replace the four crosshead screws and ...

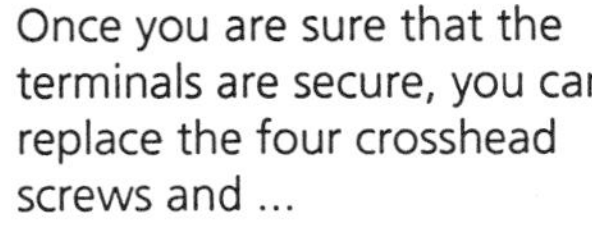

ICE3.10
... fitting is complete, although the only way to tell is to listen. It is a good idea to test the speakers before the trim is replaced ... just in case!

ICE3.11
Going further up the Sharp range, the CPS 50 can handle up to 30W maximum. The speaker is again flush-mounted although the size has risen to 5.25 inch (130mm). Almost identical to look at is the CPS 55, which is physically the same size, but with a power handling capability of 40W. The single enclosure holds no less than three speakers mounted within (tri-axial). By separating the frequencies (into bass, mid-range and treble), a much clearer sound can be heard.

ICE3.12
At the top of the speaker tree is the mighty CPM FA22, which is effectively a box housing three speakers. The woofer (bass speaker) is of the honeycomb flat diaphragm design and the mid-range speaker and dome tweeter have an acoustic screen. It is capable of handling a maximum of 80W, ten times more than the CP 53 which started this section! When you have a powerful radio/cassette unit, such as the RGF 828E shown earlier, then you owe it to your ears to use speakers of this capability.

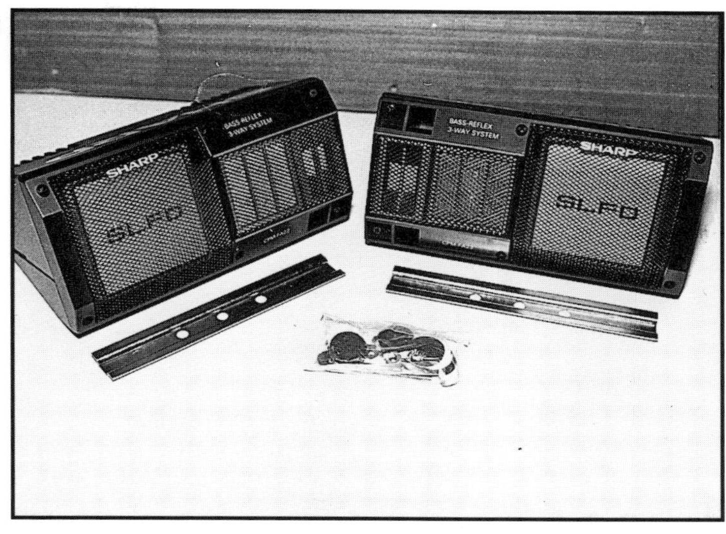

At the heart of all speakers is a magnet. You must make sure that you never get your cassette tapes anywhere near a speaker, even if it is in an enclosure, for the tape could easily be damaged. If you do manage to damage a speaker beyond repair, either electronically or physically with an errant screwdriver, you can remove the magnet and keep it in your toolbox where it will come in handy for retrieving lost screws!

ICE3.13
With the speakers come a screw-in peg and a flat metal bar which must be used when mounting on the rear parcel shelf. The speakers must be held firmly, otherwise the sound will be very muffled. Ideally you should replace the standard shelf altogether with a purpose-made, wooden unit.

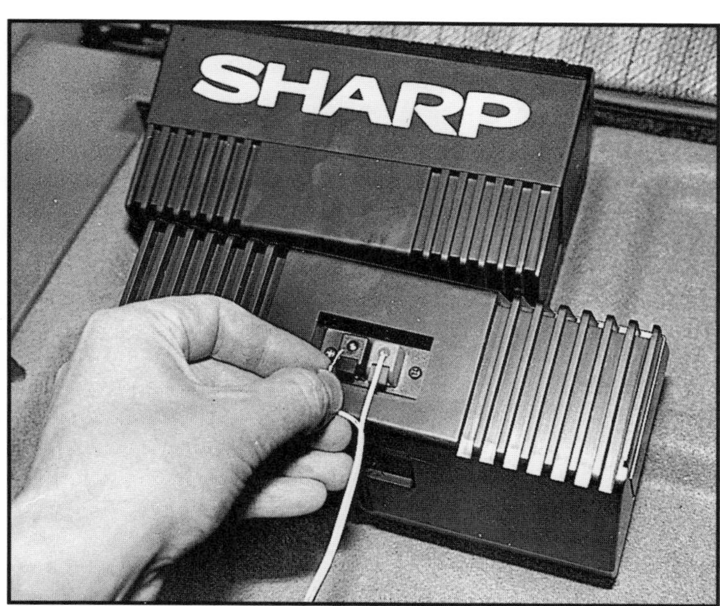

ICE3.14
Apart from the obvious difference in size, the speaker connections are no longer push-in terminals of any kind but the type more commonly used in domestic systems. The respective terminals have spring-loaded clamps, into which is placed the bared end of the speaker lead. Take great care when routing the wires that they will not become trapped when the parcel shelf or rear seat is moved.

ICE3.15
Once secured and wired correctly, they not only sound superb but look good too!

Security

The old saying, "you can't take it with you" doesn't seem to apply to the car thief who, given half a chance, would be more than happy to take your newly installed ICE equipment with him! Sharp are well aware that their in-car entertainment equipment is worth stealing and most of it comes with some form of security as standard, either the Sharp Guard (seen earlier) or the Sharp Safe and Removal system shown here. Naturally, fitting an alarm will help protect your car and its contents, but only if you use it *every* time you leave the car; this is where the Zemco system (Chapter Two) scores heavily as you simply can't forget to switch it on. Also, you can do yourself a favour by parking your car in sensible places. When leaving your car at night, for instance, parking in a dark, poorly lit street is just asking for trouble. Don't forget that your ICE accessories are valuable too. Your Fischer C-Box full of high quality cassettes would be worth breaking a window for, so either put such items in the boot, under a seat or, if they are fixtures, cover them in some way.

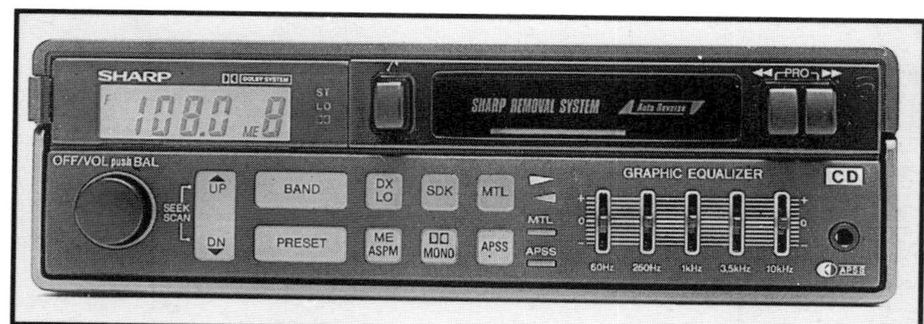

ICE4.1
Undoubtedly the best way to stop a thief taking away your front end unit is to take it away yourself! The Sharp RG F834E is a highly desirable system but the bad guys will be disappointed as it is not a permanent fixture; by lifting the handle, the unit pulls out to be stored either in the hatch of your Fiesta or taken with you.

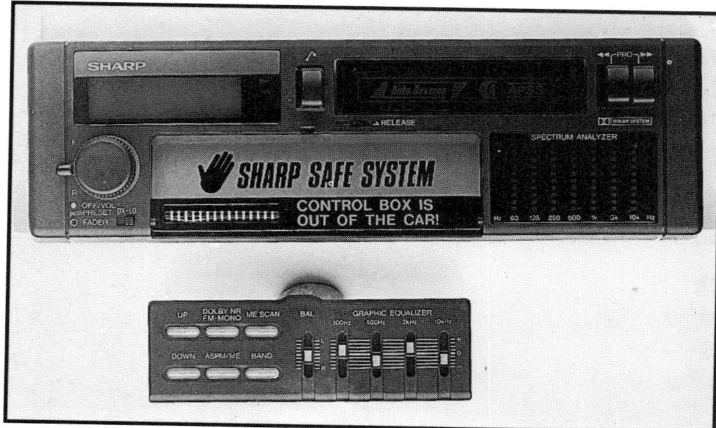

ICE4.2
A variation on that theme is the Sharp Safe system employed on the RGF 816. As well as the usual array of useful features it too can be taken with you; or rather some of it can! Part of the front of the set just unplugs and is small enough to pop into your pocket or handbag. Without it, the set is useless and not worth stealing. The window stickers and the large logo on the set itself warn the potential thief that he needn't bother.

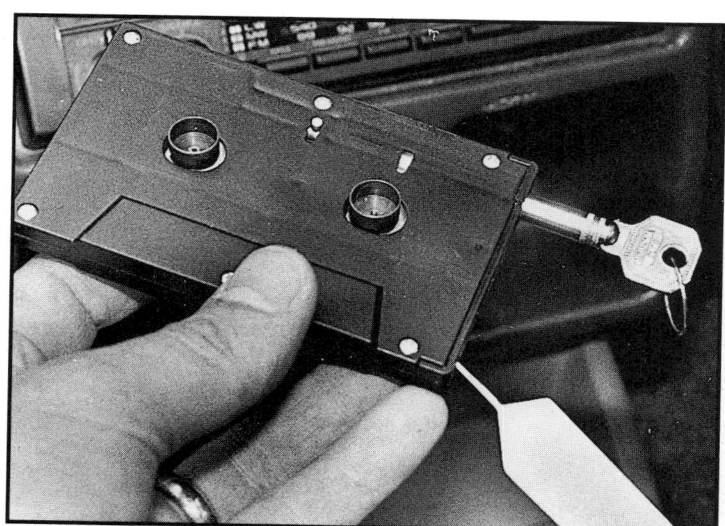

ICE4.3
If you have a set such as the RGF 284E, which has no specific form of built-in security, then you could use the Motus Security Lock, an ingenious device which uses two clamps which lock over the capstans and make it virtually impossible to remove without destroying the set.

ICE4.4
Again, warning stickers are supplied and a large yellow tag is attached to the lock which hangs from the front of the cassette deck. The Skandia Insurance Company of Sweden issues one of these devices with each motor policy, such is their effectiveness!

The car aerial has specific problems, largely because the radio tuner is constantly moving around in relation to the signals. This can lead to poor reception, not only if the transmitter is too far away, but also if it is too close. If the set is too close to a strong signal, but it is tuned into a more distant one, then it may become confused and mix up the two. The resultant audio melange is called cross modulation.

Conversely, if the set is already tuned into the near, strong signal, there is a danger of overloading. If the signal required is too far away, there is an opposite problem. (This is particularly noticeable with FM, where the signal travels in "sight" lines and therefore is easily interrupted by the horizon or tall buildings.) The volume will fall but interference will increase. The difficulties associated with all these phenomena can be largely overcome by having a quality aerial to go with your tuner.

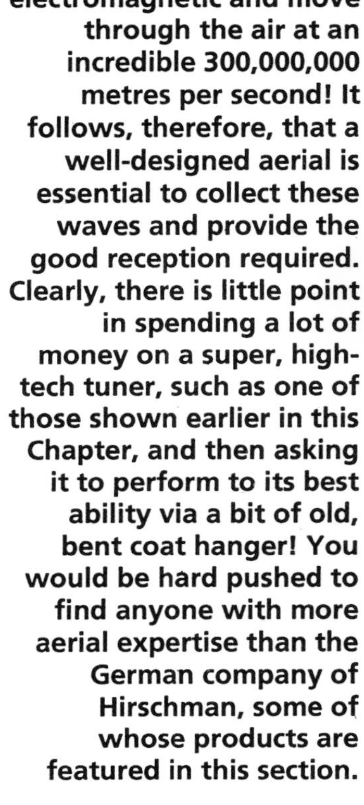

Radio waves are electromagnetic and move through the air at an incredible 300,000,000 metres per second! It follows, therefore, that a well-designed aerial is essential to collect these waves and provide the good reception required. Clearly, there is little point in spending a lot of money on a super, high-tech tuner, such as one of those shown earlier in this Chapter, and then asking it to perform to its best ability via a bit of old, bent coat hanger! You would be hard pushed to find anyone with more aerial expertise than the German company of Hirschman, some of whose products are featured in this section.

ICE5.1 As improving or modifying your aerial is generally taken to mean an electric model, that's just what we have here. The Hirschman 5091 is a universal unit, easy to fit and of superb quality. Because of the extra space required by the electric motor, always try the aerial for space before you start work. The model shown here is finished in black (no more polishing!), but is also available in chrome for those who prefer it.

ICE5.2 If you are replacing a manual aerial, then you will already have the required hole. If not, you'll have to drill one! Mark your spot carefully, using masking tape to make it clear and prevent the drill bit damaging the paintwork if it slips.

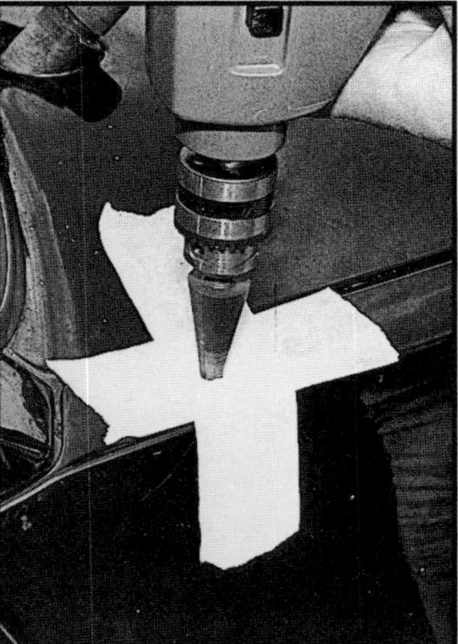

ICE5.3 Follow up the initial pilot drill with the Sykes-Pickavant "varicut" bit until the hole is the required size ...

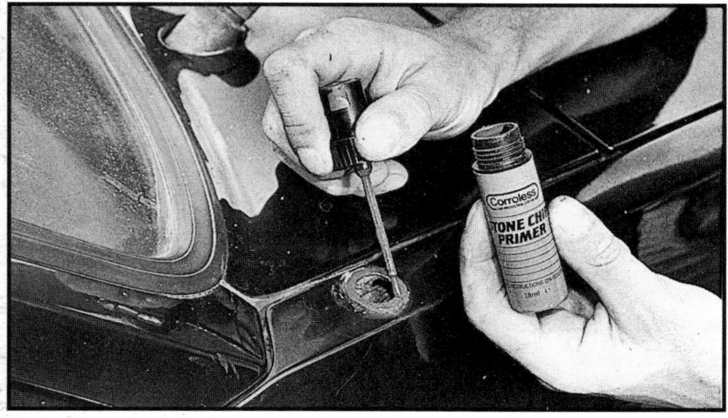

ICE5.4 ... and don't forget to rustproof the edges. Corroless Stone Chip Primer (see Chapter 5) is ideal for this.

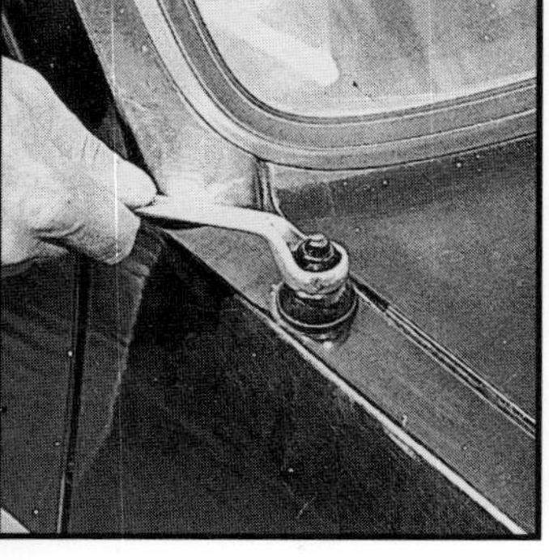

ICE5.5 Now is the time to connect the separate aerial lead to the aerial and feed it through the hole in the inner wing as you pass the aerial into the newly drilled hole. A 17mm ring spanner is required to tighten the aerial.

Aerials

No such thing as aerial maintenance? Don't you believe it! Out in all the elements, even a high quality Hirschman aerial takes quite a battering. Always retract the aerial when you park (this also helps prevent vandalism), although if you have an electric model it may do this automatically when the set is switched off. Also, a regular smear of light grease along its length will help to keep rust at bay and prevent it from sticking.

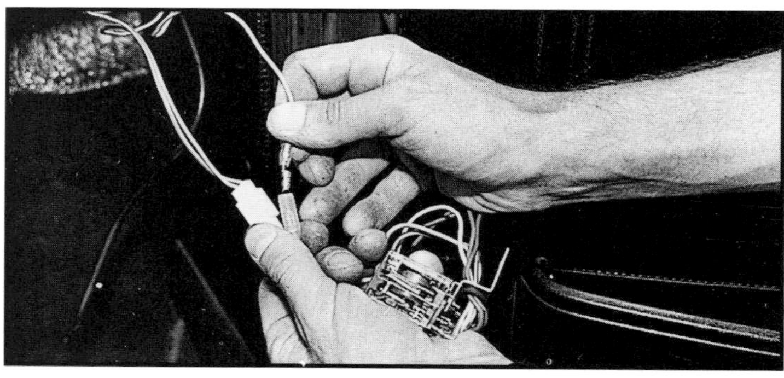

ICE5.6 There are three electrical wires which should also pass through the inner wing with the co-axial lead. These connect directly into a socket and a bullet connector which in turn are part of the relay wiring harness.

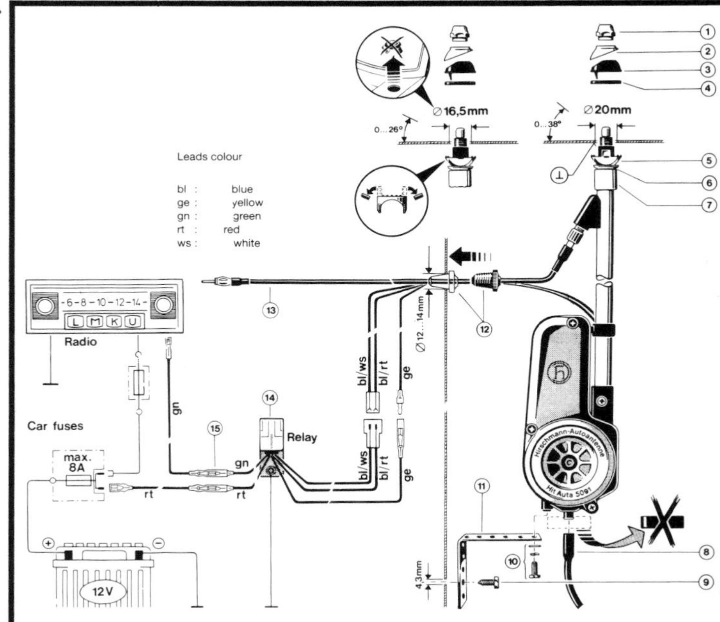

ICE5.7 As you can see from this diagram, the wiring is simple and it is designed so that the aerial automatically retracts when the radio is switched off; one method of protecting your aerial against vandalism. If you are fitting one of Hirschman's wide range of manual aerials the fitting is basically the same as that described for the 5091 electric model.
(Diagram courtesy Hirschman)

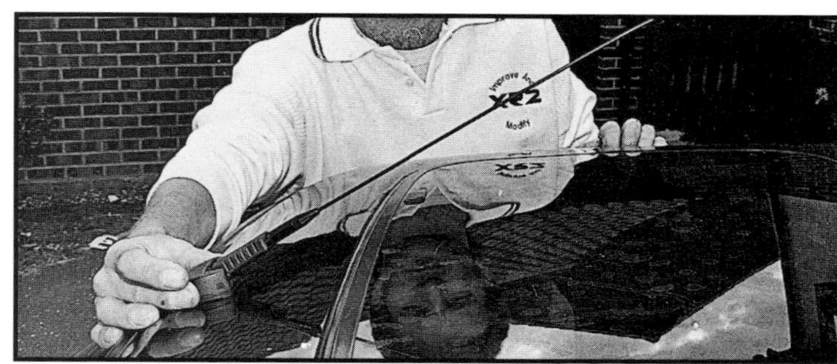

ICE5.8 Not an electric unit but still desirable, the Hirschman Auta 91 TOP model allows you to collect the radio signals from the best position possible; the roof of your Fiesta. It means that you have to be very accurate with the drill and prepared to route the lead painstakingly under the trim, but it's well worth it.

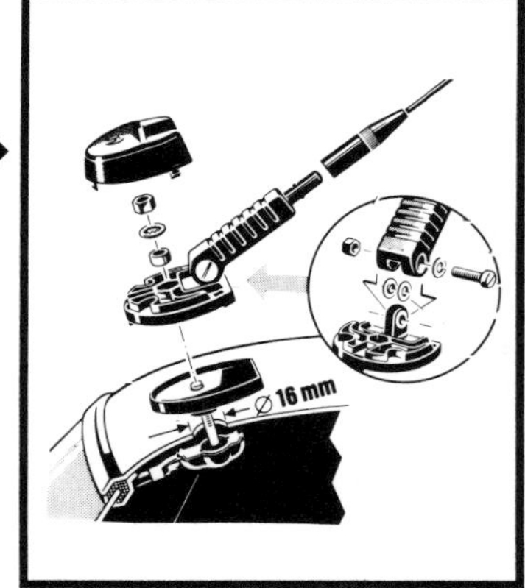

ICE5.9 This diagram shows the basic layout of the aerial and how it should be fitted. The aerial rod itself is stainless steel, 40cm long and comes in an anodised black finish. For protection against vandals and car washes, it can be unscrewed and kept in the car.
(Diagram courtesy Hirschman)

Here's a tip for sorting out "interference" on your tuner. Sometimes, an old aerial can become loose at its joints and cause a crackling sound. To check this, tune into a strong station then stand by the side of the car and flick the aerial; if there is interference on the radio then your aerial is worn out. Unfortunately, the only alternative is to buy another and at this point you will find yourself wishing that you'd looked after it better!

Fitting an in-car telephone

As with just about everything in the motoring world, today's luxury items are tomorrow's standard equipment. The in-car electronics industry is particularly prone to rapid change and so it is that in-car telephones, once the preserve of the wealthy, can now be supplied, fitted and linked into a system for less than half the price of a Compact Disc player! For this section, we visited the Milton Keynes branch of the Carphone Group plc, in order to see exactly what is involved in fitting a Motorola 4800X in-car telephone to a Fiesta XR2.

ICE6.1
The Motorola 4800X in-car phone as it comes: there's a lot of bits! The box contains all that is necessary to complete an installation. A Fiesta would typically take the skilled Carphone Group fitter a couple of hours, but this short time is only the result of many years' experience; it is not really a DIY task unless you are very well qualified.

ICE6.2
The handset cradle should be mounted where the driver can see it, and make a minimal distraction from driving. It could be mounted alongside the transmission tunnel console, but a better position ...

ICE6.3
... would be on the side of the instrument console. Care must be taken when drilling the bracket holes to ensure no damage is caused to any cables or wires in the fascia. Placed high enough, it should not cause any discomfort to a passenger.

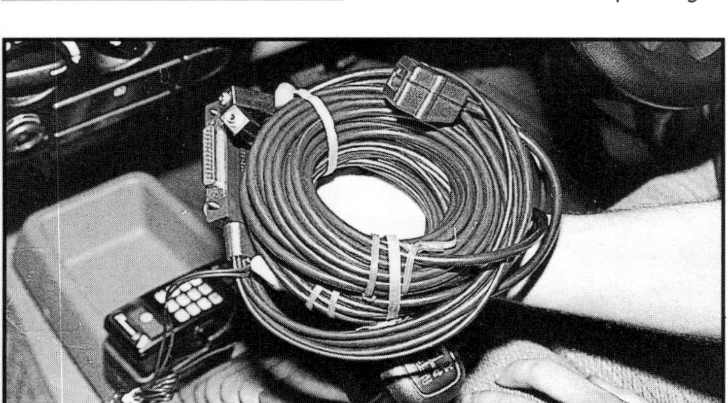

ICE6.4
The life blood of the system is this Motorola wiring loom. The large, multi-pin socket connects to the transceiver, whilst the others are for the phone itself, the remote microphone and the speaker.

As can be seen, this particular Motorola unit comes complete with a separate, remote mounted, microphone. The Carphone Group recommend that "hands-free" should always be part of any in-car telephone installation and we wholeheartedly endorse this view; there are enough accidents on the roads through in-attention, without adding any more! Here, we show the fitting of a specific in-car phone or a "mobile". Also available are trans-mobiles, which can be fitted in the car but also removed and used as portables, and "Transportables" which can be carried around but are not designed for in-car use. In essence, the more versatile the phone, the more it costs!

Fitting an in-car telephone

Unlike other items of ICE equipment, you have to pay to use it. This means renting "air time" from either Cellnet or Vodaphone, via one of around forty air time suppliers. This is paid for in the same way as a normal land line – a monthly rental and then call charges. The Carphone Group's rental charge includes itemised billing (each call listed separately along with the number called), although this is by no means universal. It is something to check before buying your phone, as is the scale of call charges. The Carphone Group charge in half minute intervals after the first minute, which can make a great difference when compared with those who charge only for whole minutes!

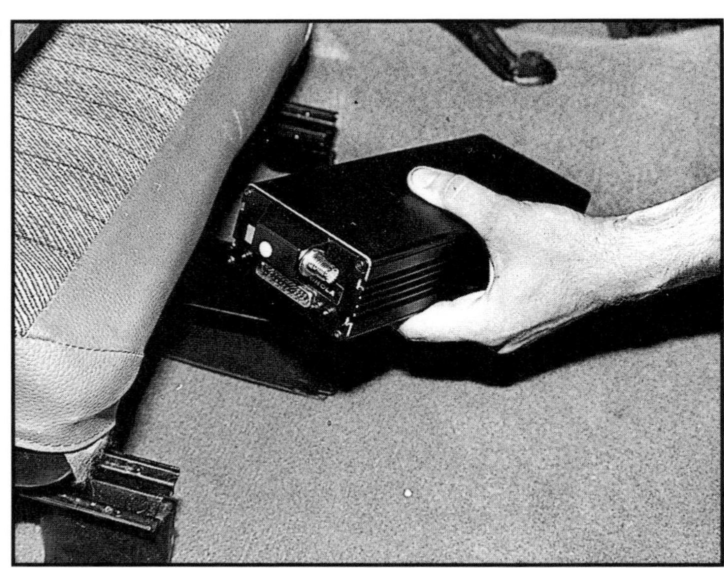

ICE6.5 The "brains" of the whole system is the transceiver. This little black box not only receives incoming calls but also makes sure your outgoing calls go to the right number. With a purpose made car installation, it is normally mounted safely out of harm's way under one of the front seats. Alternatively, it could be positioned in the tool compartment in the hatch. The unit is held by the bracket shown here and, by releasing the wing nut, can be easily removed for security purposes.

ICE6.6 The loudspeaker is usually placed on the centre console or in the transmission tunnel tray. It is held by a bracket and two self-tapping screws.

ICE6.7 The microphone lead is routed up the driver's side "A" pillar and the mike is positioned just above the door. Experience has shown that with the mike further forward (ie, at the top of the "A" pillar) poor sound can result when the sun visor is down. Alternatively, the mike can be fitted to the sun visor.

ICE6.8 All the high-tech, in-car gadgetry is as nothing without this short piece of metal rod! Ideally, a body-mounted aerial should be used with every car phone. In the centre of the car at the front is an excellent position and even with a sunroof in situ, causes no fitting problems. However, this is not always possible for various reasons, the main one being that owners do not want to drill holes in their cars!

ICE6.9

Alternatively, the optional glass mounted aerial could prove ideal. Usually mounted on the rear screen (or on a side window), the receiving unit is stuck onto the glass and ...

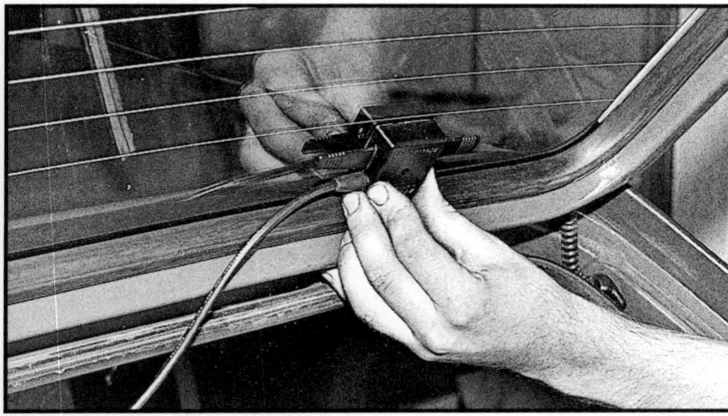

ICE6.10

... the transmitting unit stuck onto the underside directly beneath it. Note that great care is taken to avoid both the heated rear window elements and the sweep of the rear wash-wipe. No problem for an experienced Carphone Group fitter, but positioning the aerial here would mean removing a lot of the trim, in order to route the aerial lead neatly and safely to the receiver under the seat.

ICE6.11

The layout of the Carphone system can be seen better in this schematic diagram.

(Diagram courtesy Carphone Group/Motorola Inc.)

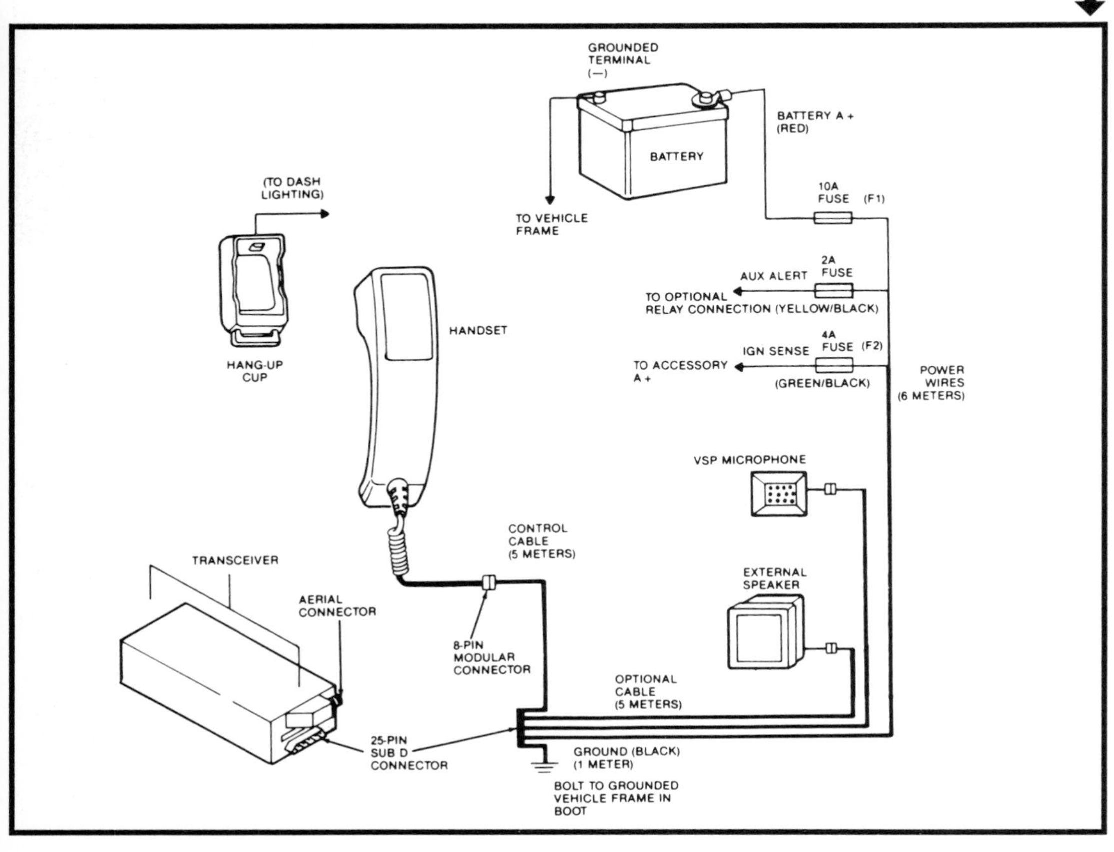

If a well earthed, good quality aerial is necessary for good radio reception, then it is doubly so for an in-car telephone, which, of course, not only receives incoming transmissions, but also sends out its own. At the Carphone Group they take great care to position it properly and make sure that there is a really good earth connection.

Chapter Four
Mechanical Uprating

Fitting a free-flow air filter

MU1.1➡
You don't have to own the powerful XR2 to benefit from a Pipercross filter. The company produce a wide range of standard replacement filters for most other models. This is a Mk II, 1100cc car, on which the first task ...

⬅MU1.2
... is to remove the two crosshead screws holding the plastic assembly in place.

MU1.3➡
The top can then be removed after it has been unclipped all around its base.

There are Pipercross filters to suit Fiestas fitted with either Weber DFT or Ford VV carburettors. It is very important that you check exactly which carburettor is fitted to your car and in many cases, the best method is to lift away the air filter and check the number on the carburettor body. If you're still in doubt, compare it with the diagrams and photos in your Haynes manual. The effect of a Pipercross filter is shown in these two graphs relating to fuel consumption and increased power respectively.

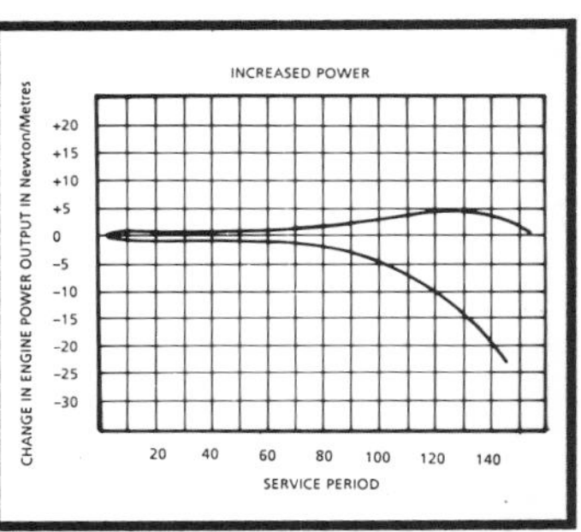

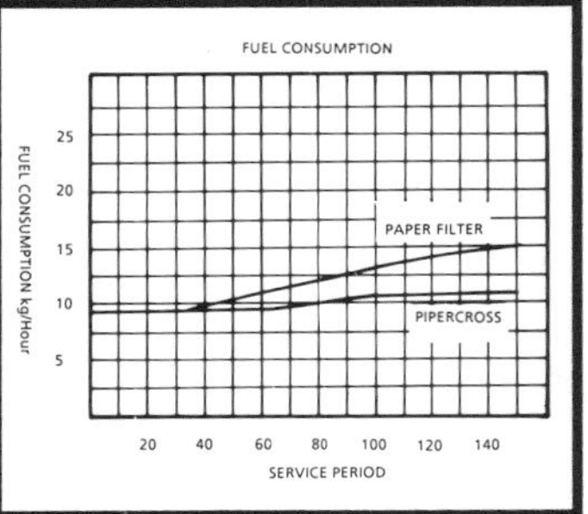

(Graphs courtesy Pipercross Ltd)

Fitting a free-flow air filter

Fitting a free-flow air filter is one of the simplest ways of "tuning" your car. A Pipercross filter will enable your car to breathe more easily and thus function more efficiently. Many filter manufacturers claim performance increases with only very subjective proof. However, Pipercross commissioned Martin Tickford Engineering (now, of course, part of the Ford Motor Company) whose report contained the comment that: "Some increase in power output was noticed." The report also said that, "... there was a noticeable improvement in fuel economy." Their research showed that the use of Pipercross filters increased and maintained engine efficiency for a longer service period when compared with standard paper filters. This graph shows the difference in service life.

(Graph courtesy Pipercross Ltd)

MU1.4 The Pipercross unit fits exactly in the space left by the standard paper filter. As you can see, although the filters are physically the same size, they are very different. The Pipercross unit is made of strong rubberised material with alloy strengthening. The most important difference is in the filter element itself, which allows the engine to breathe better and release more of its potential.

MU1.5 Unlike the standard replacement filter, the Mk I XR2 version is markedly different from the standard equipment ...

MU1.6 ... and requires this special adaptor bracket in order to match the Weber carburettor. When fitting, it means that the complete original filter assembly must be removed altogether, including the heating piping from the exhaust manifold. Naturally, this means that, in winter, carburettor icing could be a problem, although it will depend largely on where you live. We would suggest that the benefits would be worth the extra effort of creating a home-made heater arrangement.

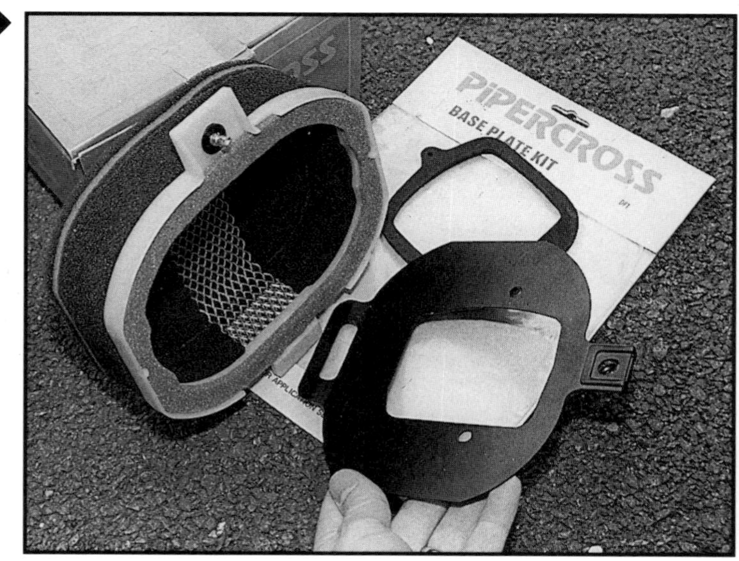

Fitting electronic ignition

The Lumenition Optronic ignition system comprises three basic components; an optical trigger, a power module and a chopper (rotating, segmented disc).

The optical switch directs an infra-red beam from its emitter (a light-emitting diode, or LED) on to its detector, a silicon photo transistor. When the detector sees the ray, it is switched on. When the ray is interrupted by the revolving chopper, the detector is switched off. The chopper, fitted to the cam, has one blade for each cylinder and the constant on-off action controls an electronic switch in the power module. This, in turn, switches the coil on and off and produces a longer lasting, high energy spark at the plugs. Because there is no physical contact, there is nothing to interfere with the accuracy of the timing and thus the engine keeps perfect timing throughout its life.

MU2.1
From the instant you put in new points, they begin to wear and the timing becomes progressively more retarded. The effects of wear are shown clearly in this diagram. The answer is either to continue replacing the points and retiming or to fit electronic ignition.
(Diagram courtesy Autocar Equipment)

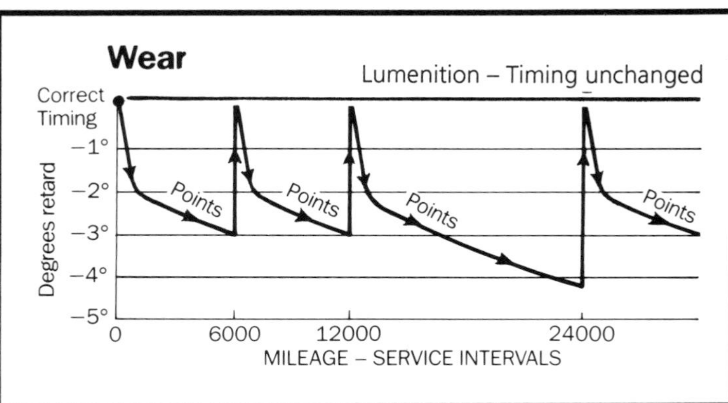

MU2.2
This is the basic power module kit for which a fitting kit is required. It is very important that you ensure that both are specific to your car, especially as various distributors have been used over the years. The main component is ...

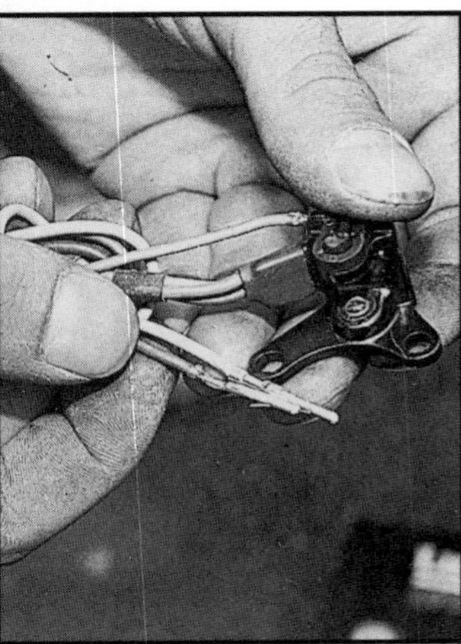

MU2.3
... the light emitting diode contained in this single section which replaces the original and complex, contact points assembly.

MU2.4
The fitting kit comprises everything required to adapt a particular power module to a specific distributor.

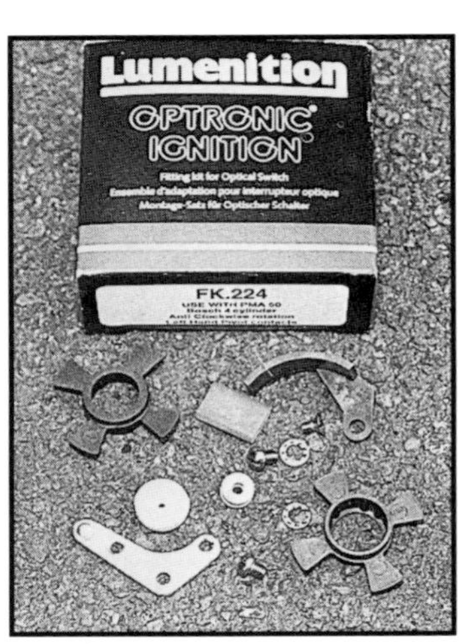

The advantages of using electronic ignition can be seen best by highlighting some of the problems caused by contact breaker points.

1 Bounce and Float
As the engine speed increases, it can be difficult for the contact points to follow the contour of the cam, and can cause bounce or float. This results in a loss of spark energy causing misfires, increased fuel consumption and increased exhaust emissions.

2 Arcing
At low engine speeds, arcing between the contact points causes inaccurate timing and loss of spark energy, most noticeable when the engine is reluctant to start on cold mornings.

3 Spark Scatter
Mechanical irregularities of the cam can be too great for the contact points to cope with. These cause spark scatter which results in rough running, incomplete combustion and poor fuel consumption.

Fitting electronic ignition

This diagram shows the simplicity of the overall wiring. The High Tension electrics on your car can be very dangerous! In some circumstances they could even kill! Damp conditions can make matters worse. Read your manual, the maker's safety notes and follow the rules for safe working.

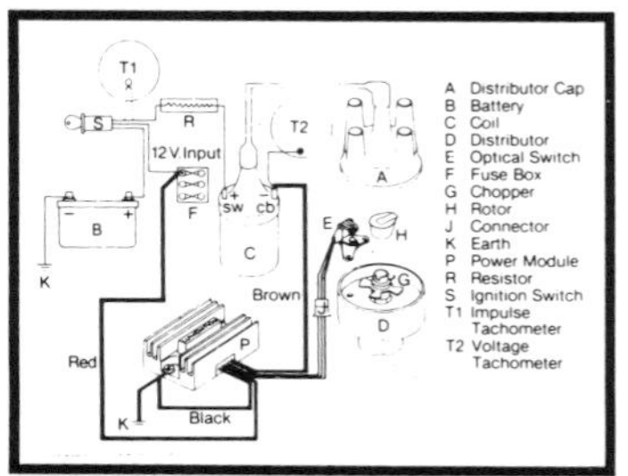

(Diagram courtesy Autocar Equipment)

The Lumenition Optronic system has been continuously developed for more than 20 years and is used by most Formula 3 racing cars! Fitted correctly, the system offers a reduction in petrol consumption, longer spark plug life, easier starting and reduced maintenance costs. All Lumenition components are covered by a comprehensive, three-year guarantee. It is extremely important that the battery be disconnected before fitting commences and that once fitted, care is taken whenever you are working in the engine compartment.

MU2.5
As the Fiesta distributor is somewhat hidden in the depths, this diagram shows more clearly the layout of the electronic system.
(Diagram courtesy Autocar Equipment)

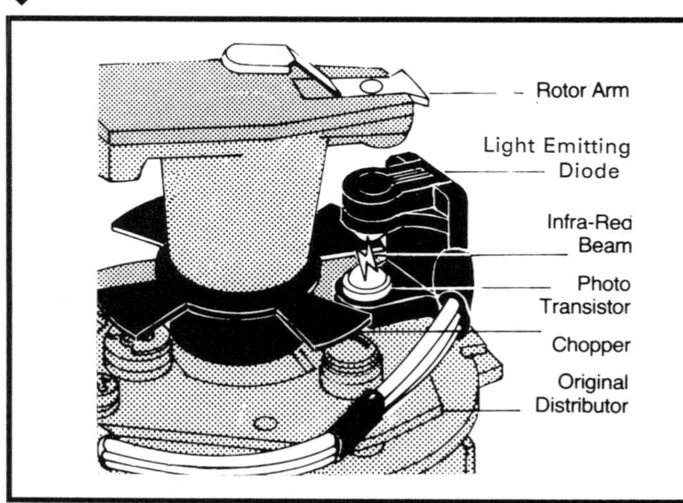

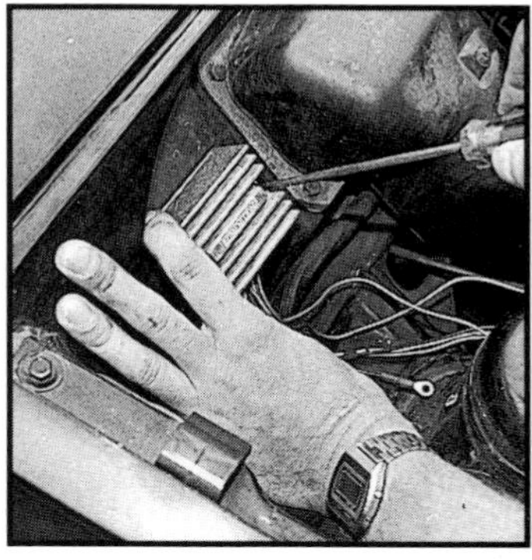

MU2.6
You have to find a dry place for the power module, close to the distributor but not the exhaust! This position on the offside bulkhead was ideal. Two small holes have to be drilled (and rustproofed) for the self-tapping screws.

Fitting an engine preheater (in cooling system)

The Kenlowe Engine pre-heater is an ingenious device which could save you a lot of trouble during the icy winter months and also save wear and tear on your engine throughout the year.

For correct operation, the car heater must be in the "on" position when the pre-heater is being used. All necessary connections for patching into the cooling system pipework are included in the kit.

Basically, the Kenlowe pre-heater is a pump and heater element which is mounted under the bonnet of your Fiesta. Approximately fifteen minutes before departure connect the appliance to your mains extension lead – the pre-heater then heats the water in the engine to 85°C. When you are ready to leave, the cable can be disconnected and your car is ready to go with a warmed up engine. All plugs and sockets and weather resistant housing are supplied and you can connect up to a standard household appliance timer the night before so it cuts out automatically just prior to departure.

The hot air heating and demisting, even on the shortest journey, are really useful, particularly in winter. However, one benefit not quite so obvious is that with the engine warm the choke will not need to come on, or, in the case of fuel injected models, the mixture need not be so rich. Thus, the usual early morning "washing of the bores" with excess petrol will not take place, saving much wear over a period of time. It could easily make a difference to overall engine life and to your fuel bill.

MU3.1
The Kenlowe kit complete, with the pump assembly in the centre. The kit includes all necessary clips and pipes.

MU3.2
Here, the pump assembly is being offered up under the bonnet of this XR2. Note that it ***must*** be installed this way up for it to function correctly. It has to be positioned below the level of the top hoses to avoid airlocks.

Fitting an oil cooler

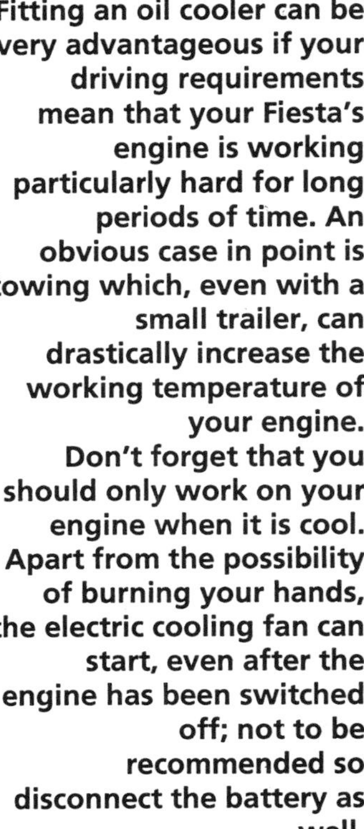

Fitting an oil cooler can be very advantageous if your driving requirements mean that your Fiesta's engine is working particularly hard for long periods of time. An obvious case in point is towing which, even with a small trailer, can drastically increase the working temperature of your engine.

Don't forget that you should only work on your engine when it is cool. Apart from the possibility of burning your hands, the electric cooling fan can start, even after the engine has been switched off; not to be recommended so disconnect the battery as well.

MU4.1
The DIY Clova cool kit comes as seen here, with cooler, piping, compression joints, brackets, fasteners and sandwich plate. Everything required, in fact.

MU4.2
The position of the cooler itself needs to be where it can receive a direct flow of cooling air. A tricky task on this XR2, but down on the nearside of the radiator should do nicely, although the horns will need repositioning. Before mounting the cooler, you should ensure that the routing of the pipework will not cause any problems.

MU4.3
Showing how to fit the thermostatic sandwich plate was going to be difficult due to its position. However ...

MU4.4
... Power Engineering came to the rescue and we were able to use one of the jig mounted engines for increased clarity. The sandwich plate fits between the oil filter and the engine block. There is a gasket supplied with the plate which must be fitted correctly in order to avoid leaks. The oil flows normally through the system without using the new cooler as long as the temperature remains fairly cool. However, when the temperature starts to rise, then the thermostat opens and allows oil to pass through the cooler.

Fitting an oil cooler

The Clova range of oil coolers uses the very latest in technology. The fluxless, high vacuum methods of brazing employed are cleaner, stronger and more efficient than old fashioned methods. Unlike some older designs, the top and bottom plates of the cooler are themselves oil carrying galleries. Extensive investigations into the optimum spacing of galleries (rows), fin pitch and turbulation have shown that size for size and row for row, the Clova cool units give better heat dissipation with less pressure drop than other units of comparable size.

MU4.5
A special adaptor is used in order that the oil filter can be screwed back into position as normal.

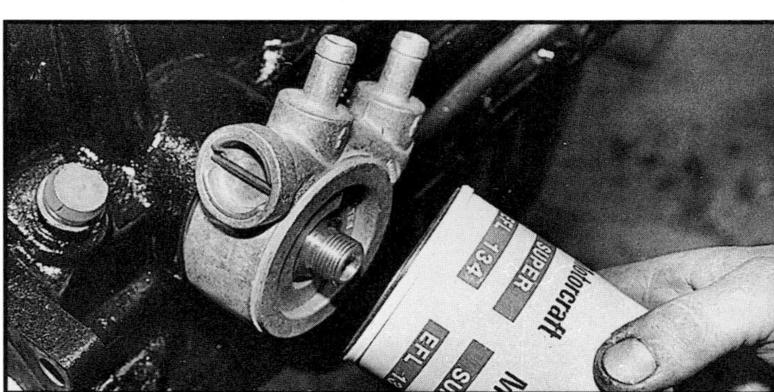

MU4.6
The half inch pipes have to be carefully measured and cut to size. They are connected here by pushing on and tightening a Jubilee clip. At the oil cooler, special angled compression joints are employed to similar effect. It is important that care be taken when tightening these to avoid damage to the joints, pipes or cooler itself. Also, you should ensure that the routing of the pipework has no sharp bends and does not foul other equipment.

MU4.7
Automatic transmissions lend themselves greatly to towing applications but the extra load can cause overheating of the gearbox oil and subsequent reliability problems. In fact, some 95 per cent of all automatic problems are caused by overheating and oil has been known to approach twice the average temperature under extreme conditions. Fitting a Pacet "Cooldrive" oil cooler can help ease the burden on the transmission. This diagram shows how the effects of increasing heat in the transmission can drastically reduce both reliability and performance.
(Diagram courtesy Pacet Products & Co. Ltd.)

Transmission Life Expectancy Chart

High Heat – Short Mileage
Transmission Temperature
315° (Seals, Clutches, Burn Out, Carbon Forms in Oil)
295° (Plates Slip)
260° (Seals Harden)
240° (Varnishes Form)
220°
195°
175°
Low Heat – Long Mileage
2000 4000 15000 25000 50000 120000 240000

MU4.8
Oil coolers operate best when placed in a direct cooling airstream, as can be seen in this diagram.
(Diagram courtesy Pacet Products & Co. Ltd.)

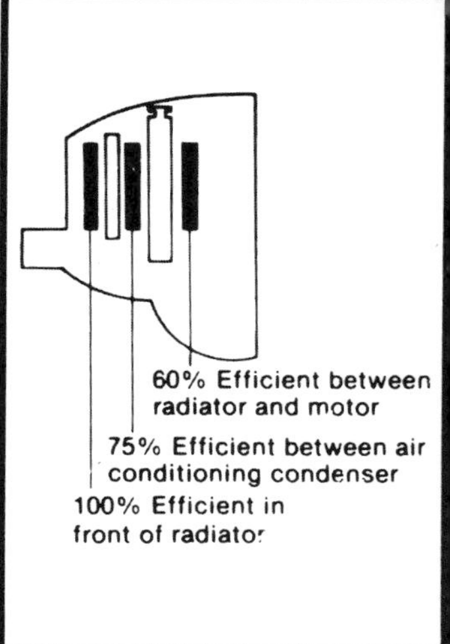

Improving the braking system

If you are thinking of making your Fiesta go faster, then you should take a look at improving your brakes first. When the Fiesta was introduced, a great deal of thought went into the design of the braking system. It must, however, be maintained in top condition and this is where many owners are found to be neglectful. A general visual check is your first task. Check around the brake pipes. After a while these tend to corrode and leak. If you have corrosion problems, skip straight to page 142 which deals with the fitting of copper brake pipes. Also check the routing of the pipes, which should be neatly positioned out of the way of anything harmful. If the pipes are all right, then check the areas around the wheel hubs. Are there any signs of brake fluid leakage? Older cars will often have worn wheel cylinder seals. If the hub area is particularly dirty then give it a good clean and then press the brake pedal several times. When you return under the car, you may see a leakage that wasn't obvious before.

By thoroughly checking the braking system and bringing it up to the manufacturer's original specification, you will, in effect, be uprating it in comparison to how it should have been when you bought the car! Ford have to be commended for their attitude to safety in making the Fiesta one of the first small cars in the world to be available with an optional low-cost anti-lock braking system. Unfortunately, this system is only available when the car is new, not as an after-market accessory.

Checking the braking system is a task you should carry out regularly, regardless of whether or not you intend to modify it in any way. Don't forget the safety rules when working under the car, making sure that it is well supported and that you have adequate hand and eye protection. Ideally, have a colleague close by just in case. Another tip; bear in mind that brake fluid (unless it is the Automec Silicone type) is potentially dangerous; keep it away from paintwork, skin and children!

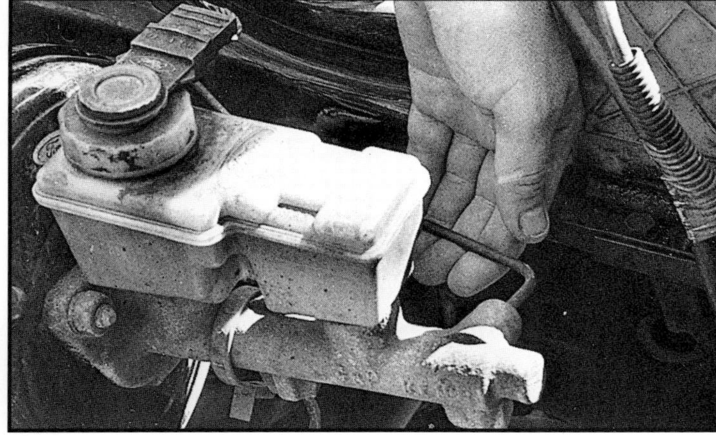

MU5.1
Check the master cylinder for leakage. Naturally, you must make sure that the master cylinder is correctly topped up with fluid and, for safety's sake, non-silicone fluid should be completely replaced every two years. See your Haynes manual for details.

MU5.2
Also, take a good look at the air lines from the servo. The hard life they have inside the engine bay can often lead to them cracking and allowing air to escape. Replacement is simple, although if the servo itself is found to be faulty, it cannot be repaired and a new one must be fitted.

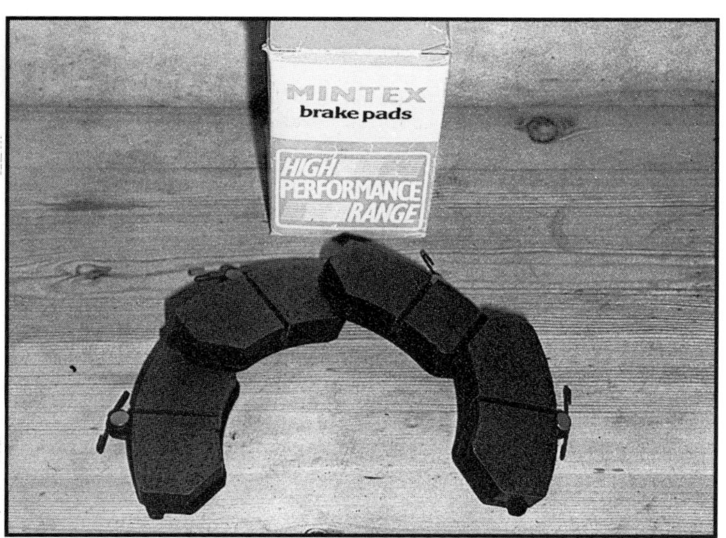

MU5.3
If you want to improve on pure stopping power, then fitting Mintex Don M171 brake pads will add some extra bite. If you are retaining the original specification pads and linings, then make sure that there is plenty of "meat" left on them. They're not expensive and regular replacement is always to be advised. Not doing so could cost you new discs and drums or worse, your life!

Fitting copper brake and petrol pipes

The best discs and pads in the world are not much use if your brake pipes are corroded. The only way to make sure that they don't corrode is to fit copper pipes, such as the Automec ones shown here.

Brake pipes are a sadly neglected area of car maintenance and, as David Power of Power Engineerin claims, it is largely a case of "out of sight, out of mind." The problem is, of course, that a damage or corroded brake pipe could lead to disastrous and tragic consequences. Even with a diagonally spl braking system, braking on two wheels is no substitute for braking on four; the system is meant fc emergencies only and neglect of your braking system is not an emergency, it is pure stupidity!

Fitting Automec copper brake pipes will ensure that they can never corrode and, to be totally saf silicone brake fluid will complete the system.

MU6.1
The Automec kits come complete and ready to fit. The lengths of copper pipe are the correct length but circular wound. Bending them to the correct shape is no problem, as we shall see later.

MU6.2
All pipes are clearly labelled as to where they fit and the brass unions have neat plastic protective caps to prevent them being damaged. It is a good move to leave these in place whilst you are measuring and bending the pipes, which also prevents dirt from getting in the threads or worse, in the pipes themselves.

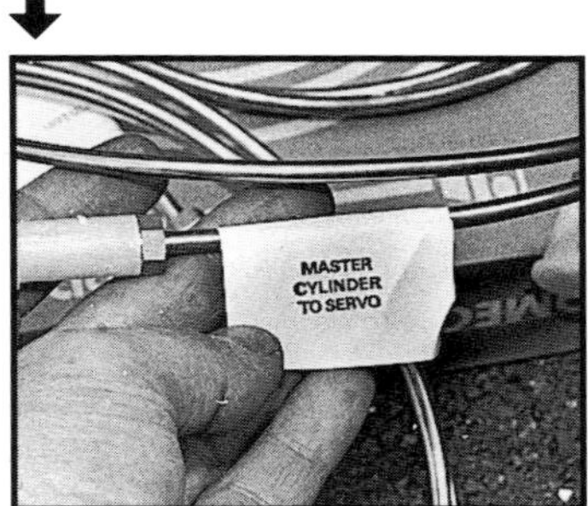

MU6.3
You can save yourself a lot of time and effort by stemming the flow of brake fluid with the Sykes-Pickavant hose clamp, which prevents any leakage. Thus, there is no need to bleed the system. However, it is a good idea to replace the fluid in the system totally when you have finished and ...

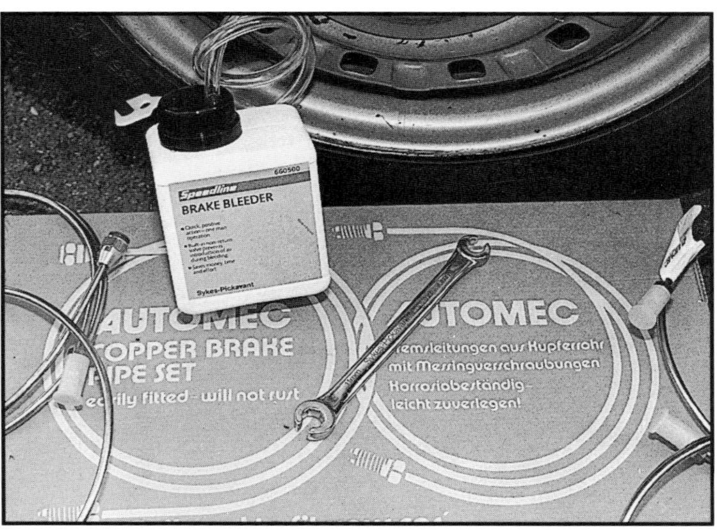

MU6.4
... if you decide to bleed your own system, there is one thing you can guarantee; no-one will be around to help by pushing the brake pedal! The simple answer is to use the Sykes-Pickavant one-man (or woman! brake bleeding kit. Also shown here is the Sykes-Pickavant brak pipe spanner of which more later.

MU6.5
Undoing the old unions is a task which should be approached with care. They are likely to be very reluctant to unscrew. Do not force them, however tempting it may seem. A dose of releasing agent and a little patience are far more effective. Using a purpose made brake spanner, like the Sykes-Pickavant one here, also makes life easier. Effectively, it is a ring spanner with a gap in it to allow the brake pipe to pass through. Alternatively, cut through the old pipe and use a ring spanner.

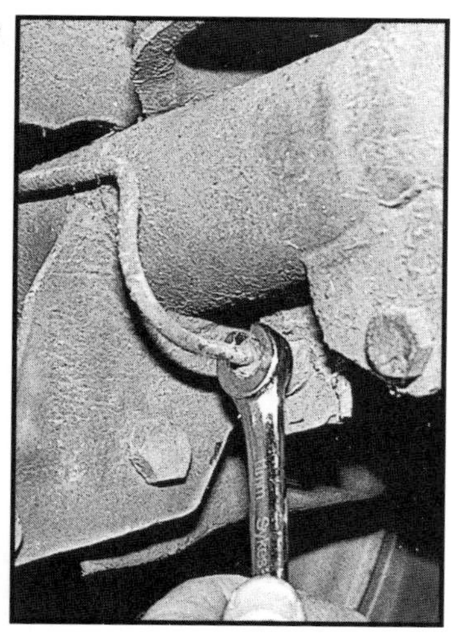

MU6.6
Once you have taken a section of pipe off, you should then bend the relevant new pipe to shape. Automec use copper, rather than anything else, largely because it is so malleable and easy to bend by hand to whatever shape is required. Take your time and make sure that you reproduce exactly the contours of the original pipe. Make equally sure that the new pipe cannot rub or chafe as the suspension works or on any moving parts. Keep it away from the exhaust.

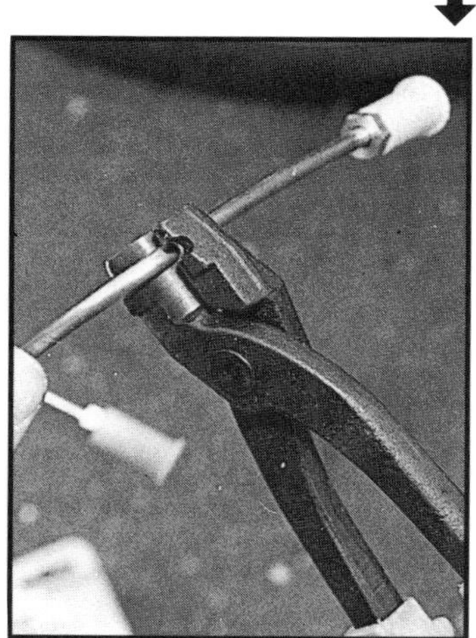

MU6.7
Once you are happy that the new pipe is exactly right, then you can fit it. Take care not to damage any of the threads as you screw on the brass union. It's easy to do and even a slightly damaged joint could result in a loss of fluid and, eventually, a loss of brakes! In this photo, you can see how the new pipe shapes up against the rusty original.

MU6.8
This diagram shows the location of the brake pipes on a Mk II Fiesta. Check your specific Haynes manual before you start dismantling your braking system!

(Diagram courtesy Haynes Publishing Group)

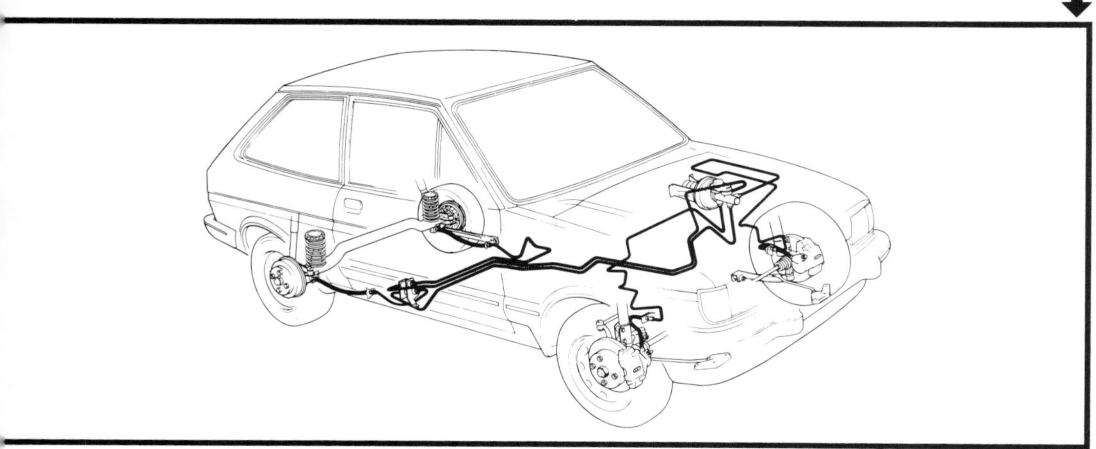

Clean! Clean! Clean! You must be almost surgical with regard to cleanliness when dealing with any part of your Fiesta's braking system. A speck of dirt in a brake pipe may seem insignificant, but it could ultimately cause untold damage, to you as well as your car. At the end of the day, if you are not totally confident that you can safely carry out the work on your car's braking system then *don't* attempt it! Even if you do all of your own work and do it properly, it would definitely pay dividends to have the job checked over by a qualified mechanic before venturing back out onto the highway.

As ever, working under the car demands the usual safety precautions with regard to ramps and axle stands and to the protection of your eyes from falling dirt and rust. *Never* work beneath a car supported only by the car jack, which is meant for emergency wheel changing only.

Fitting copper brake and petrol pipes

Automec Silicone Brake Fluid is non-hygroscopic; more simply, it does not attract or absorb water. This means that, unlike conventional fluids, it does not require changing every two years to prevent the risk of internal corrosion and the possibility of the water in the system turning to steam (because of the difference in boiling points) and leaving you with a distinct lack of brakes! Once silicone fluid is in the system, it is there for life. One extra advantage is that it will not harm your Fiesta's paintwork, unlike normal fluids which have an extremely corrosive nature. Whilst silicone fluid is completely compatible with conventional fluids, and can be used quite safely for topping up, adding normal fluid to a silicone system negates the use of using silicone fluid in the first place!

MU6.9
With the job finished, it is a wise move to check the brake fluid level. A change to silicone fluid is a wise move at any time and certainly if the fluid is two or three years old. Here, the Fiesta is being topped up with Automec's superb silicone brake fluid, described in detail elsewhere in this section. Note the plastic tag around the reservoir warning that ordinary fluid should not now be used.

MU6.10
Automec produce a range of copper pipe kits which enable you to replace the petrol pipes on your Fiesta. As you can see, the box contains all pipes and fittings required to complete the job and even ...

MU6.12
Having replaced the pipes, how about looking at what flows inside them? Little Big Shot from Mitchell Marketing is a petrol additive designed to clean and lubricate your engine. It comes in handy "one-shot" packs and you just pour it into the fuel tank when you've filled up and that's it.

MU6.11
... a special flexible screwdriver socket, ideal for those awkward to get at nuts and bolts.

MU7.1
In technical terms, Pacet solved the extremely difficult problems of fluid dynamics by creating a bell-shaped shroud and altering the skew of the blade fins to trap and move air with greater velocity. However, it requires less power to do so.
(Diagram courtesy Pacet Products & Co. Ltd.)

MU7.2
The Pacet Kit contains all you will need for DIY fitment. In fact, Pacet state that more than 80 per cent of these kits are fitted by the enthusiastic owner and that's no real surprise, for it isn't that difficult. One of the great points about the Pacet kit is that it requires no drilling or cutting near the radiator.

Although all Fiestas are fitted with electric fans, nothing lasts forever and when your fan does take a trip to that great scrapyard in the sky, it is a good time to Improve and Modify your cooling system. Fitting a Pacet Clovafan is claimed by the manufacturers to be highly beneficial, especially to your pocket! More horsepower, better fuel consumption and a quieter, more efficient engine are just some of the benefits claimed. The range of "Clovafan" units was developed over a period of two years in collaboration with the SCIRO Department of Energy and has produced a self-contained unit, mountable on either face, with specially designed mounting points and flexible "quick mounts", making installation straightforward and easy. The ratings of 60 per cent efficiency are very close to the theoretical maximum possible.

MU7.3
Before removing the original fan, disconnect the battery. Then, there are four, 10mm screws to be removed and ...

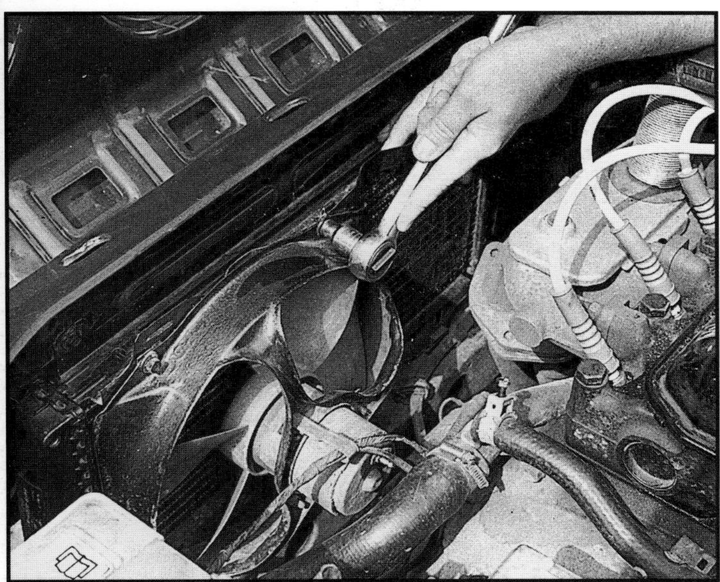

MU7.4
... this single electrical plug to be pulled away.

Fitting an electric fan

It may be obvious (to some) but a safety warning is never wasted. *Never* work on your engine when it is hot or even warm. A thermostatically-operated fan can start up many minutes after the engine has been switched off, and fans and fingers don't mix!

MU7.5
The Clovafan takes up the position of the original fan and is secured ...

MU7.6
... to the radiator by these plastic ties which are passed through to the Clovafan and then secured by the small, but very strong, discs.

MU7.7
The thermostat unit requires only simple wiring and the probe has to be inserted in the top radiator hose. It can be wired to either suck or blow, depending on whether the fan is affixed to the front or rear of the radiator. Having checked your connections, the system can then be set up by selecting the correct temperature for it to operate. The thermal switch is used to control the temperature at which the fan cuts in. This can be set by the owner and can be varied according to conditions. For example, if you are towing a caravan in summer then you will need a different setting to driving solo in the winter snow.

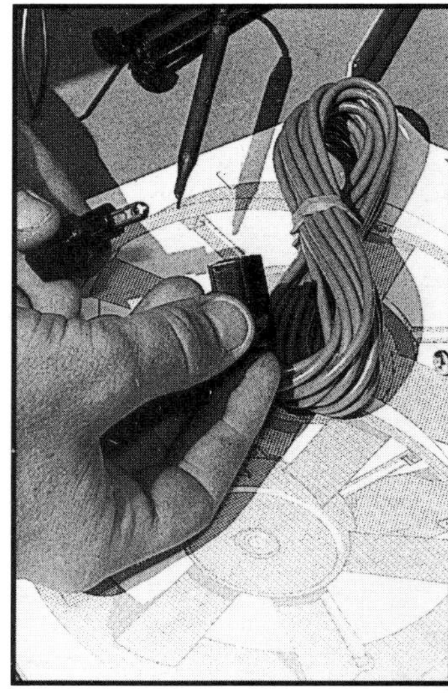

MU7.8
Full wiring instructions are given together with wire, connections and this very important, in-line fuse holder.

Fitting a Dellorto carburettor

Replacing the original carburettor may be necessary as old age takes its toll, particularly if your car is five years old or more. However, you may just want the extra benefits that the Dellorto unit can bring regardless of the age of your original carb. These benefits include an engine which breathes more easily, improved starting, idling, acceleration and economy and, state the manufacturers, up to 4bhp more at the wheels!

MU8.1
The Dellorto carb comes with everything required to fit it, including adaptors, gaskets, new choke cable assembly and full instructions. By their nature, carburettors are delicate instruments and so we were pleased to note that no re-jetting or other engine tuning is necessary. In addition, the Italian-made carbs have been specially prepared for the (RHD) UK market.

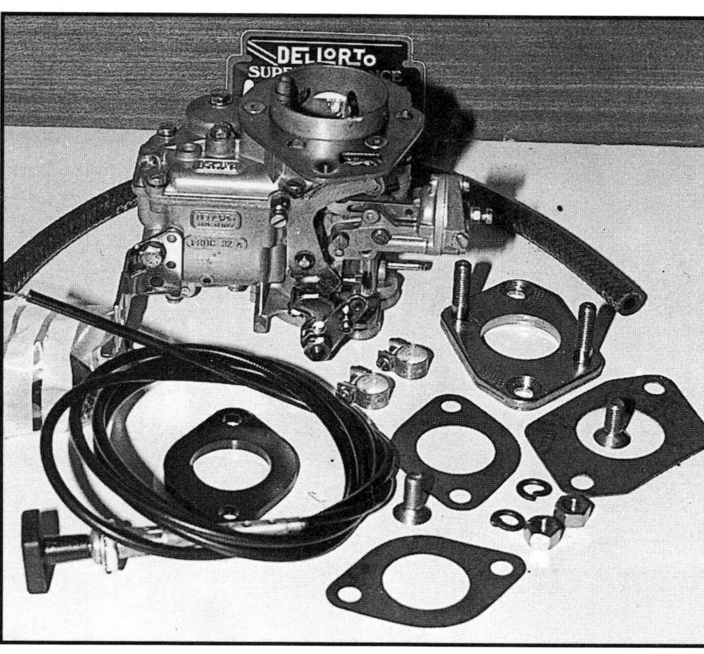

MU8.2
Removal of the original carb starts with the air cleaner which, on this model, is held by two screws on top.

MU8.3
The pipe for the vacuum advance unit has to be pulled off, as does the petrol pipe. Take care here not to spill any petrol. ***Note the safety advice given in the margin note!***

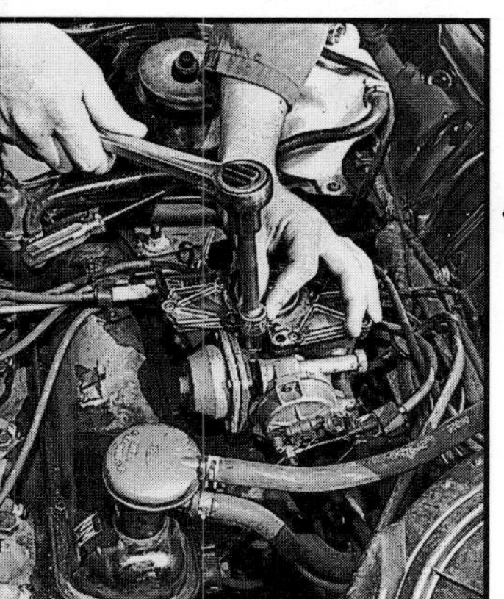

MU8.4
The Ford carburettor is secured with two 10mm nuts. There is enough room this side to use a socket with an extension, but you'll need an open ended spanner on the other side. Be careful that the latter does not slip and damage the nut or your fingers.

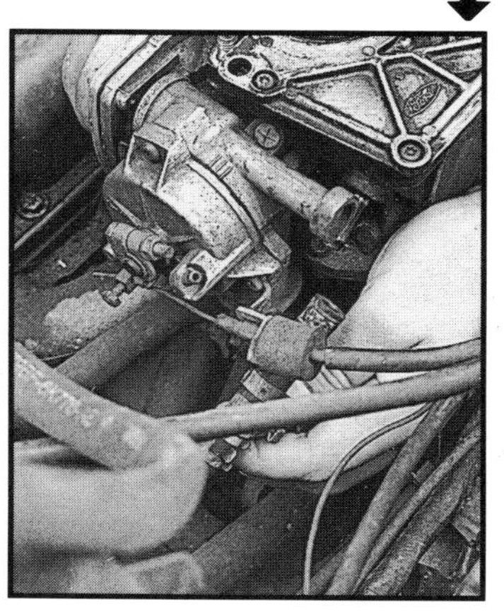

By their very nature, all carburettors need to be kept clean and on no account should anything other than fresh air and petrol be allowed to pass into them. If it does, it will then end up in the engine and you'll end up with a large invoice! Equally, petrol is the most volatile of liquids. When you're working with the fuel system, don't do it while the engine is warm, let alone hot, and don't smoke! Ideally, even following these precautions, you should have a fire extinguisher around, just in case.

Fitting a Dellorto carburettor

The Dellorto replacement kit comes with a manual choke cable. If you have a Fiesta which does not already have a choke cable (that is, fitted with an automatic choke), then you have the task of drilling the bulkhead and running the cable through. The important points here are that the cable should not to able to chafe on the new hole (fit a grommet) and that its routing should be totally smooth and kink-free. Also, as always in the engine compartment, try to avoid running the cable near sources of extreme heat or where it is likely to get very wet.

MU8.5
The throttle cable and the choke cable, shown here, have to be removed. Unlike the throttle cable, the choke cable remains on the same side on the new carburettor.

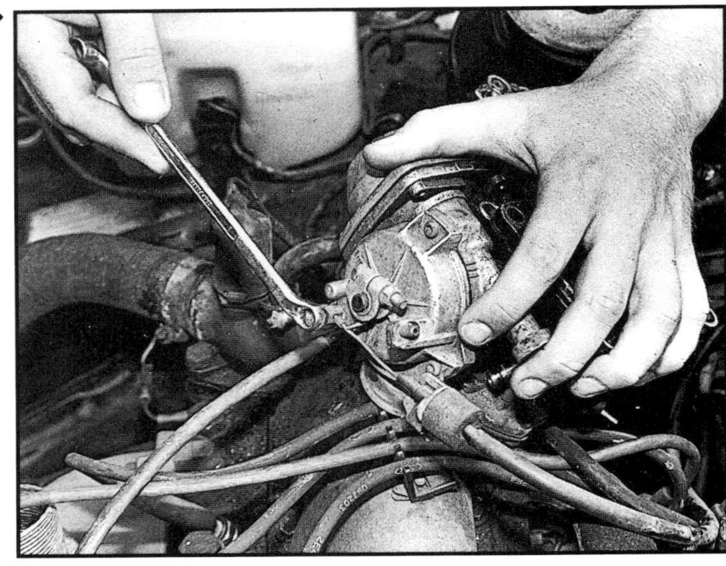

MU8.6
The studs have to be removed and you must be wary of using too much force, as it is easy to damage the aluminium manifold. Screw onto each stud in turn two 10mm nuts as far down as possible and lock the two nuts together. Apply a spanner to the lower of the two nuts and, with luck, the stud will be released and can be unscrewed from the manifold.

MU8.7
The Dellorto unit sits differently on the manifold and so this purpose-made adaptor is required. It is mounted in the original stud holes but using these countersunk set-screws with 5mm Allen key heads. A gasket is placed between the adaptor and the manifold.

MU8.8
With the adaptor in place, the Dellorto carb requires an open-ended spanner to tighten down the screws as there is not enough room to use a socket. Once again, care is needed to prevent rounding-off the heads or hurting your fingers.

MU8.9➡
The throttle cable has to be changed from the left- to the right-hand side on the new carburettor. There is plenty of cable to spare, but you must ensure that the routing does not produce any kinks or sharp bends. The small, plastic holder on the cable has to be gently prised from the Ford unit but is a tricky task, wearing on the patience and the fingernails!

Always use an air filter. It is quite easy to ruin not only the carb, but possibly the whole engine by running the engine without one. The engine might run better (though not necessarily), and it may sound better (noisier!), but its working life will be cut dramatically. See page 135 for uprated air filters.

MU8.10➡
Here you can see the T-piece in the petrol pipe. The original pipe in the Ford carb has to be removed and a new piece fitted to feed the petrol to the Dellorto unit. It is held at both T-piece and carburettor by small Jubilee clips which have to be nice and tight, for obvious reasons!

MU8.11
Dellorto supply a special lead to connect the cut-off solenoid on the new carb into the electrical system. However, in this case, the connector on the old lead was suitable and a simple push fit to connect.

⬅**MU8.12**
Whilst you have the air cleaner off, make sure that the choke is working correctly and will open the mechanism to its fullest extent, as shown here.

MU8.13➡
And that, apart from the air cleaner refitting, is that. You may find that after a test run some minor adjustments are needed to the carb. You may note that the spark plug leads on "our" Fiesta have apparently changed colour, this is because we took the opportunity to change them for Cosmic's silicone leads (see page 188).

Uprating the clutch

Having a powerful engine in your Fiesta is fine, but is only part of the overall tuning process. Tyres and suspension modifications (covered elsewhere in this Chapter) are important factors but everything is irrelevant if the power can't reach the road! Even with a fairly mild power increase, it would pay to use a tougher clutch, although Power Engineering's larger engines can hardly be said to be mild!

MU9.1
Power Engineering use clutch discs and covers originally intended for the Escort RS Turbo for uprating purposes. On the right is the unit from the Mk I Turbo, designed to take the increased power that this engine provides. On the left is the Mk II Turbo clutch and, as can be seen, is physically larger as well as having stronger springs. Early FWD Fiestas will take the Mk I Turbo clutch with no modifications, although using the Mk II version will require the fitment of a larger flywheel. Later models will take the Mk II Turbo clutch with no problem.

MU9.2
Power Engineering have found that the standard clutch release bearing is quite adequate for handling the increase in horsepower, although in all their conversions it is replaced as a matter of course.

MU9.3
This diagram shows the basic components of the Fiesta clutch system. Removal and replacement is covered in the Haynes manual. Replacement is an "engine out" job and not for the unskilled or ill-equipped. In essence, the clutch cover is bolted to the flywheel and the clutch disc is pressed up against the flywheel by the springs inside the cover assembly. Thus, the power is transferred to the road wheels by means of the frictional connection of the clutch disc. When this disc begins to wear, clutch slip occurs. To interrupt the transmission of power, the pressure plate must be lifted away from the clutch disc against the springs contained in the clutch cover. This is what happens when you press the clutch pedal – it forces a release bearing against the release levers (or diaphragm spring fingers) and the clutch disc is released.

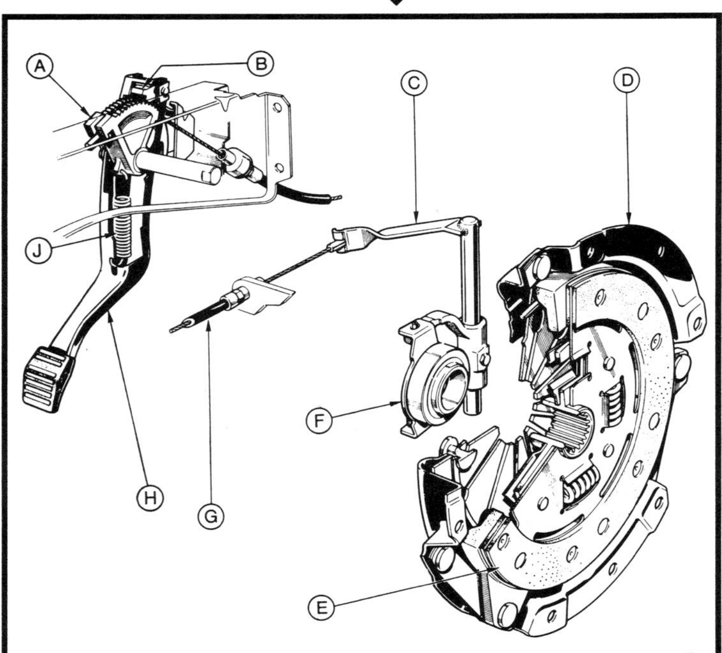

(Diagram courtesy Haynes Publishing Group)

Using Slick 50 oil treatment

MU10.1
The Slick 50 name is usually associated with the famous engine treatment, but there are, in fact, several products in the Slick 50 range, some of which are shown here. As well as the engine and gearbox additives, Slick 50 produce a PTFE enhanced grease for bearings and other long term lubrication requirements.

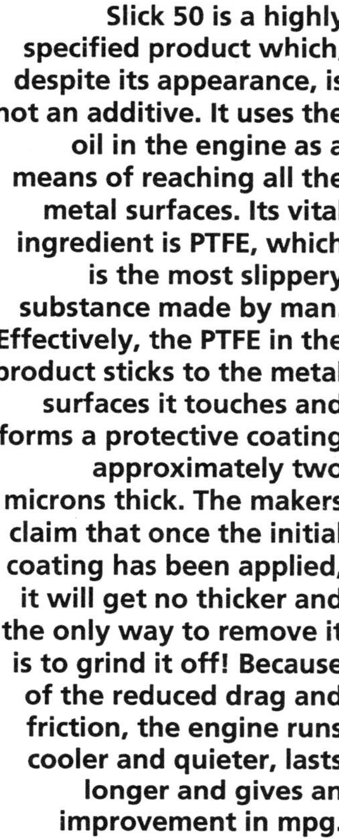

Slick 50 is a highly specified product which, despite its appearance, is not an additive. It uses the oil in the engine as a means of reaching all the metal surfaces. Its vital ingredient is PTFE, which is the most slippery substance made by man. Effectively, the PTFE in the product sticks to the metal surfaces it touches and forms a protective coating approximately two microns thick. The makers claim that once the initial coating has been applied, it will get no thicker and the only way to remove it is to grind it off! Because of the reduced drag and friction, the engine runs cooler and quieter, lasts longer and gives an improvement in mpg.

MU10.2
Adding Slick 50 to your Fiesta's engine oil is straightforward. Drain the oil when warm and fit a new filter. The plastic pack of Slick 50 should be shaken and, if the weather is cool, it should be immersed in warm water beforehand. The engine should be refilled (preferably using a branded product such as Duckhams) leaving enough room to add the Slick 50. ***Do not overfill.*** The manufacturers recommend an immediate journey of around 30 miles or leaving the engine on tickover for half an hour. After this, the engine will have received its coating of PTFE and further treatment with Slick 50 will not be necessary. Future oil changes can be carried out as normal.

MU10.3
Slick 50 also produce an aerosol can of their PTFE lubricant which is ideal for things like sliding window runners and throttle linkages. Door locks and hinges would also benefit as well as the bonnet catch shown here.

Engine conversion

This section deals with the process of producing a tuned engine for the Fiesta, either by using relatively mild tuning techniques or by converting the engine to a larger capacity. To establish exactly what is involved, we visited the Power Engineering headquarters in Uxbridge. Power Engineering have gained a reputation for producing excellent quality workmanship in their engine conversions. Formed by partners David Power and Richard Prior, the company enlisted the aid of Ian Swinyard as Development Engineer to produce their most impressive "System Two", a two litre conversion for the 1600cc CVH engine. This is the largest capacity conversion on the market at the time of writing. Power Engineering can tune any Fiesta engine, although they have spent a great deal of time (over nine months) developing a CVH conversion programme.

The System Two Conversion

This conversion forms the basis of Power Engineering's workload, and no wonder. The company started with the basic premise that the 1600cc, CVH engine in both carburettored and fuel injected form was not powerful enough. Although the most powerful Fiesta, the XR2's 96bhp is only enough to make it pleasantly lively when compared with the similarly sized Peugeot 205 GTi (with 105bhp) and the very powerful 1.9 GTi version with a stunning 130bhp on tap! So, at Power Engineering, the aim was two-fold; a) to increase the power output and b), increase the torque levels accordingly. It didn't take long for the company's researchers to decide that increasing the capacity was the best answer to the problem. During several visits to their Uxbridge workshops, we were able to see many engines at various stages of development, and to view the microscopic attention to detail that is so essential in this line of work.

MU11.1A
Parked outside Power Engineering's Uxbridge base, their XR2 demonstrator leaves the onlooker in no doubt at all as to what is under the bonnet!

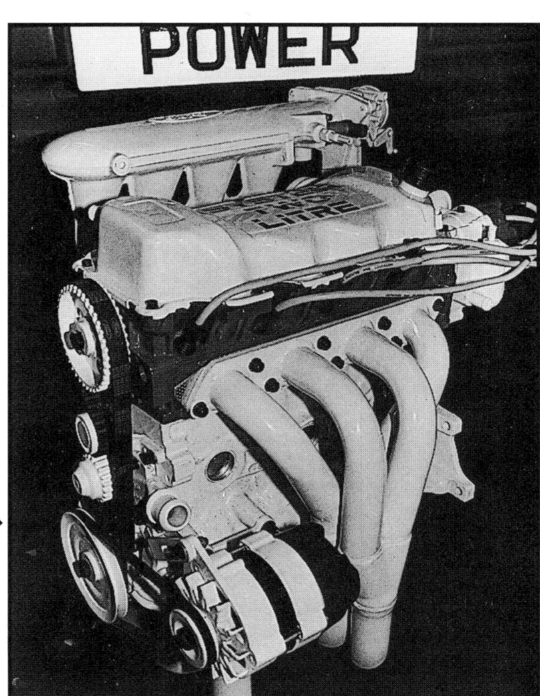

MU11.1B
This little beauty would add a little fire to your motoring life! The Power Engineering "System Two" engine in all its glory, although not normally available in white! This particular motor was a special, built for their display at the Racing Car Show.

MU11.2 ➡
Down to business ... when a customer's car is brought in for the "treatment", Ian first removes the engine from the car and then the road dirt from the engine to make life easier. Here, the rocker cover has been removed, and Ian has slackened the tensioner allowing the cam belt to be eased off.

It was also good to see that the company is progressing with a DIY engine conversion programme, enabling the skilled enthusiast to save on fitting costs by having the uprated parts delivered to his doorstep. We must emphasize, however, the word "skilled". If your technical expertise stops at changing the oil and checking a spark plug, you would be well advised to let the professionals do the job or be prepared to learn fast!

⬅ **MU11.3**
Off with its head! Removing the cylinder head is next. All the bolts have to be removed and then they ***must*** be thrown away, for they are stretch bolts and can only be used once. The washers, however, can be cleaned and re-used.

MU11.4 ➡
On checking the head, the engine appears to have been running quite well, with little carbon build-up and the valves an even brown colour.

Deciding which tuning package to choose involves many elements of personal preference and, of course, personal finances! As mentioned, much of the Power Engineering workload comprises their "System Two" conversion, but they can perform any tuning operation to suit the customer's needs.

MU11.5
Cylinder heads are made of relatively soft aluminium and can easily be damaged. Ian uses the Sykes-Pickavant cylinder head stand for holding the head whilst it is being worked on.

MU11.6
With the head on the stand and out of the way, the cylinder head/block locating dowels can be eased out and the head gasket taken off. This is another item heading for the Power Engineering rubbish bin, as head gaskets should never be re-used.

MU11.7
Removing the sump involves inverting the block and the prior removal of no less than 18 bolts. Obviously, Ian had drained the oil before commencing work! Even so, there is usually a little residue, so it pays to have a drip tray handy. With the sump on the workbench, Ian pulls the sump gasket away. There are two kinds; earlier models had gaskets with cork sides and rubber ends, whereas the later versions are all rubber. In the latter, there are holes which locate on pegs in the sump and prevent the bolt tightening pressure from damaging the gasket and causing leaks.

MU11.8 ➡
Removal of the front pulley involves jamming the crank with something such as a hammer shaft. The pulley should slide off easily, but can often be reluctant. Gentle prising with a pair of large screwdrivers is the answer, taking care not to damage the pulley.

MU11.9
This then allows access to the plastic timing belt cover which allows removal of the belt, followed by the belt pulley together with the rear washer. Note that this washer is dished and must be refitted in the correct manner, otherwise it will destroy the belt.
⬇

⬆
MU11.10
Oil pump replacement is part of the standard procedure with the "System Two" engine. The pick-up pipe has to come off so that the oil pump can be removed. Again, the drip tray has to be ready, as there could still be a little oil remaining in the system from the oil galleries. This is followed by the water pump which is also discarded, as it is replaced when the engine is rebuilt.

⬆
MU11.11
Here, the oil seal and carrier have been taken off (to allow the crankshaft to come away when the time comes), and the big-end caps are being removed. Note that they are numbered, so some care must be taken to ensure they are refitted in the same order as removed.

The two-litre "System Two" conversions offer a power output of around 135bhp, which is comparable with the 132bhp turned out by the Fiesta's big brother, the Escort RS Turbo, and represents nearly a 50 per cent increase over the standard XR2. If such an amount of power is your goal, then it could well prove to be more cost effective to look at a conversion of your present car rather than trading it in for a more expensive, and not so powerful car. For comparison, Power Engineering also work their magic on the Escort Turbo which increases the output to a heady 165bhp!

At every stage of preparation, whether the tuning is minor or a full engine conversion, Power Engineering make cleaniness the key word. Not only with regard to the engine itself but also the equipment used. Small particles of dirt included inadvertently in a rebuilt engine will cause rapid wear, and a decline in performance will result. Before entrusting your pride and joy to anyone for engine work (of any description), take a good look at the workshop first; if it is dirty and unkempt, take your valuable custom elsewhere!

MU11.12
The piston and con-rod have to be gently withdrawn. It is quite common for the piston to stick due to a step worn in the top of the cylinder bore or a build-up of excess carbon. If this happens then it is permissible to tap the assembly lightly with a hammer shaft. This particular engine was allowed to run very hot for a while (no water!) and, as a result, this piston has been very badly scored down the side.

MU11.13
With the engine once again inverted, the main bearing cap bolts can be undone and removed which allows ...

MU11.14
... the crankshaft to be lifted out. It's far from light and so Ian makes sure that he has somewhere to put it before he begins to lift! In this case, it is heading for the Power Engineering bath, where it will be given a good clean with solvent.

MU11.15
Almost there, as Ian removes the baffle (which is positioned next to an oil breather pipe and prevents oil surging back up it). After this, all that remains is to remove the oil gallery plug and core plugs. Some engine builders leave the core plugs in place. However, Power Engineering have found that the solvent cleaning agent used only softens the dirt behind the plugs, rather than washing it away. Thus, when the engine is rebuilt, the debris is swept back into the new motor where it is able to cause irreparable damage ... and all for the cost of a core plug!

MU11.16
The uprated flat-top pistons used in this conversion are made by Mahle, and are specific to the Power Engineering "System Two" engine. They are made of a special aluminium alloy and have large steel insert struts, which control the amount by which the pistons are allowed to expand when they get hot. In addition, they allow closer tolerances between the pistons and the cylinder walls, which in turn produces a quieter engine with a reduced appetite for oil. Note the difference in the new piston, shown on the right, and the old, alongside. Normally aspirated (whether carburettor or fuel injected) engines have a crankshaft stroke of 88mm and a piston diameter of 84mm, giving a new engine capacity of 1951cc and a compression ratio of 9.55:1.

MU11.17
It is interesting to note that Power Engineering's other "System Two" conversion is performed on the Turbo engine from the Escort. In order to maintain the same level of reliability as the motor used in the Fiesta, certain concessions have had to be made. In this case, a slightly smaller piston diameter is used (83mm) giving a new capacity of 1905cc and a compression ratio of 8.2:1. Here, the turbo piston can be seen on the right, next to a "standard" two-litre version. As can be seen, it is different in having a small dish in the top.

MU11.18
Clean! Clean! Clean! Ian prepares to assemble an engine, starting with a gleaming re-worked block. After the new core and gallery plugs have been fitted, the new main bearing shells are placed in the block "dry", and are then oiled on the bearing surfaces before ...

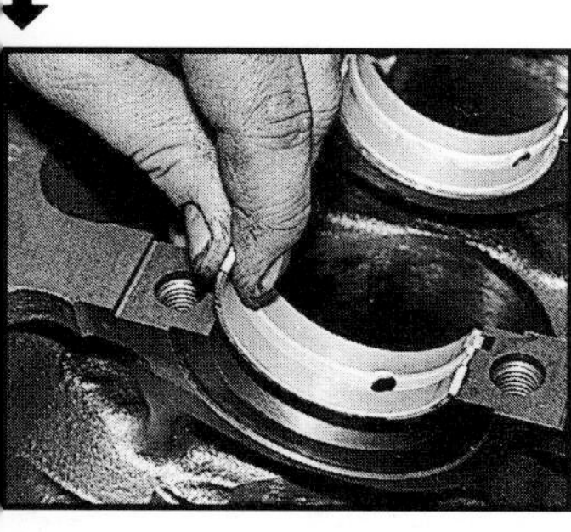

MU11.19
... the highly polished new crankshaft can be lowered carefully into position. Even more important now, the emphasis is on keeping everything clean; even the smallest amounts of swarf could eventually lead to the premature ruin of a new engine.

One way to ruin any engine tuning exercise is to use "cheap-'n'-nasty" pattern parts. Power Engineering use only what they consider to be the best. This will seldom mean that they're the cheapest, but the M25 hard shoulder is littered with those who thought they could save a pound or two by using pattern parts ...

Power Engineering use high quality tools to match the quality of the parts they fit. Sykes-Pickavant tools are among the best, although not necessarily the most expensive. The use of *cheap* hand tools is a false economy.

MU11.20
The thrust washers are fitted, with Ian taking care to ensure that the oil slots are facing the crankshaft.

MU11.21
With a new crankshaft, the tolerances should be absolutely spot-on, but perfectionist Ian checks them anyway.

MU11.22
A light coating of oil to both pieces is required when fitting the main bearing caps over the shells.

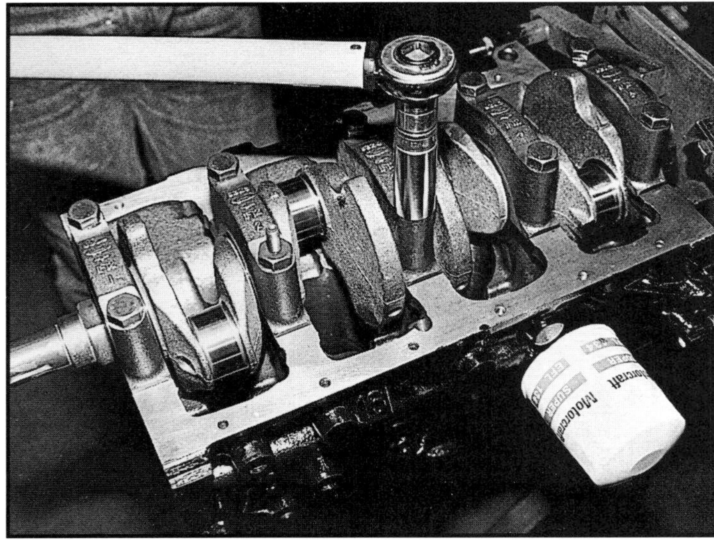

MU11.23
It is absolutely essential that everything is tightened to the exact torque figure recommended. The Sykes-Pickavant torque wrench is invaluable at this stage of tightening the main bearing cap bolts; too little or too much could be equally disastrous.

The component list for the "System Two" conversion is most impressive, with the following being just a few of the items fitted new: rocker cover gasket, exhaust manifold gasket, water pump, oil pump, timing belt, spark plugs, head bolts, inlet manifold gasket, head gasket, special cylinder sleeves, piston rings, pistons, connecting rods, big-end bearings, main bearings, small end bearings, crankshaft, oil filter and so on.

Although any engine *can* be tuned, Power Engineering will cheerfully advise that uprating the smaller engined Fiestas is not particularly cost effective. In most cases, trading up for a larger engined car would be a better proposition.

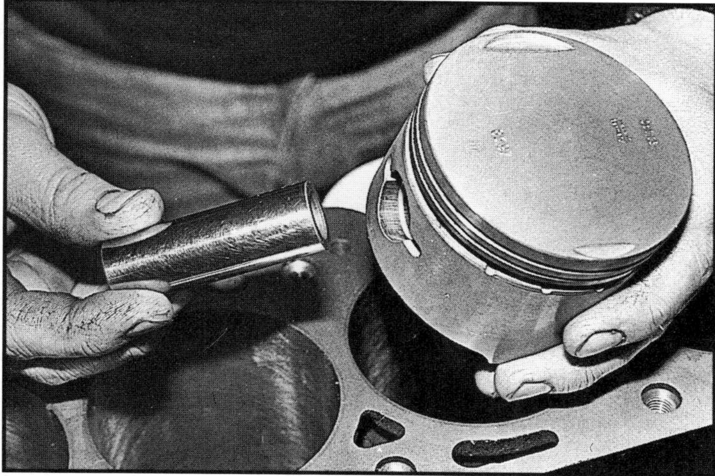

MU11.24
The Mahle pistons are fitted with fully floating gudgeon pins, meaning that they can accept higher loads than the normal press-fit type.

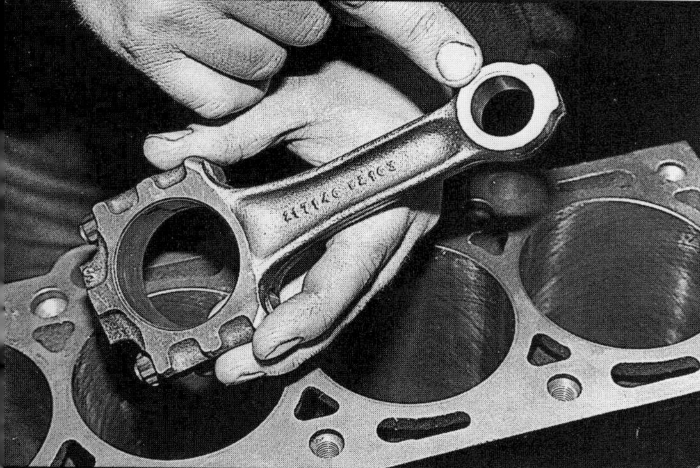

MU11.25
New forged connecting rods are fitted and have phosphor bronze little end bearings.

MU11.26
Use of a piston ring compressor – Sykes-Pickavant to the fore, once more – is essential when fitting pistons. Tighten the compressor around the rings, place the piston over the bore and tap carefully into place with the wooden handle of a hammer.

MU11.27
The Sykes-Pickavant torque wrench comes into play once more when tightening up the big-end bearing cap bolts. It is a good idea to turn the crankshaft after tightening each one – that way you can identify a tight bearing.

Engine conversion

As mentioned previously, Power Engineering can, and often do, supply their "System Two" conversions for DIY fitment. Removing your Fiesta's engine is not as difficult as it sounds; with a systematical approach and the right tools, it is well within the capabilities of the competent DIY mechanic. Refer to your Haynes manual for full details of the work involved.

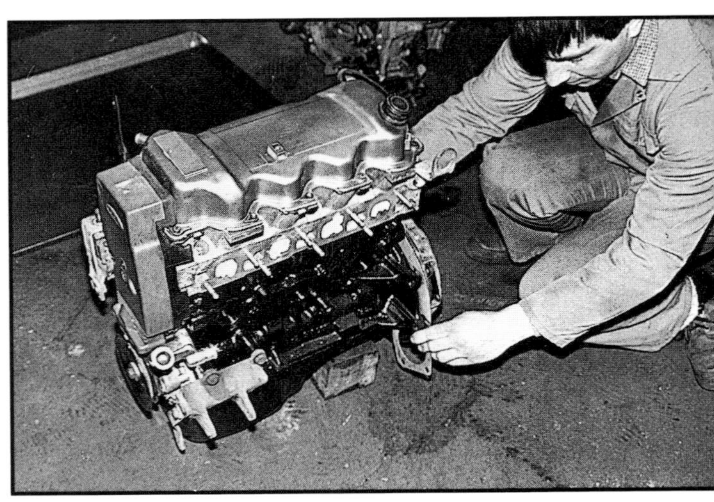

MU11.28
When the engine has been thoroughly checked and tested, it is ready to be refitted into the Fiesta. Here, Richard Prior is preparing to fit the gearbox to the uprated engine.

MU11.29
Note how clean the gearbox is. Such attention to detail will pay dividends.

MU11.30
In order to get the engine into the correct position under the engine bay of the XR2, the hoist is used (along with a little manpower!) to ease the unit on to a steel tray, which is then slid back as required.

MU11.31➡
Then the Clarke Strongarm engine hoist is re-attached and used to bring the engine gently up into the engine bay.

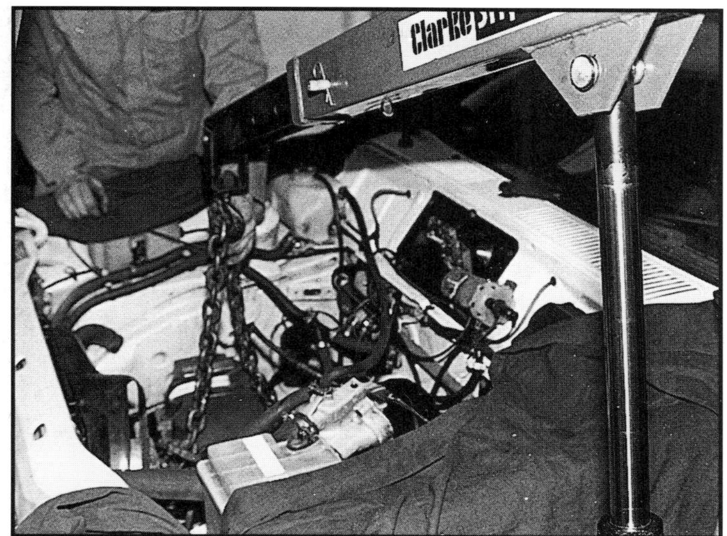

If you are removing and fitting your own engine, then masking tape and a marker should be used to label every wire and pipe you disconnect. In addition, it is a wise move to keep a clearly labelled set of boxes and tins containing all the nuts and bolts you remove.

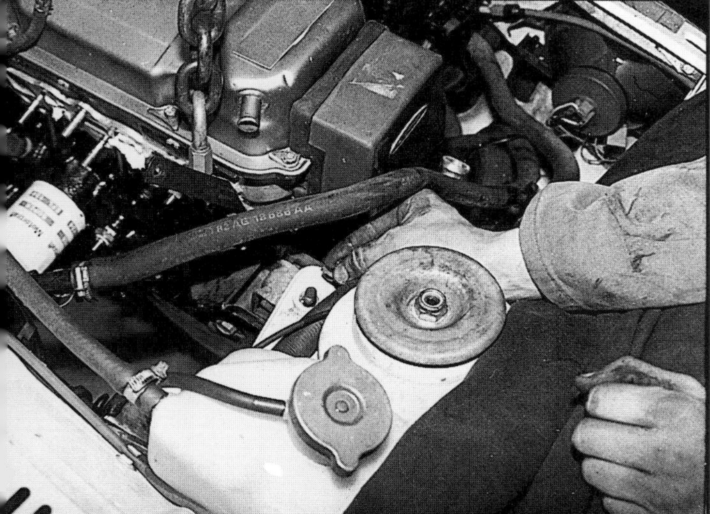

⬅MU11.32
The first engine mounting is located on the offside of the car. Once this is in and a nut screwed on, the engine is pulled up further which allows ...

MU11.33➡
... the lower crossmember to be fitted to the gearbox. In essence, all that remains to actually install the engine is to locate and tighten the remaining engine mounting which passes through the inner wing. However, connecting up the various ancillaries (driveshafts, electrics and so on), is another matter and is a work of art in itself. Again, referring to your Haynes manual will show the correct procedures where final fitting is concerned.

Engine conversion

Another question often asked is whether or not it is possible to uprate a Fiesta by fitting a larger capacity, standard engine. As the basic design of the FWD Fiesta has remained the same, it is theoretically possible to swap a smaller engine for a larger one. However, you have to be aware that changing an engine ideally requires some specialised equipment (such as hoists), a fair amount of room and no small amount of skill. Equally, if you are installing, say, a 1.6 litre engine in a 1.1 litre car, you should uprate all ancillary parts, including exhaust, brakes, wheels, tyres, engine mounts and so on, as well as the gearbox and differential. Changing to a fuel injected engine from a carburettored version is particularly tricky and, let us say, expensive. As with any such modification, an engine change will probably be frowned upon by your insurance company who will usually require a higher premium; insurers prefer standard cars. Overall, there are likely to be few cases where the cost and effort required to effect a "standard" engine swap will be financially viable. Certainly, the general advice from Power Engineering is to sell your standard smaller engined car and buy a standard, larger engined one.

MU11.34 A simple way to "tune" your engine is to help it breathe more easily. Available for either the "System Two" conversion or as a modification to a standard car, the Power Engineering stage three head will certainly increase your pulling power. A finished head is shown here on the right, alongside a standard head just removed from a customer's car.

MU11.35 All inner surfaces are painstakingly polished in order to provide a much better gas flow. The valve throat area is increased by some 11.5 per cent.

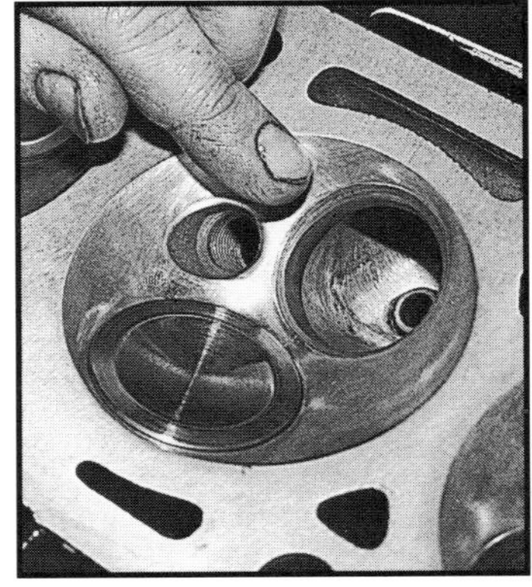

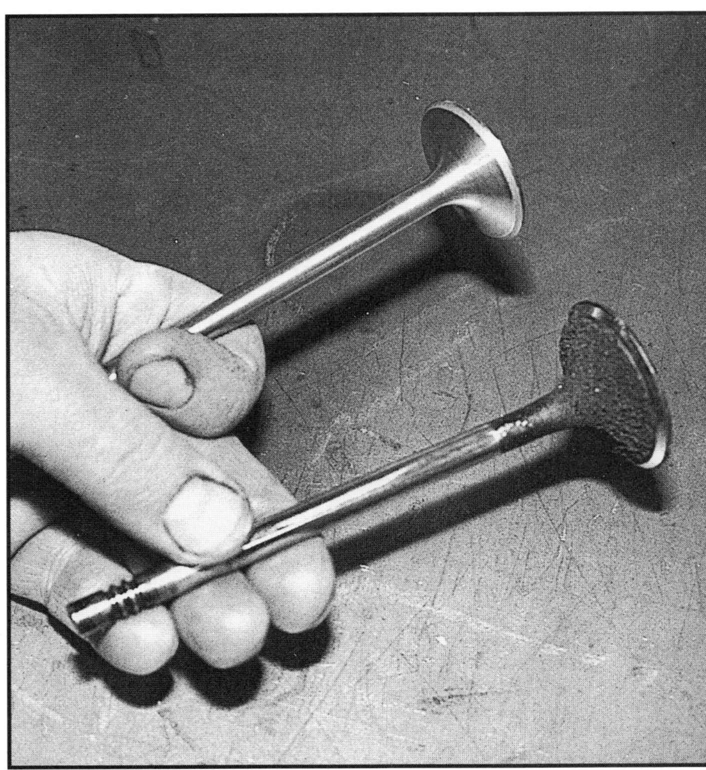

MU11.36 The stage three head uses superb, stainless steel valves, again highly polished. In case you haven't guessed, the lower valve here is a used one, shown for comparison!

MU11.37 ➡
Removing and replacing valves is always made easier by using the Sykes-Pickavant valve spring compressor.

Power Engineering always stress, as do we, the need to bear in mind the effect a power uprate or engine conversion can have on the rest of the car. In particular, the clutch, suspension and brakes should be modified to suit and, in fact, they should have been uprated *before* the power increase. The tyres may well be illegal if your car has had a large power increase (speed ratings – see page 179) and with an uprated suspension, lower profile rubber may well be required in order to make the most of the increased performance.

⬅ **MU11.38**
The stage three head has its exhaust ports widened, as can be seen here, with the standard head underneath. The exhaust manifold now takes the larger Turbo gasket.

MU11.39 ➡
A lot of work has gone into polishing these inlet ports to this mirror-like finish. They are also enlarged to exactly match the standard inlet manifold gasket.

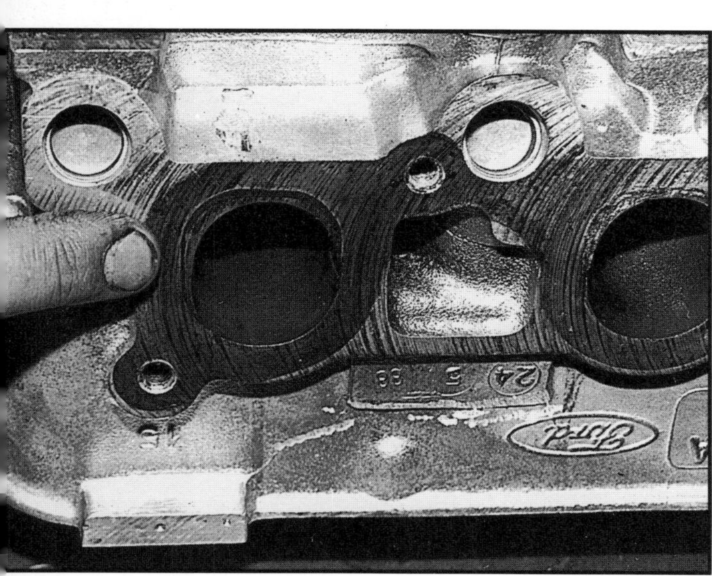

⬅ **MU11.40**
As with any car, the match between mass-produced parts is only approximate, and the marks left by the gasket can be seen on this standard head.

You must always remember to inform your insurers that you intend to modify your car. Many companies will refuse point-blank to have anything to do with uprated engines and it is best to know beforehand; driving without insurance is not only reckless and stupid, it's also illegal! Some companies will only insure such a vehicle after an independent engineer's report. Where a large power increase is in evidence, some companies may *insist* that other items (brakes, suspension and so on) are uprated accordingly. Remember that policies are issued on trust and that not declaring modifications, however small, could lead to the policy being declared void in the event of a claim. Void insurance is no insurance, and that, too, is illegal!

MU11.41
For pure performance, how about a couple of these beauties! Twin Dellorto DHLA 45 carburettors should improve your engine's power output and top speed ... but watch your fuel consumption!

MU11.42
They will, of course, need this special manifold in order to fit your existing engine. You would be most unwise to go to the expense of fitting carburettors of this nature without some thought for the rest of the engine, particularly if it has covered more than 20,000 miles.

Driving Impressions

Driving the "System Two" Fiesta is a revelation. Turning the key snaps the engine into life instantly and the healthy rasp from the Ansa exhaust tells the driver (and onlookers) that all is not standard on this one of Henry's offspring! In real terms, the biggest test of any uprated engine is not the top-end performance figure, but quite the opposite; how the car behaves itself in traffic and the more mundane driving situations. The two-litre Fiesta burbles gently away from rest with barely a trace of throttle movement, and a little restraint proves the engine to be as docile as the humblest 950cc shopper. Mid-range torque is massively improved, with third being the optimum gear for most urban situations.

However, this car is a true Jekyll and Hyde, sprouting its extra facial hair and fangs at the twitch of an impatient right foot. Applying such pressure in whatever gear, pushes your head towards the headrest and has your hand reaching for the next gear as the tachometer needle attempts to bury itself in the red zone. A watchful eye has to be kept on the speedometer, for this car is capable of defeating any UK speed limit in less than 10 seconds. At motorway speeds, the torque of the big engine again makes itself felt, with overtaking being simply a matter of operating the accelerator pedal; no gear changing, regardless of initial velocity, is required.

The demonstrator has been treated to a Spax suspension uprate and as such, the handling of the car is impeccable.

We must emphasise that the engine conversion should be viewed as just one part of a whole package; increasing the performance capabilities of a car does not just involve going quicker in a straight line.

Naturally, Power Engineering take great care to ensure that the braking system, including discs, pads, brake lines and silicone fluid, are absolutely spot-on. Wheels and tyres are standard and on our short test drive seemed to be well up to the task of holding the car on course. An increase in tyre and wheel size would be a matter for the individual and would depend on personal choice and usage.

For those who have, for instance, a three-year old XR2 and would like the extra power of the Escort XR3i or even the RS Turbo, but lack the cash, the Power Engineering "System Two" engine uprate offers an intriguing alternative and, given the disadvantages of turbo lag and the fact that the two-litre car produces more power and torque, it would be quite a choice to have!

Regardless of what car you are buying, it is not wise to take just the seller's word for its performance and capabilities. However, a flick through the motoring press will soon confirm that the "System Two" engines are held in very high regard by the often critical motoring journalists. When your job includes testing all manner of exotica, praise for this engine is high indeed.

Fitting a free-flow exhaust system

Fitting a less restrictive exhaust system is one of the simplest ways to extract a few more horses from your Fiesta's power plant. At Power Engineering, they topped off their big bore conversion with an Ansa exhaust system which allows the engine to breathe more easily and thus release even more power! The Power Engineering mechanics made life much easier for themselves by "mock" fitting the new system together whilst it was off the car and sanding down any joints that were not an easy push fit. It's a lot easier on the deck than in the air!

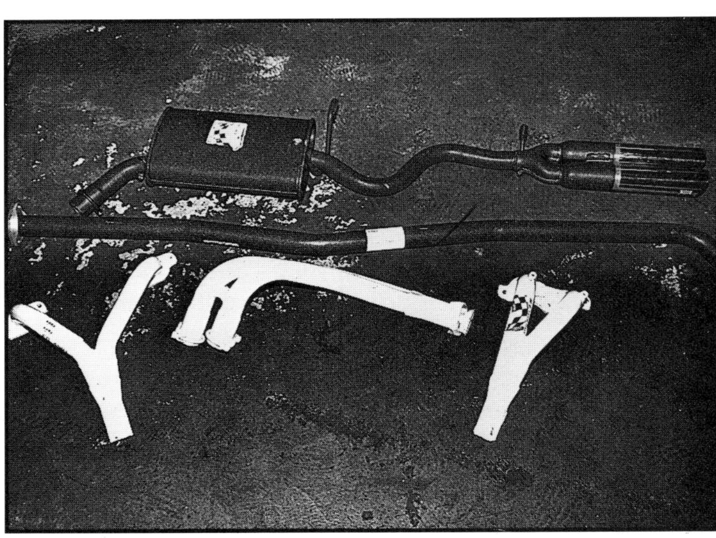

MU12.1 The basic Ansa system for the XR2 comprises these five pieces, with the manifold being in two sections.

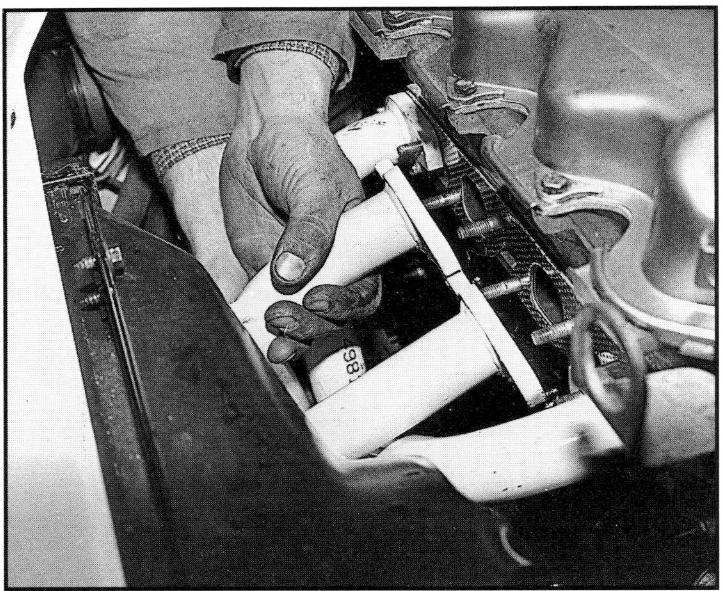

MU12.2 This particular engine was newly installed and so the worst part was over; removing the old exhaust! If you are removing your old system, remember that it will probably be well rusted and that you will need lots of releasing agent, patience and eye and hand protection. The two section manifold is installed with the outer pipes first, followed by the two inner ones.

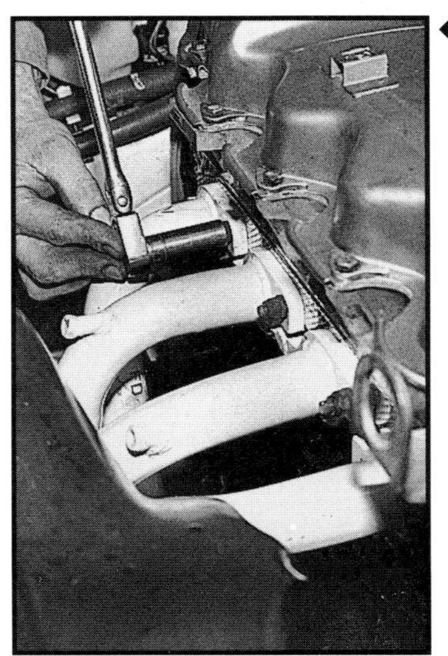

MU12.3 Tightening up should be done steadily, working crossways and having due care and consideration for that aluminium cylinder head. The Ansa manifold looks striking in white.

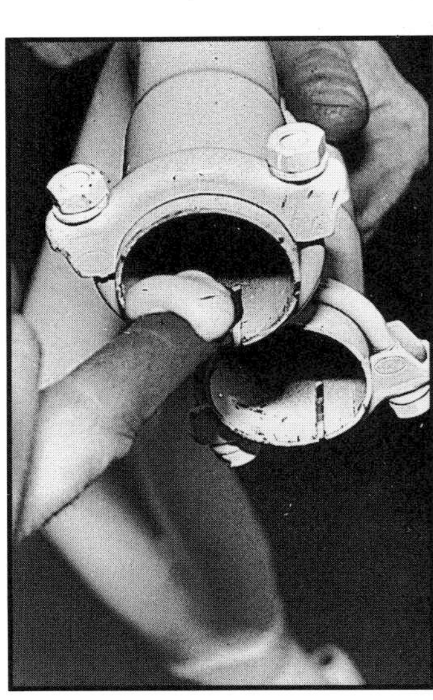

MU12.4 Before fitting the first section of the exhaust, a sealant is smeared on and ...

MU12.5
... then it can be offered up as shown. The wisdom in "pre-fitting" the system whilst it's off the car now becomes apparent!

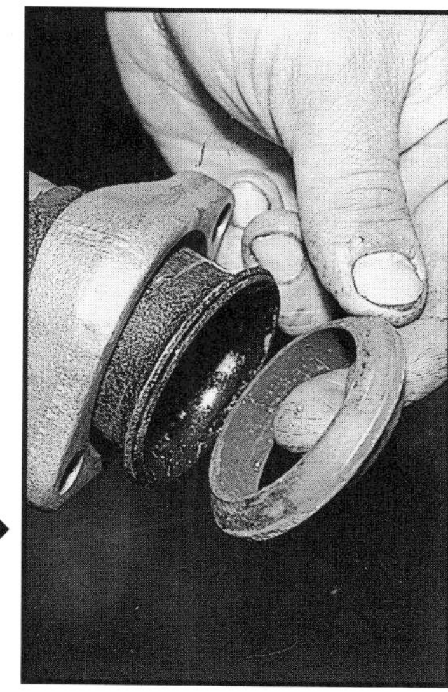

MU12.6
The sealing rings in all joints have to be correctly installed in order to prevent any dangerous, power-sapping leaks.

MU12.7
All joints must be tightened up fully. In order to keep the system at the correct angle, a helper is useful to steady the system at the rear.

MU12.8
It's a good idea to replace the rubber mounting for the last section. As you can see, it sometimes requires a little persuasion! Note that a copper hammer only should be used if this is necessary.

MU12.9
The throaty rasp of the Ansa twin pipes is music to the ears of many owners!

Whether you have your exhaust fitted for you or whether you fit it yourself, it is vital that you take the trouble to have your engine and new system properly set-up on diagnostic equipment. A meaty system like the Ansa will undoubtedly change many of the settings. Not checking them could result in an inefficient engine and an engine which is causing excess pollution.

How the suspension works

From page 170 onward we cover what is involved in replacing a standard suspension set-up with a Spax Sporting kit. However, it helps to be able to relate the modified suspension components to those of the standard suspension.

A great deal of thought should be given to exactly which sort of suspension to fit to your Fiesta. It is possible to "mix-n-match" springs and dampers in order to obtain the ideal set-up for your needs (such as sports dampers, but with more forgiving springs). However, unless you are particularly skilled in this area, we would recommend that you consult a specialist dealer, and preferably one who has some measure of experience with the Fiesta model range, such as Power Engineering. We would also suggest that any potential buyer of uprated suspension drives a car so fitted beforehand. This applies particularly with a sports kit which is *very* different to the original equipment!

MU13.1
At the front, MacPherson struts are fitted. These consist of a coil spring, in which is mounted a telescopic damper. The strut extends from the axle to the suspension turret, a specially strengthened area of the Fiesta inner wing. At the top mounting, the strut is able to swivel. The spring, when in position on the strut, is held under great pressure and under ***no circumstances*** should any attempt be made to remove it without the specialist equipment shown on page 172.
(Diagram courtesy Haynes Publishing Group)

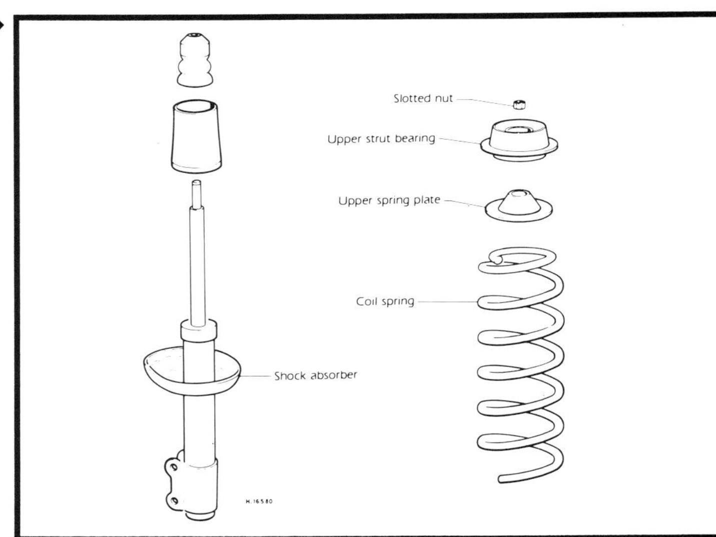

MU13.2
This diagram shows the position of the front struts in relation to the suspension components and driveshafts. Note that only certain models are fitted with an anti-roll bar, which is, in effect, a torsion bar, mounted at two points to the car body and at each end to the bottom of the struts. When the car is cornering, the spring on the outer wheel is compressed. However, the opposite spring is not loaded so heavily and thus exerts a twisting force on the anti-roll bar. The spring already under compression is stiffened by this twisting motion and so acts in a way which resists the car's natural tendency to roll.
(Diagram courtesy Haynes Publishing Group)

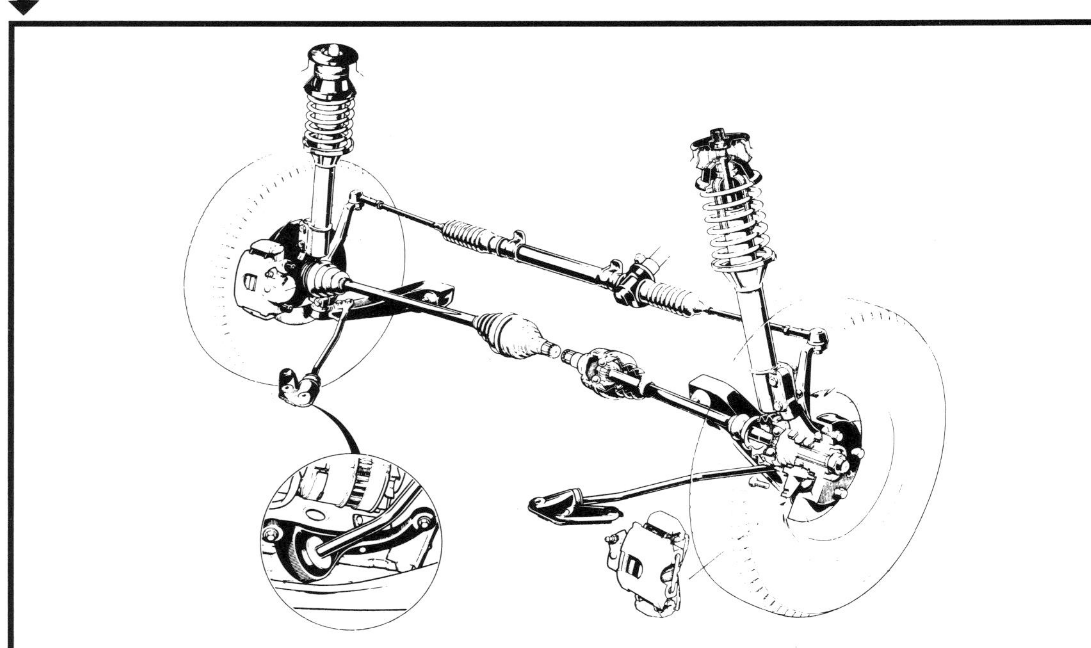

When replacing faulty suspension items, it is important that they are always fitted in pairs, providing an opportunity to uprate your suspension system on an economical basis. Whenever front struts are replaced, and especially if they have been uprated, the camber and tracking must be checked and adjusted if necessary before the car is used on the road.

Standard shock absorbers have an expected life of around 50,000 miles or four years, although this is very much dependent on the treatment they receive. Constant use on rough and unforgiving roads could lower that figure dramatically and the frequency of your safety checks should be increased. When you have uprated your suspension with high quality units, such as the Spax set-up shown earlier, then you can expect to get more mileage from them.

Safety checks should be carried out at regular intervals on both front and rear suspension units. Check that all fasteners are tight and secure and that the rubber sealing shroud is always in place on the piston tube. They should always be dry but, if not, any unit found to be leaking should be replaced immediately.

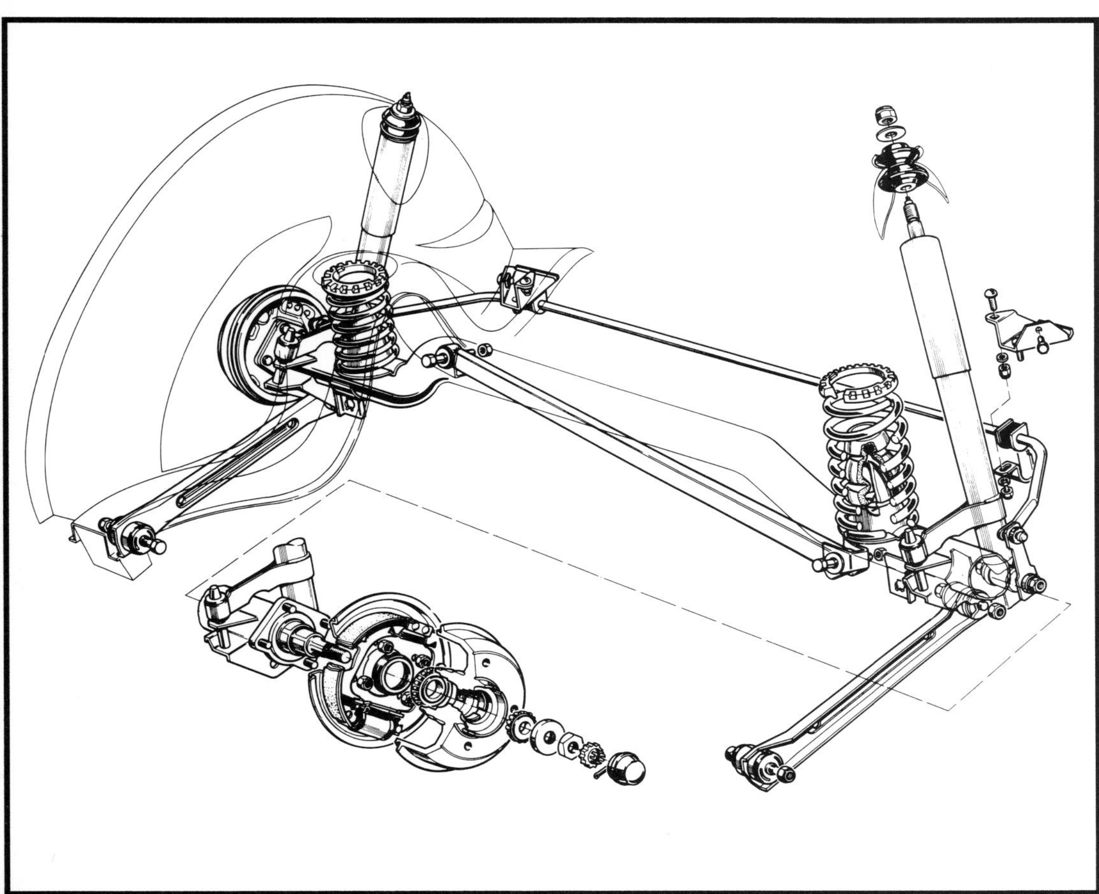

MU13.3
The rear suspension layout and axle assembly is shown here. It is the five-point link type consisting of the axle beam, coil springs, telescopic shock absorbers, Panhard rod (helping to prevent sideways movement), and trailing arms. Certain models (notably the XR2) are fitted with an anti-roll bar for improved handling characteristics. By using a separate shock absorber and coil spring, DIY swapping of either or both is made considerably easier, not least because it does not demand the use of a spring compressor.
(Diagram courtesy Haynes Publishing Group)

Uprating the suspension

Improving the suspension of your Fiesta can make it positive to drive and more fun to own, and if you have improved the performance, improving the suspension it is virtually a necessity. However, uprating the suspension usually means that the spring rates are harder and that some of Ford's original compromise with regard to ride quality is lost. The choice, as ever, is yours ...

Along with braking efficiency, a good suspension set-up should be fitted before you even think about power uprates for your Fiesta. The name of Spax has long been associated with high quality British made suspension products and it is no surprise to find that Power Engineering have the task of evaluating, advising and developing Ford suspension units for the company. In this section, we cover the fitting of a set of Spax Gas Pak shock absorbers to a Fiesta which had recently received a two-litre, Power Engineering conversion.

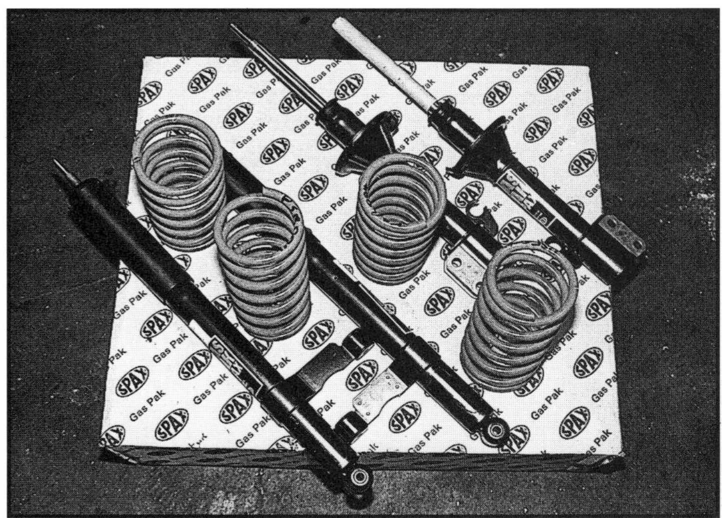

MU14.1
This is the Spax Gas Pak shock absorber kit in its entirety. This particular set is reference P004 and is suitable for all Mk II XR2 models (1983 to 1989). It includes the dampers and uprated springs and is a particularly suitable conversion for the more powerful Fiesta.

MU14.2
With the wheel removed, the first task is to remove the strut-to-axle carrier retaining bolts. Eagle-eyed readers will have noticed that there are no driveshafts in evidence! This is not a secret Power Engineering project to produce a rear-wheel-drive Fiesta, but rather the engine was so recently installed that they simply had not been refitted.

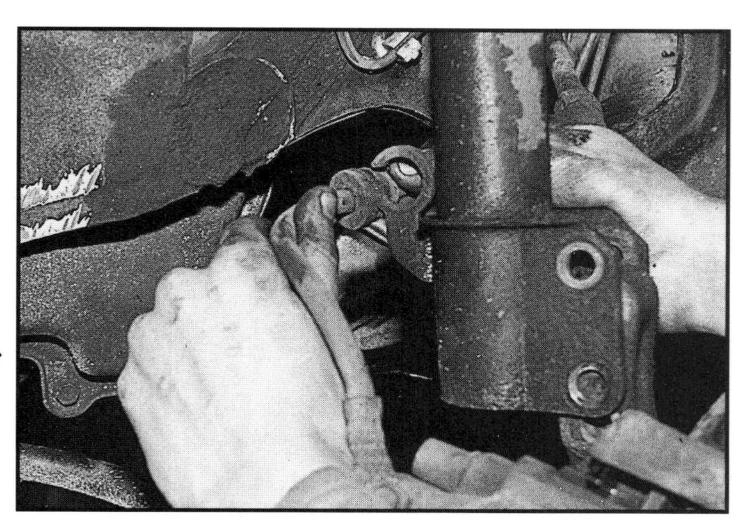

MU14.3
An important point to remember is the removal of the brake line securing mount, which fixes onto the side of the suspension leg.

Fitting your own uprated suspension is not awfully difficult to achieve, but it does demand some specialised equipment for safety and practicality. On the Power Engineering ramp, for example, the lower strut can be worked on at a level comfortable to the mechanic. As not many Fiesta owners will have such a power lift in their garage, it means working with the car on axle stands. If you do work with the car on axle stands, don't forget to keep to the safety rules and to securely chock the wheels remaining on the ground.

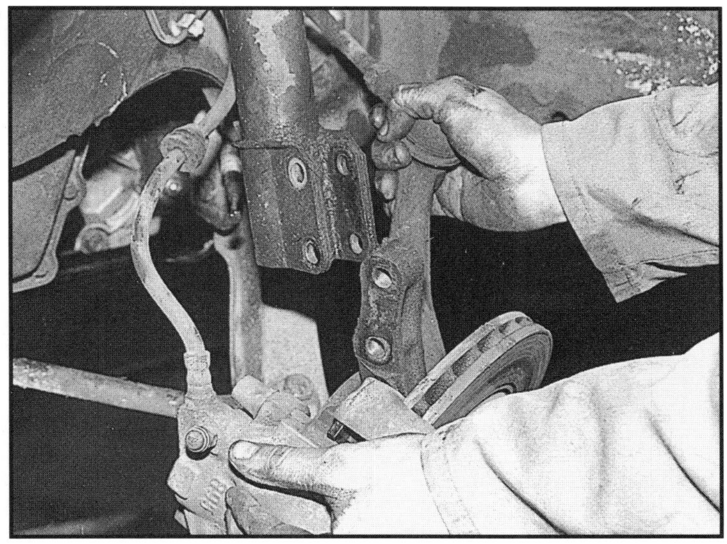

MU14.4
With this done, the stub axle can be pulled clear of the suspension unit, as shown here.

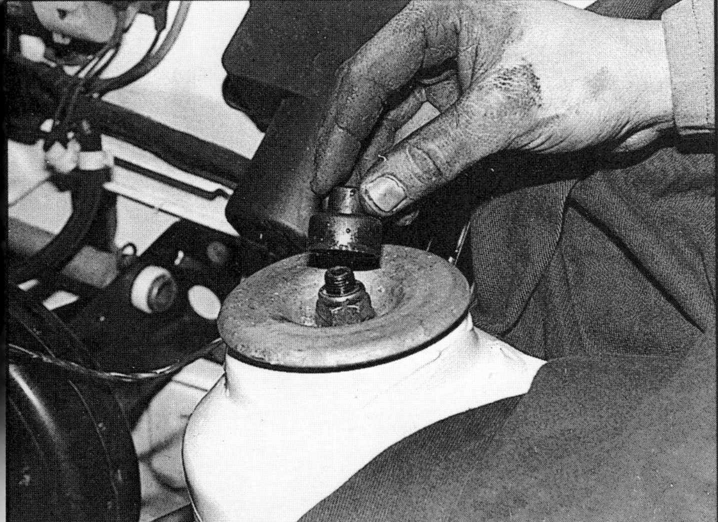

MU14.5
Then, it's time to lower the ramp and start work under the bonnet. Removal of this rubber dust cap ...

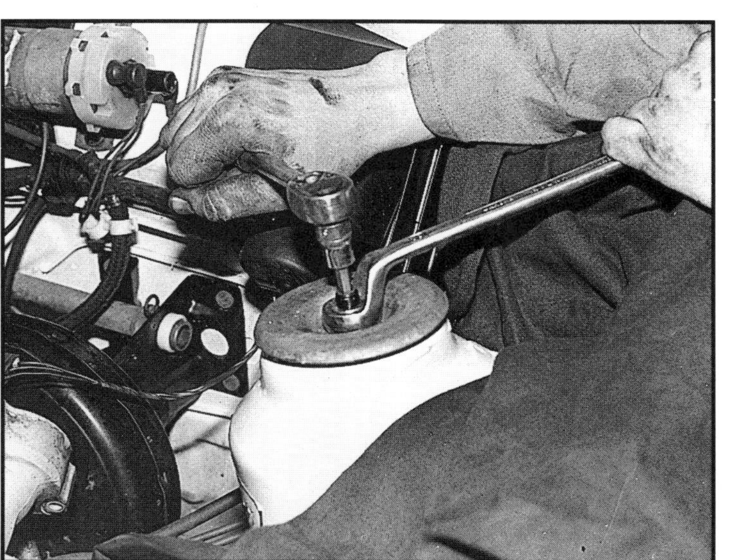

MU14.6
... allows access to the strut retaining nut. The socket here is fitted with an Allen key and the ring spanner is required to stop everything from turning. A second pair of hands is useful here, for although the suspension unit should be tight enough in position, there is the possibility that it could fall away as the nut is removed.

Compressing a shock absorber spring can be a highly dangerous operation. The DIY owner can use the appropriate compressor (shown in MU14.10) but great care must be taken whilst using it. Ensure that the locating hooks are securely in place. Tighten one pair of the Sykes-Pickavant compressors a little way and then the other. Never tighten one side so far that the other compressor runs the risk of slipping off. Release them with equal care and evenness. Unless you are absolutely sure about your competence to do this job, have it done by a garage or a trained mechanic.

MU14.7
Next, the top plate can be taken away and the suspension leg pulled out from under the car. Removing the spring can be a tricky business if you do not have the Sykes-Pickavant spring compressor that Power Engineering have. This particular model has a working load of up to 750kg and it needs all of that to contain the incredible strength of the spring.

MU14.8
With the spring securely held and compressed, an Allen key in the socket wrench and a ring spanner are used to ...

MU14.9
... remove the upper spring plate which in turn allows the damper to be pulled out of the spring.

MU14.10
There is also a Sykes-Pickavant DIY version, seen here in use. Note that eye protection is being worn; these coil springs are extremely strong and need to be treated with the greatest respect as one suddenly released from tension could cause serious injury.

This Spax sporting kit includes completely new springs and dampers for both front and rear. However, for those who want their uprate to be a little less radical, a specialist, such as Power Engineering, can advise as to which Spax combination is best for your needs. For example, you could use uprated dampers with standard springs. This would affect stiffness but not roll and indeed, each of the various options will produce a different handling characteristic. Discussions with your specialist supplier are called for, should you want to design your own system.

MU14.11
The new spring and the old. In case you haven't guessed, the new one is on the right, shiny and much shorter, hence giving a harder ride.

MU14.12
The dampers themselves look much of a muchness but the difference is immediately apparent when you drive the car!

MU14.13
Back with the Allen key and ring spanner the removal operation is reversed to assemble the new damper with the new spring and old top plate ...

It is important to realise that the fitting of any new suspension components may affect the camber and tracking. This should be checked and adjusted straight away, as a maladjusted front end can be both expensive in terms of tyre wear and very dangerous.

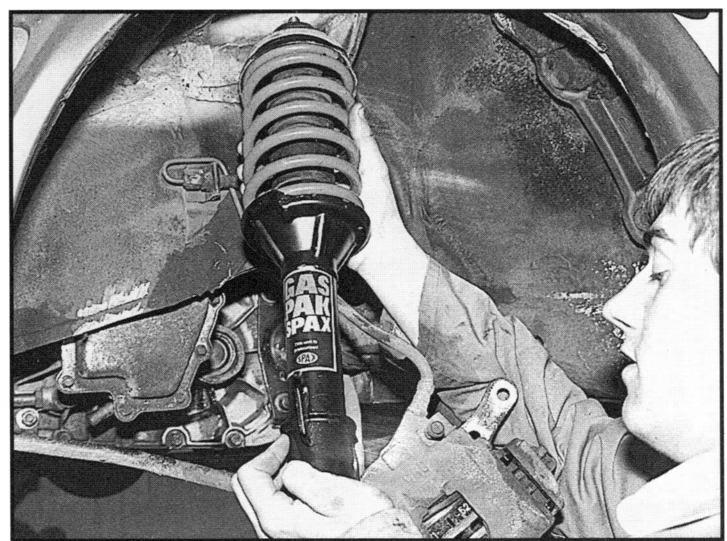

MU14.14
... and the new shock absorber assembly can be replaced as a unit.

MU14.15
Before replacing the lower strut retaining bolts, they are treated to a good covering of Comma Copper Ease in order to facilitate easy removal at some time in the future.

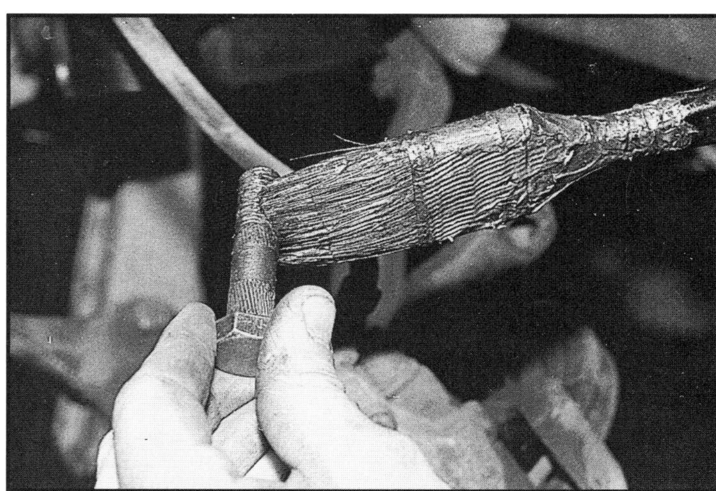

MU14.16
Having secured the new unit at the top, the damper has to be "encouraged" back into the stub axle assembly. Having done so, the nuts and bolts have to be tightened up to the correct torque setting using a torque wrench such as the Sykes-Pickavant model used by Power Engineering. Having finished both sides, it is essential to have the tracking and suspension geometry set up by a properly equipped specialist. You may also find that the steering wheel will need moving slightly on its splines; such can be the effect of a lowering of the front end.

MU14.17
Moving to the rear of the car, a similar procedure is followed. The lower damper mounting bolt is removed first and then ...

When mounting the front and rear dampers, the Power Engineering mechanic found it useful to have a second pair of hands to help with the fitting.

MU14.18
... the lower location arm has to be pulled away from the peg. It's likely to be a tight fit, but not nearly as tight as the new one will be!

MU14.19
Once the damper has been released, it is a simple task to reach in and remove the spring, which is held under no pressure at all.

MU14.20
The new spring, on the right, is shorter than the original, meaning that a much tauter, harder ride will be forthcoming.

You should only work on your Fiesta's suspension if you are certain of your own competence to do so. If you DIY your suspension, you would be well advised to have your work checked by a qualified mechanic before taking to the road. Otherwise, leave it to the experts!

MU14.21
The damper has to be released from its top location in the hatch area. This is a question of taking off the protective rubber cap ...

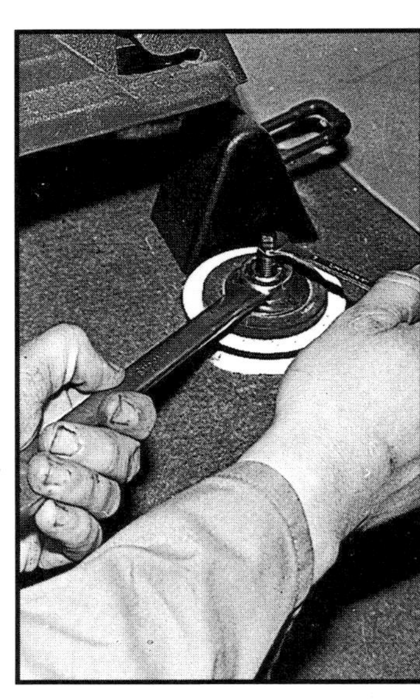

MU14.22
... and unscrewing the upper mounting locknut, washer and insulator. It's here that you will need some help to steady and retrieve the damper from the outside.

MU14.23
This photo clearly shows the great extent to which the shock absorbers are exposed to the elements, with the old unit being on the right. With all that dirt and mud around, trying all the time to penetrate the various seals, it's no wonder that we recommend frequent checking of all your shock absorbers.

MU14.24 ➡
Replacing the spring is easy. Just pop it in. Similarly ...

⬅ **MU14.25**
... the damper slides easily into place. Then simply tighten up the top locknut.

MU14.26 ➡
Fitting the lower location arm back on to the peg is not quite so easy. The rubber bush is an incredibly tight fit and requires some skill and ingenuity to overcome. Once again Copper Ease helps to lubricate it but Power Engineering have a way to cheat ...

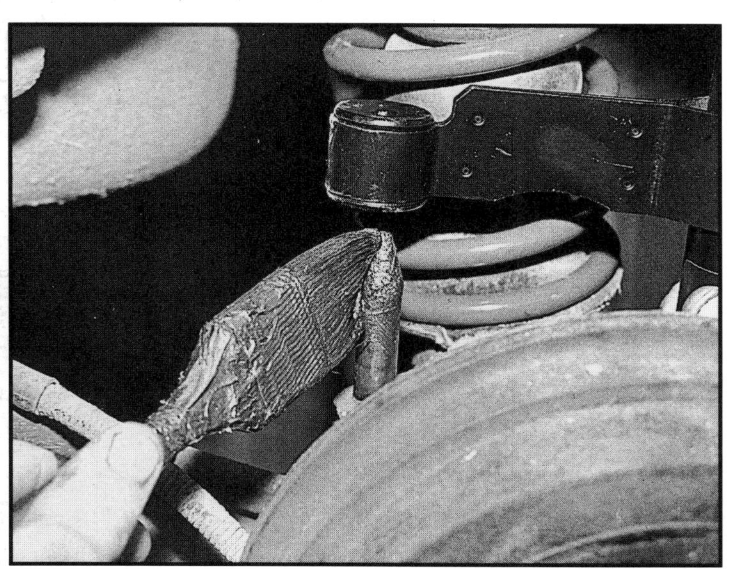

Whilst it is true to say that most uprated shock absorber kits are fitted to the sportier cars (such as the XR series), there is no reason at all why the less overtly sporting cars should not be so fitted. In fact, in many repects it is these cars which would stand to gain most, as their standard suspension is likely to be more of a compromise and therefore much more restrictive.

Spax are world renowned for their range of high quality suspension systems and there are too many to choose from to list here. The best answer, should you be unsure as to your choice, is to contact Spax direct or a specialist such as Power Engineering, either of whom will be able to advise as to what would suit your particular needs best.

MU14.27
... they use a valve spring compressor to "encourage" the errant arm into place.

MU14.28
Once this is achieved, the lower mounting bolt is replaced and tightened up to the correct torque. And that is the job finished, except for the final checks made by Power Engineering.

MU14.29
For the ultimate in totally controllable suspension, the top adjustable Pakspax kits are, as the name suggests, fully adjustable, simply by using a knurled nut which screws on to the top of the suspension unit inside the car. A rear unit is shown here on the Fiesta's big brother, the Escort, although they are available for the Fiesta and the principles still apply. So whether it's a little hard charging down the back lanes, or a gentle Sunday afternoon cruise with Auntie Maud, you have the choice!

Road Impressions

Suspension is almost invariably a compromise between the soft ride required for comfort and th harder ride for controllability when travelling at speed. The Gas Pak kit, fitted here to the Mk II XR2 makes an instantly noticeable difference. The whole car feels much more taut and "more of a piece than the original set-up. Lack of body roll whilst cornering can be a little unnerving at first, but it onl takes a short while to adapt and one soon appreciates the true joy of driving (as opposed to pilotin a car from A to B.

Such a suspension system naturally increases the tyre's workload as cornering speeds increas You should always take expert advice as to your tyre choice and their compatibility with your ne suspension. You should also think hard about your braking system, for, with improved cornerin ability, your overall speed is likely to be increased and the ability to stop is of paramount importanc A last point to bear in mind is ride height. Using shorter springs lowers the height of the car. If yo have a body kit, or large front spoiler, you may well find that it could ground much earlier. addition, if you have a body kit which includes flared wheel arches you may find that wide, lo profile tyres foul the bodywork although this is no problem with the relatively "mild" kit fitted the XR2 as standard.

In many cases, you can obtain a better handling car (especially in the wet) by using, for exampl a 185/60 series tyre with a sporty Spax kit, even though it may mean foregoing the body kit. Bu as ever, you pays your money ...

MU15.1
These pictures show how the road would "see" a tyre contact patch. This is the Michelin MX and ...

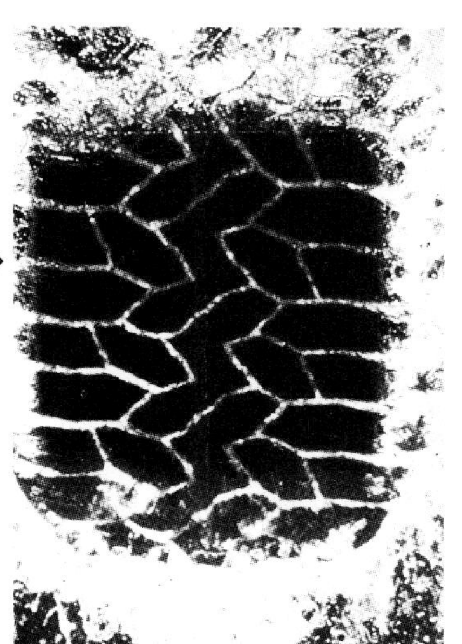

MU15.2
... this is the lower profile, MXL tyre.

MU15.3
This is the Michelin MX series for conventional rims. From left to right they are the MX, 80 series, the MXV 60 series and the MXL 70 series.

When you realise that your car's "footprint" – the small area of rubber actually in contact with the road – is in fact no bigger than a man's hand, you begin to see just how crucial the selection and care of your tyres can be. All your car's power and performance come to nothing if you can't transmit it to the road ... and keep it there!

pecification

n the side of every tyre, you will find lots of writing, including a series of markings looking ıspiciously like an MI5 code. They aren't, of course, and in fact relate to both size designation and ervice description.

This is easiest to explain with a single example. Let us use a tyre which has the reference 185/60R14 2H. Reading from left to right:

***85* refers to the nominal section width of the tyre in millimetres.**

***0* represents the aspect ratio, which is the ratio of nominal section height to the section width. In ıis case it means, roughly speaking, that the distance from the bead of the tyre to the tread is 60 er cent of the tyre's width. The lower the tyre's aspect ratio, the less sidewall flexing will occur, nproving cornering grip and steering response. On the other hand, the tyre is less able to absorb umps and could allow more road noise to be transmitted, whilst the ride could be a little firmer – lthough this is something that some owners prefer.**

indicates the tyre construction denoting "Radial".

***4* refers to the wheel diameter in inches.**

***2* is the load index, which is the numerical code associated with the maximum load the tyre can carry t the speed indicated by the speed symbol.**

is the speed symbol. This is an alphabetical code indicating the speed at which the tyre can carry load corresponding to the load index.

Tyre Load Indices/Max Loads

Load Index	Load (kg)
60	250
65	290
70	335
75	387
80	450
85	515
90	600
95	690
100	800
105	925
110	1060
114	1180

Inflation

Inflation is not just a monetary problem, it is tyre related as well. Regardless of whether you hav a 1.1L Fiesta with standard tyres or an XR2 with ultra low profiles, you must ensure that they a always inflated to the correct pressure, including the spare.

Your handbook will inform you of the recommended pressures for your particular model. No that there will be different pressures depending on the load you usually carry and the type of roa you usually travel, ie, motorway or minor roads. You should check your tyre pressures as often possible, and certainly once a fortnight. Use a reliable gauge (and not *all* forecourt gauges a reliable) and check them when the tyres are cold; tyres get hot as you drive the car and will give higher reading then when they are cold.

If you have changed your tyres and are not sure what the pressures should be, then you shou seek the advice of your conversion specialist or the vehicle manufacturer.

Prolonged under-inflation permits excessive flexing of the sidewalls, deterioration of the casin and increased wear of the tread. On the other hand, running for any length of time with an ove inflated tyre will cause excessive wear in the centre of the tread, a harsh and uncomfortable ride an the contact patch with the road will be decreased.

MU15.4
The lower the profile, the "chunkier" the appearance, as can be seen by comparing this 80 series MX tyre with ...

MU15.5
... this 70 series MXL. However, you should note also the differences in tread pattern.

Clearly, it is important that your Fiesta should be fitted with tyres which match its speed capability, and you should never fit tyres which have a lower speed rating than those fitted as standard.

If you have your car tuned so that the top speed is more than standard, you may need to change your tyres to match the performance of the car. When fitting ultra low profile tyres it is the recommendation of most tyre manufacturers that the overall diameter of the wheel and tyre combination should not vary more than +3 per cent to –5 per cent from the original equipment. Remember also that your Fiesta's speedometer and odometer are set to be accurate with the original wheels and tyres. Changing one or both will make them inaccurate to a lesser or greater extent, although by choosing carefully and consulting your local dealer, you should be able to minimise the effect. For example, the effect of an increase in wheel diameter can be largely cancelled out by a decrease in tyre aspect ratio provided that the choice is made with reference to the tables that your tyre stockist will – or should – have available.

Inner Tubes

Most tyres today are tubeless but, if your tyres are not marked "Tubeless" or have no marking at all, then an inner tube must be fitted. It should be noted that all ultra low profile tyres (65 series and below) are tubeless and Michelin do not recommend tubes to be fitted in these tyres and therefore they must be fitted to tubeless wheels. The tubeless marking will normally be directly after the tyre size details on the sidewall. If you need to replace a tubed tyre, then the tube should also be replaced.

Many tyre manufacturers build in tyre wear indicators such that, when the indicator is level with the tread, then 1.6mm of tread pattern depth is left.

MU15.6
The ability to shift large quantities of water is one of the main requirements of any tyre which is to be used in the UK. Michelin have excellent test facilities and a great deal of time and money is spent on testing to ensure that the best combination of rubber compounds and tread patterns is reached. This is the MXL on test prior to its launch.

Understanding tyres

The speed symbol indicates the speed at which the tyre can carry the load corresponding to its load index as shown in the table below. As detailed earlier in this section, there are figures relating to these on all new tyres.

Speed Symbol	Speed KPH	Speed MPH
L	120	75
M	130	81
N	140	87
P	150	95
Q	160	100
R	170	105
S	180	113
T	190	118
U	200	123
H	210	130
V	240	150
VR*	Over 210	Over 130
ZR*	Over 240	Over 150

(For conversion of kph to mph see our "Data" section in Chapter Seven).

** When the reference VR or ZR is used, it will be found within the actual tyre designation, eg, 205/60 ZR15. If you have a Fiesta which requires such rubberwear, then you've got some car!*

Tyre Repairs

It is hard for us to recommend repairing tyres, especially if you have a high performance Fiesta.

However, tyre repairs should always be carried out by an accredited tyre specialist and to Britis Standard AU159. As part of this, the tyre should be removed from the wheel and checked, inside an out, to make sure that there is no hidden damage which could cause problems at a later date.

Wheel and tyre sizes

The Eighties saw a massive increase in the popularity of big, wide, low profile tyres. Although, i the right circumstances, these will give a considerable increase in roadholding, many drivers fit the for the "mean" look it gives to their Fiesta. It is true that they improve the looks, but it is importa to ensure that you only fit tyres to your car which are the correct size for your wheel rim width. Fittin tyres either too big or too small for the rim width could be extremely dangerous to the point of bein lethal. The table here shows the tyres fitted as standard by Ford and the possible sizes of Micheli replacements. The effect of all the replacement tyre and wheel combinations shown on th speedometer readings will be negligible, if any. As you can see, some tyres require a larger ri (either width or diameter) in order for the tyre to fit correctly and safely. To cope with any increase tyre size it is essential to check all clearances under static, full lock and maximum suspension trav conditions to ensure that tyres and wheels do not foul suspension units, steering linkage, spring bodywork or any other part of the vehicle. If wheels are changed then the vehicle manufacture advice should be sought on the suitability of the existing wheel bearings with regard to ar increased bearing loads.

Talk to your local tyre fitting specialist *before* you consider changing.

	Standard OE Fitment	70 Series	65 Series	60 Series	55 Series
Up to 1984					
Fiesta 1.0 Base	135R12S	155/70R12	–	–	–
1.1 + 1.0L, GL, Ghia	145R12S	145/70R13*	165/65R13*	175/60R13*	–
1.1S + Popular + 1.3GL, Ghia	155R12S	–	–	185/60R13*	–
1.1S + 1.3S (1982-83)	155/70R13S	–	165/65R13	185/60R13	–
1.3 Supersport + XR2	185/60R13H	–	–	–	195/55R13
1984 MODELS					
1.0 + 1.1L	135R13	155/70R13	165/65R13	185/60R13*	195/55R13*
1.0 Ghia + 1.1 Ghia, 1.3 Base, L, 1.3S Ghia, 1.6 Diesel, Ghia	155/70R13	–	165/65R13	185/60R13	195/55R13*
1985 MODELS					
1.0 Popular, 1.0L, 1.1L, 1.0 + 1.1 Pop Plus	135R13S	155/70R13	165/65R13	185/60R13*	195/55R13*
1.1 + 1.3 Ghia 1.3L, 1.6L Pop Plus, 1.6 Diesel	155/70R13S	–	165/65R13	185/60R13	185/55R13*
XR2	185/60R13H	–	–	–	–
1986 MODELS					
1.0 Pop, 1.0, 1.1 Pop Plus L	135R13S	155/70R13	165/65R13	185/60R13*	195/55R13*
1.4L	165/65R13S	–	–	185/60R13	195/55R13*
1.1, 1.4 Ghia, 1.6 Pop Plus, 1.6L	155/70R13S	–	165/65R13	185/60R13*	195/55R13*
XR2	185/60R13H	–	–	–	195/55R13
1987 MODELS					
1.0 Pop + L, 1.1L, 1.0 Pop Plus	135R13S	165/65R13	185/60R13	–	–
1.1, 1.4 Ghia 1.4L	155/70R13S	–	165/65R13	185/60R13	195/55R13*
1.4S	165/65R13S	–	–	185/60R13	195/55R13*
1.6 Pop Plus, 1.6 Diesel	155/70R13S	–	–	185/60R13*	195/55R13*
XR2	185/60R13H	–	–	–	195/55R13

** **Note:** New wheels required, either due to increased diameter or width*

Lubrication – Oils, greases and fluids

Understanding lubrication

For decades, the average motorist didn't trouble his head about that dark, messy liquid that was apparently required in the engine and gearbox. As long as there was sufficient in both to cover the respective dipsticks he knew that the car would chug along quite contentedly.

However, today's enthusiastic owner knows better and that you don't have to own a high performance XR2 to make using the best oil available worthwhile. With increased performance, longer journeys and higher speeds, demands on engine lubricants have increased tenfold and can be well beyond the performance of the "economy" oils on the market. The wise owner gets to know what is required in a lubricant and makes sure he or she uses only the best available. Saving a pound or two every oil change will pale into insignificance when the engine gives up the ghost 50,000 miles too early. The moral is simple: being penny wise with engine oil could mean being hundreds of pounds foolish with your engine.

If you want the best for your Fiesta engine, then you should start with the best oil. Duckhams have a hard earned reputation for producing excellent quality engine and gear oils, grease and other associated products.

Engine oils

This section leans on the expertise of Duckhams, a company at the forefront of oil technology. They have invested enormous amounts of resources in producing a range of engine oils that satisfies the requirements of all engines, including the most advanced, with some to spare. Before explaining how they have done so, it is necessary to take a look at some of the criteria that are applied to modern oils.

Many years ago, all engine oils were "single grade". It was given an SAE rating which described its viscosity or, in other words, its thickness.

An SAE 20 oil was used in the colder winter months because it was thin and thus made the task of starting the engine first thing in the morning much easier. In the summer, a thicker SAE 40 or 50 oil was used for the opposite reasons.

Multigrade oils were first introduced by Duckhams back in the 1950s and covered the spectrum from SAE 20 through to SAE 50, making them suitable for use all year round.

These oils are still available, along with some more recently introduced variations on the theme, such as 15w/50, 10w/40 or even 5w/50.

It's relatively easy to make an oil with an SAE rating of 20w/50 when it is new. The manufacturer simply adds an ingredient called a "polymer" which acts as a thickener when the oil gets hotter. However, there are many different polymers available and some are not as good as others. The old adage applies: you only get what you pay for! Cheap polymers lose their effectiveness quite rapidly as they are subjected to the heat and "shearing" effects inside the engine. The net results of using such cheap polymers is that a 20w/50 oil loses the SAE 50 part of its viscosity which removes much of its effectiveness when the engine is working hard. The only way to avoid the potential damage this can cause is to use a top brand oil. As would be expected, Duckhams use only the highest quality polymers in their oils.

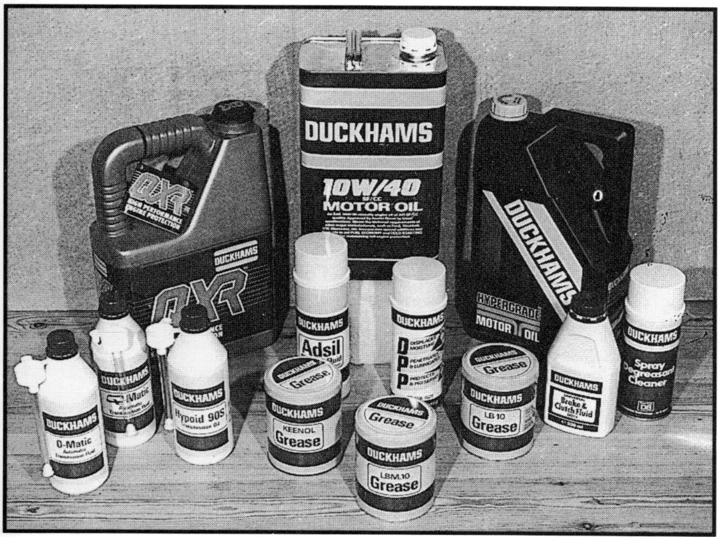

MU16.1
At the mention of Duckhams, one instantly thinks of oil. However, the company also produce a wide range of related products, such as spray degreasant cleaner, DDP penetrating fluid and Adsil silicone fluid, which is wonderful for lubricating sliding rubber parts. All come in aerosol packs. Check your Fiesta handbook to find which grade of engine or transmission oil is required for your car.

Lubrication – Oils, greases and fluids

Where the lower drag factor of a lower viscosity oil is required, but without the additional features of QXR, Duckhams also produce 10w/40 Motor Oil. It offers excellent winter starting and marginally improved fuel economy when used with a newer engine. However, 10w/40 is not intended to replace Hypergrade 15w/50 in an older or higher mileage engine for oil consumption could increase noticeably if 10w/40 is used, as it can find its way more easily past worn bores, piston rings and valve guides.

Top brand 15w/50 oils, such as "Hypergrade", are designed to satisfy the technical requirements of every engine in use today. However, Duckhams QXR is the very latest oil designed especially for use in true performance cars.

Those with fuel-injected, multi-valved, turbocharged or uprated engines will stand to gain by using QXR (although, of course, there is nothing to stop you using this super high quality oil regardless).

QXR certainly costs more than conventional oils but offers more protection from wear, the greatest possible freedom from deposits, excellent oil consumption control and the ability to perform really well over the widest extremes of temperatures and motoring conditions.

QXR is a 10w/40 oil, offering all the protection that could possibly be required along with a reduction in the "drag" effect suffered inside an engine when thicker oils are used.

Ordinarily, a 10w/40 oil would have two huge disadvantages over conventional oils; it would tend to lose viscosity at higher temperatures, and even vaporise, because 10w/40 oils are normally so much more volatile. The most expensive solution, and one which prices the oil beyond the reach of most enthusiasts, is to use a synthetic lubricant in place of the usual mineral based oils.

However, the route chosen by Duckhams is interesting, for they have developed a special process through which the normal mineral oil is put at the refining stage to give it all the properties required but at a far lower cost than that of synthetics.

Best of all, the tests which Duckhams carried out during development showed that in terms of performance, QXR proved to be comparable to highly expensive synthetic oils and, in some respects, even better!

Pat Lelliott, Duckham's Technical Manager, is so proud of QXR that he says; "Achieve those standards and you have an oil of the high performance class, such as QXR. Look around and see how many products attain such high levels. There aren't many!"

MU16.2
As this section indicates, Duckhams QXR has to be the first choice for those with a high performance Ford. The XR2 will benefit greatly from its addition.

Gearboxes (manual)

The oil specification demanded by a gearbox varies according to its design and such factors as the power transmitted, ease of gear selection and sealing, for example. In the case of the Fiesta range, Duckhams Hypoid 80 gear oil is recommended. Where low temperatures might lead to a "sticky" gearchange, a multigrade such as Hypoid 75w/90S might be preferred. Five-speed gearboxes sometimes benefit from the use of a multigrade gear oil, especially under the adverse circumstances already mentioned and, in particular, as an aid to low temperature gear selection.

Rear axles

An oil such as Duckhams Hypoid 90S is, quite simply, all that is required to withstand the extraordinary "shear" forces involved. An oil with an API GL4 specification is fine for normal use, but bear in mind that Hypoid 90S is actually produced to API GL5 spec – the different number indicating a higher level of additive treatment.

Engines with turbochargers or which have a significantly uprated specification demand the use of the very best oil you can buy. Turbochargers themselves run at incredibly high speeds (in the region of 100,000rpm!) and are driven by the searingly hot exhaust gases passing through the exhaust system. They are cooled as well as lubricated by the engine oil. To avoid loss of viscosity and gain protection you should use a top line lubricant such as QXR.

MU16.3
As well as being available in the large "oil change" 5 litre packs, QXR is also available in a smaller 1 litre pack.

MU16.4
There is a wide range of Duckhams greases available and again, you should check that you are purchasing the right type by checking in your car's handbook.

Understanding spark plugs

Carl Benz, the "Father of the Motor Car", referred to the automobile ignition system as, "the problem to end all problems."

"If the spark fails," he said, "then everything else is useless, no matter how sophisticated the design." Bosch pride themselves on having supplied that spark as early as 1902, although things have progressed just a little since then!

MU17.1
The three types of Bosch spark plug on display are (left to right): the triple electrode (which is only used in VW/Audi cars, and is not suitable for the Fiesta); the platinum-tipped plug, which is dearer to buy but much more efficient provided that it is gapped correctly before use, and finally, the standard Bosch Super plug, produced to original equipment specification.

Some spark plugs have a flat seating surface and make use of a sealing gasket; others have a conical surface and are self-sealing. Clearly the correct type of plug seating designed for your engine has to be used; they are not interchangeable. Some types are, however, and it is up to you to ensure that you know which is which. If you have any doubts, consult your Bosch dealer.

Where radio interference from spark plugs is a problem (unusual nowadays given the complexity of most radio suppression circuits, although with interference anything can happen!), it is possible to buy Bosch plugs with interference suppression built-in, these being denoted by the letter "R" in the type number. It is even possible to buy fully shielded plugs.

Other special plugs include those with multiple electrodes to satisfy some manufacturers' extremely long service intervals and also those with precious metal electrodes.

These plugs, with either silver ("S" identification) or Platinum ("P" identification) electrodes are inherently more efficient than ordinary plugs and the extra efficiency is especially useful in high performance engines, all the way up to racing specification.

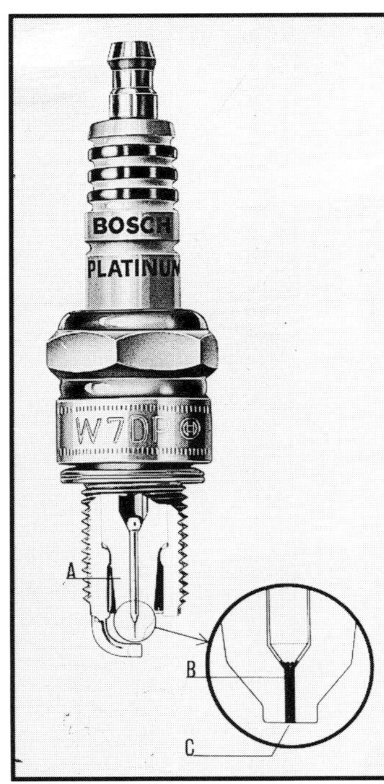

MU17.2
The advantages of platinum plugs are: ignition conditions remain practically constant throughout the recommended service life of the plugs; plugs warm up quicker and so "self-clean" earlier; and heat transfer properties are improved.
A Very long insulator nose ensures extension of the thermal operating range.
B 0.3mm diameter platinum centre electrode.
C Platinum centre electrode sintered gas tight in insulator nose.
(Courtesy Robert Bosch Ltd)

Type Numbers and Fitting

You can identify a Bosch plug by the number on the box and on the body of the plug itself. Take a typical number, such as W 7 DP (a plug with a built-in resistor would have the letter "R" after the "W"). "W" indicates the type of thread and seat, this being the most common flat seat, M14 x 1.25 thread. "7" indicates the heat range – a critical measure, because to use a plug outside the correct heat range could damage the engine. "D" shows the plug thread length, in this case 19mm or 17.5mm if the plug is tapered. The last letter indicates the electrode material, where "C" shows that the plug is a standard unit with a copper electrode. You will find a Bosch application list detailing the correct plugs for your car wherever the plugs are sold.

Working at a pressure of up to 50 bar and in temperatures of up to 3,000 degrees Celsius, the spark plug is expected to deliver in excess of 30,000 volts no less than 100 times every second when the car is at speed! Not only that, but it is expected to do this day in, day out, hot or cold, for thousands of miles on end.

This is all the more credit to Bosch, who have perfected plugs which can perform their duties perfectly for up to 20,000 miles.

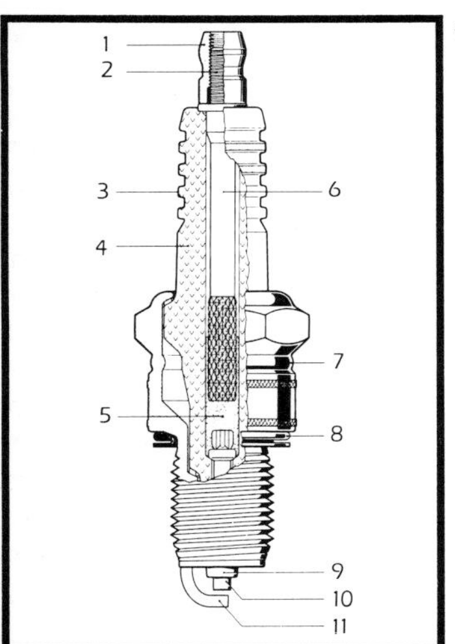

MU17.4
Construction of a Spark Plug
1 Terminal nut
2 Thread
3 Current leak barrier
4 Insulator
5 Conductive seal
6 Terminal stud
7 Fitting: swaged & heat shrunk
8 Gasket (flat seat)
9 Insulator tip
10 Centre electrode
11 Ground electrode
(Courtesy Robert Bosch Ltd.)

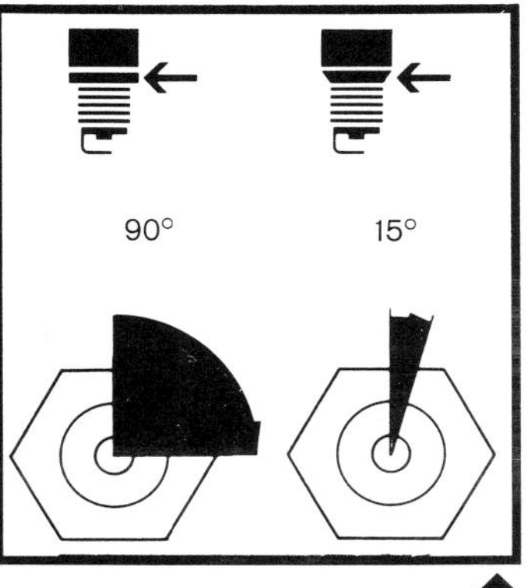

MU17.3
Always ensure the plug threads are clear, using a Sykes-Pickavant thread chaser if necessary. Screw spark plug in by hand until seated. New plugs with flat seats are turned a further 90 degrees with a spark plug wrench. Used flat and conical seat plugs should be turned a further 15 degrees with the wrench.
(Courtesy Robert Bosch Ltd.)

MU17.5
If you've read the Engine Uprate section, you'll know that the Power Engineering "System Two" engine is a demanding unit. It goes without saying that Bosch plugs are used exclusively.

Plugs in practice

In the main, spark plugs tend to break down for one of several reasons. One is that the plug's internal insulation fails, which leads to internal shorting out, although this is usually because another problem has occurred. A plug working outside its optimum temperature range will be prone to failing in this way. Therefore, it is important that you use the plug with the correct heat range to suit your car. If the engine is standard, then check against the Bosch catalogue and follow its recommendation. However, if your engine has been tuned, then refer to the specialist concerned who should be able to advise.

Leaving the plug in place for too long could also lead to breakdown. Again, it could be failure of the insulation or the centre electrode could have become contaminated, leading to reduced efficiency. Alternatively, the electrode could have become eroded.

MU17.6
Using the Bosch spark plug gap-gauge:
A Measuring the electrode gap. The measuring wire should pass through with only the slightest resistance.
B Checking Platinum plugs for wear. Bend the side electrode back; push measuring wire into hole in insulator nose; when wire goes in as far as plastic stop, wear limit has been reached.
C Opening the electrode gap with the "bottle opener" type bending device on the Bosch measuring tool.
D Close the gap by tapping lightly and carefully on a smooth hard surface.
(Courtesy Robert Bosch Ltd.)

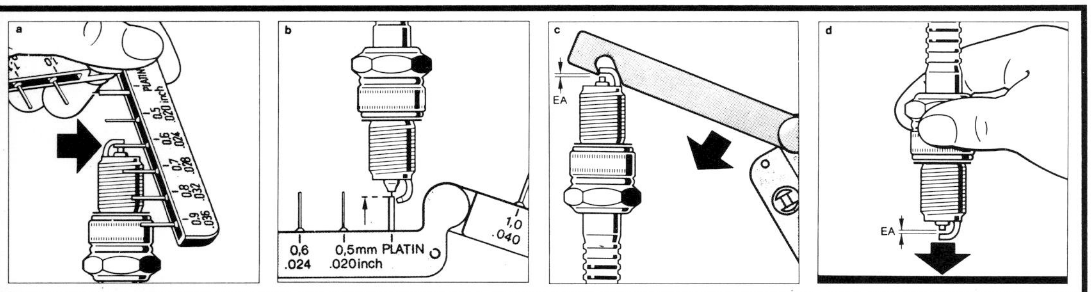

Fitting silicone HT leads

Whether or not you have "tuned" your Fiesta engine, you will certainly benefit from fitting Silicone HT leads. Normal leads have a tendency to deteriorate after a period of time and allow moisture to penetrate. This means that your precious sparks will "leak" to earth via the easiest route rather than by the plugs, especially when it is wet or damp. The Cosmic "Silicone Plus" leads shown here will remain flexible at temperatures from –50 degrees C to 260 degrees C and are not prone to hardening or cracking like conventional leads. As can be seen in this diagram, their complex construction ensures that they maintain a high spark conductivity. It also means that they are fully interference suppressed.

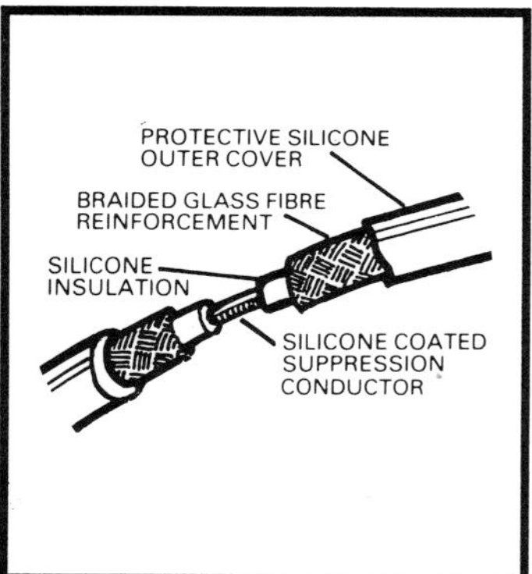

(Diagram courtesy Cosmic Limited)

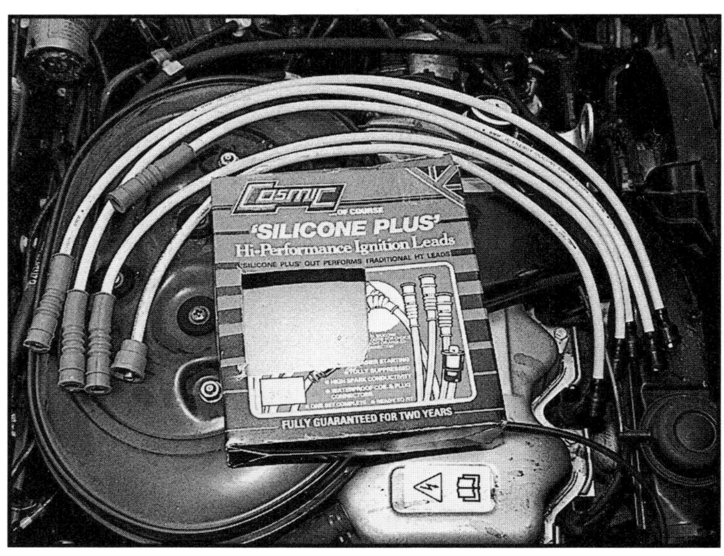

MU18.1 As can be seen here, the leads in the Cosmic set are of different lengths so as to be a custom fit for your particular car. It is a five lead set; four plug leads and one for the coil.

MU18.2 It is a wise move to replace your leads one at a time in order to avoid the possibility of mixing them up. However, there is not much danger of mixing old and new leads; the Cosmic ones are bright yellow! Similarly, it is not a job to tackle with a warm engine, for obvious reasons. Make sure that all the leads are pushed firmly into place and, although it is sensible to try to keep them clean, they are fully resistant to petrol, oil and even acid spillage.

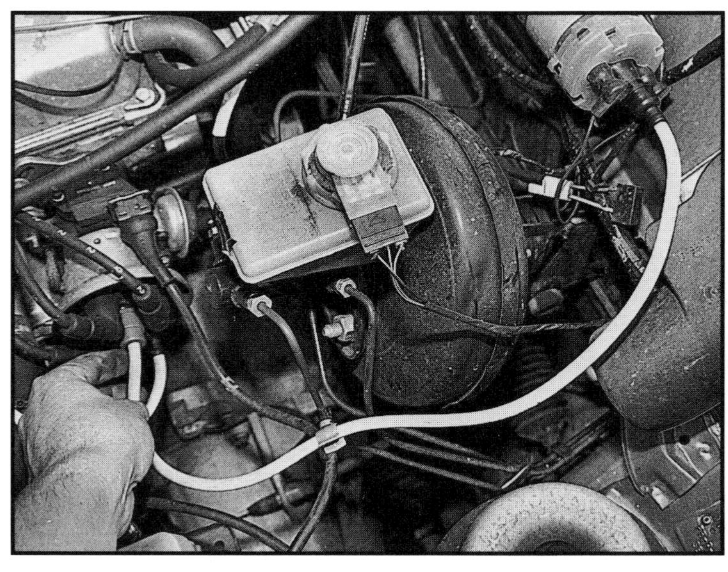

MU18.3 Don't forget the coil. Positioning of the various connections does not matter as the design of the Silicone Plus leads incorporates "bendy boots", that is, the ends of the leads can be used either straight or angled.

Improving engine bay appearance

Cleaning and protecting the engine bay is an oft neglected but very important task. Allowing it to become dirty and oily can put off the DIY owner from keeping up with those regular maintenance jobs. This importance is usually discovered following failed spark plugs, which, along with plug leads and the distributor cap, are far more likely to let you down if covered in oily dirt. On an even more serious note, excessive dirt could be concealing potentially dangerous problems such as loose nuts, worn cables and cracks in the bodywork.

MU19.1 It is vital to keep the engine bay clean. Not only will it make for a more efficient motor but also, it will make any potential faults much easier to see. As most engine compartments are covered in a fine (or sometimes not so fine!) layer of oil or grease, the first task is to remove it. Comma Hyper Clean is an active spray-on-wash-off degreasant which does the job admirably. The spray nozzle will get into the most tricky places, although for really ground-in dirt, you could assist it with an old paintbrush. So that the rinsing process does not encourage rusting, Hyper Clean contains anti-rust agent, FP3.

MU19.2 Comma Rad Clean Plus works in a similar way to Easi Flush, except that it cleans the water cooling system! It requires the radiator to be drained and filled with fresh water and the Rad Clean Plus. When drained again, you will see lots of scaly deposits, like those you get in your kettle; and wondered why your Fiesta was overheating! Also for the water system, Comma produce Rad Seal Plus, which, as its name suggests, seals leaky radiators and cylinder blocks and helps prevent rust and water pump squeaks. Just add the contents of the 300ml bottle to the radiator to seal leaks instantly.

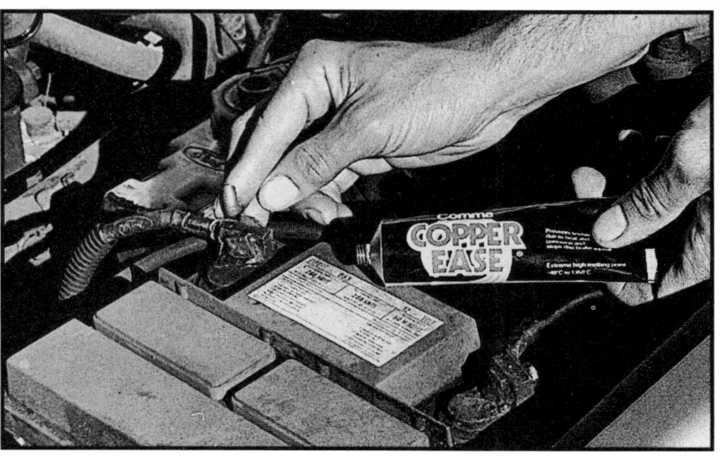

MU19.3 No toolbox should be without a tube (or a tin if you do a lot of DIY on your Fiesta!) of Comma Copper Ease. It improves sealing and facilitates easy dismantling of nuts and bolts (including road wheel bolts and spark plug threads). It is an excellent electrical conductor which makes it ideal for smearing over battery terminals to protect against corrosion, as seen here.

Chapter Five
Techniques and Tools

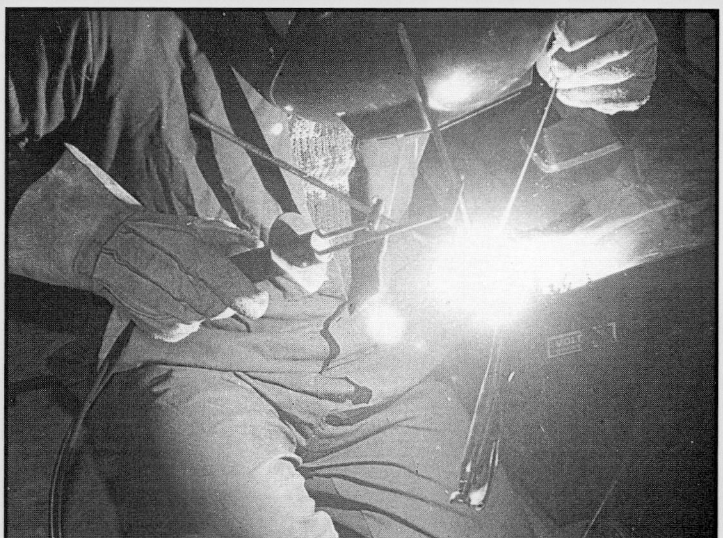

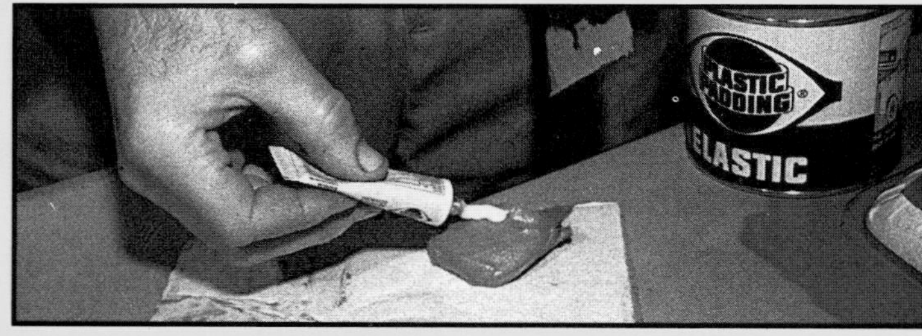

Workshop skills and equipment

Hand tools

There seem to be two approaches when it comes to buying hand tools. One is to buy the cheapest Far Eastern produced tools that can be found, preferably on special offer at the local filling station and, better still, given away free with 5 litres of oil; while the second approach is to buy tools with a sense of quality about them; tools that will last a lifetime. Some of the finest tools to be found are made in the UK by Sykes-Pickavant, who are also the producers of the Speedline economy range. We examine some of them here.

It is possible to produce a higher standard of workmanship with high quality tools than with poor ones. Not only do they fit better, causing no damage to the components that you are working on, such as nuts and bolts, but they're also designed to work efficiently. In addition there's the psychological benefit of working with good quality tools in your hands.

TT1.1
One of the exceptions to the "Made in Britain" rule is the wide range of tool boxes and chests, which are made for Sykes-Pickavant in Canada. They're made of tough heavy gauge steel, are lockable, and contain separate "filing cabinet" type drawers for tool storage. Some of the units are stackable.

TT1.2
Castors and fixing nuts and bolts come as part of the kit. Two of the castors swivel and are lockable, providing a stable base if you wish to use the cabinet top as a workbench.

TT1.3
You have to pull out the top drawer and bolt the push-pull handle to the side of the cabinet.

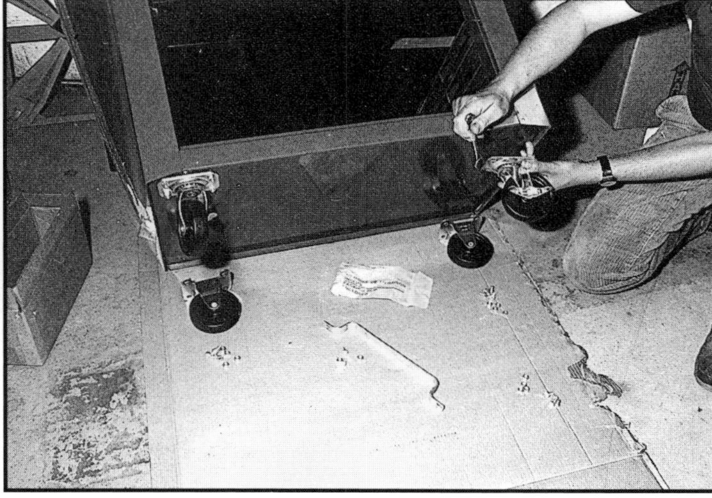

TT1.4
A nice touch this: Sykes-Pickavant also provide trim finishes for the drawer fronts which give an attractive appearance and eliminate sharp edges. The Space Maker Chest in TT1.1 contains six smaller drawers and a lift-out tote tray. It is designed to fit neatly on top of the cabinet bench.

With Sykes-Pickavant's surface drive sockets force is applied to the "flats", not the corners (see Figure A below), reducing socket and fastener wear and avoiding "rounding off". The arrows in Figure B below show those parts of the nut or bolt where the socket applies its turning force.

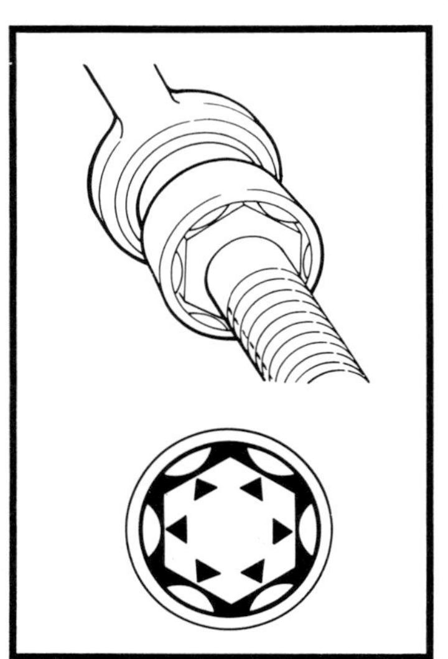

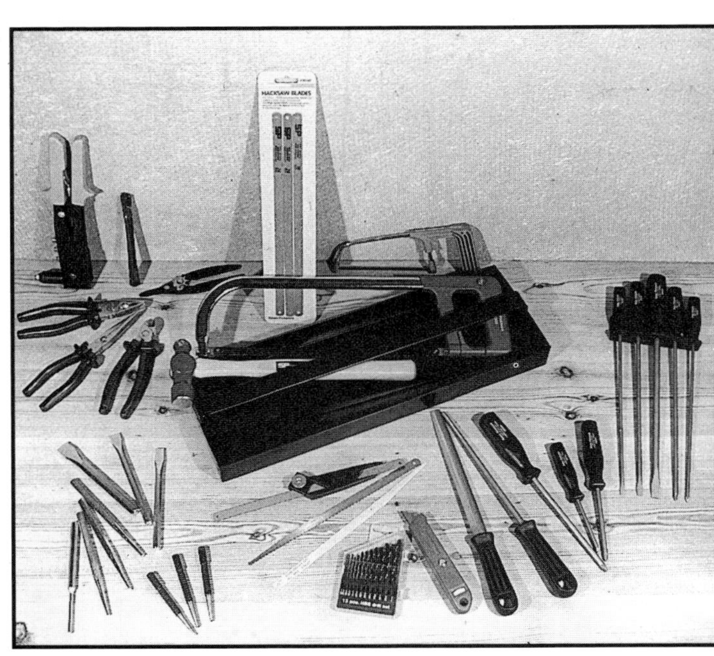

TT1.5 The tote tray from the Space Maker Chest with a selection of Speedline SP tools. Speedline are still of a very high quality, needless to say, but are designed to satisfy the enthusiastic DIYer's pocket.

TT1.6 There are no better looking or better handling ratchet sets than Sykes-Pickavant's Speedline tools. The 3/8 inch drive socket set is so well built that it's easily tough enough for most jobs yet it's lighter, easier to handle and less expensive than its 1/2 inch drive counterparts. Buy sockets in sets or individually bubble packed as shown.

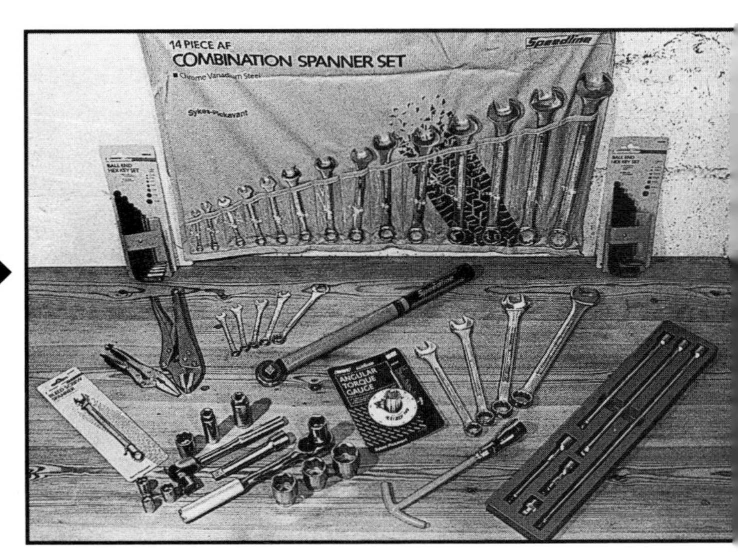

TT1.7 In the old days everyone bought open-ended or ring spanners. Now we buy combination sets like the Speedline spanners pictured in the background. The extension set, pictured right, has a wonderful "wobble" end on each one; a boon in awkward spots.

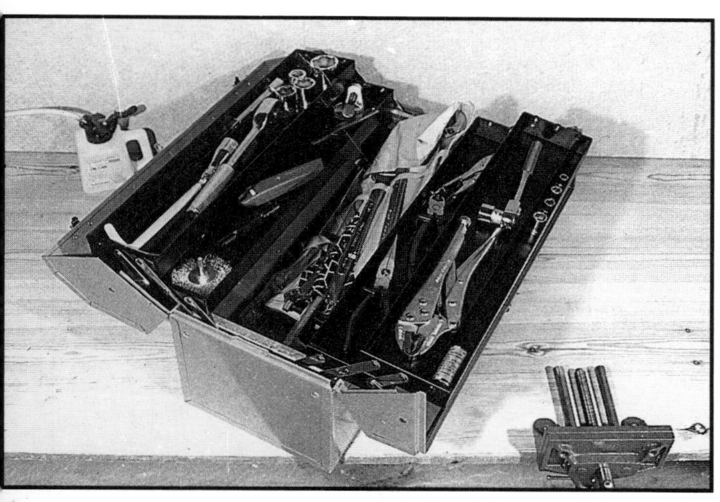

TT1.8
The Sykes-Pickavant Mechanic's Box has four cantilevered trays and an extra lower compartment. It is superbly built and there's no comparison between this and the average accessory shop tool box.

TT1.9
Power Engineering use a Sykes-Pickavant Compressor Tester to check the health of an engine before deciding whether it's a suitable case for modification or whether some reconditioning will be needed first.

Engine diagnosis and tuning is relevant to engine modifications in two ways. First, it enables you to tell whether any reconditioning work will be required on the engine before uprating its performance, and second, it allows you to keep the engine in prime condition thereafter.

TT1.10
The engine will have to be cranked so it is important to remove the HT lead from the distributor cap to avoid the risk of an electric shock. However, on cars fitted with electronic ignition the HT lead must be earthed to prevent damage to the ignition system components.

TT1.12
Faulty valves or piston rings will give variable compression readings and this indicates that some reconditioning may be necessary. A blown cylinder head gasket or – horror of horrors! – a holed piston will also give distinctive compression readings. Deep seated plugs require the accessory extension set shown here.

TT1.11
The Speedline Spark Plug Spanner has a UJ swivel which enables you to give extra leverage and aids access in awkward spots. See ***Understanding Spark Plugs*** for correct tightening procedure.

Hand tools

Here's a typical application of the 6 to 24 volt circuit tester; testing continuity in the ignition circuit. The ignition switch is in the "start" position. You can also check for breaks in a suspect wire by clipping the crocodile clip to a good earth and pushing the sharp end of the probe through the insulation at various points.

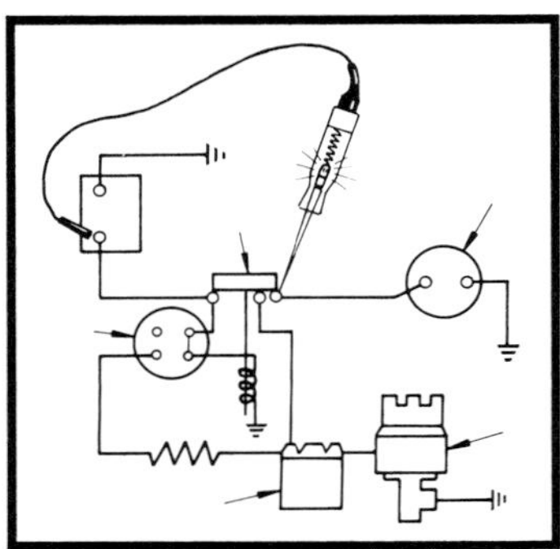

TT1.13

Apart from the compression and circuit testers mentioned and the spark plug thread chaser (bottom right) shown under ***Engine Modifications***, there's a huge range of other Sykes-Pickavant engine tools. Bottom left is the carburettor tool overhaul set while along the top (from right) are: oil filter remover, feeler gauges, piston ring compressor, and the odd-looking but extremely useful cylinder head stands.

TT1.14

It's absolutely crucial that clutch centre plates are aligned correctly. The Speedline Clutch Aligning Tool set enables just about every clutch on the market to be aligned just how it should be.

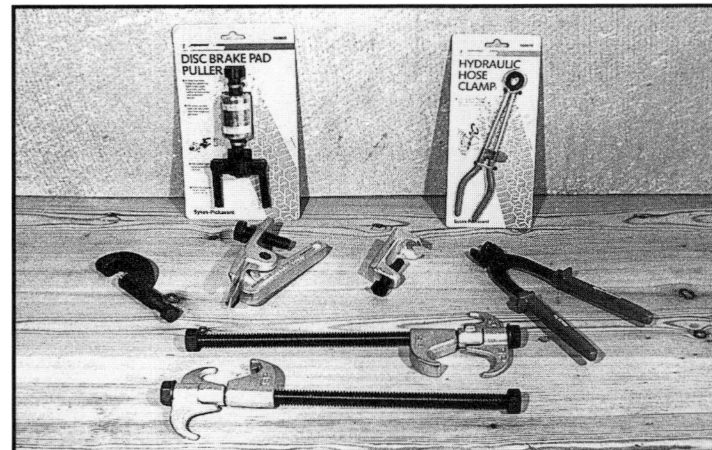

TT1.1

For "chassis work" there's th Speedline disc brake pad puller a nut splitter (a better alternativ to a sheared bolt), and balljoin remover. There are also the too seen in Chapter Four being use by Power Engineering

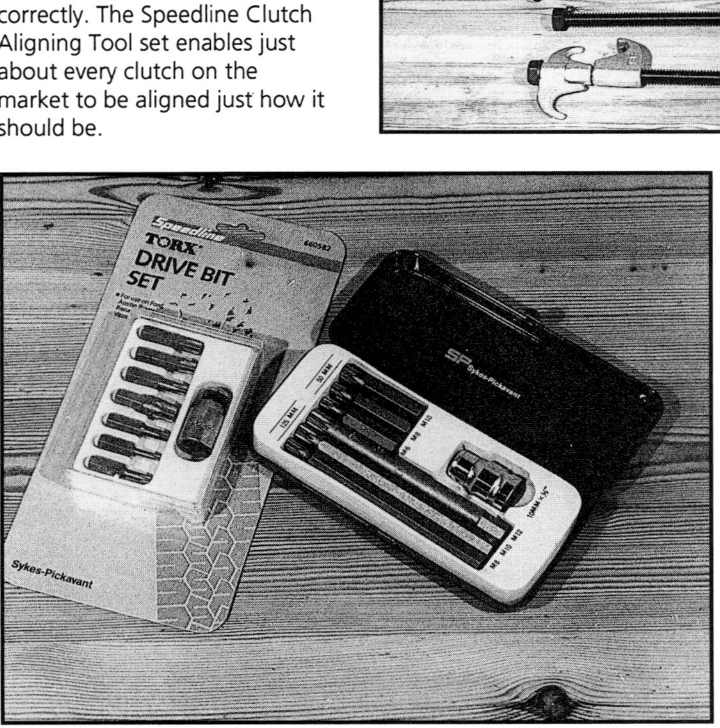

TT1.16

Torx fasteners are found in a variety of applications on modern vehicles, such as door hinges, locks and striker plates, window regulators, wiper motors, seat fixings and bumpers. Sykes-Pickavant Speedline Torx drive bit sets solve the problem.

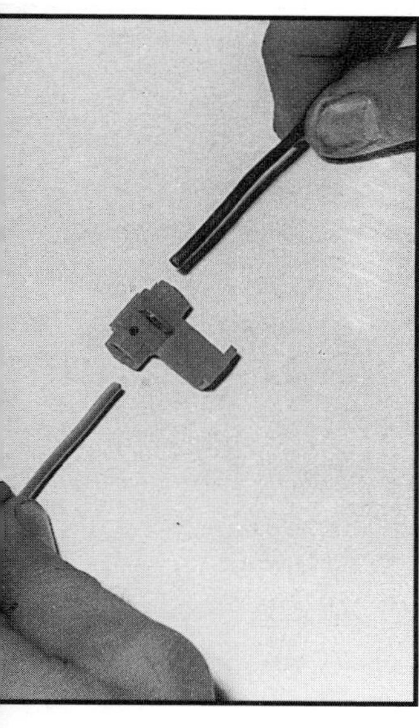

TT1.17
Even professional electricians now often use wiring clips, like the one shown, for joining two pieces of wire together. Called "Scotchloks", these connectors will also join the end of one wire into the "run" of another.

TT1.18
Speedline insulated grip pliers are shown here squeezing the clip and making contact between the two lengths of wire. It's as simple as that!

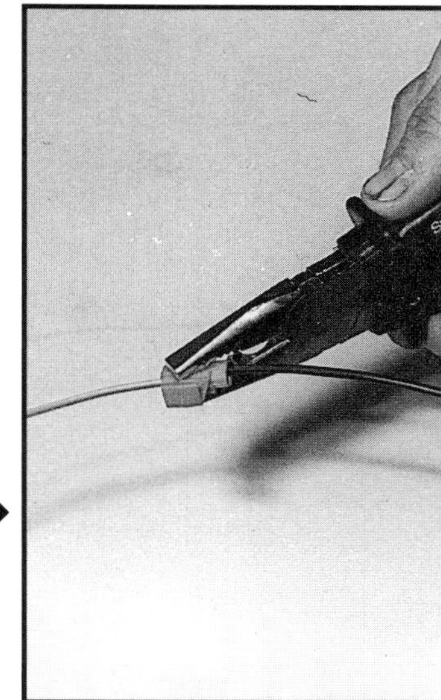

A Speedline long reach riveter will be invaluable when fitting body kits. When selecting rivets remember that the rivet should be 4mm (5/32 inch) longer than the thickness of the material to be riveted.

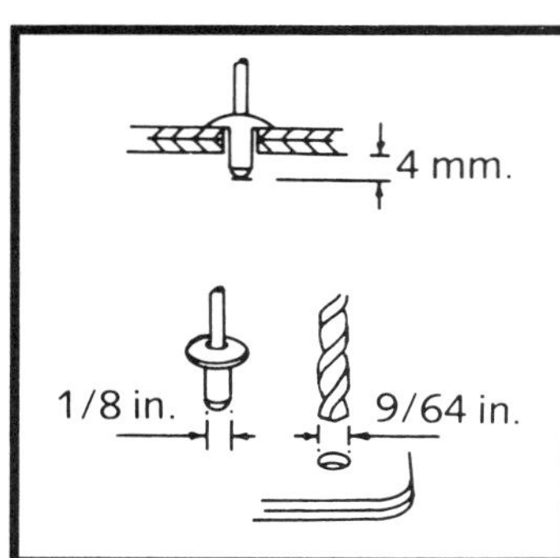

The correct selection of drill size is important; it should be 0.1mm (1/64 inch) larger than the rivet.
(Diagrams courtesy of Sykes-Pickavant)

TT1.19
The finished job is possibly only just about tolerable from the aesthetic point of view, but the electrical contact is perfectly acceptable.

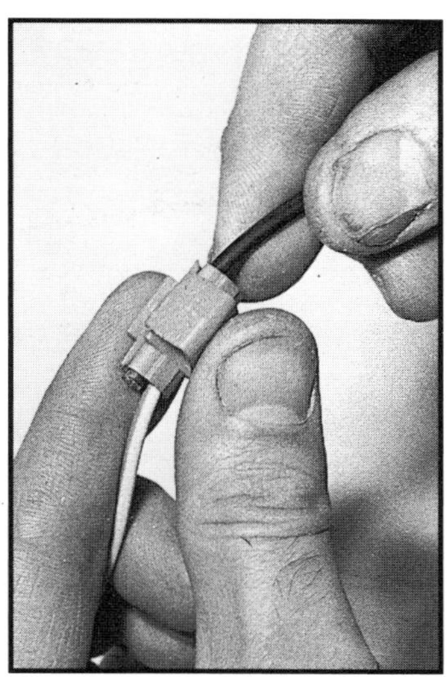

T1.20
edan market an extremely iseful box of wiring clips and asteners shown in the background. The Sykes-ickavant crimping tool is used o pinch a spade terminal to the nd of a bared piece of wire. No oldering is necessary.

TT1.21
Last in this sequence but perhaps first in priority, especially in respect of some of the items to come, is the Speedline Safety Kit. Goggles, gloves, efficient breathing mask and earplugs.

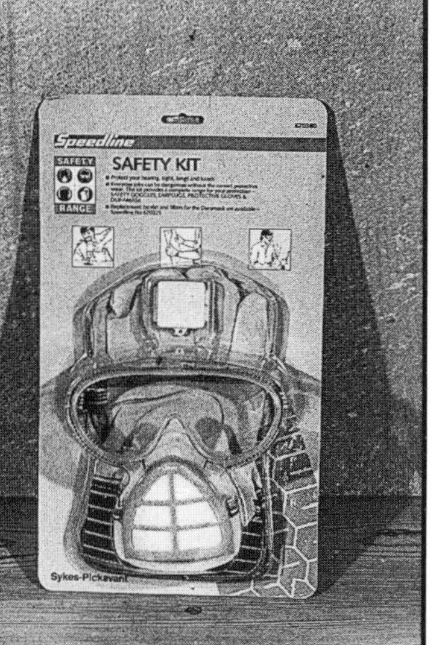

Arc, MIG and spot welding

Although the plasma cutter is only arguably relevant to the car restorer, it's worth looking at. Here is one of the latest developments in arc "welding" technology. Costs of the smaller models such as the SIP Cutmaster 25 have fallen to the level where the keen restoration enthusiast who intends carrying out more than one job could afford to buy one.

It is only a few short years ago that the only way of cutting and welding steel was with messy and relatively dangerous oxy-acetylene welding. Now there's electric arc and MIG and spot welding, and even electric cutting; quick, clean, efficient and best of all, affordable to the keen DIYer. For a combination of quality and economy, the smaller SIP unit shown here takes some beating!

TT2.1
Plasma cutters demand coupling to a compressor to supply cooling air to the torch and cutting area. This cuts down significantly on distortion. Conveniently, the jet of plasma, which carries out the cutting operation, is also formed from air; no special gases here!

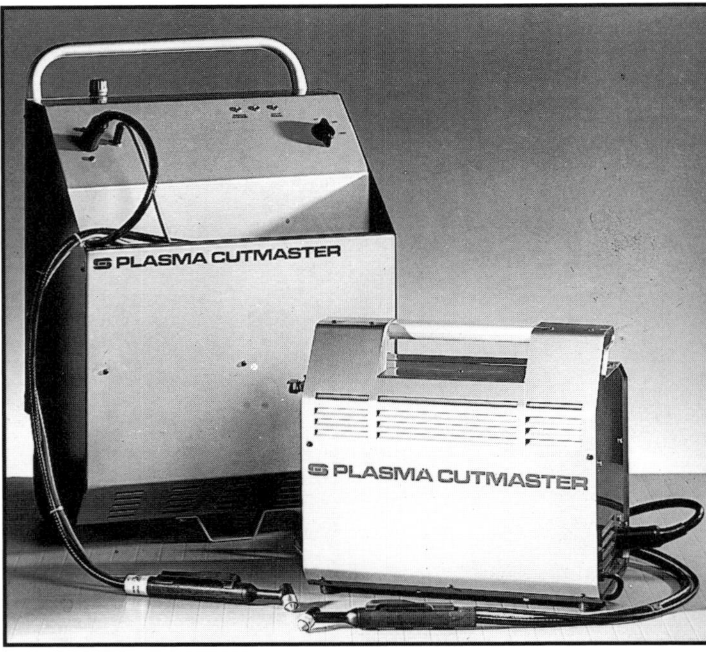

TT2.2
Because electrical contact is needed, it is best to start cutting on a piece of paint-free metal with the smaller models.

TT2.3
Once you start (note gloves and goggles), cutting is amazingly quick and clean. Edges are clean and the torch moves almost as quickly as your hand will let it.

All SIP MIG Welders come with "MIG Welding Step-by-Step", a fully pictorial book by Lindsay Porter on how to get the best from your MIG Welder.

TT2.4
Settings couldn't be easier. There's a button, far right, relating to the type of gas you use (CO_2 or Argon-Mix); three settings: "Max", "Med", "Min", and a wire feed setting being adjusted here. On later models, separate settings for Argon-Mix and CO_2 have been deleted; SIP have found them to be unnecessary.

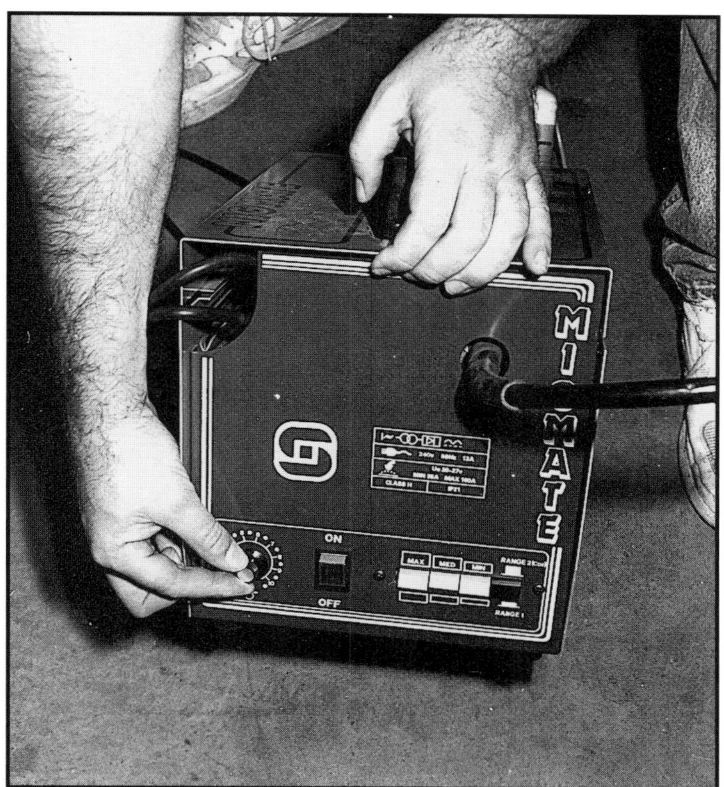

Normally, if you try MIG welding in windy conditions, the shielding gas, which is supposed to surround the weld, will be blown away leaving a weak and truly horrible weld. One solution is to weld indoors or place a wind shield around the weld area. Another is to use a gasless MIG welder such as the highly regarded SIP gasless MIG. The 0.8mm wire – the recommended size for car bodies – contains its own flux, making a separate gas supply unnecessary. Results are not quite as neat but the compromise is well worth considering for the "outdoor types" and those who don't want to have to rent a separate gas bottle.

TT2.5
Most DIYers are happy to use the small disposable gas containers shown here which are available from many DIY and auto accessory outlets. If you give the machine a lot of use, save money by obtaining a large cylinder from one of the major gas companies.

TT2.6
In the background, the British-made MigMate Super. Welding wire appears out of the end of the torch when the trigger is squeezed and that's where the welding takes place.

You'll probably find it easiest to hold the torch at the angle shown and move it steadily in the direction indicated.

(Diagram courtesy SIP)

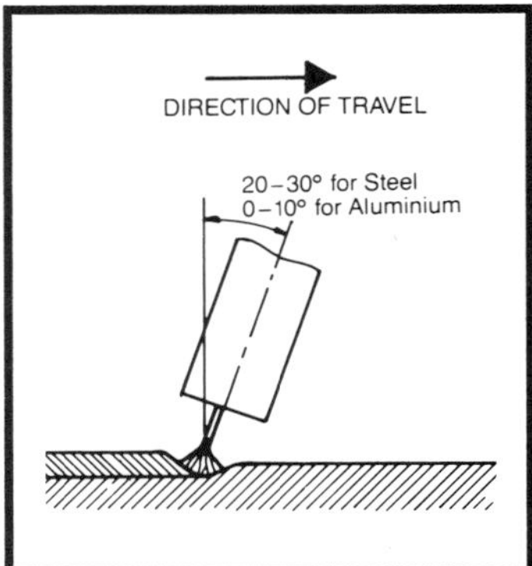

TT2.7
After a little experimentation, the correct settings will be very quickly established. Tack-weld your two work pieces together at regularly spaced intervals, then go back to the start and run a continuous seam weld, end to end. It has to be the simplest form of welding.

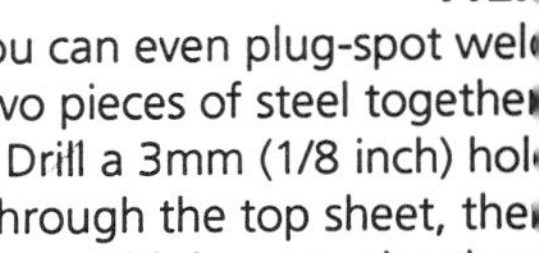

TT2.8
You can even plug-spot weld two pieces of steel together. Drill a 3mm (1/8 inch) hole through the top sheet, then weld down to the sheet beneath, "plugging" the hole.

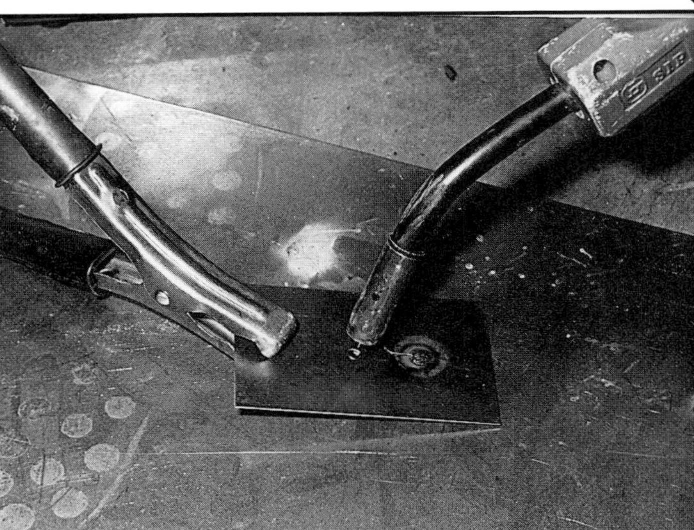

TT2.9
Here is the wire feed mechanism inside the machine. Wire is pushed along the feed pipe by the two rollers, top and bottom. Shielding gas (see pipes on right) travels along the same pipe as the welding wire.

TT2.10
Disposable cartridges of shielding gas; varying types, thicknesses and quantities of welding wire; gauges and fittings, all available from SIP.

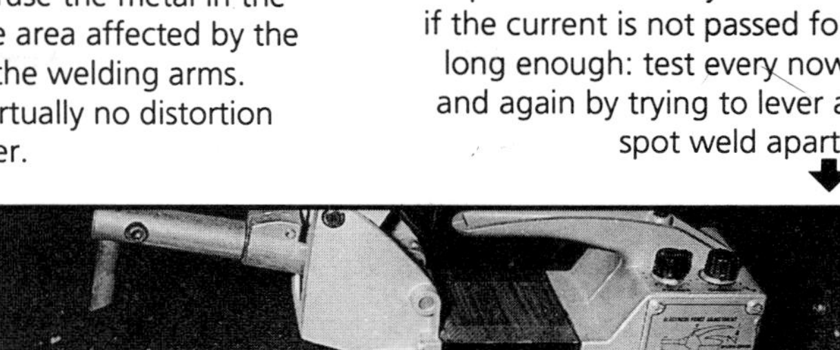

TT2.11
Spot welders, or "resistance welders" fuse the metal in the immediate area affected by the points of the welding arms. There is virtually no distortion whatsoever.

TT2.12
The spot weld will only be weak if the current is not passed for long enough: test every now and again by trying to lever a spot weld apart.

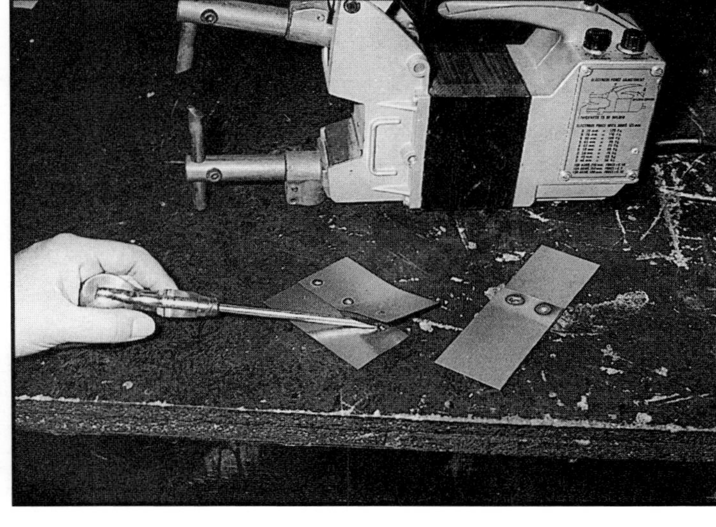

One of the smaller SIP spot welders also has a timer which consistently regulates the duration of the spot weld. It automatically compensates for slight rusting, paint residues and zinc coatings for best results.

TT2.13
The weld will also be weak if too much power has been passed, blowing a hole through the metal. The Automatic SIP model virtually refuses to do this, even when provoked!

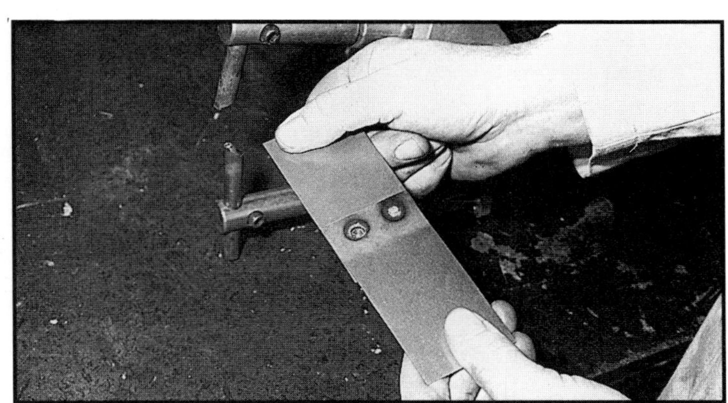

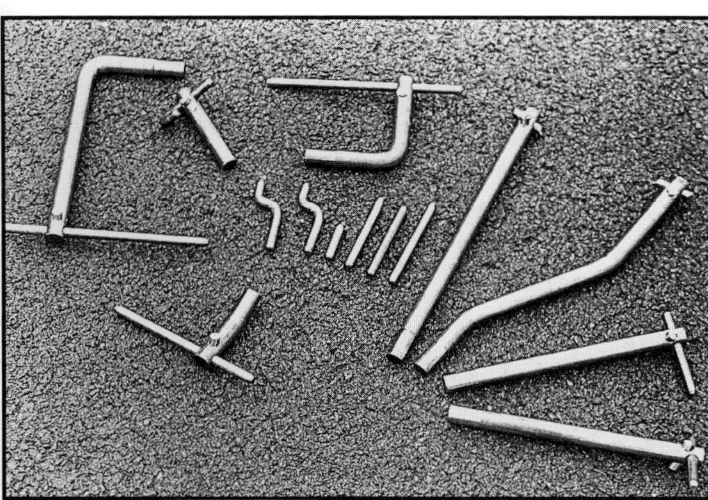

TT2.14
Manufacturers put cars together almost entirely with spot welds. But access is easy on the production line: repairers can call on a variety of extension arms to help them get around obstacles.

Arc, MIG and spot welding

"Strike an arc" by either stroking the end of the rod on the work piece or strike a hard blow with the end of the rod allowing it to bounce up to the correct distance away. It must be said that the procedure takes more practice than for MIG welding. Another problem is that you can't arc weld really thin sheet steel but the cost of the welders themselves start at less than half the price of a MIG.

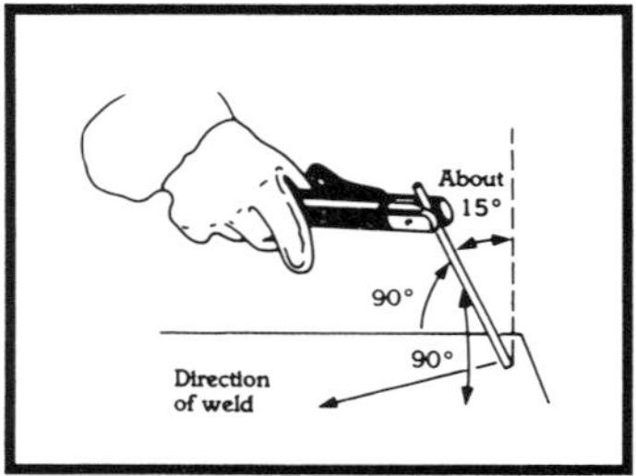

TT2.15
Current settings are easily controlled by using the sliding scale on Weldmate models.

TT2.16
As with MIG, you have to tack weld first. The slag which forms on the top of an arc weld has be to carefully and meticulously chipped away using the chipping hammer which SIP thoughtfully provide.

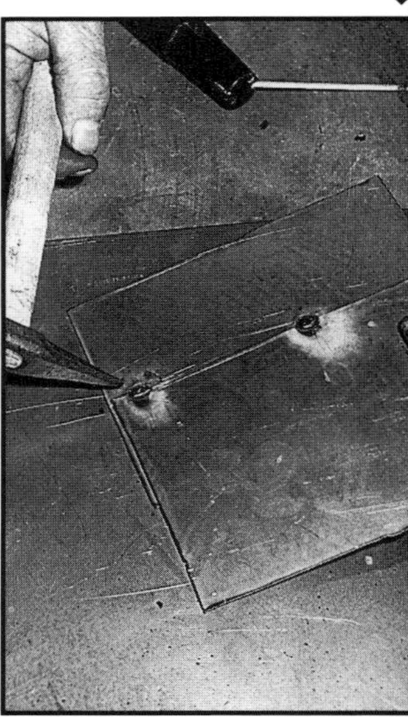

TT2.17
A full seam weld can then be run from one end of the joint to the other.

TT2.18
The layer of slag should chip away smoothly and cleanly. Erratic rod movements will introduce slag into the weld and weaken the joint.

TT2.19
All SIP welders come with full instructions to assist you in getting started. This one is also equipped with a carbon-arc brazing kit.

TT2.20
The carbon-arc rods create a heat-only arc which heats the metal and melts a brazing rod held in the hand. This enables the arc welder to successfully braze-weld thin sheet steel. It's not suitable for repairing major structural components.

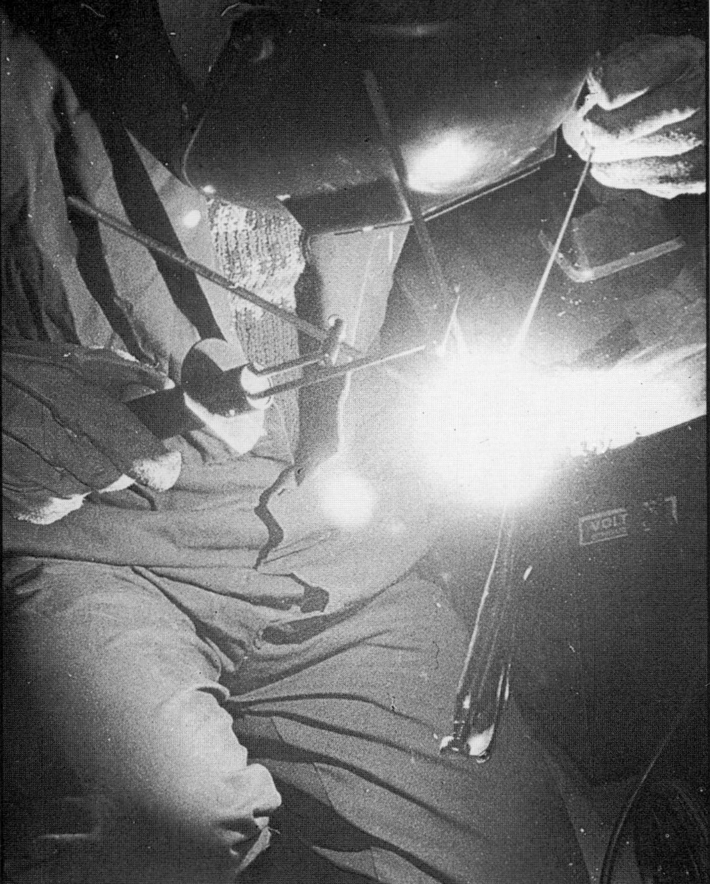

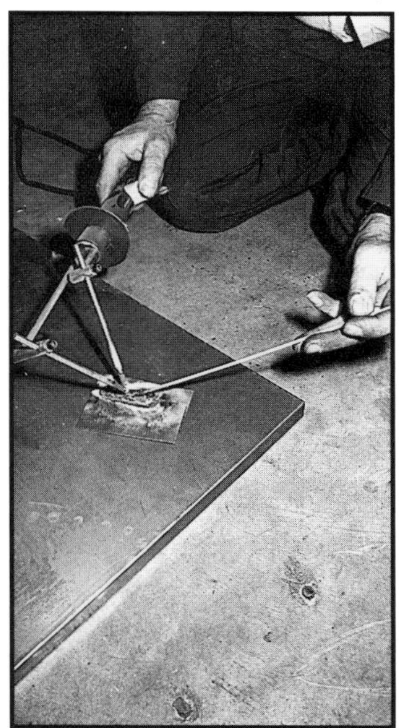

TT2.21
Repairing a stripped-down car door with carbon-arc brazing. Use of full head shield is essential because both hands are otherwise employed.

Safety

Gloves should be worn when welding. The UV rays given off can be a health hazard and hot metal can burn! Sleeves should also be rolled down. It is *vital* that a full face mask is used at all times. Looking at a welding arc with the naked eye can cause an extremely painful eye condition short term, permanent eye damage long term. Keep children, onlookers and pets away. Looking through the safety glass rapidly becomes second nature. Overalls should be of a flame-resistant material, *not* nylon.

Power tools

We are only concerned here with tools that will help you "Improve and Modify" your Fiesta. Those shown in this section are from the wide range of Hitachi DIY Power Tools. For the more adventurous enthusiast, the company also have an extensive range of industrial power tools to choose from. Many of the tools shown here have been used elsewhere in the book for various fitting tasks.

Hitachi, or to give the company its full title, Hitachi Power Tools Ltd., have been producing electric motors (which are the basis for all power tools) for the last forty years and have created the latest range to be the best in performance, reliability and handling ease. It is reassuring to note that the company take safety so very seriously, for this is a subject that should be number one on your shopping list. Read the instructions supplied with every power tool before use.

TT3.1
The Hitachi power tool range not only functions well, but looks good too! The incredibly strong plastic casings are designed to stand up to the use (and mis-use!) that the average DIYer can give. Those shown here are just a few of the most popular from Hitachi's DIY range.

TT3.2
The cordless drill is the revolution of the 80s and is manna from heaven for the regular Fiesta DIY enthusiast. Requiring no mains power, it obviously needs no mains leads or awkward (and often dangerous) extension cables. This is the FDV 10DA and is part of a three model range. For most in-car tasks, the 9.6 volt unit is more than powerful enough, as holes tend to be fairly small. Naturally, a charging unit is supplied with the drill.

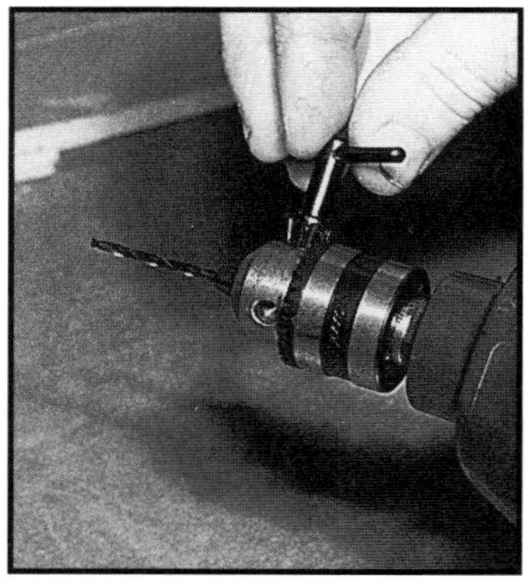

TT3.3
Any size hole requires a small pilot hole to be drilled first. Always use the correct size chuck key and if it is worn, replace it. Lost chuck keys are the bane of the DIYer, but Hitachi have provided a slot in the drill casing to store it.

TT3.4
Before drilling, it is important that the hole position is accurately marked. Use masking tape so that: (a) it is easy to see any marks made and, (b) the drill bit is less likely to slip. Then the position should be dot punched carefully, for more than a tap could result in a dented piece of bodywork!

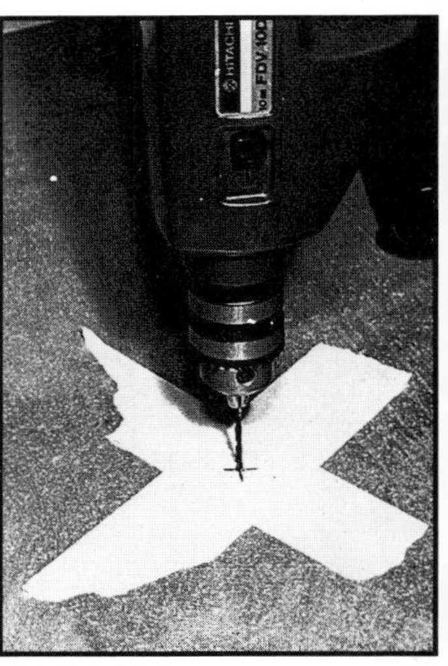

TT3.5
The lighter weight of the cordless drill makes it ideal for pilot hole drilling with such tiny drill bits.

Tools that were once purely the province of the professional are now within the price range of the keen DIYer. New technology has meant that, as features offered are on the increase, prices in real terms have fallen. The use of professional quality tools makes it possible for the home enthusiast to achieve professional standards, saving on the cost of paying someone else to do the job and more than offsetting the cost in tools and equipment.

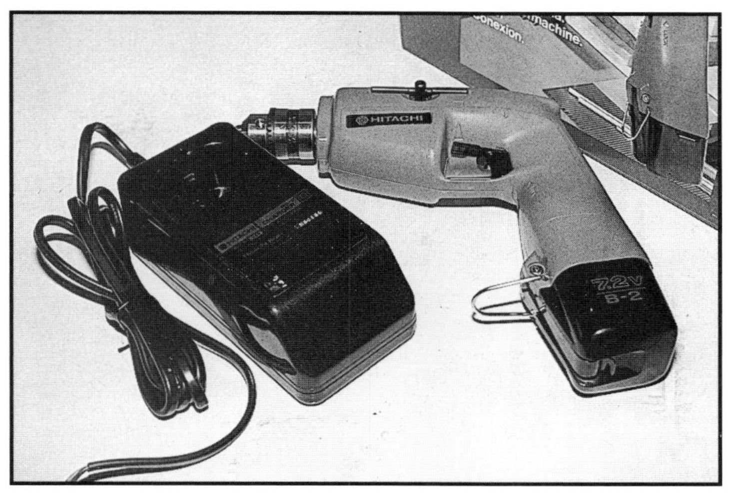

TT3.6 A variation on a theme, the DTC 10 driver/drill (from Hitachi's industrial range) is another cordless tool designed with the auto DIYer in mind. Although it can be used as a drill, it is much more suited to its role as a power screwdriver. The domestic equivalent is the FDW 10D. Unlike the FDV 10DA, the battery is a separate entity. It slots into the base of the handle and clips into place. It is simple to remove when recharging is required and slots neatly into the purpose built charging unit.

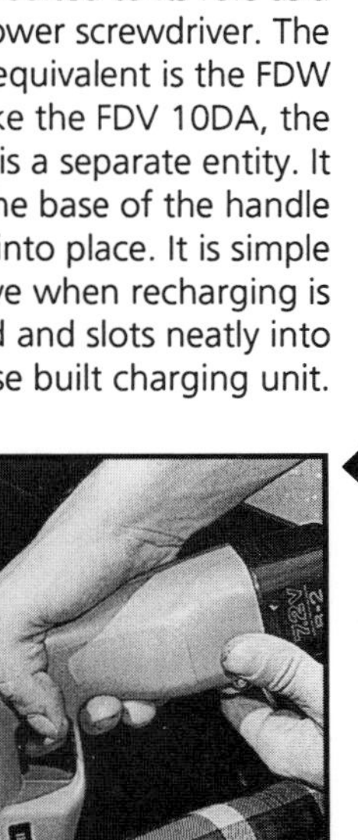

TT3.7 It doesn't take long to get into the habit of using the power "driver" on almost each and every occasion.

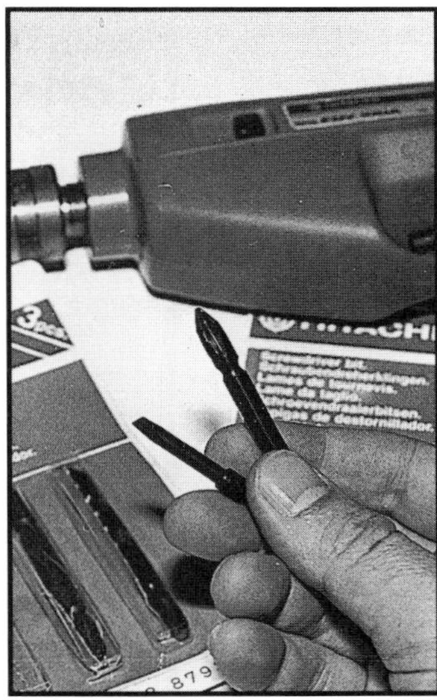

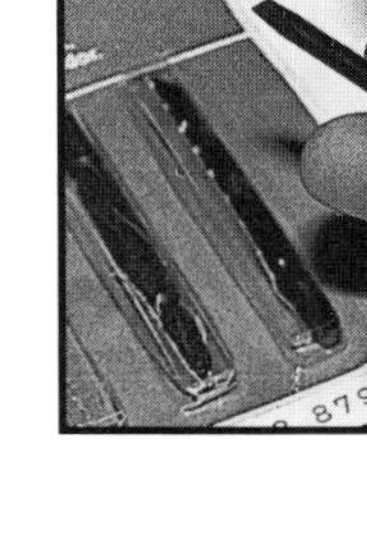

TT3.8 Whichever you use as a power screwdriver, you can use standard screwdriver and drill bits of which Hitachi produce a range of various styles and sizes. Seen here are a pack of crosshead and a pack of slotted head bits. The varieties here are sufficient to permit the average Fiesta owner to carry out most DIY tasks.

TT3.9 There are some jobs requiring more power than can be obtained from any cordless drill, but it's unlikely you'll need any more than the 600W that the FDV 16VA 16mm impact drill can offer. It has a two-speed mechanical change and the chuck has a 13mm capacity. The speed of the drill varies directly in accordance with the amount of pressure placed on the trigger. The knurled nut within it adjusts the pressure required and thus the right speed for the material you are drilling can be predetermined. A switch on the top rear of the machine controls the direction of rotation.

Power tools

Sanding dust in the air can create a definite health hazard, even if you use a machine like the Hitachi, which has a built-in dust collector. It may not be necessary to wear a face mask if an extractor system is fitted, especially if your domestic vacuum cleaner is powerful enough to take the bulk of the dust away. If the substance you are sanding presents a health hazard in itself (for example, glass fibre), then you should always wear a mask.

TT3.10
A typical job for the big drill involves using a rotary wire brush to clean up the insides of your road wheels. A painstaking task by hand, this powerful tool makes light work of it.

TT3.11
The FS 10SA orbital sander comes complete with a dust collector attachment (but not the actual bag, which is an optional extra with this model), and three sheets of sandpaper. This kind of device is particularly useful for sanding down large areas of paintwork, where the orbital motion will not create deep scratches.

TT3.12
Little could be simpler than replacing the paper in the machine. A clamp, shown here, is used to hold the paper at this end and a similar clamp holds it at the other. Make sure, of course, that you always use the correct grade for the job in hand; using too harsh a grade for a delicate job will not give a good result, regardless of machine!

TT3.13
Once solely the prerogative of the professional, the mini-grinder is now becoming much more commonplace in the DIY motorist's toolkit and no wonder! Obviously, those replacing body panels will see an immediate benefit, by being able to cut away old rusted bits of Fiesta. The grinder cuts through normal bodywork like a knife through butter. Throw out the hacksaw and use the grinder! ***Note carefully the maker's instructions when using any grinder!***

TT3.14 Sorting out a rusty tailpipe end on this Fiesta is just the sort of job for the Hitachi grinder. Note the position of the handle making operation easy for our left-handed operator.

It's worth bearing in mind when selecting power tools, that, to a great extent, they can also be put to uses around the home. For instance, the Hitachi Jigsaw shown here attacking bodywork, could just as easily be used for cutting new kitchen shelves to length, if you're ever out of your garage long enough! Cordless tools are particularly versatile making it easy to reach the places other drills cannot reach!

TT3.15 Like the orbital sander, the SP18T Sander/Polisher will be of benefit to those who intend to work on the bodywork of their Fiesta. The rubber disc is fitted to the machine by means of this arbor which is turned by a two-pronged tool (similar to the grinder) whilst the chuck is held by a special spanner, also provided. It can then either be used with a sanding disc or ...

TT3.16 ... the special, soft buffing pad included. It takes the effort out of polishing the car with no less than 1200 watts as opposed to "one elbow power"!

TT3.17 Fancy a sunroof? You'll get a good idea of how to fit one in Chapter Two and if you think you could fit it yourself, you'll need a jigsaw. More commonly, the jigsaw is put to good use in creating holes in interior trim for speaker mounting. This is the Hitachi FCJ55V which has a maximum cutting depth of 55mm, variable speed and four-step orbital action. The angle of the blade can be varied in relation to thickness of the material.

Power tools

All of the Hitachi tools shown here are well designed and superbly built to give you a good result every time. Naturally, all are covered by a comprehensive, one year guarantee. However, you have to know how to use them and this means reading the instructions. Getting the best out of your power tools should not be a matter of "hit and miss" and not studying the operating instructions before using any powered item could result in poor work or, worse, personal injury!

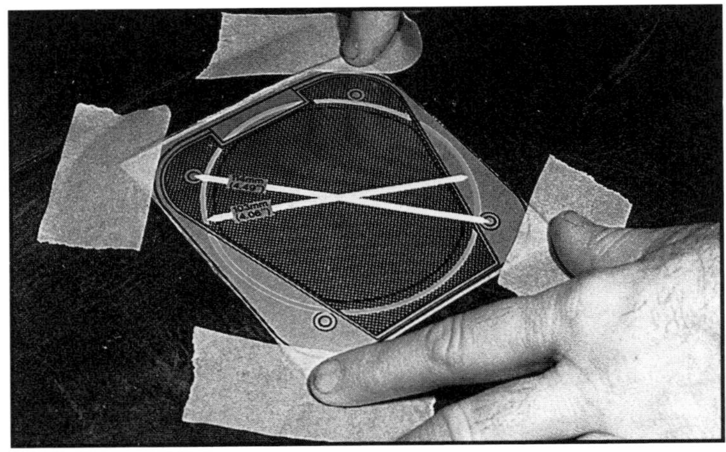

TT3.18
More commonly, the jigsaw is put to good use in creating holes in interior trim for speaker mounting. In the case of this Sharp speaker, a handy template is supplied and the first task is to use masking tape to secure the template to the trim.

TT3.19
Before cutting out the centre hole, the four speaker mounting holes have to be drilled.

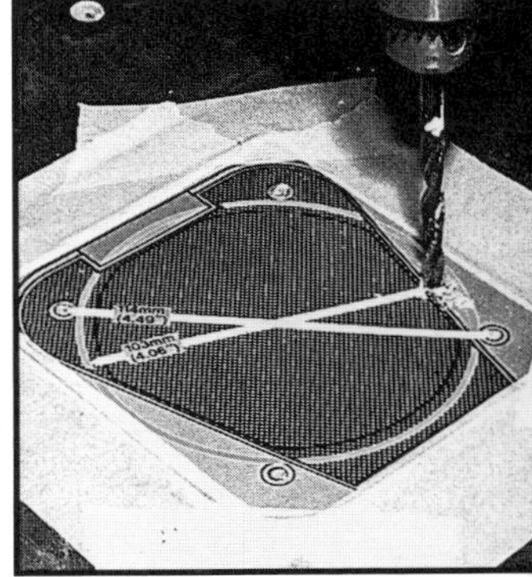

TT3.20
Yet another drilling operation. This time, a larger size bit is required in order to provide ...

TT3.21
... a starting point for the jigsaw blade. By using a smooth action and keeping strictly to the line marked on the template ...

When using a jigsaw take the same precautions as you would when drilling; check carefully that you will not saw through operating cables or wires before starting. And always ensure that the plate through which the blade passes is held down firmly to the surface being cut.

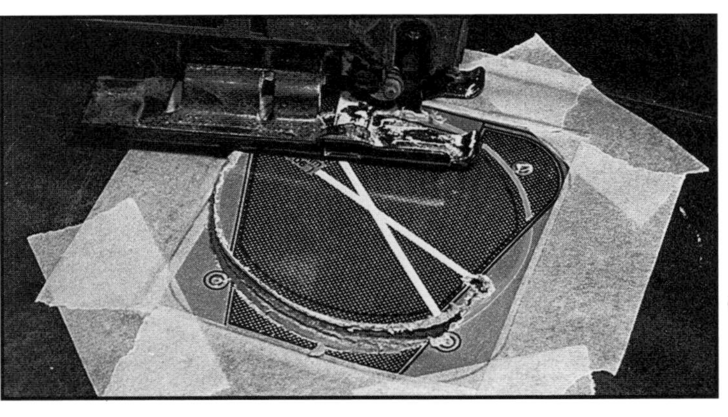

TT3.22
... cutting a smooth hole of exactly the right size is simplicity itself.

Working with filler and glass fibre

Blending in with resin, mat and filler

We chose Plastic Padding products for this part of the work, partly because they are readily available from just about any auto accessory shop in quantities which are just sufficient for projects of this size, and also because Plastic Padding type Elastic Filler is noted for its ability to flex and to withstand shock and vibration without cracking or coming adrift.

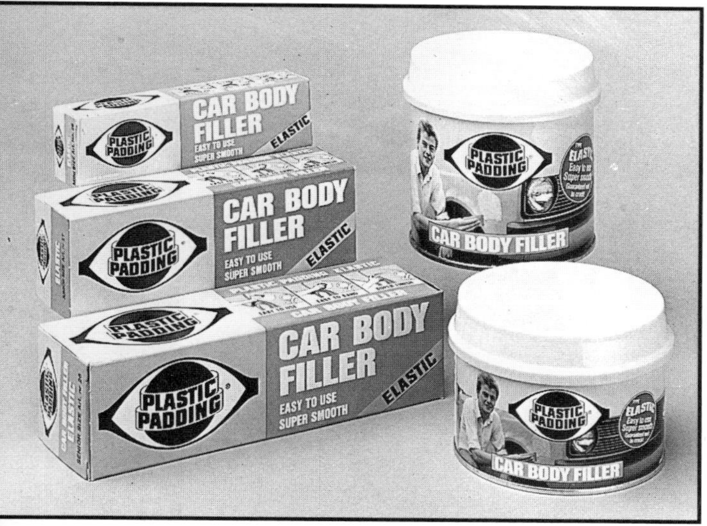

TT4.1
This is part of the large Plastic Padding range and it's worth mentioning that they also sell aerosol cans of Stonechip Protect for spraying onto sills, valances and other vulnerable areas.

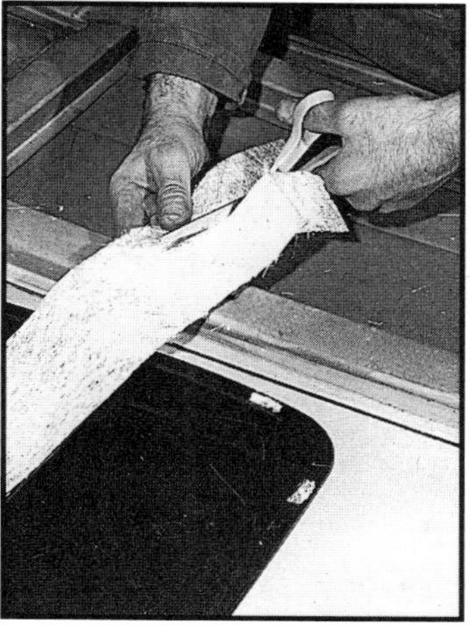

TT4.2
You won't get in too much of a mess if you carry out work in the right order. Cut strips of glass fibre mat to the width and length required before mixing the resin.

Weight for weight, glass fibre is stronger than steel and yet is far easier to work with. It can be persuaded to adopt any shape that you wish and yet bonds with great tenacity. Its close cousin, body filler, is the perfect medium for filling gaps and smoothing out imperfections to give a perfect finish.

Before applying filler or resin to a previously painted surface, remove all paint and rust back to bare, shiny metal. "Key" a plastic surface by rubbing carefully with abrasive paper, then rub over with a spirit wipe on a clean cloth.

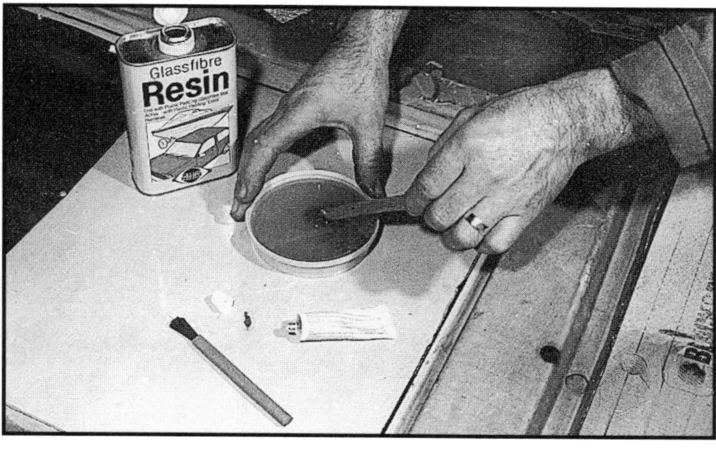

TT4.3
Add the recommended amount of hardener with the resin in a suitable container (this is the lid from the tin of Plastic Padding filler), and stir thoroughly until the hardener is well mixed.

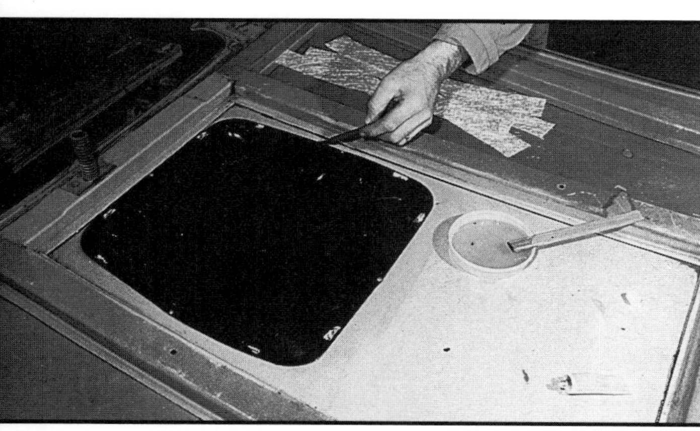

TT4.4
Brush resin generously onto the areas to receive the glass fibre. Don't brush it out like paint; leave enough to soak into the mat.

Blending in with resin, mat and filler

Resin will come off your hands after a generous application of hand cleaner, although it's strongly recommended that you to use a barrier cream first as well. Alternatively, use disposable plastic gloves or even plastic bags tied around the wrists.

TT4.5
Place the mat in position and add more resin. You're now at stage one, where you need to add a fairly generous amount of resin to break down the bonding agent in the mat allowing it to go floppy.

TT4.6
After you've "wetted-out" all of the mat, go back and stipple it vigorously with a brush. It will then follow the contours of the panel beneath, taking on its shape and the removal of any air bubbles will add strength.

TT4.7
The SP craft knife comes in handy for removing any excess glass fibre but only if you catch the glass fibre ***after*** it has ceased to be "wet" and before it sets hard.

TT4.8 ➡
When the glass fibre has gone hard, the Hitachi angle grinder comes into its own, but be careful not to go straight through! You will see further on in this section that the Plastic Padding hardener is yellow in colour. If the resin and the glass fibre are yellow all through, this shows that you've mixed the resin thoroughly.

If you find that you need more resin or more hardener separately (although you shouldn't if you use it in the proportions recommended by Plastic Padding), there are individual cans of resin available in various sizes from your auto accessory shop.

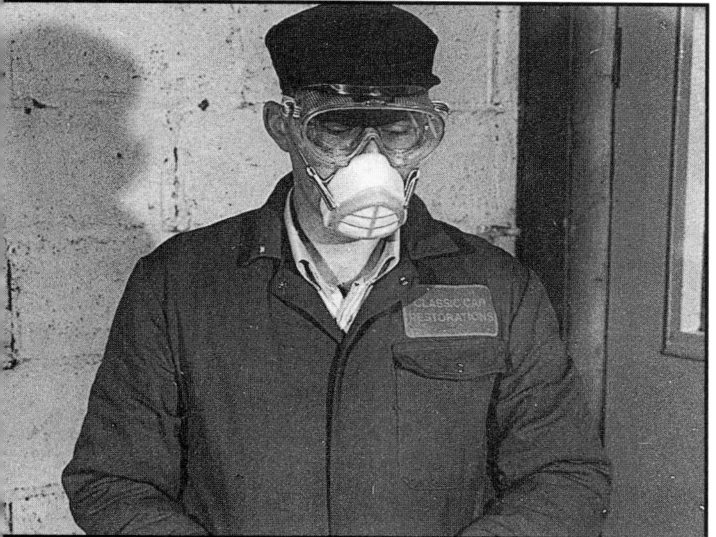

⬅ **TT4.9**
All glass fibre dust can be harmful if inhaled during sanding, and therefore you should always wear goggles and a face mask during grinding or sanding operations. This is the SP kit featured earlier.

TT4.10 ➡
Being determined to obtain a good finish underneath the bonnet as well as on top, we spread a layer of Plastic Padding type Elastic Filler over the glass fibre and then sanded it smooth before painting it. On the top side, the protuding self-tapping crews were trimmed by fitting a cutting wheel to the Hitachi angle grinder. Plastic Padding ecommend cutting off any resin that may have oozed through with a craft knife before it goes too hard. If left until later it would have to be ground away.

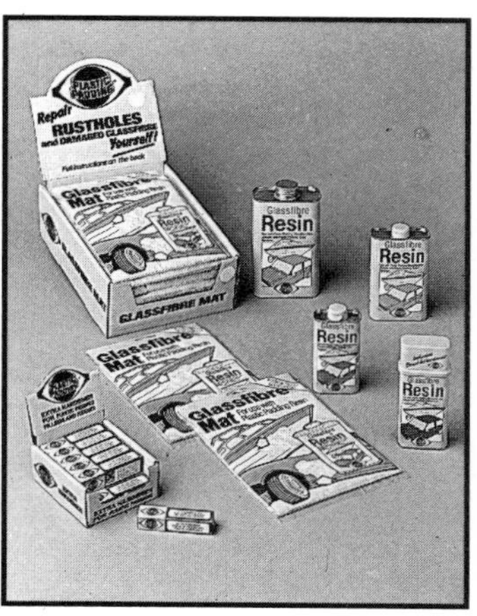

Plastic Padding Glass Fibre Mat, Resin and Hardener can be obtained from most car accessory shops.

Filler "goes off" (sets) by chemical reaction. The warmer the weather, the quicker the reaction and the less hardener you need. It is not recommended that you use excess hardener in the mixture. In cold conditions apply moderate heat by a blow fan to start setting.

TT4.11
Plastic Padding type Elastic comes in a tube or in a tin with its own spreader and sufficient hardener for the filler in that particular pack.

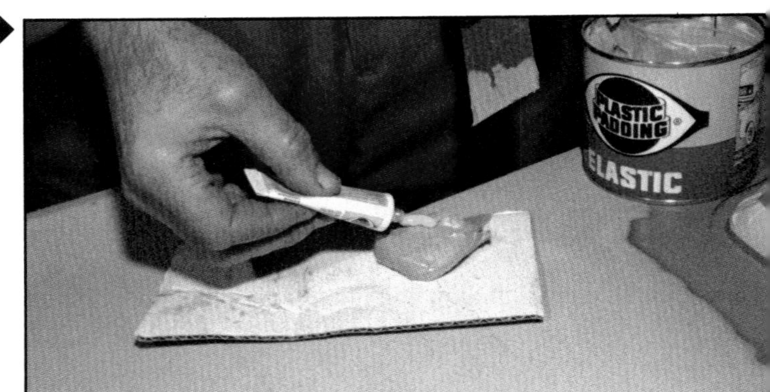

TT4.12
Take a piece of clean card, scoop out sufficient filler and squeeze on top as much hardener as you will need. Don't get hardener into the open tin, nor, if you can help it, on your fingers since it can be harmful.

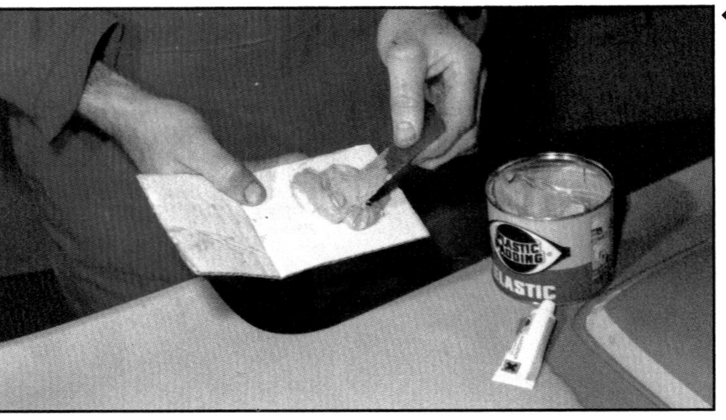

TT4.13
Again, the Plastic Padding trick of including a strongly coloured hardener pays off because you can see clearly when the pigmented hardener has been mixed thoroughly with the filler

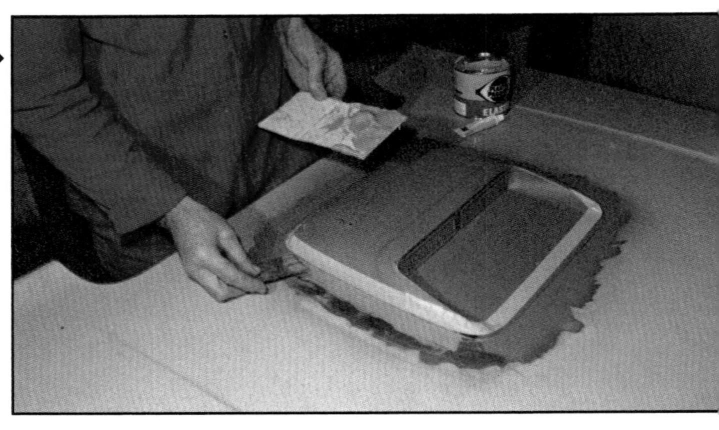

TT4.14
Carefully spread filler into the joint, leaving it very slightly proud but not so high that you have an enormous amount of sanding to do. Plastic Padding filler has the great advantage that it sands particularly easily giving a smooth finish. After sanding, you will invariably find a few dips and hollows which will have to be filled with a further application of filler.

Plastic Padding also produce aerosol Stonechip Protect for protecting sills, spoilers and the underside of panels vulnerable to stone chipping.

Aerosol paint is the ideal way of spraying anything up to a single panel at a time. After all, you don't need to buy any expensive equipment, only the can that the paint comes in.

TT5.1
The "wet-or-dry" paper was used with water to feather out the Plastic Padding filler, leaving no trace of a hard edge..

T5.2
efore starting to spray, the rimer was taken outside, haken vigorously, and the ozzle cleared.

TT5.3
The can was held about six inches away and red oxide sprayed onto bare metal.

Spraying with aerosol

Illustration TT5.8 shows why it's essential to shake an aerosol paint can for several minutes before using it. The agitator ball has the job of mixing the paint pigment, which may be quite thick at the bottom, thoroughly with the solvent. In very cold weather you may also have to immerse the can in warm (not boiling) water for several minutes before use. Never puncture an aerosol can nor expose it to direct heat.

TT5.4
This was magical (or, at least, the results of sanding it later were). High Build Spray Putty was sprayed onto the whole area ...

TT5.
... and then, extending a litt wider than the area of th original red oxide primer, second coat of spray putty wa applied after the first had driec

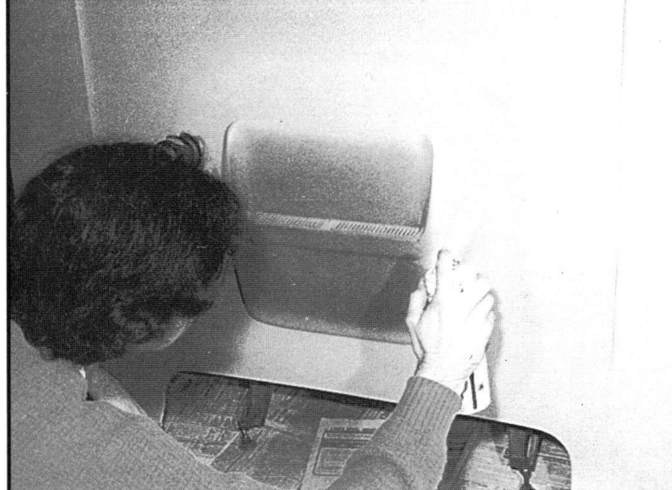

TT5.6
It's best to practice your spraying on a spare scrap of sheet metal. Hold the can too close and the paint will run, too far away and you'll have a "dry" look finish.

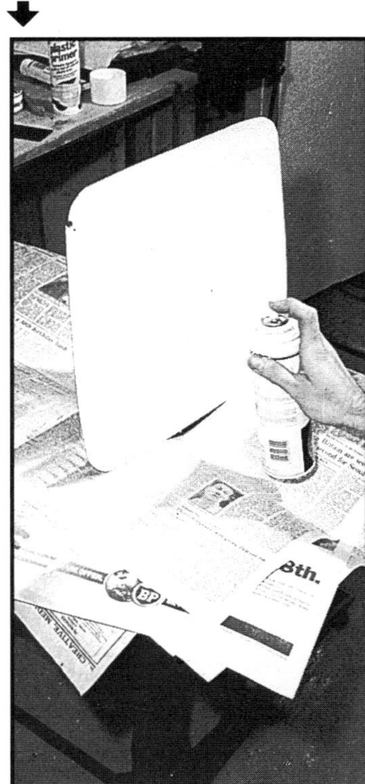

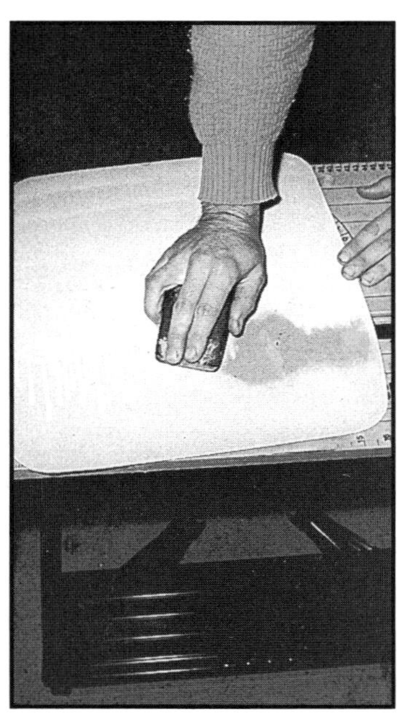

TT5.7
Very slight runs may be polished out but most will have to be sanded out when the paint is dry using fine "wet-or-dry" paper.

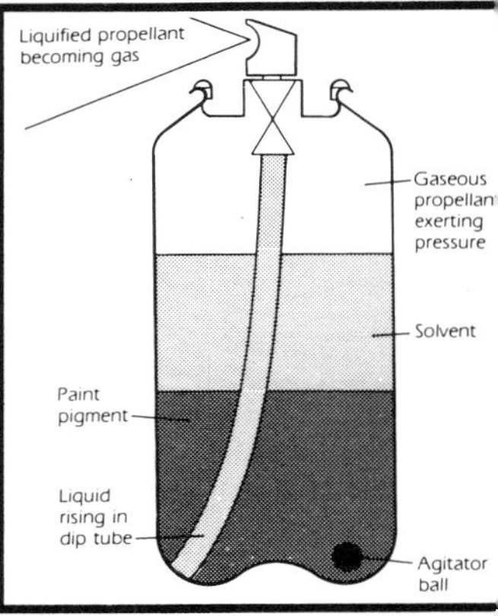

TT5.
How an aerosol works. If you ti the can upside down, the pai flow ceases. At the end c spraying, use this technique t clear the nozzl

When choosing your primer colour, use red for dark shades, grey for lighter coats, and grey or preferably white for white top coats and metallics.

TT5.9
Provided that the filler work was carried out properly, the use of High Build Spray Putty will allow you to remove every last blemish when you sand it out with fine "wet-or-dry" supported on a flat rubbing block.

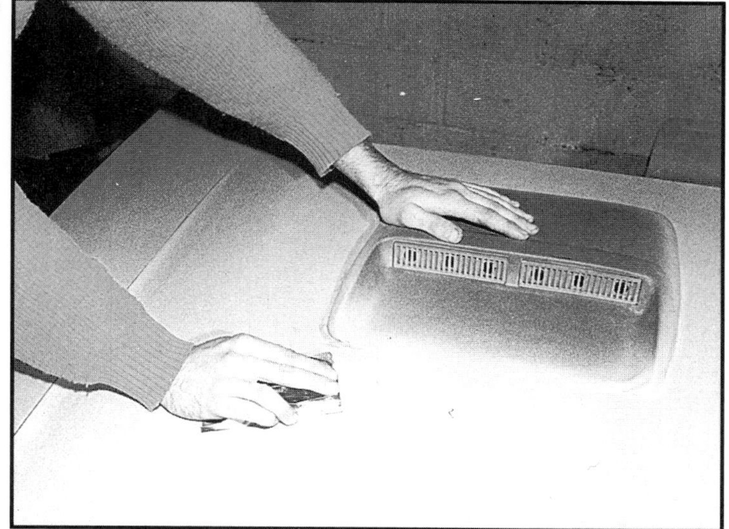

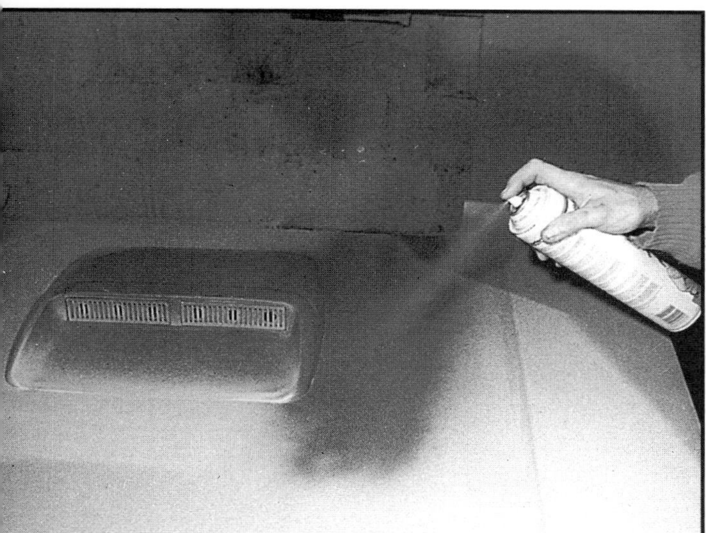

TT5.10
By now, and for no apparent reason, we were working with the bonnet laid horizontally. We chose to spray on grey primer paint as a barrier colour between the yellow and the white top coat to follow. Red and yellow have a nasty habit of "grinning through" white surface coats above them.

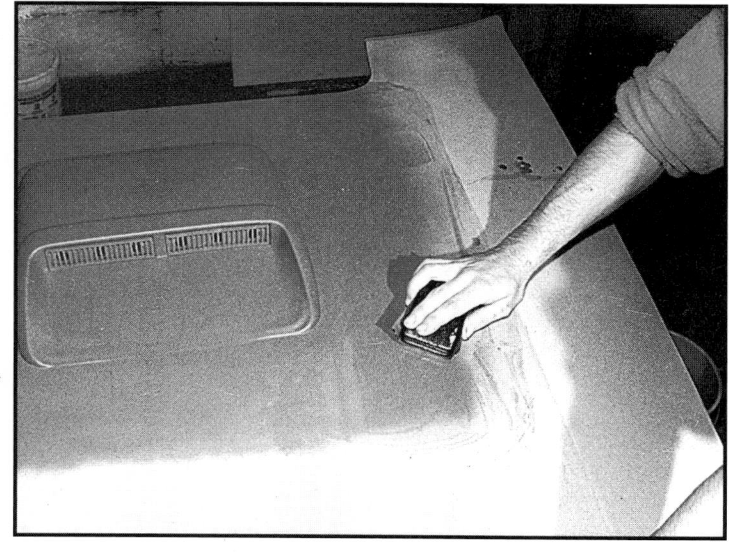

TT5.11
Plenty of water, a few spots of washing-up liquid and the finest grade of "wet-or-dry" and the final primer coat was prepared for finish painting.

You should make sure that you choose high quality aerosol paint containers which are specially designed not to clog and not to spit blobs of paint onto the work. There's nothing more frustrating.

TT5.12
Now here's a tip from the experts. Holding a tin of black spray paint about a foot or more away from the job, a light coat was dusted onto the work surface.

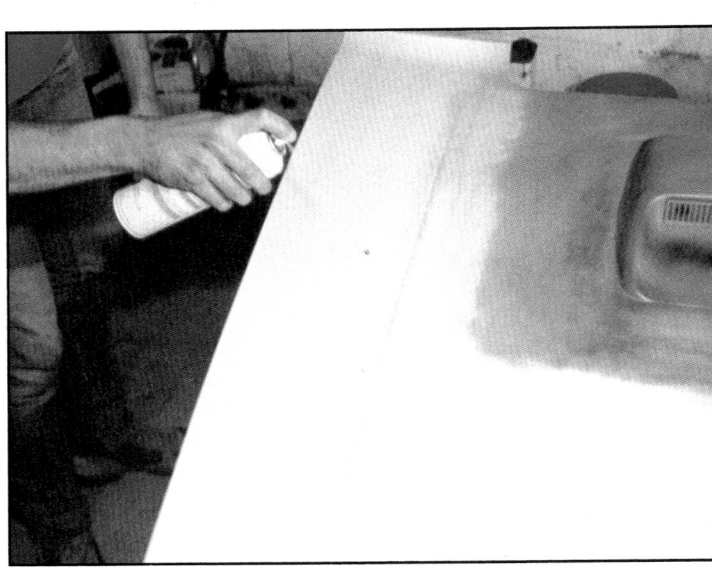

TT5.13
The idea is not to change the colour of the panel but just to put an even sprinkling of paint over the whole panel.

TT5.14
Sand the entire panel all over once more with the finest grade of paper and the guide coat, as it is called, will be sanded off in all but the low areas. After you wipe off with a dry cloth, any low spots and blemishes will stand out like a sore thumb!

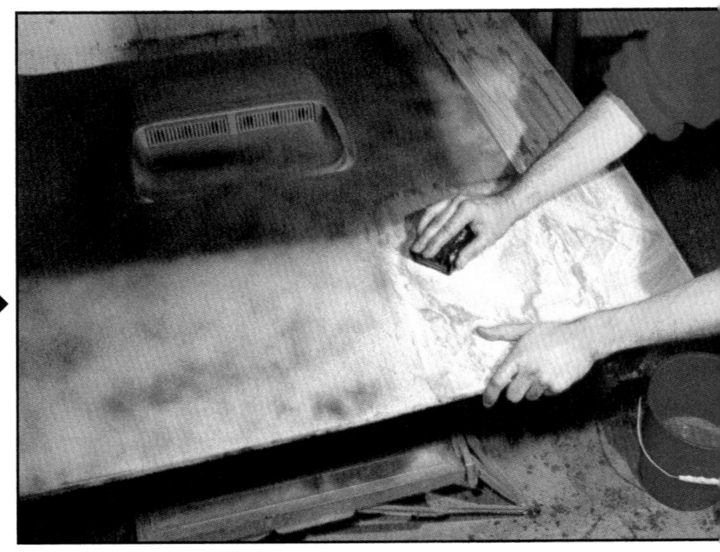

TT5.15
It might look uncomfortable but you should always hold the nozzle down with the very tip of your finger. Alternatively, try the aerosol trigger, shown on page 224.

TT5.16
If you do what comes naturally, the part of your finger sticking forwards catches the edge of the spray which builds up into a drip which is then shot forward as a blob onto your lovely handiwork. Most annoying!

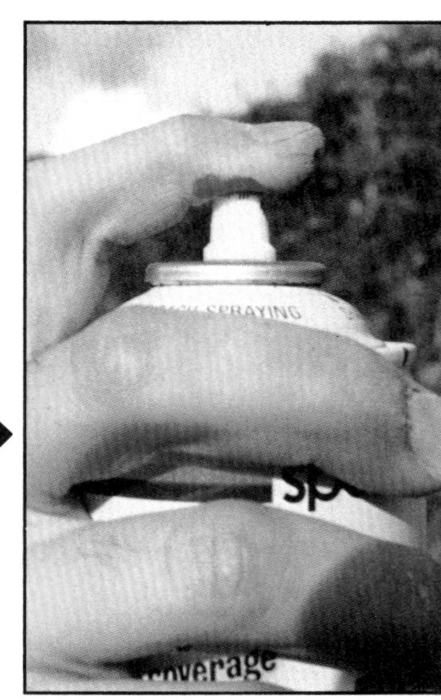

You can spray the first two finish coats on in fairly quick succession, just leaving a few minutes between them for the first coat to "flash off". The second coat should be sprayed at right angles to the first.
(Diagram courtesy Spectra)

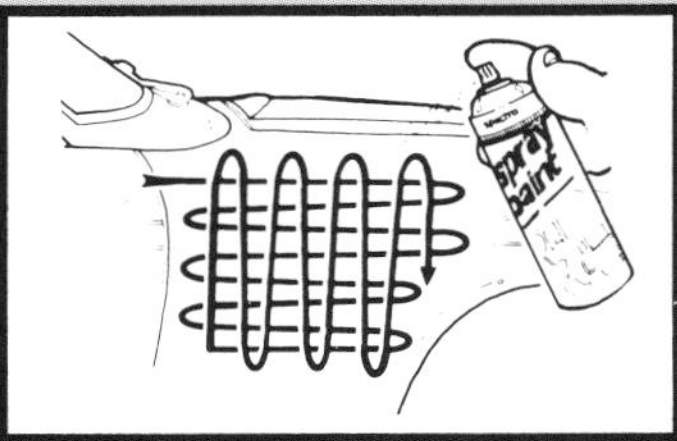

Safety Note
Read the safety notes on page 217. They apply to aerosol spraying too!

TT5.17
The first coat was applied in regular strips up and down the bonnet, concentrating on obtaining an even coat without trying to blanket out the colour underneath. That's the way to achieve runs!

TT5.18
The second coat, as already suggested, followed in a pattern which criss-crossed the first (see margin note), and this time the colour beneath did disappear from view. Ideally, you may want to give another one or two coats. If any little bits of dust land in the paint surface, you may be able to polish them out with fine cutting compound, but be most careful not to go right through the paint and don't try it until the paint has had several days to dry really hard.

Using special paints

As well as the paint types already shown, there is a wide variety of others to consider. Extra high gloss chrome or gold paint, for customising, black heat resistant paint for cylinder blocks, engines and exhaust systems to aid cooling and impove efficiency, and clear acrylic lacquer, most useful for forming a protective coating on alloy wheels. However, we could not really advocate using heat resistant paint on manifolds, as the extra heat there would probably be too much for the paint to handle.

TT6.1
Using a hammer finish paint is a good way to provide some extra rustproofing and also makes the surface easier to clean. Used direct from the aerosol, it gives an even finish without needing a primer beforehand.

TT6.2
Only the plastic components shown earlier would need plastic primer. A second coat, sprayed at right angles to the first, gives a full, even coat. Do it within a few minutes of spraying the first coat but after the first coat's solvent has "flashed off"

TT6.4
Treating your road wheels to a new coat of paint is a cheaper alternative to replacing them with alloys. However, the effect is ruined if you cover your tyres with paint as well! The obvious answer is to use masking tape and newspaper to mask off the tyre, although it's not easy to do. An alternative is to cover the tyre with hand cleaner or washing-up liquid. When the paint has dried thoroughly, give the tyres a good wash. To match the tyres to the wheels, a coating of Comma's Tyre Black will bring them up a treat.

TT6.3
Use a cellulose clear lacquer for sealing styling stripes (see page 16) or for keeping the gloss on cellulose paint finishes.

Do-it-yourself spraying

Cellulose paint is not as durable as the 2-pack paint which DIY enthusiasts are advised not to use, but it has the virtue of being able to be sprayed on a DIY basis and it can also be polished to give the best shine of any paints.

TT7.1
If many coats of paint have previously been applied, they will have to be stripped back to bare metal before being repainted. Very minor blemishes such as pin holes or scratches in the paint should be filled with a thin scrape of Valentine G112 stopper which can be sanded down after drying thoroughly.

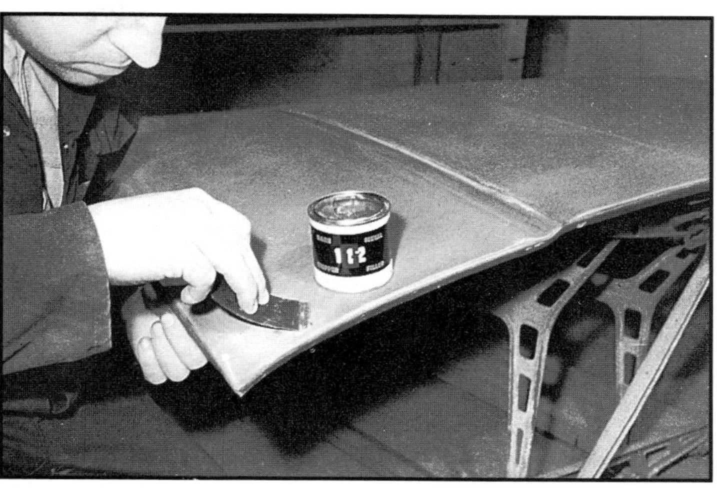

TT7.2
Hand sanding should always be carried out with the aid of a rubbing block, other than in the corners of fluted panels such as those shown here, where your fingers make an ideally shaped tool.

TT7.3
With no attachment on the end of the hose, you can use the SIP Airmate compressor to blow any remaining sanding dust off the panel.

Safety

All filler contains skin irritants so you should wear gloves when handling them. When sanding paint or filler, particularly with a power sander, you must always wear an efficient particle mask, because otherwise the inhalation of sanding dust could damage your health. Nitro-cellulose paints, those made by Valentine for instance, and shown here, are suitable for DIY work, unlike 2-pack paints which must only be used by a professional bodyshop. However, take full note of Valentine's own safety precautions and, in particular, never spray in other than a well-ventilated work area. Also, bear in mind that paint, thinners and spray vapour are all highly flammable. Do not use near flames, sparks (including those created by central heating boilers), or any naked flames. Always wear a face mask when spraying cellulose or aerosol paint.

NB. The Valentine paints shown here have since been superceded by cellulose paints from their sister company, Glasurit.

PREPARATION

Tools required:
Grinder, sander, P120 and P240 grit discs, P600 "wet-or-dry" paper, dust particle mask.

Materials required:
197-1005 degreasing fluid (this is essential for removing silicones which will most certainly ruin the finished paint surface if allowed to remain on the work), G112 stopper.

Before using primer check the existing paint to find out whether it is compatible with cellulose. Rub a small area of paint with cellulose thinner. If the paint film dissolves go ahead; if the paint wrinkles it is affected by cellulose and will have to be sprayed all over with isolating primer 200-6 to seal it.

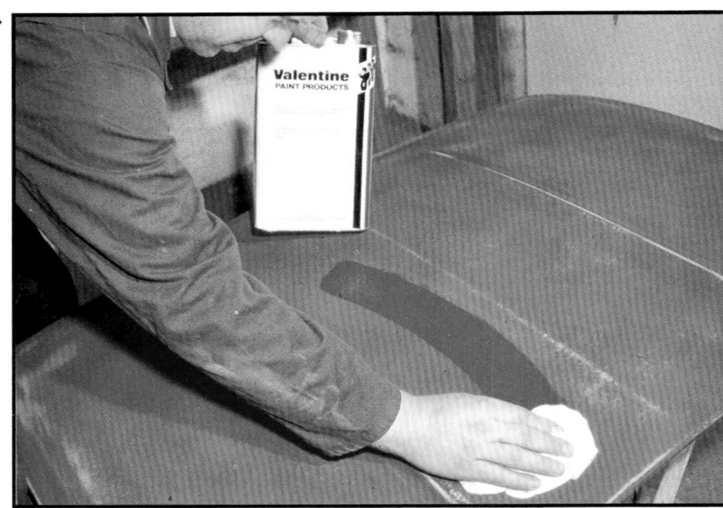

TT7.4
The Valentine Degreasing Fluid should have been used before you started and should now be used again to remove any traces of silicones or other grease contamination. Silicones, which are contained in all domestic polishes, cause dreadful and irremovable "fish eye" marks in the final paint finish.

TT7.5
The Hitachi Cordless drill was used with a paint stirrer in the chuck to stir the Valentine Primer Filler to an even consistency. Note the steel rule placed in the pot to aid accurate measurement when thinning the paint. Start initially with a 50/50 thinning, but be prepared to readjust to suit the requirements of the SIP spray gun.

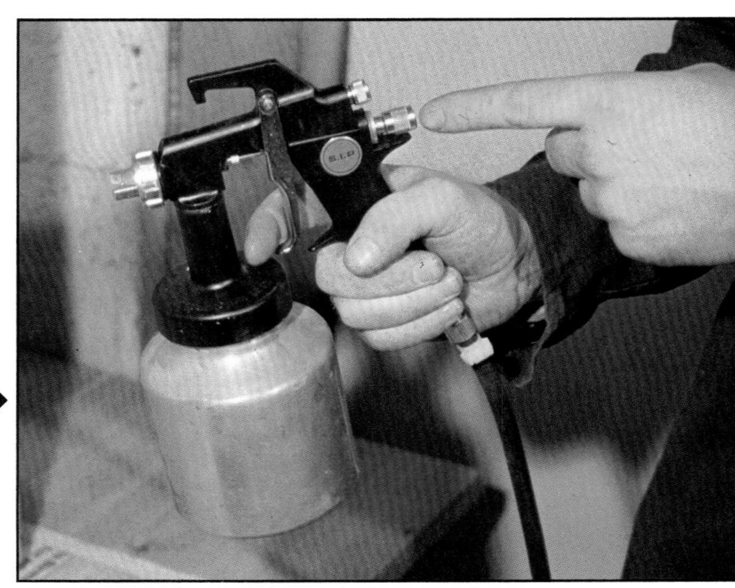

TT7.6
The SIP gun has two adjustment screws at the rear. The top one is for the width of the spray pattern, while the lower one adjusts the quantity which comes out of the gun.

TT7.7➡
Adjust the two spray gun screws so that the spray pattern and spray density are as you require. Test it out thoroughly upon a piece of scrap board or a cardboard box.

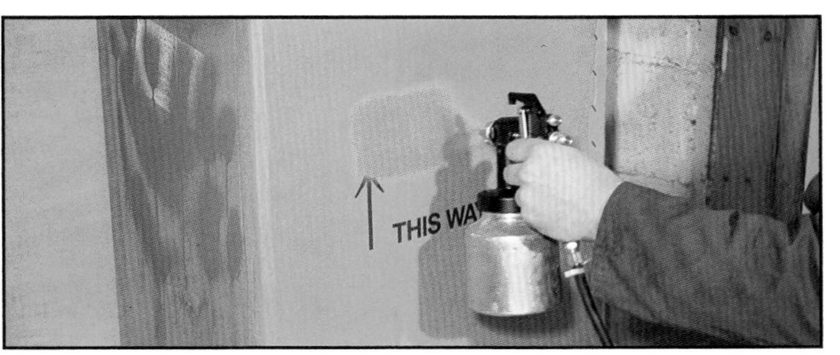

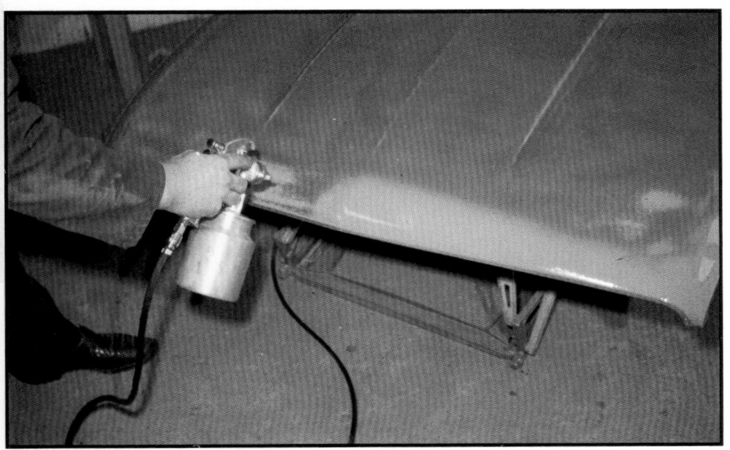

⬅TT7.8
The edge of this panel dipped away from the user so that part, the curved edge, was sprayed first. The SIP gun has a light trigger action and is easy to use.

TT7.9➡
The whole panel was painted in consistent, even bands, each one half overlapping the previous one.

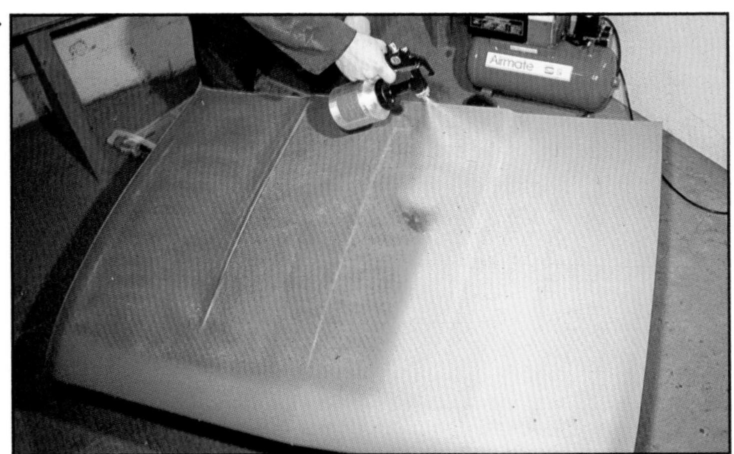

⬅TT7.10
The next day, after the two full coats of primer had thoroughly dried, a very light, heavily thinned coat of black paint was sprayed on with the SIP gun.

PRIMING

Tools required:
Masking tape, masking paper (such as newspaper), paint strainer, SIP spray gun, SIP compressor, spray mask, tack rag.

Materials required:
As well as those shown earlier and on these pages: cellulose thinner 199-207 for any additional thinning above 50/50 (don't use 199-6 for more than 50/50), Glasurit Red Oxide Primer.

TOP COAT

Tools required:
The same SIP equipment and other "hardware" as was previously used. Top coat paint must be strained. Add P1200 "wet-or-dry" paper and polishing compound for polishing out any dirt particles that may get into the final coat.

Materials required:
Spragloss 178 solid colour paint; Spragloss thinner 199-18 (mix 50/50). For further thinning, add more 199-18 thinner.

Ask your stockist about Glasurit cellulose equivalents.

TT7.11
When the primer was "blocked" down with medium grit paper, the thin "guide" coat, which was sprayed on with the SIP gun (although you could have used aerosol for greater speed), was sanded off as the primer filler coat was made smooth. It remained visible in the low spots, however.

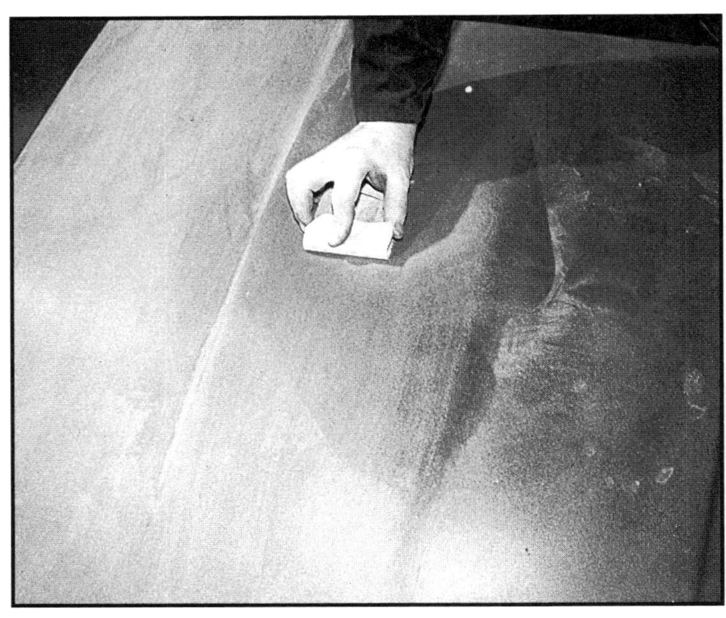

TT7.12
Before spraying the top coat, wet the floor to prevent dust but take care to avoid electrical connections.

TT7.13
Use an air line to blow any dust from around the top of the tin. SIP produce a trigger operated "air duster", if you prefer.

TT7.14
The cordless drill is again used for several minutes to mix the entire contents of the Spragloss paint.

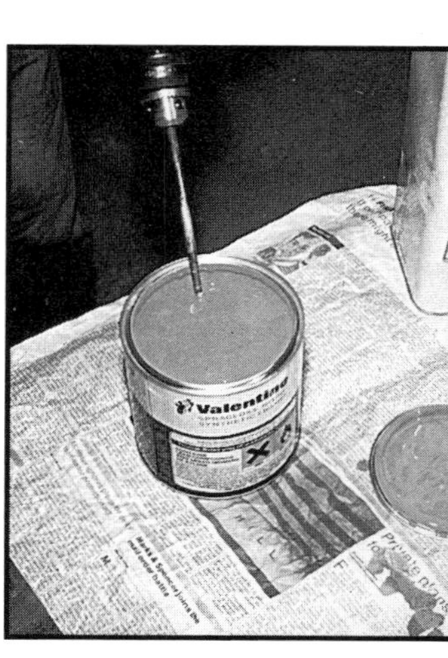

TT7.15
Use a steel rule, if you haven't got the correct painter's measuring stick, to measure the correct amount of Spragloss paint and thinners.

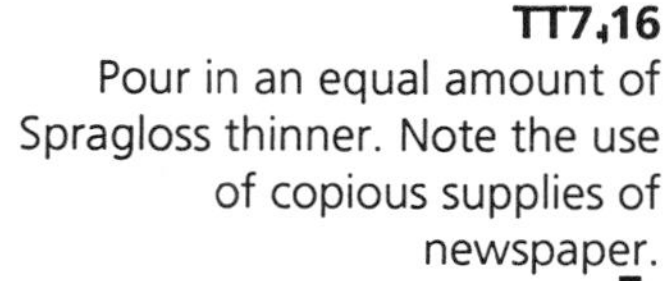

TT7.16
Pour in an equal amount of Spragloss thinner. Note the use of copious supplies of newspaper.

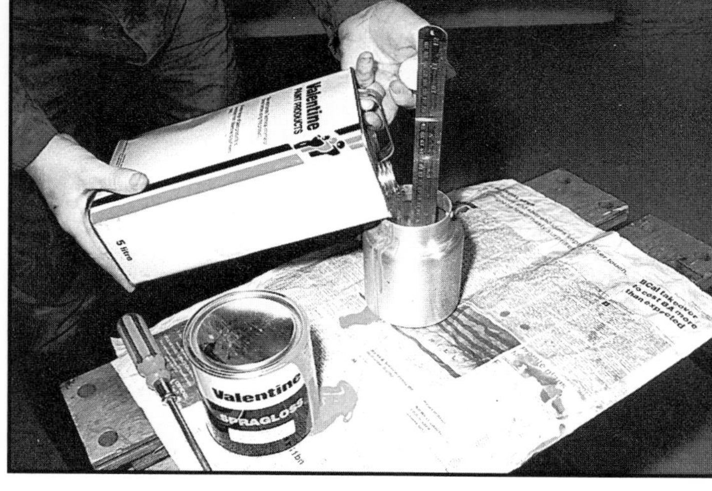

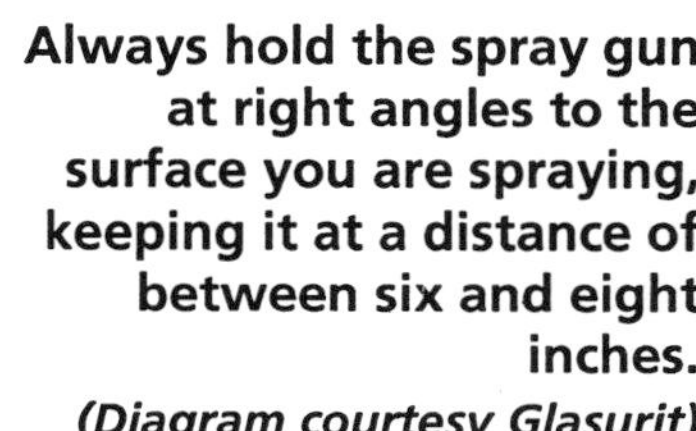

Always hold the spray gun at right angles to the surface you are spraying, keeping it at a distance of between six and eight inches.
(Diagram courtesy Glasurit)

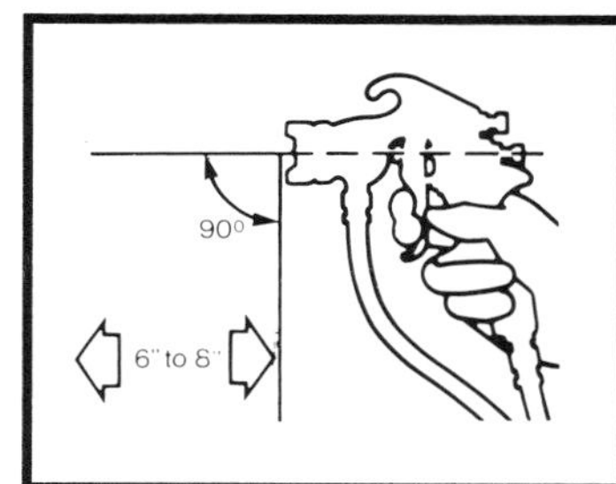

TT7.17
After using the Air Mate air line to blow off the panel once more, wipe it down yet again with Valentine spirit wipe ...

TT7.18
... followed by a wipe down with a tack rag to remove every trace of dust and dirt.

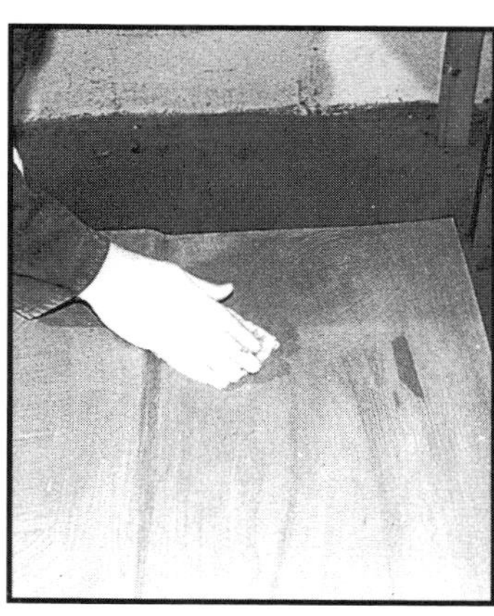

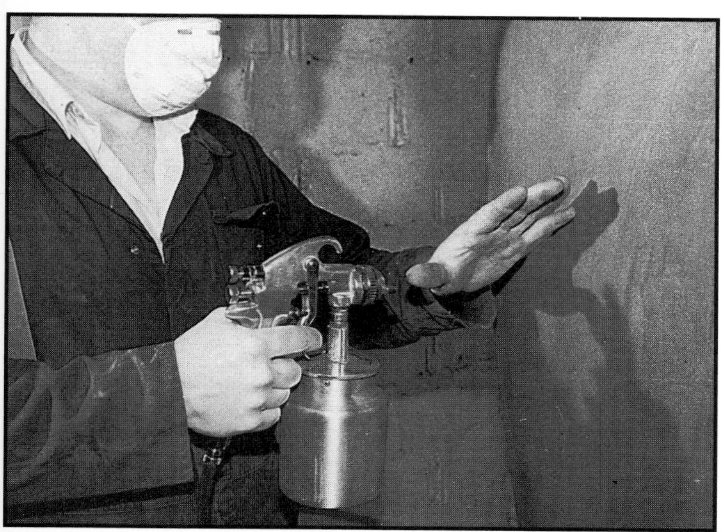

TT7.19
An accepted way of checking that the SIP gun is held the correct distance away (see margin note), is to use a hand span as a measure.

Keep your wrist stiff and avoid swinging the gun in an arc from your elbow, to ensure even spraying. Always spray at a steady, even pace.
(Diagram courtesy Glasurit)

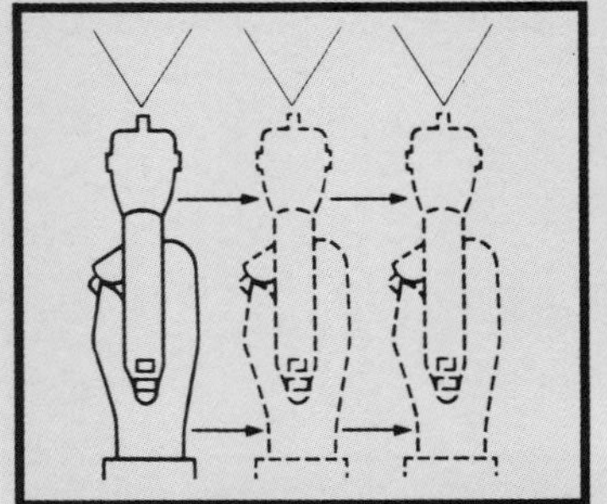

TT7.20
Spraying starts with a "half-coat" – a thin coat to aid adhesion without causing runs – sprayed in vertical, overlapping bands.

TT7.21
After this has "flashed off" (that is, the thinners has evaporated), a full coat is sprayed in overlapping horizontal bands. The suspended panel reduces dirt contamination and an open door aids ventilation.

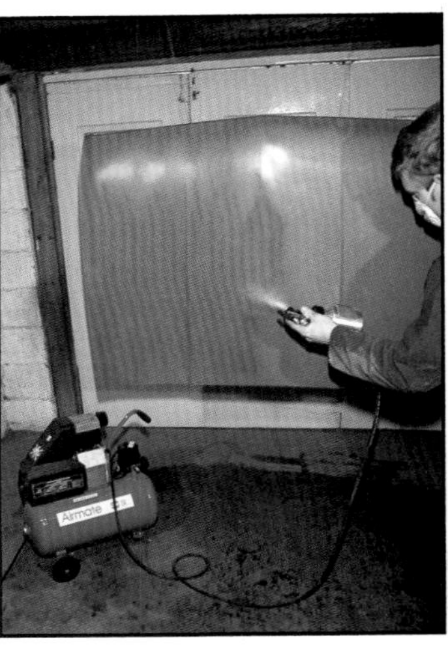

TT7.22
The Valentine Spragloss solid colour has given an excellent depth of gloss and proves that the DIY SIP equipment can give fully professional results.

TT7.23
Valentine paints, shown here in their new livery, are professional paints perfectly suitable for the DIY enthusiast to use. Follow the safety regulations printed on every can.

If you try spraying aerosol spray paint onto a plastic component without preparing it properly, the paint will simply peel off again soon afterwards. Spectra produce a special plastic primer, with a pre-treat solvent all in one pack. After using the plastic primer you can spray your finish coat straight on top. Aerosol tins of paint to match your car's body colour can be purchased from your Ford dealer.

TT8.1
We used a Richard Grant accessory for this section. Plastic primer treatment works just as well on any other plastic component, of course. Start by wiping over every nook and cranny with "Pre-treat fluid" on a clean rag.

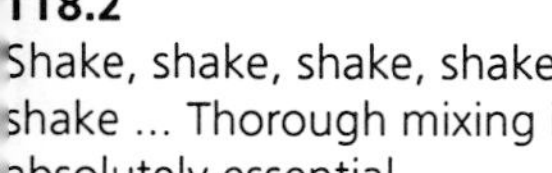

TT8.2
Shake, shake, shake, shake, shake ... Thorough mixing is absolutely essential.

TT8.3
The plastic primer can now be sprayed over the whole air intake cover.

TT8.4
Once the primer is dry, your car's body colour or any finish colour you choose can be sprayed on without fear of paint flaking off.

Preserving bodywork

Injecting rustproofing fluids

In common with many manufacturers, Ford are taking steps to ensure that their cars are now much less prone to corrosion. However, any steel bodywork can, and eventually will, rust so it's up to you to protect it! Using Corroless stabilising cavity wax is recommended, for not only does it prevent more rust from starting, it also contains a rust inhibitor which tackles the existing rot and is said to stop it in its tracks. Whether you have a recent car or an older model, you can't start too early when it comes to defeating the rust bug!

TT9.1
For enclosed bodywork sections and seams, Corroless produce their highly effective Rust Stabilising Wax, whilst for exposed underbody areas and for paint chips there are other specially produced Corroless products such as Rust Stabilising Body Primer, Underbody Finish and Stone Chip Primer.

TT9.2
Each Corroless can comes with two types of spray nozzle. One allows it to be used as a normal spray can, whilst the other incorporates a long plastic tube used for injecting the fluid into enclosed, tricky-to-get-at sections. However, their latest development is ...

TT9.
... this "trigger" type hand gri which fits any aerosol an makes usage much easier an cleane

TT9.4
Using the trigger grip on the Rust Stabilising Wax can we gave the first dousing to the "ledge" that you can feel by running your hand inside the front wings. This can be treated from inside the engine bay as shown.

TT9.5
Use the "wide spray" nozzle to give a good covering to the bulkhead.

TT9.6
At the front of the wing, look out for the wing mounted flanges.

Corroless wax has two crucially important plus points in its favour. First, it "creeps" particularly well, getting into spot welded seams where corrosion likes to take hold. Second, it has unique rust killing properties. Many other rustproofers don't necessarily stop rusting that may have already taken place.

TT9.7
Scrape the heavy mud encrustations from under the front wings, then seek out the strut support seams and joints between the wing and bodywork.

T9.8
he front of the bonnet is prone
ɔ rusting and so you should use
ıe many holes in the panel
ressing to get the fluid deep
ıto the edges of the bonnet.

TT9.9
Similarly, the tailgate can rot quite easily so inject as much as you can through the hole in the edge, accessed by removing the small, rubber bung. Removing the trim panels at either side of the tailgate gives access to the lower edge, which is another "rot-spot".

Injecting rustproofing fluids

All rust preventatives evaporate over a period of time and so "topping them up" should be regarded as part of your Fiesta's maintenance schedule. After all, bodywork is far more valuable than mechanical components, yet there is a tendency to spend little time and money maintaining it! Factory applied protectors harden in time, yet Corroless will creep into and seal any rust inducing cavities or cracks. If re-treated every year, your Fiesta could go on and on, although it must be said that Corroless are adamant that annual re-treatment is not necessary in enclosed areas.

TT9.10
Take some time over the doors, especially around the lower parts. There's another rubber bung in the edge of the door and removal ...

TT9.11
... allows you to get the long nozzle well inside and give it a good spray. Make sure that it gets behind the plastic film lining the inner door and always remember to wind the window up first!

TT9.12
The door pillars are also prone to rust and they too have bungs which can be removed. Again, the long nozzle allows the rust stabilising wax to reach the most awkward areas.

TT9.13
You may find it necessary to actually drill a few new holes in order to inject the Corroless fluid. Drill holes just large enough to get the long nozzle i at stragegic places along the sill Don't forget to treat the hole with Corroless primer before capping with a rubber bung.

TT9.14
The metal behind the loose rubber door seals is in an ideal place to cultivate rust. Pull the rubber gently away and squirt the fluid in.

TT9.15
You can use the spray to protect the inside of your road wheels. If they are steel, this will prevent rusting but even if you have alloy wheels it would still be useful, for they too can corrode, usually in the form of a light surface flaking. By sealing the inside of the wheel with Corroless fluid, you should be able to avoid this. Note that the conventional nozzle is being used here in order to cover a wide area quickly. Don't forget the spare as well.

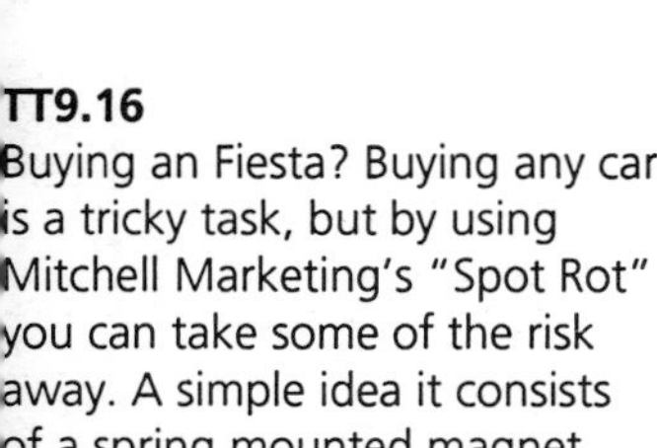

TT9.16
Buying an Fiesta? Buying any car is a tricky task, but by using Mitchell Marketing's "Spot Rot" you can take some of the risk away. A simple idea it consists of a spring mounted magnet which ...

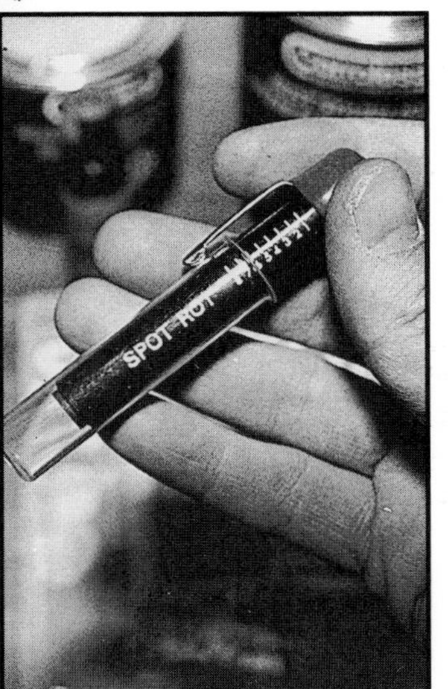

TT9.17
... is simple to use. Just hold the magnet against the bodywork of the car in question. As you pull it away the scale on the side provides a pointer to the composition of the "metal". Included with the "Spot Rot" is a very handy booklet showing how to interpret the various readings (fibreglass, rusty metal and so on), and what to look out for when buying a used car in general.

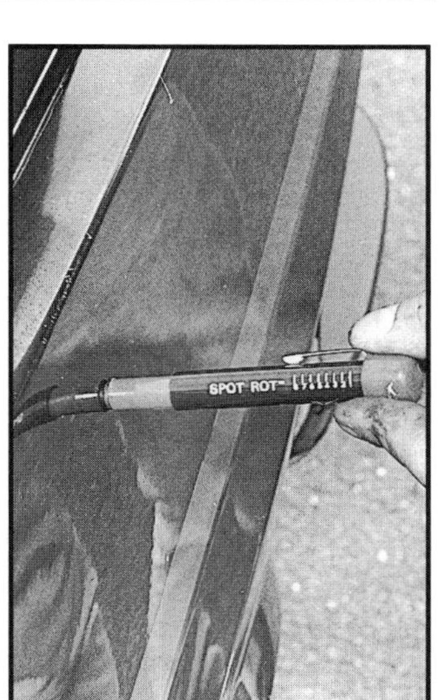

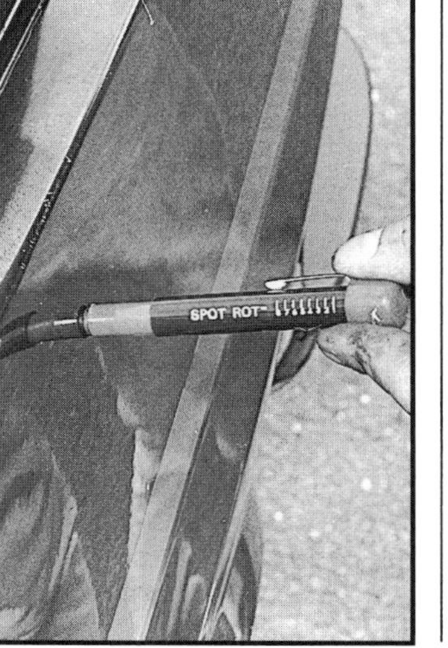

As well as structural seams and box sections, pay particular attention to chrome sections (spray behind them) and other body trim which could trap moisture. If you can get to the other side of the trim, spray the fluid into any fixing holes you come across.

SAFETY WARNING

Never work beneath a car supported only by a jack. Always use axle stands or a ramp, apply the handbrake, leave the car in gear and always chock the wheels carefully.

Using rustproofing primers and paints

Corroless Rust Stabilising Body Primer contains the same amazingly effective rust killer as the Cavity Wax, and actually contains tiny glass flakes which give it far more resilience than any conventional paint. Stones and hard objects simply bounce off!

TT9.18
Rust Stabilising Body Primer is sprayed on in the conventional way, after cleaning the area well and removing any loose paint or road dirt from the surface. Here the sill is being protected so it is important that the door is covered by newspaper carefully taped in position.

TT9.19
One place that paintwork will always chip is at the front of the car, particularly on the leading edge of the bonnet. If you can't stop the paint coming off, at least you can stop the rust spreading from the chips by using the aptly named Corroless Stone Chip Primer. In the top of the can is a handy little brush made specifically for dealing with small areas.

TT9.20
The built-in brush unscrews and you can treat the affected areas in seconds. Whilst the Primer will stop the rust spreading, it is in your own interest to get some paint onto the damaged area as soon as possible, even if it's just a spot of the maker's touch-up paint.

Chapter Six
History and Development

The Fiesta Story

The Research, the Development and the Launch

Given the sales figures of Ford's Fiesta range, and indeed, those of its big brother, the Escort, it is hard to believe that until the 1970s, Ford had never produced a front-wheel-drive car! In fact, the company as a whole were most reluctant to get involved with small car production at all. Historically, profits on small cars are similarly small and so producing such vehicles made little financial sense.

However, as the sixties drew to a close, there appeared to be more and more small cars on the scene. The Mini, introduced in 1959, was still going strong in various guises and its BL production partner, the Austin/Morris 1100 was also selling rather well.

In addition, there was a growing number of "foriegn" cars in this class, in particular, the Renault 5.

The buying public were growing increasingly impressed with of this type of vehicle, which offered a reasonable amount of space, good performance for the price and excellent handling capabilities.

Ford decided to take a long hard look at the possibility of building a sub-Escort sized car.

It was clear from the start that front-wheel-drive was the only way to go; both handling and space were by-products of this, although also a by-product was the need for Ford to invest around $100,000,000 in a production plant to build them!

The Detroit design study project was given the official go ahead in 1972 and the original code name for the Fiesta was the Bobcat.

Within the year, the project became a working reality and Ford decided that a new Spanish plant (in Almasufes, Valencia) should be the site chosen to produce the components for the new car. At many stages throughout its development, the Ford designers constantly used the Fiat 127 as a yardstick and, in fact, the Italian company suggested that they should enter into a partnership to produce the transmission units. However, Ford rejected this and continued with their original plans.

The forthcoming Bobcat was announced to the chiefs of Ford in Europe in 1973, when it was also announced that the car would be launched in the Autumn of 1976.

As it happened, the timing could hardly have been better, for it was just about the time of the first "oil crisis" which meant that there was a boom in small, economical cars.

It was decided that Bobcat assembly should take place in two more European plants, to supplement the production from Spain; Saalouis in West Germany and Dagenham, in the UK.

The choice of the name (Bobcat was simply a project name), had still not been decided. At the time, Metro was one under consideration and Sierra was another; clearly, someone thought that was a good name! At the end of the day, it came down to a choice of two, Bravo or Fiesta.

It was Henry Ford himself who made the decision, although it is interesting to note that "Bravo" has appeared on Limited Edition Fiestas in the 1980s.

The Ford publicity machine made sure that the whole world knew about the car well before its launch date (which had to be brought forward) and by September 1976, "Ford's New baby" was on sale though Britain had to wait until February '77.

The Angular lines of "Ford's new baby" proved immensely popular and attractive as on this 'S' model

The Car

Inside the car, silver dash trim was all the rage. Note the lurid striped seats!

In the Fiesta engine bay, there seemed to be lots of room for such a (relatively) small engine. Perhaps a larger power plant was envisaged by the company? Although no announcement was made, it was clear that someone had seen the potential of a small car with a large engine; an XR2, of course!

Initially, the car was technically quite mundane. However, this was certainly not because the company lacked the necessary skill or expertise in engine development and design! It was simply a question of horses for courses; their early research had led them to the simple conclusion that the market for the small car was one where the owner wanted simple, economical and reliable mechanical components.

The range was available with two versions of the old "Kent" pushrod engine, with capacities of 957cc and 1117cc, producing 40/47bhp and 53bhp respectively.

It was a year after its introduction that the Fiesta was available with a 1300cc engine. With the assistance of a twin-choke Weber carburettor borrowed from the Escort 1300 Sport, it produced 66bhp. Clearly, in such a small body, the performance was much improved and most impressive for 1977. Among the many changes made to the car for the installation of the bigger engine unit was an enlarged cooling system, braking and suspension modifications and an uprated exhaust system.

The Mk II Fiestas

To call those Fiestas made from 1983 onwards Mk IIs is an exaggeration, for they were, in effect, facelifted Mk Is. However, Mk II we shall call them, for simplicity, if nothing else. Ford has never been a company to let the grass grow under its feet and the need to introduce new models at regular intervals has always been high on its list of priorities. The history books are full of motor manufacturers who are no more, simply because they relied for too long on a single model or a single range. The Ford record stands proud in terms of timing and market knowledge.

In its second incarnation, the Fiesta kept the family look but lost the sharp edges. Once more it was an instant success. This is a 1984 Ghia

But truly new cars demand a massive investment in plant and machinery, not to mention research and design. So, updating an existing car is considerably cheaper and, to a great extent, serves the same purpose.

So the Mk II first saw the light of consumerism in the September of 1983. Under the bonnet, the company took the opportunity to discard the ageing Kent ohv engine and replace the larger versions with the ultra modern CVH range, whilst the smaller capacity models received reworked, Valencia made engines, producing more power and torque. The latter were much more economical (up to 25 per cent) and similar performance was available from the CVH units. In addition, the Mk II Fiestas gained a five-speed gearbox on all 1.3 and 1.6 litre petrol and 1.6 litre diesel engined models.

The interiors too were updated, seen on this 1987 1.4S

The diesel version of the Fiesta was available for the first time, and soon found great favour with fleet buyers.

In 1986 the Mk II was available with the Lean Burn 1.4 litre engines (ousting the 1.3 litre variants in the sales catalogue) and a year later, the first Automatic Fiesta was on sale. This was fitted with the revolutionary CTX, variable transmission gearbox.

The change in the look of the car was to soften the sharp and angular lines of the Mk I whilst retaining the Fiesta style. This smoother silhouette not only made it look more modern but also helped in reducing the drag coefficient. The wheels were increased in diameter to 13 inches and many changes to suspension and chassis were made in order to improve ride quality.

Inside the car, "modernisation" continued, with a brand new dash layout and a split rear seat facility on all but the most basic models.

The new car, but still recognisably as a Fiesta and, as the sales figures show, still just as popular. During the twelve year lifespan of the first two models, over twelve million cars were sold (more than 1.2 million in the UK). Inevitably, this put more pressure on the designers when it came to the Mk III.

A lot of research time and money went into producing superb interiors which would do justice to many "luxury" cars

The Mk III Fiesta

Five hundred and fifty million pounds: say it slowly – it's a lot of cash! However, it is just this amount that Ford ploughed into the development of the Mk III Fiesta, introduced to the UK in the Spring of 1989. The new car is the first Fiesta available in five-door format and has better performance, improved mpg, reduced emissions and more interior space.

The drag coefficient has been reduced by 15 per cent and the new body features impact resistant polycarbonate front and rear bumpers and side protection mouldings on all models. Inside the car there is 45 per cent more luggage space, a 10 per cent increase in glass area and Ford claim that it has more passenger space than any vehicle in its class.

The Mk III Fiesta comes with a choice of five petrol engines, from 1.0 litre to 1.6 litre and a 1.8 litre diesel unit. Naturally, all petrol engines will operate on unleaded fuel and the lower capacity engines feature the Lean Burn HCS (High Compression Swirl) system, whilst the XR2i and diesel engines are CVH units with electronic fuel injection. Despite the increase in technology, Ford claim that routine servicing costs should be cut by some 27 per cent!

In order to take the risk out of buying a new, untried car, Ford have tested the new Fiesta for over two million miles, half of which has been undertaken on public roads by high mileage, private motorists rather than test engineers.

The XR2 – The Quick One!

It was five years after the car's launch in 1976, that a truly sporting version was introduced. For some while, the company had been concentrating on the Escort, firstly with the Mexico and RS series of rear-wheel-drive cars and then with the front-driven XR3. However, with the Ford Special Vehicle Engineering (SVE) department having finalised their work on the 2.8i Capri, they were free to start another project; the Fiesta XR2.

Often asked is the question, "Where is the XR1?". Effectively, although the big Capri was never given an "XR" number, as it was the first vehicle that SVE had worked on, it was the mythical XR1.

The SVE, under the control of Rod Mansfield, were given strict guidelines with regard to what the sporty Fiesta should be. They were not allowed to make dramatic revisions to the chassis or transmission and although 100mph plus performance was expected, the engine was required to come up to all existing emission controls.

The engine used in the XR2 was basically that used in the American Fiesta, a 1599cc ohv "Kent" unit, employing a Weber 32/34 carburettor (also seen on the contemporary XR3) and producing a very handy 84bhp. Naturally enough, this made the small Ford both quick and fast; a 0–60mph time of 9.4 seconds and a top speed of around 105mph. The gearbox, albeit mounted slightly lower than in other models, used the same four ratios found in the XR3 but with a higher final drive.

The looks and handling of the car were uprated to suit, with 6 inch alloy wheels, 60 Series tyres and several suspension modifications. Curiously, there was still no front anti-roll bar.

The front brakes were ventilated discs, á la Escort XR3. Visually, the XR2 could be spotted a mile away. Naturally, the wider wheels and tyres combination gave the car a more purposeful stance, accentuated by the revised suspension geometry. Down the sides of the car were graduated stripes and the rear was graced by a rubber spoiler. At the front, it was the first model to use circular rather than rectangular headlamps and had two driving lamps as standard fitments. Not unnaturally, the XR2 found many buyers at its original launch price of £5,500 (the XR3 cost £6,246) and by the time the face-lifted version was introduced in 1984, more than 20,000 XR2's had been sold in the UK alone.

The King is dead ... We all know the saying and it applies here, for although the Mk II XR2 appeared to be everything the small "Hot Hatch" owner could want, Ford did not agree and as early as 1982 the SVE were working on its replacement. The new XR2 was shown at various motor shows (in face-lifted, Mk II form) throughout the end of 1983 and the beginning of 1984, but eager buyers had to wait until June of that year before they could taste the "fruit". The new car carried on where the old left off, with spoilers, wider wheels and tyres and body graphics differentiating the XR2 from its less powerful brethren. Unlike its predecessor, the Mk II car was not fitted with alloy wheels as standard. However, the wheel trims looked that good, that most people couldn't tell anyway!

The body adornments were more in evidence, with a full body kit (front and rear spoilers, side skirts and wheel arch extension) being standard. In the engine compartment , the new engine bay was able to accept the new, overhead cam (rather than ohv) CVH engine and better still, the five-speed gearbox. Naturally, this gave SVE much more scope. However, they were not able to use the 1600cc, fuel injected engine for fear of upstaging the XR3i, but they were able to use the

The changing face of Ford's small sports hatch. From this ...

... to an updated Mk II to ...

... a radically new, fuel-injected Mk III model, with shattering performance

nside the car too, the dash layout has been given serious consideration and is superbly ergonomic

old" XR3 CVH engine which, with its Weber carburation, gave an increase of 12bhp over the revious model's 84bhp. A combination of this engine, the revised and much tauter suspension nd the five-speed gearbox made the Mk II car even better to drive than the Mk I and this was eflected in the sales figures which show that more than 10 per cent of all Mk II Fiesta sales were he XR2.

As yet, we don't know much about the latest XR2 but, significantly, it gains an "i" for injection nd, because of this, the power is up to an impressive 110bhp. A glance down the XR2 erformance figures will show that, from first to last, the top speed has risen by 14 per cent, and he power output by an incredible 30 per cent. To counter some of this power increase, the XR2 as put on some weight, although at 1960lb, the Mk III can hardly be called obese!

It's early days yet, but we don't think it imprudent to say that the XR2i is bound to be a vinner. A final note relates to a sentence to be found in the company's press pack relating to he new Fiesta. It reads, "By the end of 1989, Ford plans to unveil a limited production, urbocharged version of the new car which is being developed by Ford Special Engineering (SVE) t Dunton in Essex".

A Turbocharged XR2i, from the manufacturers? Shades of the Escort RS Turbo. As we await like you, with bated breath!) we can only surmise what form it will take. However, given the istorical sharing of components between Escort and Fiesta, it is fair to assume that the engine nd possibly drive train will draw much from the existing Escort RS Turbo. This would put its ower output at between 130–140 bhp and put the cat among the pigeons for the opposition!

XR2 Performance Data

	Mk I (1981–83)	Mk II (1984–88)	Mk III (1989–)
Engine	***1.6 ohv Kent***	***1.6 CVH ohc***	***1.6 Injection***
Power output	84bhp	96bhp	110bhp
Maximum speed*	104mph	112mph	119mph
0–60mph*	9.5 secs	9.3 secs	9.0 secs
Kerb weight	1848lb	1851lb	1960lb

** Performance figures for Mk I & II cars taken as an average of contemporary road tests. Mk III figures from manufacturer.*

The "Special" Fiestas

The "Special Edition" model is a motoring phenomenon which has grown enormously over the past fifteen years. There can be many reasons for offering a car with a slightly different name and with the promise of limited production numbers, the most common being to sell off stocks of a particular model prior to the introduction of a new one. However, there are others, including special promotions linking cars with other products (the Fiesta Dash, for example) or simply to boost sales in a traditionally slack period. Whatever, Ford have never been slow to spot a marketing opportunity, and to date the Fiesta has been the subject of no less than twenty two special edition models! What is a Special Edition? In essence, the purchaser should get a lot of extra car for little extra money. For example, he buys a base level car but for only £200 extra, he gets £500 worth of "extras" which usually include sunroofs, stripes, spoilers, radios and so on. The listing shows the names and numbers of all Fiesta Specials produced up to the time of writing.

Fiesta Mk I & II Production

Year	Production Total (Germany/UK/ Spain)
1976	109,838
1977	440,969
1978	449,807
1979	444,402
1980	450,927
1981	357,015
1982	327,568
1983	356,517
1984	365,248
1985	343,419
1986	362,753
1987	386,587
1988	407,292

Special Edition	*Year of Introduction*	*Number Manufact.*
Solitaire	1978	2000
Kingfisher	1978	2500
Millionth Edit.	1979	3100
Sandpiper	1979	4000
Firefly (base)	1980	2000
Supersport	1980	3000
Festival	1980	4000
Sandpiper	1981	4000
Bravo	1981	3000
Special Launch	1981	2000
Bravo II	1982	4000
Quartz	1983	4000

Special Edition	*Year of Introduction*	*Number Manufact.*
Finesse	1983	15500
Dash	1985	8600
Finesse II	1986	12000
Holiday	1986	4000
Firefly (Ghia)	1986	2000
Festival	1987	15000
Bonus	1987	5000
Frescoe	1987	3000
Festival II	1988	15000
Firefly (Ghia)	1988	4400
Bonus	1988	7000
Olympus	1988	1009

As can be seen from the listing, not all Limited Editions are *that* limited and names appear more than once. This makes life difficult for the prospective used car purchaser, as often a name is reused, but on a totally different base model.

In addition, almost 100,000 Fiesta vans were produced in the period from their introduction in 1977 to the end of 1988. The total production of over 5,000,000 vehicles in eleven years is no mean feat and it will be interesting to see whether the Mk III can maintain this incredible record.

The special edition models began with the Mk Is, this being a "Bravo" from 1981

The Festival was so popular that For
repeated the formula with the Festival I

Specialists and Manufacturers

Allen Continental Limited, Unit 6, Eastcote Autocare Centre, South Ruislip, Middlesex **01-422 9612**
"Ansa" performance exhaust systems and manifolds

Autocar Electrical Equipment Ltd, 77-85 Newington Causeway, London SE1 6BJ **01-403 5959**
Hirschman manual and electric aerials, Lumenition electronic ignition

Automaxi Limited, Chiltern Trading Estate, Grovebury Road, Leighton Buzzard, bedfordshire LU7 8TU
"Mountney" steering wheels, specialist roof racks and sunroofs **0525 383131**

Automec Equipment and Parts Ltd, Stanbridge Road, Leighton Buzzard, Bedfordshire LU7 8QP
Copper brake, petrol and clutch pipes and also Silicone Brake Fluid **0525 376608 & 375775**

Autostyle Unique, Unit 128, Commercial Centre, Pickett Piece, Andover SP11 6LU **0264 333491**
Tailored floor mats, embroidered sweatshirts and rally jackets

Robert Bosch Ltd, PO Box 98, Broadwater Park, Denham, Uxbridge, Middlesex UB9 5HJ **0895 833633**
Range of automotive electrical equipment including spark plugs

Branyl Ltd, Unit 17, Kimberley Way, Redbrook Lane Trading Estate, Brereton, Rugely, Staffordshire WS15 1RE
Self-adhesive car stripes, badges and decals

Cannon Rubber Ltd, Ashley Road, Tottenham, London N17 9LH **01-808 6261**
Rubber car mats and mudflaps, etc

Carflow Products Ltd, Leighton Road, Leighton Buzzard, Bedfordshire LU7 7LA **0525 383543**
Wheel clean discs and locking wheel nuts

Carphone Group plc, Unit 16, Darin Court, Crownhill, Watling Street, Milton Keynes, Bucks. MK8 0AD
Suppliers and installers of in-car telephonic equipment **0908 560148**

Cobra Superform Ltd, Unit D1, Halesfield 23, Telford, Shropshire TF7 4EW **0952 684020**
Producers of a wide range of car seats and sub-frames

Comma Oil & Chemicals Ltd, Comma Works, Denton Industrial Area, Lower Range Road, Gravesend, Kent DA12 2QX **0474 64311**
A full range of valeting products for the private and commercial user

Cosmic car Accessories Ltd, Sadler Road, Brownhills, Walsall WS8 6NA **0543 452626**
A wide range of auto accessories, interior and exterior

Dellorto Ltd, 13 Boult Street, Reading, Berkshire RG1 4RD **0734 598955**
A full range of standard replacement and performance carburettors

Dreamwheelers, Chepstow Place, Harrold, Bedfordshire **0234 720068**
Suppliers of high quality alloy wheels including Wheelwrights and Borbet

Duckhams Oils Ltd, Duckhams House, 157/159 Mason's Hill, Bromley, Kent BR2 9HU **01-290 0600**
Producers of high performance oils and lubricants for high performance engines

Fibresports, 34-36 Bowlers Croft, Crancs Industrial Area, Basildon, Essex SS14 3ED **0268 27331/282723**
Manufacturers of high quality Fiesta bodykits and accessories and fitting specialists

Artur Fischer (UK) Ltd, Hithercroft Road, Wallingford, Oxon OX10 9AT **0491 330000**
Manufacturers of Fischer C-Box, high quality cassette holders

Ford Motor Company Ltd, Eagle Way, Warley, Brentwood, Essex CM13 3BW **0277 253000**
Ford US, The Ford Motor Company, The American Road, Dearborn, Michigan, 48121, USA **313 845 2279**
Manufacturers and distributors of Ford Cars and a range of improve and modify components

Gemini Elettronica Ltd, 12 North Street, Droitwich, Worcs WR9 8JB **0905 794565**
Central door locking systems and electric window kits for two and four door vehicles

Specialists and Manufacturers

- **Glasurit Valentine, Automotive Refinish, BASF Coatings and Inks Ltd, Albany House, 73-89 Station Road, West Drayton, Middlesex UB7 7LT** **00895 43115**
  Specialists in Glasurit automotive finish paints for the DIY and professional markets

- **Hella Ltd, Daventry Road Industrial Estate, Banbury, Oxon OX16 7JU** **0295 27223**
  A wide range of auto accessories including fog and spot lamps, spoilers, Optilux bodykits and electrical items

- **Hitachi Power Tools (UK) Ltd, Precedent Drive, Rooksley, Milton Keynes, Bucks MK13 8PJ** **0908 66066**
  Manufacturers of all types of power tools, both domestic and industrial

- **Holt-Lloyd Ltd, Lloyds House, Alderley Road, Wilmslow, Cheshire** **0625 52683**
  Car care products, aerosols, touch-up paints and Autofilm

- **Kenlowe Ltd, Burchetts Green, Maidenhead, Berkshire SL6 6QU** **062882 330**
  The "Hotstart" engine preheater

- **Link Sedan Ltd, Bone Lane, Newbury, Berkshire RG14 5TD** **0635 4479**
  A wide range of automotive accessories for the DIY enthusiast, customiser and family

- **Michelin Tyres plc, Davy House, Lyon Road, Harrow, Middlesex HA1 2DG** **01-861 212**
  Manufacturers of car, truck and motorcycle tyres and tubes

- **Mitchell Marketing, 140 Leicester Road, Wigston, Leicestershire LE81DG** **0533 88152**
  Corroless products, full range of unique rustproofing fluids and paints. Also, Slick 50, Protectalines and Backflashes

- **Pacet Products and Company Ltd, Wyebridge House, Cores End Road, Bourne End, Buckinghamshire SL8 5HH** **06285 2675**
  Oil coolers, replacement cooling fans, heated windscreen washer jets

- **Pipercross Ltd, Pipercross House, Leicester Road, Lutterworth, Leics. LE17 4HB** **0455 55481**
  Foam air filters for competition and road-going Fiestas

- **Plastic Padding Ltd, Woburn Industrial Park, Woburn Green, High Wycombe, Buckinghamshire HP10 0PE** **06285 2791**
  Full range of glass fibre and fillers for bodywork

- **Polco Products Ltd, Brent Works, Catherine Wheel Road, Brentford, Middlesex TW8 8BB** **01-560 640**
  A range of automotive products, including Harada car aerials

- **Power Engineering Ltd, The Power House, 8 Union Buildings, Wallingford Road, Uxbridge, Middlesex** **0895 5569**
  Ford tuning specialists producing their own conversion and kits

- **Quickfit 70 Ltd, Fearnhead Street, Bolton BL3 3PE** **0204 62381/6201**
  A wide range of centre consoles

- **Rye Mill Coachcraft, 70-76 London Road, High Wycombe, Bucks HP11 1DD** **0494 45061**
  Paint and body shop using Glasurit paints and primers

- **Safety Devices Ltd, 176 Exning Road, Newmarket, Suffolk** **0638 66142**
  Competition and road-use roll cages

- **Sharp Consumers Electronics (UK), Sharp House, Thorp Road, Manchester M10 9BE** **061-205 233**
  All types of in-car entertainment equipment

- **SIP (Industrial Products) Ltd, Gelders Hall Road, Shepshed, Loughborough, Leicestershire LE12 9NH** **0509 50314**
  Welding and spraying equipment

- **Sound Service (Oxford) Ltd, 55 West End, Witney, Oxon** **0993 498**
  Makers of Auto-Sound, DIY insulation kits and materials

- **Spax Ltd, Unit E11, telford Way Industrial Estate, Launton Road, Bicester, Oxon OX6 0UU** **086 92 4477**
  Manufacturers and suppliers of adjustable and standard replacement shock absorbers

- **Sykes-Pickavant Ltd, Kilnhouse Lane, Lytham St. Annes, Lancashire FY8 3DU** **0253 721291**
  Manufacturers of DIY automotive and industrial service tools and Speedline hand tools
- **Trimoco Ltd, 326 Dunstable Road, Luton, Beds. LU4 8JR** **0582 31133**
  Ford main dealer with approved paint and bodyshop facilities
- **C. P. Witter Ltd, Chester, Cheshire CH1 3LL** **0244 341166**
  Manufacturers of a wide range of towing brackets
- **Zemco Ltd, 509 Walsgrave Road, Coventry CV2 4AG** **0203 441428**
  High quality electrical automotive products including alarm systems, cruise controls and driving computers

Clubs and Magazines

- **XR Owners Club, Tony Trent, 20a Swithland Lane, Rothley, Leicestershire**
- **Performance Ford Magazine, PO Box 14, Hazel Grove, Stockport, Cheshire SK7 6HL**
- **Fast Ford Magazine, A&S Publishing, Central House, 154-162 Southgate Street, Gloucester GL1 2EX**

Helpful Data

Vhen performing any of the DIY tasks and fitments included in this book, you should always take great care to ensure that you ead the instructions carefully, particularly with regard to measurements and capacities. One problem which frequently occurs is hat some manufacturers give the relevant information in metric whilst others prefer imperial. Some actually mix the two within ne document! UK readers are going to be specially vulnerable to this kind of confusion as the "United Europe" of the 1990s ets under way.

he tables given here list some of the more commonly used technical data together with a single figure which can be used to onvert metric to imperial and vice versa. For example, if you wish to convert an amount in inches to millimetres, you will see that he conversion factor for one inch is 25.4. Therefore, if you have, say 6 inches, the calculation is 25.4 x 6 = 152.4mm. onversely, if you have, say, 300mm and want to convert it to inches, then you divide the figure by 25.4. So, 300 ÷ 25.4 = 11.81 nches.

Convert	Units 1	2	5	10	20
Inches to Millimetres	25.4	50.8	127.0	254.0	508.0
Miles to Kilometres	1.61	3.22	8.05	16.09	32.19
Pints to Litres	0.57	1.14	2.84	–	–
Gallons to Litres	4.55	9.09	22.73	45.46	–
Lb f ft to Kgm	0.138	0.276	0.691	1.382	2.765
Lb/in^2 to kg/cm^2	0.07	0.14	0.35	0.70	1.41

English/American terminology

Because this book has been written in England, British component names, phrases and spellings have been used throughout. American usage is quite often different and whereas normally, no confusion should occur, a list of equivalent terminology is given below.

English	American
Accelerator	Gas pedal
Aerial	Antenna
Air filter	Air cleaner
Alignment (headlamp)	Aim
Allen screw/key	Socket screw/wrench
Anti-clockwise	Counter-clockwise
Anti-roll bar	Stabiliser/sway bar
Bonnet/engine cover	Hood
Boot/luggage compartment	Trunk
Bottom/top gear	Low/high gear
Bulkhead	Firewall
Bush	Bushing
Cam follower/tappet	Valve lifter/tappet
Carburettor	Carburetor/carbureter
Catch	Latch
Choke/venturi	Barrel
Circlip	Snap ring
Clearance	Lash
Clutch drum	Clutch housing
Crownwheel	Ring gear/differential
Damper	Shock absorber/shock
Disc/brake	Rotor/disc
Distance piece	Spacer
Drop arm	Pitman arm
Dynamo	DC generator
Earth	Ground
End float	End play
Engineer's blue	Prussian blue
Estate car	Station wagon
Exhaust manifold	Header
Fault diagnosis	Trouble shooting
Float chamber	Float bowl
Free play	Lash
Freewheel	Coast
Gearbox	Transmission
Gearchange	Shift
Grub screw	Setscrew/Allen screw
Gudgeon pin	Wrist/piston pin
Halfshaft	Axleshaft
Handbrake	Parking brake
Hood (Cabrio)	Soft top
Hot spot	Heat riser
Indicator	Turn signal
Inlet	Intake
Input shaft/mainshaft	Mainshaft

English	American
Interior light	Dome lamp
Layshaft (gearbox)	Countershaft
Leading shoe (of brake)	Primary shoe
Locks	Latches
Methylated Spirit	Denatured alcohol
Motorway	Freeway, turnpike, etc
Number plate	License plate
Paraffin	Kerosene
Petrol	Gasoline (gas)
Petrol tank	Gas tank
"Pinking"	"Pinging"
Prise (force apart)	Pry
Propeller shaft	Drive shaft
Quarterlight	Quarter window
Retread	Recap
Reverse	Back-up
Rocker cover	Valve cover
Saloon	Sedan
Seized	Frozen
Sidelight	Parking light
Silencer	Muffler
Sill panel	Rocker panel
Small end/little end	Piston pin or Wrist pin
Spanner	Wrench
Split cotter (for valve spring cap)	Lock (for valve spring retainer)
Split pin	Cotter pin
Steering arm	Spindle arm
Sump	Oil pan
Swarf	Metal chips/debris
Tab washer	Tang or lock
Tappet	Valve Lifter
Thrust bearing	Throw-out bearing
Top gear	High
Trackrod	Tie or Connecting rod
Trailing shoe	Secondary shoe
Transmission	Whole drive line
Tyre	Tire
Van	Panel wagon/van
Vice	Vise
Wheel nut	Lug nut
Windscreen	Windshield
Wing/mudguard	Fender

An oil seal is fitted to components lubricated by grease. A damper is a shock absorber, it damps out and absorbs shock of bump impact. Both names are correct and used haphazardly.